AI and Digital Technologies Transforming Global Industries

Patricia Ordóñez de Pablos
The University of Oviedo, Spain

Xi Zhang
Tianjin University, China

Muhammad Anshari
Universiti Brunei Darussalam, Brunei

Mohammad Nabil Almunawar
Universiti Brunei Darussalam, Brunei

IGI Global
Scientific Publishing
Publishing Tomorrow's Research Today

Vice President of Editorial Melissa Wagner
Director of Acquisitions Mikaela Felty
Director of Book Development Jocelynn Hessler
Production Manager Mike Brehm
Cover Design Jose Rosado

Published in the United States of America by
IGI Global Scientific Publishing
701 East Chocolate Avenue
Hershey, PA, 17033, USA
Tel: 717-533-8845
Fax: 717-533-7115
Website: https://www.igi-global.com E-mail: cust@igi-global.com

Library of Congress Cataloging-in-Publication Data

LCCN: 2025033155 (CIP Data Pending)
ISBN13: 9798337360973
Isbn13Softcover: 9798337360980
EISBN13: 9798337360997

British Cataloguing in Publication Data
A Cataloguing in Publication record for this book is available from the British Library.

Editorial Advisory Board

N Sneha, *Aster Health Academy, India*
Sachin Suknunan, *University of KwaZulu-Natal, South Africa*
Shanmuga Sundari M, *Bvrit Hyderabad College of Engineering for Women, India*
Hamza Yusuf, *RMIT, Australia*

Table of Contents

Detailed Table of Contents

operations, military missions, and coastal monitoring showcase AI's practical benefits. Challenges, including maintaining stability, overcoming unpredictable environmental factors, and ensuring safety protocols, are also discussed. The chapter concludes by outlining pathways for future advancements that could revolutionize hovercraft efficiency and expand their operational landscape.

As Electronic Health Records (EHRs) become integral to modern healthcare, concerns regarding security, privacy, and scalability have emerged. Conventional centralized systems face vulnerabilities and lack patient data control, necessitating innovative decentralized solutions. This research introduces a novel AI-blockchain-based architecture for permissioned health networks, leveraging zero-knowledge succinct, non-interactive arguments of knowledge (zkSNARKs). The framework integrates AI-blockchain, InterPlanetary File System (IPFS), and zkSNARKs to enhance EHR security, privacy, and scalability. IPFS is employed for off-chain storage, improving scalability alongside blockchain's tamper-proof logging. Encryption and smart contract-based access controls preserve privacy.

The rapid rise of artificial intelligence (AI) and new technologies is transforming the global economy, offering opportunities for inclusive growth and sustainable development. Media plays a crucial role in shaping how the public views AI, influencing policies, and driving societal change in the digital age. This chapter explores how media impacts public opinion and policymaking around AI, focusing

This study investigates the adoption of Islamic FinTech services by integrating multidimensional Islamic religiosity into a predictive behavioral model. Drawing on data from Muslim consumers in the UAE, the study applies Partial Least Squares Structural Equation Modeling (PLS-SEM) to examine how various aspects of religiosity influence behavioral intention. Findings reveal that religiosity significantly shapes trust, perceived usefulness, and attitude toward Islamic FinTech adoption. The study addresses key barriers such as cybersecurity concerns, opaque Shariah governance, and limited financial literacy, while highlighting the need for transparency, ethical alignment, and culturally sensitive design. Theoretically, it advances understanding of FinTech adoption through a faith-based lens. Practically, it offers actionable insights for FinTech providers, regulators, and policymakers aiming to enhance financial inclusion and ethical innovation. Future research is encouraged to explore cross-religious and cross-sectoral applications of this model.

The gaming industry has witnessed tremendous growth over the last few years. This increased revenue has brought about significantly more sophisticated techniques for retaining players and struggle against churn. This chapter clarifies the study of game player behavior and how these studies can be applied to predict churn, and highlights the importance of churn in the gaming industry, examining high-grossing games offered on different platforms that dominate the industry in the context of churn. However, privacy and data sharing are perceived as critical barriers that hinder effective churn analysis. In summary, churn studies in online environments are not common due to the rarity of publicly available data, primarily because developers choose not to share details about players. Furthermore, the chapter presents some

Preface

INTRODUCTION

To successfully navigate the digital age, governments and corporations must not only seize the opportunities presented by artificial intelligence (AI) and emerging digital technologies, but also systematically assess associated risks and anticipate future trends. Understanding the experiences of both public and private sector actors in the deployment of AI and advanced digital tools can enrich discourse on these critical issues and facilitate the exchange of knowledge. Such strategic knowledge is essential for shaping the digital transformation agenda and promoting more resilient and inclusive societies.

Objectives of the book

The book offers valuable conceptual frameworks, introduces innovative digital tools, and presents case studies and practical examples to enhance understanding of the critical role that artificial intelligence (AI) and digital technologies play in accelerating industrial transformation and fostering more inclusive societies. Specifically, the book:

- Discusses challenges, opportunities and trends of AI in the green economy.
- Explores experiences of AI in different industries (e-commerce, healthcare, manufacturing, etc) and discusses lessons to learn.
- Addresses emerging topics in the field of AI.

Contents of the book

The book is formed by a collection of 8 chapters that address key issues to understand the importance of artificial intelligence and digital transformation in the green and digital transition. From artificial intelligence and blockchain, to e-commerce, fintech and sustainability in the digital age, the chapters offer knowledge and insights from different industries and countries.

Chapter 1, titled "Application of AI Technology in the Electronic Commerce Industry for Sustainable Business Growth in India" (by Sivasubramanian K, Shreya Acharjee, Roopa Adarsh, Kumarasamy P, Thamilmani R and Hepsibah Vani) studies "the application of AI technology in the e-commerce industry and its impact on business growth and sustainability. The application of AI technology in e-commerce for convenient shopping, mapping of products, add-on product suggestions, delivery of the product, and promotion will help business growth and sustainability. Many major online sellers are integrating AI into their businesses to provide the best services, a wide range of products, and more accessibility to remote and rural areas. It will help to reach the unreachable and needy people in the country. It analyzes it to conclude that AI intervention positively impacts the business sustainability and growth of electronic commerce in India. This review-based research work followed a descriptive approach to articulate the paper with the support of existing literature. Based on the analysis, the present chapter provides appropriate suggestions for future development in the research area".

Chapter 2, titled "Integration of AI for Autonomous Navigation in Hovercrafts" (by Chikesh Ranjan and Kaushik Kumar) focuses on "the integration of artificial intelligence (AI) for enhancing autonomous navigation in hovercrafts, highlighting key design frameworks, technologies, and algorithms. It explores how AI optimizes the complex interplay between propulsion, lift, and steering systems, enabling adaptive real-time decision-making for efficient manoeuvring over various terrains. Emphasis is placed on sensor fusion techniques, machine learning for environmental recognition, and control systems to handle dynamic conditions. Applications in search and rescue operations, military missions, and coastal monitoring showcase AI's practical benefits. Challenges, including maintaining stability, overcoming unpredictable environmental factors, and ensuring safety protocols, are also discussed. The chapter concludes by outlining pathways for future advancements that could revolutionize hovercraft efficiency and expand their operational landscape".

Chapter 3, titled "VitaChain: An AI-Blockchain-Based EHR Management Framework with Zero-Knowledge Proofs for Enhanced Privacy" (by Anand Motwani, Nilamadhab Mishra, Aditya Patil, Anshika Sinha, Harsh Pailkar and Himanish Mandrekar), affirms that "as Electronic Health Records (EHRs) become integral to modern healthcare, concerns regarding security, privacy, and scalability have emerged. Conventional centralized systems face vulnerabilities and lack patient data control, necessitating innovative decentralized solutions. This research introduces a novel AI-blockchain-based architecture for permissioned health networks, leveraging zero-knowledge succinct, non-interactive arguments of knowledge (zkSNARKs). The framework integrates AI-blockchain, InterPlanetary File System (IPFS), and zkSNARKs to enhance EHR security, privacy, and scalability. IPFS is employed for off-chain storage, improving scalability alongside blockchain's tamper-proof logging. Encryption and smart contract-based access controls preserve privacy".

Chapter 4, titled "Media's Role in Shaping Digital Transformation and Inclusive Economies: Leveraging AI and Emerging Technologies for Sustainable Development" (by Yasir Ahmed, Tanvir Ahmed and Angel Kasonta), state that "the rapid rise of artificial intelligence (AI) and new technologies is transforming the global economy, offering opportunities for inclusive growth and sustainable development. Media plays a crucial role in shaping how the public views AI, influencing policies, and driving societal change in the digital age. This chapter explores how media impacts public opinion and policymaking around AI, focusing on its potential to promote fair and equitable digital participation. It examines media narratives, challenges, and strategies, revealing regional differences: high-income countries often focus on AI's economic benefits, while low- and middle-income nations emphasize its potential for development. However, corporate-driven stories tend to overshadow critical ethical issues like bias, privacy, and inequality. By analyzing these trends, the chapter provides insights for media professionals, policymakers, and tech leaders on using media to foster responsible and inclusive digital transformation".

Chapter 5, titled "Digital Leadership- Challenges and Promises of Digital Transformation for Higher Education through a Critical Review" (by Sachin Suknunan and Pavla Macháčková), observes that "the advent of Industry 4.0 and the Covid-19 pandemic created a disruptive shift towards digital leadership in promoting digital transformation across many sectors. However, there remains a paucity of related research especially within the Higher Education Sector. Through a critical review method, this chapter contributed to addressing this gap to create more understanding of the opportunities, challenges and factors informing the adoption of Digital Leadership the sector. Key findings suggest that Digital Leadership can positively reshape Higher Education by fostering innovation, improving efficiency and enhancing teaching and learning experiences. Digital Leadership connects stakeholders and breaks down silos. Challenges hindering Digital Leadership included lack of clear vision, resistance to change, fragmented strategies and ethical concerns. Factors for successful adoption of Digital Leadership requires a clear vision aligned with strategic goals, investment in digital literacy skills development and fostering a digital culture that supports continuous learning and adaptability".

Chapter 6, titled "Bridging Faith and Digital Financial Technologies: A Predictive Multidimensional Analysis of Islamic FinTech" (by Mohamed Bouteraa, Abderrahmane Baddou, Mohammed Soufiane Benmoussa, Anes Hebbaz, Abderrahmane Elkheloufi, Mourad Boudiab, Meshari Al-Daihani, and Brahim Chekima), studies "the adoption of Islamic FinTech services by integrating multidimensional Islamic religiosity into a predictive behavioral model. Drawing on data from Muslim consumers in the UAE, the study applies Partial Least Squares Structural Equation Modeling (PLS-SEM) to examine how various aspects of religiosity influence behavioral intention. Findings reveal that religiosity significantly shapes trust, perceived usefulness, and attitude toward Islamic FinTech adoption. The study addresses key barriers such as cybersecurity concerns, opaque Shariah governance, and limited financial literacy, while highlighting the need for transparency, ethical alignment, and culturally sensitive design. Theoretically, it advances understanding of FinTech adoption through a faith-based lens. Practically, it offers actionable insights for FinTech providers, regulators, and policymakers aiming to enhance financial inclusion and ethical innovation. Future research is encouraged to explore cross-religious and cross-sectoral applications of this model".

Chapter 7, titled "Understanding Player Churn in The Gaming Industry with Key Drivers and Prevention Strategies" (by Kaan Arik), affirms that "the gaming industry has witnessed tremendous growth over the last few years. This increased revenue has brought about significantly more sophisticated techniques for retaining players and struggle against churn. This chapter clarifies the study of game player behavior and how these studies can be applied to predict churn, and highlights the importance of churn in the gaming industry, examining high-grossing games offered on different platforms that dominate the industry in the context of churn. However, privacy and data sharing are perceived as critical barriers that hinder effective churn analysis. In summary, churn studies in online environments are not common due to the rarity of publicly available data, primarily because developers choose not to share details about players. Furthermore, the chapter presents some possible avenues to overcome these challenges and expands the view on how game developers can implement tactics such as personalized experiences, socialization, leveraging technology, and transparency around data usage to reduce churn".

Finally, Chapter 8, titled "Applications, Challenges, and Future Prospects of Enhancing Medical Imaging with Neural Networks" (by Aman Dubey, Mohit Choubey, Yogesh Guptaa and Jigyendra Yadav) observes that "acute and accurate disease diagnosis is of utmost significance in modern healthcare but is generally not possible with conventional imaging techniques. As AI-based techniques offer higher diagnostic accuracy and speed, their adoption is increasingly becoming vital. Through automated processing, recent advances in deep learning have revolutionized medical imaging, enhancing anomaly identification, organ segmentation, and disease detection. Convolutional neural networks (CNNs), generative adversarial networks (GANs), transformer models, hybrid models, and more are introduced in this chapter. Revolutionary methods like Federated Learning (FL) and Self-Supervised Learning (SSL) are also discussed, along with their usage in different imaging modalities. The chapter also discusses issues including data sparsity, model interpretability, and ethics. A detailed case study on the application of transfer learning for medical image classification also showcases the capability of artificial intelligence to augment clinical diagnosis".

Patricia Ordóñez de Pablos
The University of Oviedo, Spain

Muhammad Anshari
Universiti Brunei Darussalam, Brunei

Mohammad Nabil Almunawar
Universiti Brunei Darussalam, Brunei

Chapter 1

Application of AI Technology in the Electronic Commerce Industry for Sustainable Business Growth in India

K. Sivasubramanian
https://orcid.org/0000-0001-6137-0847
Kristu Jayanti College, India

P. Kumarasamy
Dhanalakshmi Srinivasan University, India

Shreya Acharjee
Kristu Jayanti College, India

R. Thamilmani
https://orcid.org/0009-0004-7630-602X
Vel Tech Rangarajan Dr. Sagunthala R&D Institute of Science and Technology, India

Roopa Adarsh
Mount Carmel College, India

Hepsibah Vani
Kristu Jayanti College, India

ABSTRACT

This chapter aims to evaluate the application of AI technology in the e-commerce industry and its impact on business growth and sustainability. The application of AI technology in e-commerce for convenient shopping, mapping of products, add-on product suggestions, delivery of the product, and promotion will help business growth and sustainability. Many major online sellers are integrating AI into their businesses to provide the best services, a wide range of products, and more accessibility to remote and rural areas. It will help to reach the unreachable and needy

DOI: 10.4018/979-8-3373-6097-3.ch001

people in the country. It analyzes it to conclude that AI intervention positively impacts the business sustainability and growth of electronic commerce in India. This review-based research work followed a descriptive approach to articulate the paper with the support of existing literature. Based on the analysis, the present chapter provides appropriate suggestions for future development in the research area.

INTRODUCTION

Artificial intelligence (AI) is an integral part of all businesses worldwide. The integration of AI technology in business has a range of positive impacts on the online business world, including e-stores and e-commerce (Aditi et al., 2021). The application of AI enabled technology in e-commerce business enhances the sustainability for producers, sellers, buyers, and the environment. There are various applications of AI in e-commerce that significantly contribute to business and sustainability. Recommendation engines driven by AI examine past purchases, preferences, and customer behaviour to offer tailored product recommendations. E-commerce companies may boost the average value of orders and client retention by making relevant product recommendations. For instance, 35 percent of Amazon's revenue comes from its recommendation engine. Chatbots and virtual assistants driven by AI offer immediate customer service by responding to questions, assisting clients with the buying process, and making tailored suggestions. A large number of client encounters may be handled by chatbots, which speeds up response times and raises customer satisfaction. For example, H&M's chatbot offers styling tips and product discovery assistance to clients (Jatmika et al., 2024). Large volumes of data can be analysed by AI systems to find trends and abnormalities suggestive of fraud. E-commerce companies may safeguard their earnings and uphold client confidence by promptly identifying and stopping fraud. AI is used by businesses like *PayPal* and Stripe to stop fraudulent transactions. By anticipating demand, estimating stock levels, and automating replenishment procedures, artificial intelligence (AI) can improve inventory management. Businesses can cut expenses and boost operational effectiveness by reducing stockouts and overstocking. Walmart has reduced the number of out-of-stock items by 15 percent as a result of using AI to improve its inventory management (Farhat et al. 2025). Artificial intelligence (AI)-driven dynamic pricing algorithms dynamically modify product prices in real time by analyzing consumer demand, competition prices, and market trends. Businesses can increase profitability and maintain their competitiveness by basing price optimization on market conditions. Amazon makes price adjustments millions of times every day using dynamic pricing. AI systems can identify which clients are likely to leave by examining engagement metrics and behavioral trends. Businesses can proactively interact with at-risk clients by identifying them and implementing focused retention tactics. Businesses that employ AI to anticipate and stop client attrition include Netflix and Spotify (Chugh & Jain, 2024).

Background

In India, e-commerce is expanding quickly. It's altering consumer purchasing patterns, making life simpler for them, and opening up new business opportunities. E-commerce in India has expanded quickly as a result of shifting consumer habits and rising internet usage (Raman et al. 2024). Managing the increased number of products effectively and sustainably is the problem. To reduce environmental impact and guarantee long-term profitability, sustainable practices are essential. However, there are drawbacks to this expansion as well, particularly when it comes to meeting the rising demand and operating in an environmentally friendly manner (Yadav et al. 2024). With major ramifications for sustainable development, the advent of e-commerce has completely changed how companies conduct their operations. The growth of e-commerce has significantly impacted many facets of the financial system and society, according to the sources. Nowadays, practically every economy views e-commerce as a key area for growth. Furthermore, several industries have benefited from e-commerce, such as the promotion of price discovery and market openness in the distribution of agricultural goods. Additionally, e-commerce has become the primary means of putting the new economy into practice and has played a big part in the digital market. It's crucial to remember that e-commerce levels differ amongst nations, especially in emerging ones (Park & Yoon, 2025). Artificial intelligence (AI) is the development of computer systems that can do tasks that have historically required human intelligence, such as pattern recognition, problem solving, and decision making. AI is a potent tool in many fields because it allows robots to gain knowledge from data, adjust to new data, and make decisions on their own (Fu et al. 2023). The practice of running online company operations to lessen negative environmental and social repercussions is known as sustainable e-commerce. It comprises putting in place eco-friendly practices across the whole e-commerce value chain, including waste management, sourcing, production, packaging, and shipping. Reduced carbon emissions, resource consumption, social responsibility, and ethical labour standards are the goals of sustainable e-commerce (Zhong et al. 2024). The potential of computational intelligence (AI) to revolutionize e-commerce while rendering it more efficient, customized, and sustainable is what makes it so significant. To deliver customized recommendations and ads, e-commerce platforms may employ data analytics and artificial intelligence algorithms to track customer behavior, preferences, and past purchases (Sak et al. 2025). This increases sales conversion rates, decreases product returns, and enhances customer happiness. AI-powered management of supply chains may also enhance route planning, delivery schedules, and inventory control, lowering carbon emissions and transportation expenses. To reduce waste and save the environment, AI algorithms may also identify and remove inefficiencies in garbage and packaging management procedures (Ramanathan et al. 2024). The goal of machine learning is to replicate human learning processes with data and algorithms to gradually improve accuracy. An input layer, several hidden layers, plus an output layer make up the node layers of a neural network. Every node, or synthetic neuron, has its weights and limit and is linked to the others. A node becomes operational and starts sending data to the following network stratum if its output surpasses the predetermined threshold. Otherwise, no information is transmitted to the next network layer (Qiu et al. 2024). Neural networks of three or more layers are used in deep learning. With limited effectiveness, these neural networks attempt to mimic how the human brain functions so that it can "learn" from vast amounts of data. The goal of natural language processing, or NLP, is to enable computers to comprehend spoken and written language like that of humans. NLP integrates statistical in nature, machine learning, and machine learning models with computational linguistics, which is the rule-based modelling of human language. Expert systems are made to solve complicated issues and make decisions at the expert level. It does this by applying reasoning and inference procedures to retrieve information from its knowledge base in response to the user's queries. Speech recognition is a feature that allows a computer software to convert spoken language into written text. It is also known as computer speech recognition, automatic speech recognition (ASR), or speech-to-text. In computer science and engineering, robotics is a multidisciplinary field. Robotics is the study of building, repairing, using, and controlling robots. The goal of robotics is to develop tools that can help and assist people (Kumar, & Chidambaram, 2024). Businesses are incorporating Artificial Intelligence (AI) more and more into their everyday operations as technology develops. They are coming to appreciate how important AI is for generating leads, understanding audiences, cutting costs, and boosting productivity. Customer satisfaction is also increased when these solutions are integrated into their systems (Esmeli & Gokce, 2025).

Objectives

To review the integration of artificial intelligence (AI) in the e-commerce industry for business sustainability and growth.

To evaluate the multi-dimensional significance of technology in the online retail business

Research Framework

The research methodology or framework is a structure or logical format that guides the execution of research work. In this process, various steps have been involved, namely problem identification, sourcing relevant information, evaluation, and finding new information. This review-based research work followed a descriptive approach to articulate the paper with the support of existing literature. Earlier research works and their findings have been collected and arranged in a specific order based on the core objectives of this work. Existing research works were critically and carefully studied and analyzed to reveal their significance, relevance, similarities, and uniqueness. Based on the analysis, the present paper provides appropriate suggestions for future development in the research area.

LITERATURE REVIEW

Using modern communication tools, such as money transfers, telephone systems, electronic payments, fax machines, electronic data exchange, and the Internet, to manage a firm is known as e-commerce. This article aims to explore the essential growth drivers needed for e-commerce and highlight the many challenges online shopping faces in India. This report is the outcome of examining several e-commerce search investigations (Dai et al. 2022). It looks at many e-commerce opportunities, such as e-commerce, e-learning, education, integration, e-insurance, the internet for emerging and WTO nations, and e-commerce's future media. It brings up important difficulties that customers confront about e-commerce, such as ethical concerns, identifying danger in e-services experiences, e-commerce challenges, and education. The business process of purchasing and selling products, services, and data online is known as electronic commerce (Ullal et al. 2021). Examples include online ordering, online paid content delivery, and financial activities, including money transfers between bank accounts. E-commerce is the process of crafting and redefining interactions between business transactions and individuals via the application of digital information processing strategies and electronic transactions (Ratta et al. 2025). We think that the following major technological and market trends will characterize e-commerce shortly: Brand allegiance. In the Indian market, price has dominated, and consumers aren't afraid to switch brands regularly to take advantage of the attractive deals that rival companies are offering (Amit & Zott, 2017). E-commerce companies in India must take great care to make their clients feel valued to keep them around, because customer loyalty quickly wanes when they are presented with offers and incentives. Online merchants must make the most of technology to attract, keep, and grow their client base. Creating strategies based on big data analytics will help customers feel valued and boost brand loyalty. Businesses can gather a lot of customer data, thanks to the growing popularity and usage of smartphones, which can then be used for target-based advertising and marketing (Kwilinski et al. 2019).

E-Commerce

E-commerce includes the services and activities associated with sending money via the Internet and purchasing and selling goods and services. It highlights how transactions are facilitated by digital and technological platforms such as social media, smartphone apps, and websites. By offering easy and accessible channels for online commerce, e-commerce has completely changed how businesses operate and how consumers behave (He & Liu, 2024). Due to the potential for a competitive advantage and the rising demand for online products and services from customers, businesses are increasingly participating in e-commerce activities. However, businesses encounter difficulties in this area because of their connection with quickly changing and incredibly affordable technological advances (IT), which calls for constant business model adaptation to changing customer demands (Alotaibi, 2023). By enhancing consumer interactions and streamlining business processes, artificial intelligence (AI) has had a significant impact on the field of e-commerce and improved the customer experiences both on and off the business's website. Using artificial intelligence, e-commerce services may be customized to each client's tastes and interests, increasing the value of gathering and analyzing customer data. AI has filled the void left by e-commerce enterprises' typically lack of human touch, enabling them to provide better customer service than traditional physical sales (Patil et al. 2024). Artificial intelligence (AI) has altered the e-commerce industry and the way businesses operate. This study examines the application of artificial intelligence (AI) in online retail to enhance the shopping experience by suggesting products based on the preferences and behaviours of individual customers. Chatbots and artificially intelligent assistants with AI capabilities speed up the process of answering client queries and concerns. E-commerce businesses may measure client happiness and make wise decisions by using sentiment analysis. Voice commerce allows users to make purchases using voice commands, which streamlines the purchasing process. AI algorithms are also essential for identifying fraud and security threats, protecting consumers and companies from possible risks. Product list management and AI-driven search improve the search capabilities of the organization (Gidh, 2020). The continuous development of the web and the remarkable improvement of network basics have led to the overgrowth of e-commerce. Online shopping is currently the most common form of electronic commerce. These days, online recommender systems based on user profiles are widely used in research and engineering domains

(Li et al. 2023). Creating suggestions requires accurate user profiles. Nowadays, gaining, serving, and keeping clients is crucial for every organization to succeed. The demand for e-commerce has grown in the global market as a result of the number of users for commercial purposes. E-commerce has advanced significantly as a result of globalization and technology breakthroughs, which have produced a sustainable volume of business at reasonable prices (Dhanalakshmi et al., 2020).

Significance of AI Technology

Between these years, there have been significant changes in the e-commerce industry, including the encouragement of online sales by retailers, the rise in small enterprises, the use of social media by local sellers, and the reduction of operating expenses in the business-to-business (B2B) sector. However, as the e-commerce sector has grown, parcel delivery prices have increased significantly (Desai & Ganatra, 2022). With the emergence of numerous e-commerce marketplaces, many vendors are now able to sell online. Artificial intelligence and automation tools are being introduced in logistics. Due to its ability to boost sales and brand recognition, social media is becoming increasingly important in e-commerce. Customers' purchasing patterns have changed significantly as a result of e-commerce (Kakkar, 2017). Since the late 1960s, electronic data interchange, or EDI, has been in use for many years. In the simplest sense, electronic document interchange (EDI) is the exchange of standard company records in a digital form between two firms. Electronic document exchange offers many advantages, such as improved efficiency through transaction automation, decreased errors from manual data entry, and validation of content to ensure transactions contain all necessary information for proper processing, traceability, lower costs, and quicker processing (Aditi et al. 2021)

Figure 1. Internet Penetration from 2014 to 2024

Source: *A. Minhas, 2024*

Table 1 emphasizes the significance of the tremendous growth of internet usage from 2014 to 2024. It is observed that internet penetration has consistently grown from 13.5 percent in 2014 to 28.5 percent in 2018. The growth rate was doubled in internet usage was doubled globally. Again, it was further moved to a new height of 52.4 percent in 2018, which is double the growth rate of 2018 (28.5%).

Figure 2. Market Size of E-Commerce in India from 2014 to 2024

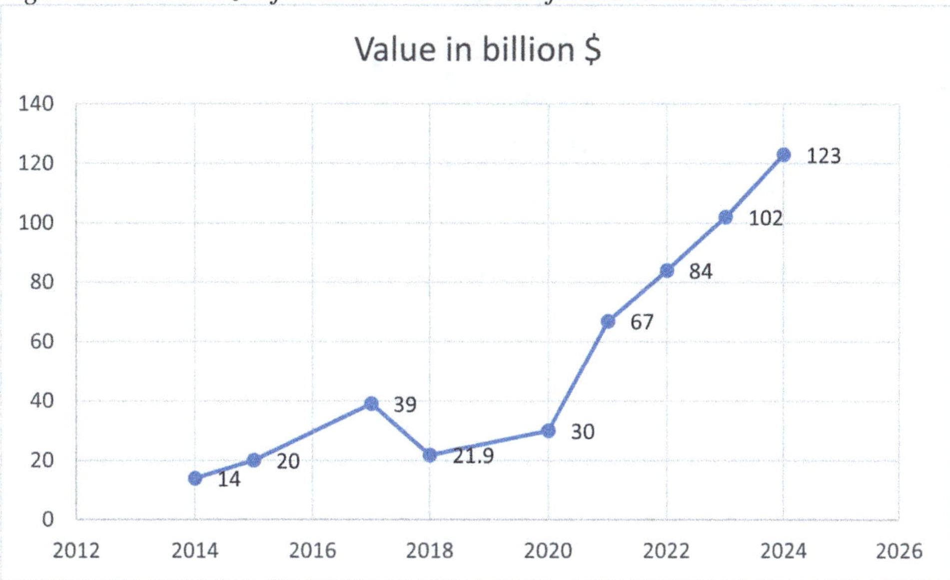

Source: *Same as the previous table.*

The market size of e-commerce has seen a crucial growth from 14 percent in 2014 to 39 percent in 2016. There was a big drop in 2018 in the e-commerce business. Again, the e-commerce business has shot up in 2020 with 30 percent of value growth, and it continued to 67 percent in 2021 due to the COVID-19 lockdown. It continues to be 123 percent of the value growth in 2024 (Table 2).

Figure 3. Revenue Growth of E-Com

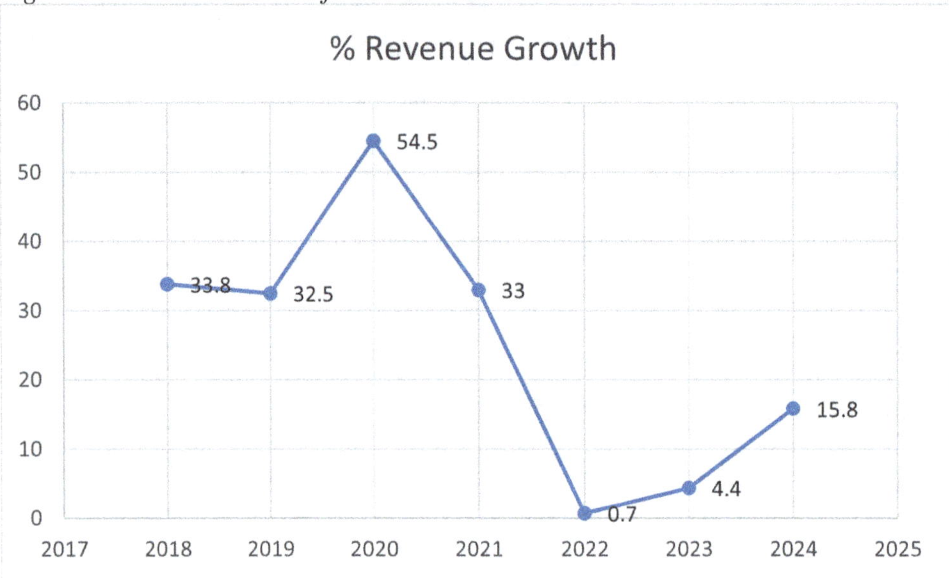

Source: *Same as the previous table.*

The revenue growth had a huge fluctuation from 2018 to 2024, starting from 33.8 percent to 32.5 percent, and suddenly hiked to 54.5 percent in 2020 due to the lockdown. Again, the value started declining due to the purchase of low-valued commodities through e-shopping. After 2022, it again started to improve from 0.7 percent to 15.8 percent in 2023 and 2024, respectively.

Application of AI in E-Com Retail

With the emergence of technologies like blockchain, massive data sets, artificial intelligence, and the Internet of Things (IoT), society is currently at the start of the Fourth Industrial Revolution. Even though some of these advances have been around for more than 20 years, progress has been difficult due to a lack of cloud computing, high-performance computing, open-source software, and transparency in code sharing. However, in the last several years, the scene has completely shifted (Gururaj, 2021). These days, technology is utilized in every industry, including management, business, healthcare, finance, and education. This illustrates how widely used the technology is and how many different uses it has. However, just 63 percent of the population is aware they have been interacting with artificial intelligence, even though it influences how we use the internet (Deng & Guo, 2024). It would take decades for an individual to evaluate and analyse the enormous amount of data created across many platforms. Because AI can evaluate vast amounts of data in a matter of seconds and reduce the likelihood of human mistakes, it can help organizations make better decisions. AI has several benefits for businesses, including the ability to visualize information and quickly identify trends in vast amounts of data (Mandala et al. 2023). Additionally, huge businesses like Amazon, Alibaba, and Rakuten use AI for big data processing, comment mining, and the creation of additional AI technologies like chatbots and recommendation engines. Retail establishments will rapidly lag behind rivals and AI developments if they don't research and adjust to new ways to provide their customers with what they want, as they demand it. However, the accuracy, fairness, and ethics of these systems can still be improved because AI technologies are still in their early phases of development (Kumar & Chidambaram, 2024). Additionally, managers and organizations must learn more about implementing AI software since a lack of information about how these systems work will prevent them from demonstrating their full potential and power (Lari et al., 2022).

AI Chatbots in E-Tail Business

The running and handling of a business by electronic methods, especially the internet, is referred to as "e-business." However, there are different settings in which the term "e-business" is applied. E-business is defined as technology that enhances internal and external business communications, especially for businesses that do not conduct all of their operations online. However, under the e-business paradigm, businesses mainly execute their major operations online with a minimum or no human connection (Bawack et al. 2021). Finding a balance between service quality and efficiency is a major difficulty for customer service providers: The potential benefits of client self-service, such as improved customer experience, lower costs, and increased time efficiency, are emphasized by both researchers and practitioners. Consumers typically seek individualized attention in addition to self-service channels that are convenient and easily accessible (He X & Liu Y, 2024). Because the lack of a personal social player in online purchases can result in lost revenues, businesses should avoid making the full transition to consumer self-service channels, especially when a customer relationship is just getting started. Nonetheless, by imitating social actors, CAs can actively impact service interactions and act as stand-ins for service professionals by doing tasks that were previously performed by human service staff (Adam et al. 2020). By evaluating data and using insights to make intelligent decisions and accomplish particular objectives, artificial intelligence (AI) is transforming e-commerce. AI can function as a system, instrument, or algorithm that gives businesses a competitive edge by enabling them to use massive data to satisfy client needs and personalize services (Patil, 2025). AI applications have become indispensable in e-commerce, transforming how companies function and engage with their clientele. Through product recommendations and data-driven marketing message customization, they tailor experiences. Using intelligent tools, methods, or algorithms to enhance and streamline online transactions for purchasing and selling goods or services is known as integrating AI with e-commerce (Song et al., 2023).

AI in demand and sales Forecasting

The goods and services that enable a business to conduct business online are known as e-commerce solutions. E-commerce solutions come in a wide variety, including ones that let conventional companies build, manage, and design websites. Certain solutions concentrate on a particular issue. For instance, to devote high resources to real commerce activities rather than to any other applications, a business that sells its goods online may buy a bandwidth optimization solution from a provider (Chen et al. 2024). Integrating the inventory control system with the CRM software that is already in place is advantageous. CRM software and inventory management were once handled by companies as two distinct systems. While CRM software handles front-end business operations like tracking sales, managing the pipeline of sales, creating marketing campaigns, and recording customer details and interactions with the company, inventory management systems are limited to managing essential back-end business operations like billing, transporting, shipping & delivery details, history of purchases, accounts and financial information, and supply chain data and details (Lee et al, 2024). Demand planning is the process of projecting future demand using market trends, historical data, and other pertinent variables (Zavyalova et al. 2023). It gives information about the amount of a product that will probably be needed in different places and at different times. For supply chains to operate efficiently, demand planning and logistics must work together. For transportation to make well-informed decisions, demand planning must provide timely and reliable information. Numerous advantages arise from incorporating AI into demand forecasting, including enhanced production scheduling, smart inventory distribution, risk reduction, and the creation of new products. Support vector machines, artificial neural networks, neural networks, and tree-based decisions are examples of machine learning approaches that use data-informed insights to provide more accurate forecasts and provide businesses with the means to create dynamic inventory policies that meet constantly shifting demand. The auto-regressive cumulative moving average, extended short-term memory systems, gradient boosting devices, support vector algorithms, and deep neural networks are the AI methods utilized for demand forecasting in another study. The vastly disparate attributes of many product categories present a challenge to the development of demand forecasting models today. Demand forecasting is difficult for relatively short-lived products, including those in the high-tech, fashion, and beauty sectors, because there is little to no past information available. Because they are more likely to experience stockouts or excess inventory, as was the case with Barbie items, these products also present a greater risk to businesses (Jena, 2025). On the other hand, long-life products like furniture and basic home appliances benefit from a longer market presence and offer a wealth of past data to predict their demand. When demand changes, these items need to be adjusted less frequently. Demand forecasting techniques must take into account the fact that different products within a category may exhibit distinct demand trends. Beauty items and other high-risk, hard-to-predict products are usually associated with higher demand volatility. Businesses that sell these products deal with poorer service levels and frequent stockouts. To stay ahead of shifting customer demand trends, they strive for an adaptable supply chain approach. Lower demand volatility, on the other hand, translates into consistent and more predictable demand, such as for toilet paper. As a result, the supply chain's focus shifts to efficiency through the reduction of vendor and delivery costs (Zhao, et al. 2025).

AI in E-Com Marketing

The emergence of artificially intelligent marketing in the last 12 months demonstrates a significant technological breakthrough and its ability to improve marketing strategies. Through maximizing product purchases and customizing client interactions, virtual personal shopping assistants, or VPSAs, began to transform marketing. Although the foundation for comprehending AI's potential in tailoring marketing campaigns was established by these early studies, their influence was constrained by the technology's infancy and the comparatively basic applications that were then accessible (Labib, 2024). The concept of "Ad Empathy" envisions the use of emotion detection and affective computing to develop emotion-sensitive technology that will impact future personalized marketing (Wu & Monfort, 2023). The idea of adding emotional intelligence to AI systems highlighted a significant trend toward more humanlike interactions (Madanchian, 2024). Over the past ten years, customer contact with 4.0 technologies, particularly AI, has advanced significantly. This circumstance changed how businesses interact with clients and make decisions. AI provides crucial customer feedback on products and services that are necessary for drawing in new clients and keeping existing ones. Using AI for promotional research is essential, given how quickly customer behavior and market dynamics are changing (Anayat & Rasool, 2022). Analysing human behaviours or the psychological actions, reactions, emotions, and imitations in technological integration is a section of the psychosocial mechanics of AI techniques in marketing. The adoption of machine learning and deep learning and the acceptability of AI-driven methodologies bring a complicated interaction between customer engagement and intention, where people's insights into these advances are influenced by mental factors related to competence and communication (Gonca et al. 2023). In the field of feelings and psychology, it gets increasingly more entwined with the engagement process as AI's capacity to understand and respond to user emotions can significantly affect the entire user experience. A complex web that stretches to service robots, technical proficiency, and the emotional bonds formed impact the adoption and usage of this technology (Vidani, 2024). Since societal pressure and corporate responsibility can have a big impact on consumer behaviour and perceptions, it is important to take these factors into account when creating strategies to use AI in marketing (Ali & Johl, 2023). The basic mechanisms defining the interaction between AI technology and human beings in marketing contexts are explained by the psychosocial area, which includes concepts of behaviour, engagement, and intent. As the AI-driven promotional paradigm evolves, understanding these dynamic features is essential to creating tactics that engage customers on an emotional and cognitive level. This will impact marketing interactions in the future (Ali et al., 2023). One of the main areas of AI in marketing is the cluster "AI-enhanced market dynamics & strategies," which captures the fusion of contemporary technology and the nuances of market behaviour. This cluster looks at the intricate web of competition, relationships, and networks where AI-powered insights and forecasts are transforming the oversight of supply chains and market laws (Lemon & Verhoef, 2016). As AI's predictive powers grow, the market's response methods shift, improving understanding of customer behaviour, impacting sales trends, and promoting rational decision-making. The amplifying effect of AI, which helps disseminate dynamic information and shifts market dynamics, gives word-of-mouth new dimensions (Chandran et al. 2024).

E-Commerce and Sustainability

Willingness and ability to meet and interact present requirements without sacrificing the capacity to meet those of future generations and their possibilities, as well as the endeavour to lessen negative effects on the nation, society, and environment through the effective application of natural assets within both domestic and foreign contexts, is known as sustainability or the sustainable method of utilising the non-renewable natural resources (Zhang, & Liu, 2024). A growing number of businesses are using sustainable business methods. Developing e-commerce strategies that don't affect the environment is known as sustainable electronic business or e-commerce. For instance, it could do so via employing environmentally feasible shipping or delivery practices that will reduce pollution-causing carbon dioxide emissions (Wang et al. 2023). Creating superior, long-lasting, and environmentally sustainable products. Customers are becoming more aware of the advantages of turning green and connecting with companies that support green products as a result of company social engagement. by putting laws into place that promote open, environmentally friendly production and shipping methods. In the same way, businesses will only collaborate with enterprises that use sustainable e-commerce methods. A focus on business competitiveness strategies that assist the e-retail industry can lead to the realization of sustainable e-commerce (Coussement et al. 2024). Merchants' purpose, vision, and primary goals must include policies that support sustainability or sustainable e-commerce. It should also inform all parties involved that it will collaborate with manufacturers, suppliers, and logistical supply providers who adhere to sustainability and green standards (Zaman et al. 2023). Customers who are eager to support sustainable e-commerce will be drawn to retailers who make sure of this. Large market shares will go to merchants who provide higher-quality, longer-lasting, and environmentally responsible goods. This study indicates that customers favor online retailers who follow sustainability guidelines in their operations (Musa et al. 2024). Retailers must realize that eco-friendly items are essential to sustainable e-commerce if they hope to attract and keep this sizable consumer base. Recent studies have shown that consumers are more likely to work with businesses that prioritize environmental sustainability, which influences their purchase decisions (Fu et al. 2023).

Impact of AI-Enabled E-Commerce

The "AI for consumer services" cluster contains a ground-breaking sector where the combination of technology and human-centred interactions is transforming the marketing industry. As AI bridges the gap between machines and users, anthropomorphism takes centre stage and enables individualized access to e-commerce experiences. As AI-driven suggestions and interactions are customized to each user's preferences, trust or satisfaction becomes intertwined, promoting reliability. Augmented reality offers another degree of immersive interaction by blurring the line between virtual and actual experiences (Singh et al., 2022). AI's ability to understand customer behavior and preferences revitalizes brand engagement and opens the door for targeted marketing initiatives that establish a personal connection with consumers. In this cluster, technologies increase brand resonance, satisfaction, and trust in a human-like way (Fu et al. 2023). Additionally, this cluster serves as an example of how AI and customer service can work together. In the ever-evolving world of e-commerce, the use of AI challenges traditional paradigms and creates an environment where client needs are anticipated and skillfully handled, elevating the customer experience to unprecedented levels (Mehta, 2021). The "AI for decision-making" cluster offers a paradigm-shifting field where the environment of well-informed decision-making is transformed by the successful combination of AI and marketing strategies (Kumar et al. 2018). The use of AI in CRM ushers in a new age by using big data to internalize complicated consumer behaviours and giving organizations dynamic capabilities. A key component of this cluster is predictive analytics, which gives decision-makers insight and enables them to identify patterns, identify opportunities, and reduce risks (Ullal et al. 2021). To rethink innovation and knowledge-sharing paradigms, marketing and AI interact in a critical area that is the focus of the “AI for value-transformation” cluster. This cluster coordinates a shift in the way perspectives are formed and value is jointly created in the marketing industry. It is impossible to overestimate the significance of AI's catalytic role in value co-creation since it leverages insights from large databases to develop innovative solutions that are highly responsive to customer needs (Chintalapati & Pandey, 2022).

Negative Impacts

(Ganapathy et al. 2023). Businesses are attempting to market environmentally friendly products, and consumers are paying more attention to the environment when they shop. Eco-friendly options are another way that online purchasing is participating. In addition to being beneficial for the environment, this can increase revenue for companies.

Millennials and other young people are very interested in supporting companies that are concerned about the environment. They search for environmentally friendly products when they shop online (Lopes et al. 2025). These green products are now featured in particular sections of online stores' catalogues. In addition to selling environmentally friendly products, they guarantee to distribute them using recyclable materials in a way that benefits the environment. New Indian internet marketplaces are also entering the market by offering environmentally friendly goods, such as electronics, toys, and personal hygiene products (Bueno-Ferrer et al. 2025). Large volumes of high-quality data are necessary for AI systems to produce precise forecasts and suggestions. E-commerce businesses frequently have trouble gathering, cleansing, and maintaining data privacy. Managing client data raises serious privacy and security issues. Data breaches can have serious repercussions; thus, it is imperative to ensure compliance with laws like the CCPA and GDPR. Legacy systems are still in use by many e-commerce companies. It may be necessary to completely redesign the current infrastructure to integrate artificial intelligence (AI) tools with these systems, which can be difficult and expensive. It can be costly to develop and execute AI solutions, particularly for smaller e-commerce companies. Expenses include buying technology, developing or acquiring AI models, and employing data scientists and engineers (Paun et al. 2024). Talent in AI and machine learning is in short supply. It can be difficult to find and keep talented data scientists and engineers, and there is intense rivalry for the best people. Biases in training data may be inherited by AI systems, which could result in unfair or discriminatory results. To preserve fairness and trust, e-commerce businesses must aggressively confront and reduce algorithmic prejudice. Customers may become concerned about data security, privacy, and the moral application of AI if it is used in e-commerce. Gaining and retaining the trust of customers is essential. Since AI is so sophisticated, this is usually taken care of right away. While customizing recommendations and expediting procedures are two ways AI may improve the user experience, improper use or an excessive dependence on AI might result in a negative consumer experience (Mei et al. 2025)

Ethical Consideration

AI ethics and legislation present a challenging environment for e-commerce businesses to traverse. Avoiding legal and reputational hazards requires adherence to a variety of regional and industry-specific legislation. An e-commerce company's AI systems must expand to accommodate more data and interactions between customers as it expands. Both the computer system and the AI algorithms themselves may experience scalability issues (Majeed & Sharif, 2024). Competition increases as more e-commerce companies use AI. To stay front of the Intelligence game, one must constantly innovate and adapt. Return on investment measurements for AI solutions can be difficult. Some AI initiatives could not provide the anticipated advantages, and it could take some time to observe noticeable changes (Lazić et al. 2024). One of the main pillars of the ethical application of AI in e-commerce is data privacy. E-commerce platforms gather and analyse enormous volumes of customer data as a result of the growing reliance on AI for customer analytics, targeted marketing, and personalized recommendations. Better shopping experiences are made possible by this data, but consumers are also at serious risk from data breaches, illegal data sharing, and abuse of personal data. Resolving these issues is crucial to building customer confidence and guaranteeing adherence to moral and legal requirements. AI is frequently used by e-commerce platforms to examine consumer preferences, behavior, and buying trends. However, concerns around data ownership and informed consent are brought up by the gathering of such detailed information. A lack of openness and possible privacy rights violations result from the fact that many customers are ignorant of how their data is collected, processed, and shared. Additionally, through re-identification strategies or shoddy data anonymization procedures, AI systems may unintentionally reveal private customer information (Li et al. 2025; Li et al, 2023). E-commerce is depending more and more on artificial intelligence (AI) technologies for user segmentation, dynamic pricing, and tailored recommendations. These systems may, however, unintentionally reinforce or magnify biases present in the data that are trained on, which could result in the unfair treatment of particular customer groups. For AI applications to support justice and inclusivity in the e-commerce ecosystem, fairness algorithms and bias avoidance are essential. Rapid artificial intelligence (AI) integration in e-commerce poses two challenges: protecting consumer privacy and encouraging innovation to improve customer experiences. E-commerce platforms must resolve this fundamental ethical conundrum between privacy and innovation to preserve customer confidence and adhere to legal requirements. In e-commerce, machine learning (AI) is changing how consumers behave and what their rights are. Businesses can provide highly customized services, optimize workflows, and improve user experiences with AI-powered tools and systems. But this change has moral and legal ramifications that have an immediate impact on individual autonomy, privacy, and equity (Narayanan & Shmatikov, 2010).

Findings from Comparative Review Analysis

The application of AI-enabled technology in e-commerce business enhances the sustainability for producers, sellers, buyers, and the environment. There are various applications of AI in e-commerce that significantly contribute to business and sustainability. AI systems can identify which clients are likely to leave by examining engagement metrics and behavioral trends. Businesses can proactively interact with at-risk clients by identifying them and implementing focused retention tactics. E-commerce companies in India must take great care to make their clients feel valued to keep them around, because customer loyalty quickly wanes when they are presented with offers and incentives. Online merchants must make the most of technology to attract, keep, and grow their client base. Creating strategies based on big data analytics will help customers feel valued and boost brand loyalty. Businesses can gather a lot of customer data, thanks to the growing popularity and usage of smartphones, which can then be used for target-based advertising and marketing. Chatbots and artificially intelligent assistants with AI capabilities speed up the process of answering client queries and concerns. E-commerce businesses may measure client happiness and make wise decisions by using sentiment analysis. The continuous development of the web and the remarkable improvement of network basics have led to the overgrowth of e-commerce. Online shopping is currently the most common form of electronic commerce. Electronic document exchange offers many advantages, such as improved efficiency through transaction automation, decreased errors from manual data entry, and validation of content to ensure transactions contain all necessary information for proper processing, traceability, lower costs, and quicker processing. AI can function as a system, instrument, or algorithm that gives businesses a competitive edge by enabling them to use massive data to satisfy client needs and personalize services. AI applications have become indispensable in e-commerce, transforming how companies function and engage with their clientele. Analysing human behaviours or the psychological actions, reactions, emotions, and imitations in technological integration is a section of the psychosocial mechanics of AI techniques in marketing. The adoption of machine learning and deep learning and the acceptability of AI-driven methodologies bring a complicated interaction between customer engagement and intention, where people's insights into these advances are influenced by mental factors related to competence and communication The ability to meet present needs without sacrificing the capacity to meet those of future generations, as well as the endeavour to lessen adverse effects on the economy, society, and environment through the effective use of natural assets within both domestic and foreign contexts, is known as sustainability. A growing number of businesses are using sustainable business methods. Developing e-commerce strategies that don't harm the environment is known as sustainable e-commerce. For instance, it can do so by employing environmentally friendly shipping practices that will lower pollution-causing carbon dioxide emissions.

CONCLUSION

In conclusion, AI-supported technology is revolutionizing e-commerce business by improving the sustainability of the stakeholders, such as producers, suppliers, consumers, and the environment. Through AI-integrated analytics, customized marketing, chatbots, and other behavioral analyses, businesses could enhance customer engagement and retain them for future business. Additionally, e-commerce has become the primary means of putting the new economy into practice and has played a big part in the digital market. It's crucial to remember that e-commerce levels differ amongst nations, especially in emerging ones. Moreover, sustainable e-commerce policies and practices, such as eco-friendly shipping and effective resource use, contribute to reducing environmental effects. As AI-driven technologies evolve, their integration into online e-commerce platforms will significantly perform a key role in fostering long-term business growth and sustainability. AI ethics and legislation present a challenging environment for e-commerce businesses to traverse. Avoiding legal and reputational hazards requires adherence to a variety of regional and industry-specific legislation. An e-commerce company's AI systems must expand to accommodate more data and interactions between customers as it expands. Both the computer system and the AI algorithms themselves may experience scalability issues. Notwithstanding its possible advantages, e-commerce carries several risks and difficulties. These difficulties include the possibility of cybercrime, customer demand analysis, and security concerns. Delivery delays, warehouse maintenance, and lack of access in rural areas due to network problems are further issues. Some villagers still lack access to reliable internet and are not familiar with its usage. E-commerce finds it challenging to expand in certain regions as a result. AI models, and employing data scientists and engineers (Paun et al. 2024). Talent in AI and machine learning is in short supply. It can be difficult to find and keep talented data scientists and engineers, and there is intense rivalry for the best people. Biases in training data may be inherited by AI systems, which could result in unfair or discriminatory results. To preserve fairness and trust, e-commerce businesses must aggressively confront and reduce algorithmic prejudice. Customers may become concerned about data security, privacy, and the moral application of AI if it is used in e-commerce.

Future Research Directions

While building on the present status of AI technology adoption in India's electronic commerce industry, various promising directions for future research can be identified to enhance a better and deeper understanding of how artificial intelligence tools could foster sustainable business growth. India's vast infrastructural and geographical diversity creates a significant area for AI-driven innovation. Future research studies must be related to empirically examining how specific AI instruments, such as predictive analytics, optimization algorithms, and demand forecasting techniques, increase the efficiency of logistics. Secondly, while large electronic commerce platforms aggressively employ AI technology, Indian SME face resource capacity, technical knowledge, and implementation issues. There is a wider scope for research focusing on the various decision-making models and strategic formulations available for SME while adopting innovative AI technologies in business. Thirdly, there is emerging evidence that AI-driven personalisation not only enhances sales but could also nudge consumer attitudes towards a more sustainable way. Future research work could evaluate the psychological and behavioural impacts of artificial intelligence instruments on Indian consumers to assess their trust and satisfaction level in AI-based recommendations, privacy, security, and willingness to engage with brands that foreground sustainability in their technology. Longitudinal research that works in this direction could strengthen the influence of AI on sustainable consumption patterns.

REFERENCES

Adam, M., Wessel, M., & Benlian, A. (2020). AI-based chatbots in customer service and their effects on user compliance. *Electronic Markets, 31*(2), 427–445. DOI: 10.1007/s12525-020-00414-7

Aditi, B., Hafizah, H., & Hermansyur, H. (2021). The Role of E-Services, Quality System, and Perceived Value on Customer Satisfaction: An Empirical Study on Indonesian SMEs. *Journal of Industrial Engineering & Management Research, 2*(3), 193–205. DOI: 10.7777/jiemar.v2i3.195

Ali, K., & Johl, S. K. (2023). Driving forces for industry 4.0 readiness, sustainable manufacturing practices, and circular economy capabilities: Does firm size matter? *Journal of Manufacturing Technology Management, 34*(5), 838–13. DOI: 10.1108/JMTM-07-2022-0254

Ali, O., Abdelbaki, W., Shrestha, A., Elbasi, E., Alryalat, M. A. A., & Dwivedi, Y. K. (2023). A systematic literature review of artificial intelligence in the healthcare sector: Benefits, challenges, methodologies, and functionalities. *Journal of Innovation & Knowledge, 8*(1), 1. DOI: 10.1016/j.jik.2023.100333

Alotaibi, F. M. (2023). A machine-learning-inspired opinion extraction mechanism for classifying customer reviews on social media. *Applied Sciences (Basel, Switzerland), 13*(12), 7266. DOI: 10.3390/app13127266

. Amit, R., & Zott, C. (2017). Value drivers of e-commerce business models. *Creating Value in a New Business Environment*, 13–43.

Anayat, S., & Rasool, G. (2022). Artificial intelligence marketing (AIM): Connecting-the-dots using bibliometrics. *Journal of Marketing Theory and Practice, 32*(1), 114–135. DOI: 10.1080/10696679.2022.2103435

Bawack, R. E., Fosso Wamba, S., & Carillo, K. D. A. (2021). A framework for understanding artificial intelligence research: Insights from practice. *Journal of Enterprise Information Management, 34*(2), 645–678. DOI: 10.1108/JEIM-07-2020-0284

Bueno-Ferrer, Á., De Pablo Valenciano, J., & De Burgos Jiménez, J. (2025). Unveiling the potential of metaheuristics in transportation: A path towards efficiency, optimization, and intelligent management. *Infrastructures, 10*(1), 4. DOI: 10.3390/infrastructures10010004

Chandran, S. M. C., Mukesh, V. M., Chandran, R., Sathiyabama, B., & Santhoshkumar, N. (2024). Mediating role of green finance in transforming banking activities to environmental performance. *Srusti Management Review, 17*(2), 19–36.

Chen, S., Ke, S., Han, S., Gupta, S., & Sivarajah, U. (2024). Which product description phrases affect sales forecasting? An explainable AI framework by integrating Wave Net neural network models with multiple regression. *Decision Support Systems, 176*, 114065. DOI: 10.1016/j.dss.2023.114065

Chintalapati, S., & Pandey, S. K. (2022). Artificial intelligence in marketing: A systematic literature review. *International Journal of Market Research, 64*(1), 38–68. DOI: 10.1177/14707853211018428

Chugh, P., & Jain, V. (2024). Artificial intelligence (AI) empowerment in e-commerce: A bibliometric voyage. *NMIMS Management Review, 32*(3), 159–173. DOI: 10.1177/09711023241303621

Coussement, K., Abedin, M. Z., Kraus, M., Maldonado, S., & Topuz, K. (2024). Explainable AI for enhanced decision-making. *Decision Support Systems, 184*, 114276. DOI: 10.1016/j.dss.2024.114276

Dai, H., Xiao, Q., Yan, N., Xu, X., & Tong, T. (2022). What influences online sales across different types of e-commerce platforms. *International Journal of Electronic Commerce, 26*(3), 311–330. DOI: 10.1080/10864415.2022.2076196

Deng, Z., & Guo, M. (2024). Research on the impact of the application of artificial intelligence technology on the sustainable development of mobile e-commerce. *Benchmarking, 31*(9), 3349–3372. DOI: 10.1108/BIJ-11-2022-0697

Desai, P., & Ganatra, K. (2022). *Artificial intelligence in strengthening the operations of e-commerce-based business. Interdisciplinary Research in Technology and Management.* IRTM., DOI: 10.1109/IRTM54583.2022.9791598

Dhanalakshmi, A., Hui, X., Roopini, R., & Supriya, R. (2020). Technological Advancements in E-Commerce and Customer Relationship Management. *International Journal of Engineering and Management Research, 10*(6), 9–20. DOI: 10.31033/ijemr.10.6.2

Esmeli, R., & Gokce, A. (2025). An analysis of consumer purchase behavior following cart addition in e-commerce utilizing explainable artificial intelligence. *Journal of Theoretical and Applied Electronic Commerce Research, 20*(1), 28. DOI: 10.3390/jtaer20010028

Farhat, R., Yang, Q., Ahmed, M. A. O., & Hasan, G. (2025). E-commerce for a sustainable future: Integrating trust, product quality perception, and online-shopping satisfaction. *Sustainability (Basel), 17*(4), 1431. https://doi.org/10.xxxx/su17041431. DOI: 10.3390/su17041431

Fu, L., Li, J., & Chen, Y. (2023). An innovative decision-making method for air quality monitoring based on big data-assisted artificial intelligence technique. *Journal of Innovation & Knowledge*, *8*(2), 100294. DOI: 10.1016/j.jik.2022.100294

Ganapathy, V., Gupta, C., & Chavadi, C. (2023). Building a sustainable e-commerce grocery business model in India: Challenges and opportunities. *Journal of Services Research*, *23*(2), 125–151.

Gidh, P. G. (2020). A multi-dimensional research study in E-commerce to capture consumer expectations. *International Journal for Research in Applied Science and Engineering Technology*, *8*(11), 411–415. DOI: 10.22214/ijraset.2020.32169

. Gururaj, P. (2021). Artificial intelligence application in the field of e-commerce, *International Journal of Research- GRANTHAALAYAH*, 9(4), 170-177.

He, X., & Liu, Y. (2024). Knowledge evolutionary process of Artificial intelligence in E-commerce: Main path analysis and science mapping analysis. *Expert Systems with Applications*, *238*, 121801. DOI: 10.1016/j.eswa.2023.121801

Jatmika, R. T. D., Ratnasari, V., & Nadlifatin, R. (2024). Empowering micro-entrepreneurs through artificial intelligence: A conceptual framework for AI-based marketing. *Procedia Computer Science*, *234*, 1087–1094. DOI: 10.1016/j.procs.2024.03.103

Jena, R. K. (2025). Factors influencing the adoption of FinTech for the enhancement of financial inclusion in rural India using a mixed methods approach. *Journal of Risk and Financial Management*, *18*(3), 150. DOI: 10.3390/jrfm18030150

Kakkar, V. M. S. (2017). A study on artificial intelligence in e-commerce. *International Journal of Advances in Engineering & Scientific Research*, *4*(4).

Kumar, I., & Chidambara, . (2024). A systematic literature review and bibliometric analysis of last-mile e-commerce delivery in urban areas. *Urban, Planning and Transport Research*, *12*(1), 2357577. DOI: 10.1080/21650020.2024.2357577

Kumar, N., Anusara, J., Hossin, M. A., Sarkar, M. K., Chanthamith, B., Shah, S., & Russel, M. I. H. (2018). Challenges and opportunities of E-Commerce in India: Pathway for sustainable e-commerce. *International Journal of Engineering Business Management*, *2*(2).

. Kwilinski, A., Volynets, R., Berdnik, I., Holovko, M., & Berzin, P. (2019). E-commerce: Concept and legal regulation in modern economic conditions. *Journal of Legal, Ethical and Regulatory Issues*, 22(1).

Labib, E. (2024). Artificial intelligence in marketing: Exploring current and future trends. *Cogent Business & Management, 11*(1), 2348728. Advance online publication. DOI: 10.1080/23311975.2024.2348728

Lari, H. A., Vaishnava, K., & Manu, K. S. (2022). Artificial Intelligence in E-commerce: Applications, Implications and Challenges. *Asian Journal of Management, 13*(3), 235–244. DOI: 10.52711/2321-5763.2022.00041

Lazić, A., Milić, S., & Vukmirović, D. (2024). The future of electronic commerce in the IoT environment. *Journal of Theoretical and Applied Electronic Commerce Research, 19*(1), 172–187. DOI: 10.3390/jtaer19010010

Lee, N. T., Lee, H. C., Hsin, J., & Fang, S. H. (2024). Prediction of customer behavior changing via a hybrid approach. *IEEE Open Journal of the Computer Society, 5*, 27–38. DOI: 10.1109/OJCS.2023.3336904

Lemon, K. N., & Verhoef, P. C. (2016). Understanding customer experience throughout the customer journey. *Journal of Marketing, 80*(6), 69–96. DOI: 10.1509/jm.15.0420

Li, C., Hao, R., Li, N., & Zhang, C. (2025). Measuring customer experience in AI contexts: A scale development. *Journal of Theoretical and Applied Electronic Commerce Research, 20*(1), 31. DOI: 10.3390/jtaer20010031

Li, Y., Liang, Z., Wang, Y., & Chang, Y. (2023). The negative effect of service robots' affective human-likeness on consumer satisfaction in frontline service encounters. *International Journal of Hospitality Management, 115*, 103603. DOI: 10.1016/j.ijhm.2023.103603

Lopes, J. M., Massano-Cardoso, I., & Granadeiro, C. (2025). Festivals in the age of AI: Smarter crowds, happier fans. *Tourism and Hospitality, 6*(1), 35. DOI: 10.3390/tourhosp6010035

Madanchian, M. (2024). The impact of artificial intelligence marketing on e-commerce sales. *Systems, 12*(10), 429. DOI: 10.3390/systems12100429

Majeed, M. T., & Sharif, F. (2024). The role of digitalization in driving green growth: A global panel data perspective. *Pakistan Journal of Commerce and Social Sciences, 18*(2), 435–467.

Mandala, V., Rajavarman, R., Jamunadevi, C., Janani, R., & Avudaiappan, T. (2023). *Recognition of E-commerce through big data classification and data mining techniques involving artificial intelligence*. IEEE., DOI: 10.1109/ICCES57224.2023.10192673

. Mehta, R. R (2021). An analytical study on e-commerce for sustainable development in India. *Elementary education online*, 20(5), 9555-9560.

Mei, L., Tang, N., Zeng, Z., & Shi, W. (2025). Artificial intelligence technology in live streaming e-commerce: Analysis of driving factors of consumer purchase decisions. *International Journal of Computers, Communications & Control, 20*(1). Advance online publication. DOI: 10.15837/ijccc.2025.1.6871

Musa, H. G., Fatmawati, I., Nuryakin, N., & Suyanto, M. (2024). Marketing research trends using technology acceptance model (TAM): A comprehensive review of research (2002–2022). *Cogent Business & Management, 11*(1), 2329375. DOI: 10.1080/23311975.2024.2329375

Narayanan, A., & Shmatikov, V. (2010). Myths and Fallacies of "Personally Identifiable Information". *Communications of the ACM, 53*(6), 24–26. DOI: 10.1145/1743546.1743558

Park, S., & Yoon, S. (2025). Cross-national findings of factors affecting the acceptance of AI-based sustainable fintech. *Sustainability (Basel), 17*(1), 49. DOI: 10.3390/su17010049

Patil, D. (2025). Artificial intelligence in retail and e-commerce: enhancing customer experience through personalization, predictive analytics, and real-time engagement, *SSRN*, 1-10. DOI: 10.2139/ssrn.5057420

Patil, S. M., Kharat, A. M., Jain, S., Tripathi, V. V. R., Bisen, G. K., & Joshi, A. (2024). Investigating the influence and function of artificial intelligence in contemporary marketing management: Marketing in the AI era. In Proceedings of the 2024 *International Conference on Advances in Computing, Communication and Applied Informatics,* 1-5

Paun, C., Ivascu, C., Olteteanu, A., & Dantis, D. (2024). The main drivers of e-commerce adoption: A global panel data analysis. *Journal of Theoretical and Applied Electronic Commerce Research, 19*(3), 2198–2217. DOI: 10.3390/jtaer19030107

Qiu, H., Zhang, X., Feng, M., Zhang, Z., Wang, J., & Wang, Z. (2024). Exploring the income-increasing benefits of rural e-commerce in China: Implications for the sustainable development of farmers. *Sustainability (Basel), 16*(17), 7437. DOI: 10.3390/su16177437

Raman, R., Lathabai, H. H., & Nedungadi, P. (2024). Sustainable development goal 12 and its synergies with other SDGs: Identification of key research contributions and policy insights. *Discover Sustainability, 5*(1), 150. DOI: 10.1007/s43621-024-00289-0

Ramanathan, U., Mathirajan, M., & Balakrishnan, A. S. (2024). Role of e-tailing: A new way of business during the COVID situation in India – A critical view. *Benchmarking*, *31*(3), 1062–1072. DOI: 10.1108/BIJ-04-2024-785

Ratta, R., Sodhi, J., & Saxana, U. (2025). The relevance of trust in the implementation of AI-driven clinical decision support systems by healthcare professionals: An extended UTAUT model. *Electronic Journal of Knowledge Management*, *23*(1), 47–66. DOI: 10.34190/ejkm.23.1.3499

Sak, T., Mylko, I., Ivashko, O., Chulipa, I., Wołowiec, T., & Sokołowska-Woźniak, J. (2025). How the digital economy is revolutionizing marketing management and driving sustainable development. *Sustainability (Basel)*, *17*(3), 1130. DOI: 10.3390/su17031130

Singh, P., Nandi, P., Jaiswal, R. S., & Padhi, A. (2022). Impact of the E-Commerce business of India. *Journal of Emerging Technologies and Innovative Research*, *9*(6).

Song, M., Zhang, H., Xing, X., & Duan, Y. (2023). Appreciation vs. apology: Research on the influence mechanism of chatbot service recovery based on politeness theory. *Journal of Retailing and Consumer Services*, *73*, 103323. DOI: 10.1016/j.jretconser.2023.103323

Ullal, M. S., Spulbar, C., Hawaldar, I. T., Popescu, V., & Birau, R. (2021). The impact of online reviews on e-commerce sales in India: A case study. Economic Research-. *Ekonomska Istrazivanja*, *34*(1), 2408–2422. DOI: 10.1080/1331677X.2020.1865179

Vidani, J. (2024). Evaluating the influence of social media advertising on e-commerce sales. *SSRN*, *11*, 52–58. DOI: 10.2139/ssrn.4849890

Wang, C., Ahmad, S. F., Ayassrah, A. Y. B. A., Awwad, E. M., Irshad, M., Ali, Y. A., Al-Razgan, M., Khan, Y., & Han, H. (2023). An empirical evaluation of the technology acceptance model for Artificial Intelligence in E-commerce. *Heliyon*, *9*(X), e18349. DOI: 10.1016/j.heliyon.2023.e18349 PMID: 37520947

Wu, C. W., & Monfort, A. (2023). Role of artificial intelligence in marketing strategies and performance. *Psychology and Marketing*, *40*(4), 484–496. DOI: 10.1002/mar.21737

Yadav, U. S., & Vyas, S. Kanchan, Ghosal, I., & Yadav, A. K. (2024). Impact of entrepreneurial leadership, social media, digital technology, entrepreneurial orientation, and innovation on business performance in the handicraft sector: Talent management as mediating construct. Journal of Innovation and Entrepreneurship, 13(1). https://doi.org/10.xxxx/jie13011234

Zaman, S. I., Khan, S. A., Qabool, S., & Gupta, H. (2023). How digitalization in banking improve the service supply chain resilience of the e-commerce sector? A technological adoption model approach. *Operations Management Research : Advancing Practice Through Research, 16*(2), 904–930. DOI: 10.1007/s12063-022-00341-0

Zavyalova, E. B., Volokhina, V. A., Troyanskaya, M. A., & Dubova, Y. I. (2023). A humanistic model of corporate social responsibility in e-commerce with high-tech support in the artificial intelligence economy. *Humanities & Social Sciences Communications, 10*(1), 274. DOI: 10.1057/s41599-023-01764-1 PMID: 37273417

Zhang, Y., & Liu, C. (2024). Unlocking the potential of artificial intelligence in fashion design and e-commerce applications: The case of Mid-Journey. *Journal of Theoretical and Applied Electronic Commerce Research, 19*(1), 654–670. DOI: 10.3390/jtaer19010035

Zhao, M., Wang, S., & Xia, T. (2025). The social welfare effect of e-commerce product reputation information asymmetry from the perspective of network externality. *PLoS One, 20*(1), e0313852. DOI: 10.1371/journal.pone.0313852 PMID: 39746014

Zhong, Y., Guo, F., Wang, X., & Guo, J. (2024). Can e-commerce development policies promote the high-quality development of agriculture?—A quasi-natural experiment based on China's e-commerce demonstration city. *PLoS One, 19*(5), e0299097. DOI: 10.1371/journal.pone.0299097

KEY TERMS AND DEFINITIONS

Artificial Intelligence: Artificial Intelligence (AI) is well understood as a multidisciplinary and contemporary field concerned with enhancing non-human entities, especially digital computers or software systems that could perform various tasks which, if carried out by humans, would require intelligence. Traditional foundational perspectives, such as those by Prof. McCarthy and Mr. Minsky, defined AI as a Science and Engineering domain of making intelligent machines or technologies do various things that would require intelligence if done by humans. However, recent scholarly efforts have expanded these definitions to accommodate various technological advances, human-AI collaborations, and domain-specific applications.

Chatbots: A chatbot is a computer-based automated conversational element or agent, software developed and designed to engage in textual or voice-based assistance with human users. It was rooted in early computational linguistics and symbolic AI; chatbots nowadays leverage advances in natural language processing.

Electronic Commerce: Electronic commerce or e-commerce refers to the conduct of various commercial activities online, including selling, buying, and exchanging goods and services through electronic networks, notably the internet. However, scholarly discourse exhibits the inadequacy of limiting e-commerce to mere online transactions, highlighting instead a multifaceted digital environment encompassing the entire spectrum of value chain activities, digital business practices and processes, and inter-business activities.

Sustainability: Sustainability is a multi-dimensional framework that guides actions and policies to assure the ongoing viability of ecological, economic, and social structure both present and future. Its core indicates the practice of meeting the requirements of today's society without compromising future generations and their needs.

Chapter 2
Integration of AI for Autonomous Navigation in Hovercrafts

Chikesh Ranjan
https://orcid.org/0000-0003-1197-601X
National Institute of Technology, Rourkela, India

Kaushik Kumar
https://orcid.org/0000-0002-4237-2836
Birla Institute of Technology, India

ABSTRACT

This chapter delves into the integration of artificial intelligence (AI) for enhancing autonomous navigation in hovercrafts, highlighting key design frameworks, technologies, and algorithms. It explores how AI optimizes the complex interplay between propulsion, lift, and steering systems, enabling adaptive real-time decision-making for efficient manoeuvring over various terrains. Emphasis is placed on sensor fusion techniques, machine learning for environmental recognition, and control systems to handle dynamic conditions. Applications in search and rescue operations, military missions, and coastal monitoring showcase AI's practical benefits. Challenges, including maintaining stability, overcoming unpredictable environmental factors, and ensuring safety protocols, are also discussed. The chapter concludes by outlining pathways for future advancements that could revolutionize hovercraft efficiency and expand their operational landscape.

DOI: 10.4018/979-8-3373-6097-3.ch002

1. INTRODUCTION

The integration of Artificial Intelligence (AI) in autonomous navigation systems represents a paradigm shift in the capabilities of hovercrafts. Hovercrafts, as amphibious vehicles capable of operating across diverse terrains such as water, ice, and land, are uniquely positioned to benefit from advanced navigation technologies. However, their operational complexity, stemming from dynamic and variable environments, presents significant challenges for traditional navigation systems.

AI-driven autonomous navigation addresses these challenges by leveraging machine learning algorithms, computer vision, sensor fusion, and real-time decision-making frameworks. These technologies enable hovercrafts to adapt to unpredictable conditions, optimize routes, and ensure operational safety and efficiency without human intervention. For instance, neural networks can analyze data from LiDAR, cameras, and inertial sensors to identify obstacles and generate safe paths in real time.

This chapter explores the transformative role of AI in enhancing hovercraft navigation, focusing on the key technologies, methodologies, and applications. It delves into the integration of deep learning for perception, reinforcement learning for control, and edge computing for real-time processing, highlighting their collective impact on achieving full autonomy. Additionally, the discussion extends to the potential use cases in areas such as search and rescue, environmental monitoring, and military operations, where hovercrafts' unique capabilities are amplified by AI.

The synergy between AI and hovercrafts not only advances autonomous navigation but also contributes to broader developments in autonomous systems. By addressing technical challenges such as robust localization, obstacle avoidance, and energy efficiency, this integration sets the stage for a new era of intelligent and versatile hovercraft operations (Okafor, B. E.2013).

2. HISTORICAL BACKGROUND OF HOVERCRAFT

The history of the hovercraft reflects a remarkable evolution of technological innovation and engineering ingenuity. Early conceptual ideas can be traced back to 1716, when Emanuel Swedenborg, a Swedish philosopher, proposed a flying machine that incorporated air-cushion principles, though it was never built. In the 1870s, Sir John Isaac Thornycroft, a British engineer, made significant strides by experimenting with air-lubricated hulls, laying the foundation for hovercraft technology. Further theoretical developments occurred in the early 20th century when Russian scientist Konstantin Tsiolkovsky described an air-cushion vehicle in 1915, and Austrian engineer Dagobert Müller von Thomamühl advanced the concept by experimenting with ground-effect vehicles during the 1920s. Sir John Thornycroft and Sir Christopher Cockerell are key figures in this journey of hovercraft development, as they made critical contributions to making the hovercraft concept practical.

The modern hovercraft owes much to Sir Christopher Cockerell, a British engineer credited with its invention in the 1950s. In 1955, Cockerell demonstrated the "wall-jet" principle using tin cans and a vacuum cleaner to show how an air cushion could reduce friction. His groundbreaking idea, combined with the use of a flexible skirt to trap the air cushion, made hovercraft practical for both land and water travel. The first functional hovercraft, the SR-N1 (Saunders-Roe Nautical 1), was designed by Saunders-Roe and successfully crossed the English Channel in 1959, proving the feasibility of air-cushion vehicles. Sir John Thornycroft's earlier work on air-lubricated hulls further strengthened the foundations of hovercraft engineering.

The 1960s marked the beginning of hovercraft's commercial and military applications. Passenger and cargo transport began using hovercraft, and the SR-N4 "Mountbatten-class" hovercraft, introduced in 1968, could carry cars and passengers across the English Channel. By the 1970s and 1980s, hovercraft gained prominence in military operations, particularly in amphibious assaults, mine-sweeping, and patrol missions, with countries like the USA and USSR developing advanced models such as the LCAC (Landing Craft Air Cushion) and Zubr-class hovercraft. As part of modern developments, it is notable that the Zubr-class hovercraft, developed by Russia, holds the distinction of being the world's largest hovercraft. Additionally, in the 2000s, hovercraft technology began to evolve further, with air cushion vehicles (ACVs) partially replacing traditional hovercraft, and electric hovercraft prototypes emerging, signaling the next phase of innovation in this field.

3. DESIGN PRINCIPLES OF HOVERCRAFT

Hovercraft operates on the fundamental principle of generating a high-pressure air cushion that lifts the vehicle above the surface it is traversing. The hovercraft design incorporates various elements to ensure its efficient operation across multiple terrains. Figure 1: Hovercraft Design illustrates a conceptual model of a hovercraft that integrates advanced lift and thrust mechanisms for efficient operation on diverse terrains, including land, water, and ice. This design combines functionality and efficiency, making it adaptable for various applications, such as transportation, rescue missions, environmental monitoring, and recreation (Ganesan, et al.2019). The layout demonstrates a systematic approach to balancing lift, propulsion, and stability, which are the core principles of hovercraft operation. Below is an expanded explanation of the design's key components:

Central Fan System (Lift Propeller)

The central fan plays a crucial role as the primary lift-generating mechanism in a hovercraft. It functions by creating a high-pressure air cushion beneath the vehicle, lifting the entire structure off the ground or water surface. This air cushion significantly reduces friction, enabling the hovercraft to hover and glide effortlessly over rough terrains, water bodies, and minor obstacles. By minimizing surface contact, the central fan enhances the hovercraft's capability to operate in environments where traditional vehicles might struggle.

To optimize efficiency, the central fan is typically enclosed within a duct. This design helps streamline airflow, minimize energy losses, and improve the thrust-to-lift ratio. The uniform distribution of the high-pressure air cushion beneath the hovercraft ensures stability during operation, preventing sudden tilts or imbalances. This stability is essential for maintaining control when traversing uneven surfaces, icy terrains, or choppy waters.

Figure 1 illustrates the working mechanism of the central fan and its role in generating lift for the hovercraft. The central fan, enclosed within a circular or rectangular duct, plays a crucial role in drawing in atmospheric air. This enclosure helps optimize airflow and reduce energy losses. Once the air is drawn in, the fan forces it downward, creating a high-pressure air cushion beneath the hovercraft. This air cushion serves as the primary lift mechanism, allowing the vehicle to hover slightly above the ground or water surface.

A flexible skirt surrounds the base of the hovercraft, effectively trapping the air cushion. This flexible structure prevents the air from escaping and ensures that the high-pressure layer remains uniformly distributed beneath the vehicle, enhancing stability. By maintaining this cushion, the hovercraft is lifted off the surface, reducing friction significantly. As a result, the hovercraft can hover and glide smoothly over diverse terrains, including rough ground, water, ice, or swampy regions, making it highly versatile in various environments.

Figure 1. Central Fan Mechanism in a Hovercraft

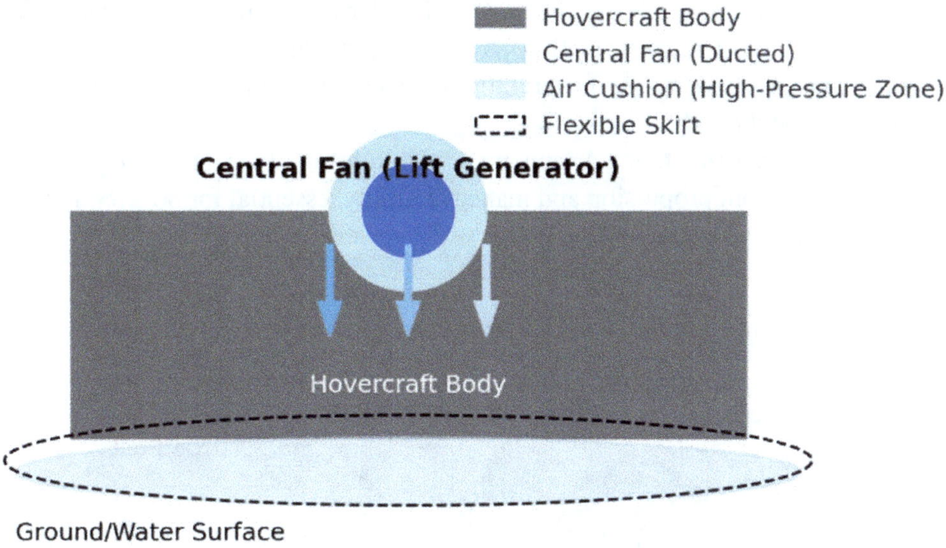

Twin Rear Fans (Thrust Propellers)

The two rear-mounted ducted fans play a crucial role in providing the thrust necessary for both forward movement and directional control of the hovercraft. These fans generate the forward thrust required to propel the vehicle at varying speeds, depending on the operational demands. Their strategic placement and size ensure efficient propulsion, allowing the hovercraft to perform effectively even in challenging environments, such as rough terrains, water surfaces, or icy conditions.

In addition to propulsion, the rear-mounted fans contribute to the hovercraft's steering mechanism. By adjusting the thrust between the two fans or employing rudders attached to the ducts, the hovercraft can execute sharp turns, change direction smoothly, or maintain a straight path. This dual-fan configuration enhances the overall maneuverability and stability, making the hovercraft suitable for applications that require precise navigation, such as rescue operations, military missions, and passenger transport across uneven terrains.

Figure 2 illustrates the mechanism of the twin rear fans in a novercraft, also known as thrust propellers, in a hovercraft propulsion and steering system. The diagram shows the key components and their functional relationships. The two large blocks represent the twin rear fans, which are responsible for generating the forward thrust required to propel the hovercraft. These fans direct airflow backward, as indicated by arrows labeled "Airflow Thrust," enabling forward movement.

The central block labeled "Hovercraft Body" connects to the twin fans and forms the core structure. Below the fans, a "Rudder Mechanism" is shown, which helps control the direction of airflow. By varying the thrust between the two fans or adjusting the rudders, the hovercraft can steer efficiently, execute turns, and maintain a straight path.

This simple yet functional arrangement highlights the twin-fan configuration's contribution to both propulsion and maneuverability, essential for hovercraft operation across different terrains.

Figure 2. Mechanism of the twin rear fans in a Hovercraft

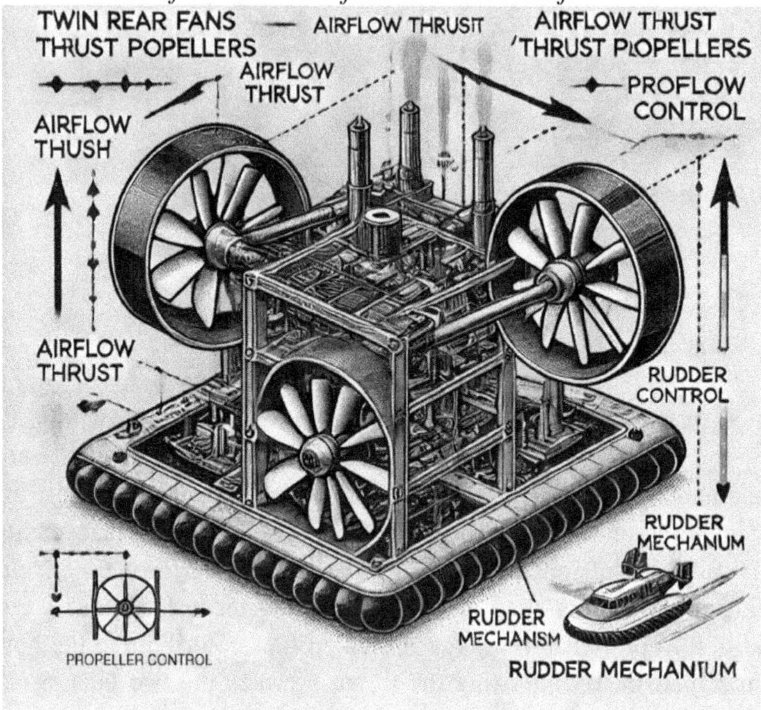

Ducted Fan Enclosures

The fans in a hovercraft are housed within ducts to enhance performance, improve safety, and reduce noise. These ducts play a crucial role in optimizing the airflow generated by the fans, resulting in greater aerodynamic efficiency. By channeling the airflow more effectively, the ducts help to minimize turbulence and energy losses, thereby increasing the overall thrust and lift efficiency. This design contributes to smoother, more stable operation, especially when traversing difficult terrains or water surfaces.

In addition to improving performance, the duct enclosures serve as a protective shield for the fan blades. This is particularly important in rugged environments, where the fans may otherwise be at risk of damage from debris, stones, or other external objects. The added protection ensures the durability and reliability of the hovercraft's propulsion system.

Another significant advantage of the ducted fan design is noise reduction. By guiding the airflow in a controlled manner, the ducts help to dampen noise levels. This is particularly valuable in applications where quieter operation is essential, such as during rescue missions, military operations, or wildlife monitoring. Lower noise emissions improve the hovercraft's stealth and reduce environmental disturbance (Lovesey, 1970).

Base Structure (Hull)

The flat hull serves as the primary structural framework of the hovercraft, ensuring stability, adaptability, and overall performance. This hull not only houses the essential lift and thrust systems but also distributes their loads evenly across the craft, which enhances balance and prevents instability during operation. By containing and spreading the air cushion uniformly beneath the vehicle, the hull plays a critical role in maintaining stable and consistent hovering.

To improve efficiency and durability, the hull is typically constructed from lightweight and robust materials, such as reinforced composites, aluminum, or advanced polymers. These materials reduce the craft's overall weight, contributing to better energy efficiency while also enhancing its structural strength to withstand various environmental conditions.

The flat design of the hull further enhances the hovercraft's surface adaptability, allowing it to glide effortlessly over diverse terrains, including water, sand, ice, or uneven ground. This design ensures consistent contact between the air cushion and the surface, facilitating smooth, stable hovering even in challenging environments, making the hovercraft highly versatile for both commercial and rescue applications.

Potential Skirt Attachment

The hovercraft's structure is designed to accommodate the integration of a flexible skirt system, a vital component for efficient and stable operation. While not explicitly visible in some designs, the potential attachment points and structural framework suggest its essential role in hovercraft performance.

The primary purpose of the skirt is to trap and maintain the air cushion beneath the hovercraft, which is critical for lifting the vehicle off the surface and reducing friction. By containing the pressurized air, the skirt helps stabilize the hovercraft and enhances its efficiency. Additionally, the flexible skirt plays a crucial role in adapting to uneven terrains. It compensates for surface irregularities, preventing air leakage that might otherwise reduce lift and stability when operating over rough, swampy, or icy surfaces.

Typically made from durable, flexible materials like reinforced rubber, nylon, or neoprene, the skirt is designed to withstand wear and tear during operation. This flexibility allows the hovercraft to glide smoothly over obstacles, absorb shocks, and endure challenging conditions, making it suitable for applications in diverse environments such as flood zones, deserts, or ice-covered landscapes.

Figure 3 illustrates a conceptual hovercraft design showcasing the key components essential for lift, thrust, and stability. The central feature is the circular, ducted fan located at the center of the hull. This fan is responsible for generating the air cushion beneath the hovercraft, which allows it to hover by lifting the entire structure off the ground or water surface. Surrounding the central fan are attachment points where a flexible skirt could potentially be integrated to trap and maintain the air cushion for stable operation.

At the rear of the hovercraft, two large, rear-mounted ducted fans are visible. These fans provide the forward thrust necessary to propel the hovercraft at varying speeds and allow for steering and maneuverability. By adjusting the thrust or using rudders within the ducted fans, the hovercraft can turn or maintain a straight path, enhancing its directional control.

The hull itself has a flat, streamlined design to optimize airflow and ensure even weight distribution. This shape supports the lift and thrust systems while improving surface adaptability, allowing the hovercraft to glide over water, sand, or uneven terrains with minimal friction. The ducts enclosing the fans help enhance aerodynamic efficiency by channeling airflow, reducing turbulence, and protecting the fan blades from external debris. This design is suitable for a variety of applications, including rescue missions, transport, and amphibious operations.

Figure 3. Hovercraft Design

3.1 Lift System

The lift system is the fundamental aspect of hovercraft design, enabling the vehicle to hover above various surfaces. This system operates by generating a sufficient air cushion beneath the hovercraft, lifting it off the ground or water. Powerful blowers or fans draw in atmospheric air and force it downward beneath the vehicle, where it accumulates to form a high-pressure layer. This air cushion reduces friction and enables smooth, frictionless gliding. The trapped air is sealed by a flexible skirt, typically made of durable materials like reinforced fabric or rubber. The skirt plays a critical role by preventing the air from escaping, thus maintaining the necessary pressure beneath the hovercraft.

For effective lift generation and stable operation, the lift system must adapt to changes in weight distribution and varying surface conditions. A consistent air pressure beneath the vehicle is essential to prevent tilting or sudden instability. Achieving this balance requires a finely tuned system that optimizes airflow, power input, and air distribution. This balance allows the hovercraft to maintain steady lift, whether traversing rough terrain, icy surfaces, or water.

Figure 4. Lift System Mechanism in a Hovercraft

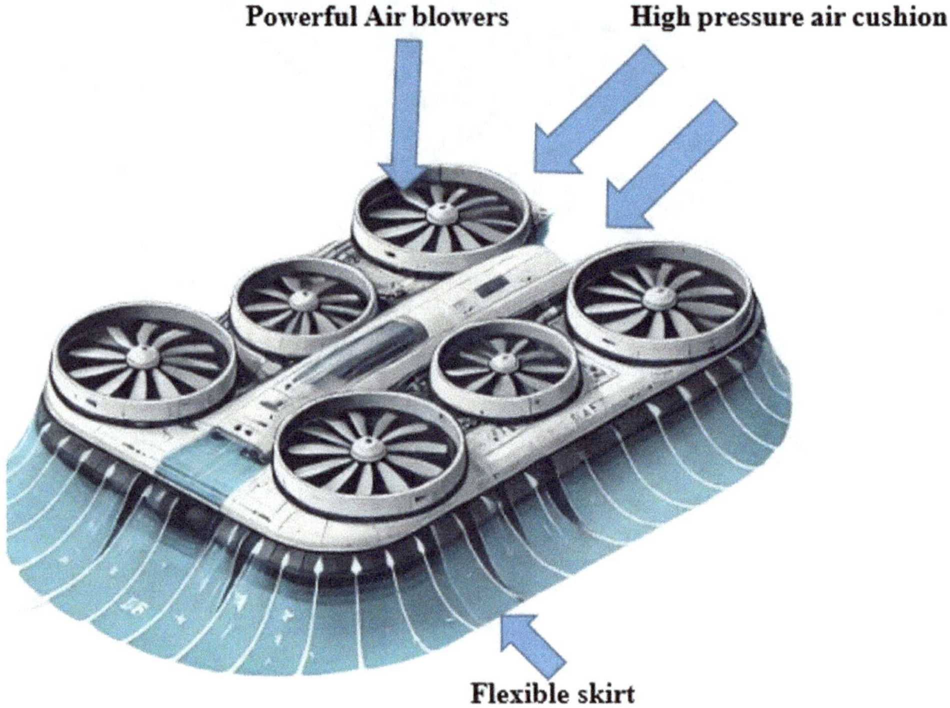

3.2 Propulsion System

In addition to generating lift, hovercraft also require a propulsion system to move the vehicle across surfaces. Typically, hovercraft employ large ducted fans or propellers located at the rear of the vehicle. These fans provide forward thrust, enabling the hovercraft to glide over surfaces with minimal friction. The placement and design of the propulsion system are critical to achieving both effective thrust and stability. The propulsion system must be powerful enough to overcome drag, particularly when moving over water or rough terrain. It also needs to be adaptable, with variable speed controls that allow the hovercraft to maintain the desired speed and direction. The configuration of the propulsion fans influences the craft's maneuverability, as directional control can be achieved by adjusting the thrust or using rudders (Fantoni, et al.1999).

3.3 Steering and Maneuverability

Hovercraft are steered using various mechanisms, including rear flaps, rudders, and differential thrust from the fans. These systems allow the vehicle to change direction while hovering over a surface. The steering system's effectiveness is vital for ensuring precise control and stability, particularly in environments like water or mud where traditional steering methods (like wheels or tracks) are ineffective. In most hovercraft designs, the rear fans are used not only for propulsion but also for maneuvering. Adjustable flaps or rudders allow the pilot to control the direction of thrust, and therefore, the movement of the vehicle (Sira, et al.2000). The challenge in steering lies in maintaining stability during sharp turns or when operating in windy or turbulent conditions, which can disrupt the air cushion.

3.4 Hull and Material Selection

The hull of a hovercraft must be designed to reduce drag while providing structural integrity and buoyancy. The materials used in hull construction must be lightweight, yet durable enough to withstand collisions with rocks, debris, or other obstacles commonly encountered on rough terrain. A streamlined hull design reduces resistance and helps the hovercraft achieve higher speeds with less fuel consumption. For hovercraft operating on water, the hull must also provide buoyancy, as the air cushion alone may not be sufficient in extreme conditions. The hull's ability to withstand impact without compromising its function is a key design consideration, particularly in harsh environments or when landing on rugged surfaces.

3.5 Energy Efficiency

Since hovercraft require substantial amounts of power to generate lift and thrust, energy efficiency is a key consideration in their design. Modern hovercraft designs are increasingly focused on optimizing fuel consumption while maintaining performance. Power management systems must be capable of adjusting the output based on the vehicle's weight, terrain type, and operational demands. Balancing the size of the engines with the craft's weight and intended use is a challenging task. Oversized engines increase fuel consumption and weight, while under-powered engines compromise performance. Designers must consider the trade-offs between power, efficiency, and operational cost (Hein, et al.2013).

4. COMPONENTS OF AUTONOMOUS NAVIGATION

4.1 Sensors and Perception

Sensors are the cornerstone of autonomous navigation, providing the hovercraft with the ability to perceive its surroundings and make informed decisions (Siderits,.2011). The effectiveness of an autonomous system depends on the quality and integration of its sensory inputs. Below are key sensor types and their roles in hovercraft navigation:

LIDAR (Light Detection and Ranging)

- **Function**: Creates precise 3D maps of the environment by measuring distances to surrounding objects.
- **Advantages**: High accuracy, long-range capabilities, and excellent performance in obstacle detection.
- **Applications**: Used for terrain mapping, collision avoidance, and localization in dynamic environments.

Cameras

- **Function**: Capture visual data for object recognition, classification, and scene analysis.
- **Types**: Monocular, stereo, and infrared cameras.
- **Advantages**: Rich contextual information and compatibility with deep learning algorithms.
- **Applications**: Essential for detecting landmarks, interpreting signs, and recognizing obstacles.

IMU (Inertial Measurement Unit)

- **Function**: Measures linear acceleration and angular velocity to determine the hovercraft's orientation and motion.
- **Advantages**: Real-time data with high responsiveness.
- **Applications**: Used for stability control, trajectory estimation, and dead reckoning in GPS-denied environments.

GPS and GNSS (Global Navigation Satellite Systems)

- **Function**: Provides precise geolocation and velocity data.
- **Advantages**: Reliable in open environments for global positioning.

- **Applications**: Enables route planning, waypoint navigation, and localization.

Sonar (Sound Navigation and Ranging)

- **Function**: Emits sound waves to detect objects and measure distances underwater or near surfaces.
- **Advantages**: Effective in detecting submerged obstacles or features in aquatic environments.
- **Applications**: Ideal for maritime operations and underwater exploration.

Radar (Radio Detection and Ranging)

- **Function**: Uses radio waves to detect objects, their speed, and distance.
- **Advantages**: Works in low visibility conditions, such as fog or rain.
- **Applications**: Used for obstacle detection, speed estimation, and collision avoidance.

Sensor Fusion: To enhance reliability and accuracy, autonomous hovercrafts utilize sensor fusion, combining data from multiple sensors. Techniques include:

- **Kalman Filters**: For integrating IMU and GPS data to improve localization.
- **Bayesian Networks**: To handle uncertainty and enhance decision-making.
- **Deep Sensor Fusion**: Uses AI to merge LIDAR, camera, and radar data for robust perception.

4.2 AI Algorithms

The “AI Algorithms” section delves into various computational methods enabling autonomous navigation for hovercrafts. Here's a detailed explanation of each algorithm type and its relevance:

Machine Learning (ML): ML involves algorithms that learn patterns from data to make predictions or decisions. Common methods include:

- **Support Vector Machines (SVM)**: Used for classification tasks like distinguishing between safe and hazardous paths.
- **Decision Trees**: Help in sequential decision-making, such as choosing optimal maneuvers based on environmental conditions.

Deep Learning (DL): DL leverages neural networks to handle complex, high-dimensional data:

- **Convolutional Neural Networks (CNNs)**: Process visual inputs from cameras to detect and classify obstacles, recognize landmarks, and interpret environmental cues.

- **Recurrent Neural Networks (RNNs)**: Analyze sequential data like sensor streams for predicting future trajectories or patterns in hovercraft movement.

Reinforcement Learning (RL): RL enables the hovercraft to learn by interacting with its environment:

- **Application**: Training models to optimize navigation strategies by rewarding desired behaviors (e.g., obstacle avoidance, energy-efficient routes).
- **Simulation Training**: RL is particularly effective in virtual environments where trial-and-error learning does not risk damage.

Bayesian Networks: These probabilistic models handle uncertainties in sensor data and decision-making:

- **Role**: Assess risks in uncertain environments, such as navigating through fog or variable water conditions.
- **Output**: Probabilities that inform safer and more reliable navigation paths.

Genetic Algorithms (GAs): Inspired by natural selection, GAs optimize solutions to complex problems:

- **Application**: Path planning and resource allocation, where multiple parameters (e.g., fuel efficiency, shortest route) need to be balanced.
- **Process**: Iteratively refines solutions by simulating selection, crossover, and mutation of potential paths.

Hybrid Approaches: Combining multiple AI techniques often yields better results:

- **Example**: Using CNNs for visual perception and RL for decision-making ensures accurate obstacle detection and efficient route selection.

5. DESIGN CALCULATIONS

Designing a hovercraft involves several calculations to determine its performance parameters, including lift, thrust, power requirements, and stability. Here's a structured approach:

5.1 Lift System Calculation

The lift system generates an air cushion beneath the hovercraft to support its weight.

Key Equations

- **Cushion Pressure (P):**

Cushion pressure (P) is the pressure generated beneath the hovercraft due to the action of the central lift fan. It plays a critical role in maintaining the air cushion, which lifts the hovercraft off the surface. This pressure is typically higher than the surrounding atmospheric pressure and helps counteract the weight of the hovercraft, ensuring that it hovers at the desired height.

The cushion pressure must be carefully regulated to balance the lift and prevent excessive air leakage. It depends on factors such as the hovercraft's weight, the surface area of the air cushion, and the efficiency of the skirt in trapping the pressurized air. Maintaining an optimal cushion pressure is essential for stable operation, particularly when navigating uneven or soft surfaces.

$$P = \frac{W}{A} \tag{1}$$

where, W: Weight of the hovercraft (N) and A: Area of the air cushion (m^2).

- **Lift Fan Power (P_{lift}):**

Lift fan power (P) refers to the energy required to operate the central lift fan, which plays a vital role in creating and maintaining the air cushion beneath the hovercraft. This cushion, formed by pressurized air, is responsible for lifting the hovercraft off the surface, allowing it to hover and move smoothly over land or water. The amount of lift fan power needed depends on several key factors. First, the hovercraft's weight directly affects the power demand, as heavier hovercrafts require more energy to generate a sufficient cushion pressure (P) to achieve and sustain lift.

Additionally, the airflow rate produced by the fan must be adequate to fill the cushion volume and compensate for any air loss due to leakage, especially when navigating uneven surfaces. The efficiency of the fan also plays a critical role; well-designed fans, incorporating aerodynamic blades and optimized ducts, reduce power consumption while enhancing lift performance. Lastly, environmental conditions such as air density, altitude, and terrain type can impact the power required. Maintaining the optimal lift fan power is essential for balancing energy efficiency, operational stability, and performance, ensuring that the hovercraft remains effective across diverse applications and challenging conditions.

$$P_{lift} = \frac{\dot{m}\Delta P}{\eta} \tag{2}$$

where, P_{lift}: Mass flow rate of air (kg/s); ΔP: Pressure difference (Pa); and $\dot{m}$: Efficiency of the fan (dimensionless)

Design Considerations:

- The area of the air cushion is determined by the hovercraft's footprint.
- Select a fan capable of providing sufficient airflow and pressure.

5.2 Thrust System Calculation

The thrust system propels the hovercraft forward.

Key Equations

- **Thrust Force (F):**

Thrust force (F) is the forward-driving force generated by the hovercraft’s rear-mounted propulsion system, typically comprising one or more ducted fans or propellers. This force propels the hovercraft forward and allows it to glide over surfaces such as water, sand, ice, or marshy terrain. Thrust force is essential for overcoming drag forces, maintaining forward momentum, and enabling directional control.

The magnitude of the thrust force depends on several factors, including the speed and power of the thrust fans, the aerodynamic design of the propellers, and the efficiency of the duct enclosures that help channel airflow. By varying the thrust produced by each fan or using additional steering mechanisms such as rudders, the hovercraft can achieve precise maneuverability, making sharp turns or maintaining a straight path. Optimizing thrust force is crucial for efficient propulsion, ensuring that the hovercraft can reach desired speeds while minimizing energy consumption and drag. This balance enhances the hovercraft’s overall performance, whether it is used for transportation, rescue missions, military applications, or recreational purposes.

$$F = \frac{1}{2}\rho A_{prop} V^2 \tag{3}$$

where, ρ: Air density (kg/m^3); A_{prop}: Propeller area (m^2); and V: Air velocity through the propeller (m/s)

- **Thrust Power (P_{thrust}):**

Thrust power ($P^{hr\ s}$) is the amount of power required by the hovercraft’s propulsion system to generate sufficient thrust force (F) for forward movement. This power drives the rear-mounted fans or propellers, which push air backward to propel the hovercraft forward. The efficiency and effectiveness of the thrust power directly impact the hovercraft's speed, acceleration, and overall fuel or energy consumption.

The required thrust power depends on several factors, including the hovercraft's total weight, aerodynamic drag, and the terrain or surface over which it is traveling. When operating over rough terrains or against headwinds, additional thrust power may be necessary to maintain stability and forward momentum. The design of the propulsion system, including the blade shape, fan speed, and duct efficiency, also influences how much power is needed to achieve optimal thrust. Efficient management of thrust power is essential for enhancing performance, reducing operational noise, and ensuring smooth and energy-efficient hovercraft operation across various conditions.

$$P_{thrust} = \frac{F.V}{\eta} \tag{4}$$

Design Considerations:

- Choose a propeller size and RPM to achieve the required thrust.
- Account for drag and surface resistance in determining thrust requirements.

5.3 Weight and Balance

The hovercraft's total weight must be supported by the lift system and evenly distributed for stability.

Weight Calculation:

$$W = m.g \tag{5}$$

where: m: Total mass of the hovercraft (kg) and g: Gravitational acceleration (9.81 m/s^2)

Skirt Design:

- The skirt should be designed to distribute the cushion pressure evenly and adapt to surface irregularities.

5.4 Power Requirements

The total power needed is the sum of lift and thrust power.

$$P_{total} = P_{lift} + P_{thrust} \tag{6}$$

Engine Selection:

- Choose an engine or motors capable of providing P_{total} with some margin for inefficiencies.

5.5 Skirt Design

The skirt retains the air cushion and must be designed to minimize leakage and handle wear.

Leakage Loss:

$$Q_{leak} = C_d A_{leak} \sqrt{\frac{2P}{\eta}} \tag{7}$$

where, C_d: Discharge coefficient (dimensionless) and A_{leak}: Leakage area (m^2)
Material Selection:

- Use durable, flexible materials that can withstand wear and tear.

5.6 Stability and Maneuverability

Stability:

- The center of gravity (CG) must be below the center of pressure (CP) for stability.
- Analyze the hovercraft's response to lateral forces using moments and balance equations.

Turning Radius:

$$R = \frac{m.v^2}{F_{Side}} \tag{8}$$

where, v: Velocity (m/s) and F_{side}: Side force during turning (N)

6. DESIGN CONSIDERATIONS FOR HOVERCRAFT DESIGN

When designing a hovercraft, various practical considerations must be addressed to ensure optimal performance, efficiency, and safety. Below are key factors to consider:

6.1 Motor Selection

Selecting the right motor is crucial, as it directly affects the hovercraft's thrust and lift capabilities. The motor must have adequate power output to generate sufficient airflow for both lift and propulsion, and this power requirement varies based on the hovercraft's size, payload, and operating environment. Choosing the appropriate motor type is another key consideration. Electric motors are lightweight, efficient, and low-maintenance, making them ideal for short-range, quieter operations, though they are limited by battery capacity. On the other hand, internal combustion engines offer higher power output and longer endurance, but they tend to be heavier, noisier, and more complex to maintain. Another important factor is the motor's revolutions per minute (RPM); while higher RPM enhances thrust, the motor should also be efficient at lower speeds to minimize power consumption. Additionally, the weight-to-power ratio plays a vital role in determining overall efficiency, as a high ratio leads to better lift and propulsion performance, contributing to the hovercraft's stability, speed, and payload capacity.

6.2 Power Margin

A sufficient power margin is essential for handling unexpected loads and adverse conditions, such as rough terrain, water drag, or headwinds. To ensure reliable performance under varying conditions, it is generally recommended to include a power margin of 20-30% over the calculated theoretical power requirements. This extra capacity helps accommodate several critical factors. One of these is payload variations, which may involve additional passengers, cargo, or fuel that can increase the load beyond initial estimates. Environmental factors, such as increased resistance when navigating uneven terrain, water surfaces, or facing strong winds, also necessitate additional power to maintain stability and control. Furthermore, this margin enhances operational safety by ensuring that the hovercraft can respond effectively to emergency situations, such as rapid deceleration or sudden increases in drag. By accounting for these variables, the power margin plays a vital role in ensuring the hovercraft's reliability, efficiency, and overall safety.

6.3 Lift and Thrust Allocation

Most hovercraft designs employ either separate systems for lift and thrust or a combined system, and this choice significantly influences motor selection and power distribution. In designs with separate systems, the lift system is dedicated to generating enough airflow to maintain a stable air cushion, which is essential for keeping the hovercraft suspended above the surface and minimizing friction. The thrust system, on the other hand, focuses on providing sufficient power to propel the hovercraft forward at the desired speed. In combined systems, a single power source is used to manage both lift and thrust, which may simplify the design but requires careful balancing to ensure that neither function is compromised. Whether separate or combined, optimizing power allocation between these systems is key to achieving efficient, stable, and responsive hovercraft performance.

6.4 Battery or Fuel Efficiency

When designing an electric hovercraft, the primary focus should be on optimizing battery efficiency and maximizing range. Since electric motors rely on stored battery power, it is crucial to choose high-capacity, lightweight batteries that can provide sufficient energy while minimizing overall weight. Efficient power management and regenerative technologies can also help extend the hovercraft's operational range. In contrast, fuel-powered hovercraft designs must carefully account for fuel consumption rates and tank size. Selecting an engine with good fuel efficiency ensures longer endurance without frequent refuelling, while an appropriately sized fuel tank balances extended operational time and added weight. Whether electric or fuel-powered, energy storage and consumption directly impact performance, range, and overall operational efficiency.

6.5 Propeller/Fan Design

The design of the propeller or fan plays a crucial role in the overall performance and efficiency of a hovercraft. Since the motor's power output must be effectively converted into thrust and lift, selecting the right propeller or fan configuration is essential. Key considerations include the size, pitch, and material of the propeller or fan. A larger diameter propeller can move more air and generate greater thrust, but it requires more power and may increase the hovercraft's overall weight. Similarly, the pitch, which determines how far the propeller moves air with each rotation, must be carefully matched to the motor's RPM to avoid overloading the motor while maintaining optimal airflow. Lightweight, durable materials, such as carbon fiber or reinforced composites, are often used to enhance performance while minimizing weight. A well-designed propeller or fan maximizes the motor's efficiency, ensuring stable lift, effective propulsion, and smoother operation across different terrains.

7. ENVIRONMENTAL FACTORS FOR HOVERCRAFT DESIGN

Designing a hovercraft requires considering various environmental factors that influence its performance, safety, and durability. Since hovercraft operate over diverse terrains such as water, sand, ice, mud, and uneven ground, their design must account for challenges posed by the external environment. Below are key environmental factors and their impact on hovercraft design:

7.1 Terrain and Surface Conditions

Hovercraft design must account for varying terrain and surface conditions to ensure optimal performance and durability. When operating over water, the hovercraft must maintain adequate buoyancy while minimizing water resistance to enhance efficiency. The skirt design plays a crucial role here, as it should effectively prevent water spray from entering the air cushion, which could compromise lift stability. On rough or uneven terrain, the hovercraft must adapt to surface irregularities, necessitating a flexible skirt system that can maintain a stable air cushion while minimizing excessive air leakage. Additionally, operations on sand and mud pose specific challenges due to the abrasive nature of dust and sand particles, which can accelerate wear on the skirt and damage sensitive components like motors and fans. To address these issues, air filters and abrasion-resistant materials are essential for protecting key systems and enhancing the hovercraft's longevity and reliability across diverse environments.

7.2 Wind and Air Resistance

Hovercraft performance can be significantly affected by wind conditions, particularly headwinds and crosswinds, which can reduce thrust efficiency and compromise stability. To counteract these effects, it is essential to design an aerodynamic hull that minimizes wind resistance and improves the hovercraft's ability to maintain directional control. Additionally, optimizing the thrust system helps the hovercraft handle sudden gusts and maintain efficient forward motion even in challenging wind conditions. Drag reduction is another critical consideration, as excessive drag can increase energy consumption and reduce overall efficiency. By shaping the hull to minimize air resistance and ensuring that air leakage from the skirt and cushion is kept to a minimum, the hovercraft can enhance energy efficiency and maintain smooth, stable operation in windy environments

7.3 Temperature Variations

Hovercraft design must account for temperature extremes to ensure consistent performance and operational reliability. In hot climates, extreme heat can lead to overheating of critical components such as motors, engines, and batteries, potentially causing power loss, reduced efficiency, or system failure. To mitigate these risks, effective cooling systems and the use of heat-resistant materials are essential for maintaining optimal temperature control and preventing thermal damage. Conversely, in freezing temperatures, cold conditions pose different challenges, including the risk of icing, which can reduce skirt flexibility, block air intakes, and impair the functionality of fuel systems. To address these issues, low-temperature-resistant materials and anti-icing systems should be incorporated into the hovercraft design, ensuring that the vehicle remains operational and stable even in sub-zero environments. By addressing these temperature-related factors, hovercraft can achieve greater resilience and adaptability across a wide range of climatic conditions.

8. CHALLENGES IN HOVERCRAFT DESIGN

Despite the innovative capabilities of hovercraft, their design and operation come with numerous challenges. These challenges stem from the complex interactions between lift, propulsion, stability, and the variable conditions under which the hovercraft must perform.

8.1 Skirt Design and Durability

One of the primary challenges in hovercraft design is the creation and maintenance of an effective skirt. The skirt must be durable enough to withstand environmental wear and tear, while also being flexible to accommodate changes in surface contour. Damaged or inefficient skirts can lead to a loss of air pressure beneath the hovercraft, compromising lift and stability.

Furthermore, the skirt needs to maintain a consistent seal under different conditions—whether the hovercraft is on water, ice, or rough terrain. Designers face the challenge of creating a skirt material that balances flexibility with strength, and can also endure repeated exposure to abrasion, moisture, and temperature extremes.

8.2 Complex Propulsion and Lift Systems

Hovercraft rely on both lift and propulsion systems to function, and these systems must be carefully integrated for optimal performance. The complexity of designing and maintaining two powerful fan systems can be costly and technically challenging. These systems need to be able to work together to provide consistent thrust and lift across various terrains.

Moreover, hovercraft are often used in harsh environments, such as military operations or rescue missions, where systems need to function reliably under stress. The challenge lies in ensuring that both the lift and propulsion systems are robust enough to handle frequent usage, temperature fluctuations, and exposure to environmental elements.

8.3 Weight Management

The balance between power and weight is a critical consideration in hovercraft design. A heavier vehicle requires more power to maintain lift, but adding too much power increases fuel consumption and operational costs. The weight of the hovercraft also impacts its maneuverability and speed, especially when operating in confined spaces or on uneven terrain.

Reducing the overall weight of the vehicle while maintaining strength, durability, and safety is a challenging task. Material innovations, such as lightweight composites, are helping to address this issue, but weight remains a critical factor in hovercraft performance (Sira, et al.2002).

8.4 Surface and Terrain Limitations

Hovercraft perform best on smooth, even surfaces but struggle with rough or uneven terrain. For instance, when traversing sand dunes, thick vegetation, or rocky surfaces, hovercraft may experience instability or inefficient air cushion performance. Over water, waves and strong currents can disrupt the vehicle's ability to maintain lift and stability (Xie, et al.2018).

Designing hovercraft to operate effectively in a wider range of environments often requires compromises in other areas, such as weight or fuel efficiency. Designers must consider the specific operational needs of the vehicle and tailor the design to meet those demands.

8.5 Noise and Vibration Control

The large fans used in hovercraft are noisy and generate significant vibrations, which can be uncomfortable for passengers and distracting in certain operational scenarios. In military or rescue missions, noise levels can be a concern, as they may compromise stealth or communication. Additionally, excessive vibrations can cause wear and tear on the vehicle's components (Stomberg, et al.2024).

Effective noise-damping and vibration-isolation systems are necessary to mitigate these issues. Designers often use specialized materials and vibration control technologies to reduce the impact of noise and ensure smoother operation (Cabecinhas, et al.2017).

8.6 Cost and Maintenance

Hovercrafts are expensive to design, build, and maintain. The complex systems, combined with the need for specialized materials and components, make hovercraft costly to manufacture. Additionally, maintenance can be expensive due to the wear and tear on the skirt, fans, and propulsion systems (Hussein, et al.2024).

Operational costs, including fuel consumption and crew training, can also be high. Therefore, balancing performance with cost efficiency is a major challenge in hovercraft development, especially for commercial or military applications where cost-effective solutions are essential.

9. APPLICATION OF HOVERCRAFT

9.1 Military and Defense

In Military and Defense, hovercrafts are used for:

- **Amphibious Assaults**: Quickly transporting troops, vehicles, and equipment from ships to shore, bypassing traditional ports and navigating over water, sand, and marshy terrains (Tanaka, et al.2001).
- **Patrol and Surveillance**: Operating in coastal, riverine, and shallow water regions where conventional boats can't go, providing flexibility for border security and reconnaissance missions.
- **Minesweeping and Logistics**: Safely navigating mine-laden waters and delivering supplies to remote or difficult-to-access locations, ensuring operational continuity in diverse terrains.

9.2 Rescue and Emergency Services

In Rescue and Emergency Services, hovercrafts are crucial for:

- **Flood and Disaster Relief**: Navigating flooded areas, debris-filled waters, and unstable ground to deliver aid, evacuate people, and transport emergency personnel.
- **Ice and Water Rescues**: Operating on thin ice, swift currents, or swampy regions where boats or land vehicles can't reach, making them ideal for rescuing stranded individuals.
- **Access to Remote Areas**: Reaching isolated or inaccessible locations during natural disasters, ensuring timely medical assistance and supply delivery.

9.3 Commercial Use

In Commercial Use, hovercrafts serve in:

- **Passenger and Cargo Transport**: Moving people and goods across rivers, lakes, and coastal areas where traditional infrastructure like bridges or docks is limited.
- **Ferry Services**: Providing reliable transport in tidal regions, shallow waters, and areas with shifting shorelines, where boats may struggle.
- **Oil and Gas Exploration**: Accessing offshore platforms, wetlands, and remote drilling sites without damaging sensitive environments, especially in marshy or icy regions.

9.4 Recreational and Sports

In Recreational and Sports, hovercrafts are used for:

- **Personal Leisure Craft**: Offering a unique, fun way to explore lakes, rivers, beaches, and other terrains for outdoor enthusiasts.
- **Hovercraft Racing**: Competitive sports events where participants race hovercrafts on mixed surfaces like water, grass, and mud, testing speed and maneuverability.
- **Adventure Tours**: Providing guided excursions in areas difficult to access by traditional vehicles, such as wetlands, shallow rivers, and coastal zones.

9.5 Environmental and Scientific Research

In Environmental and Scientific Research, hovercrafts are valuable for:

- **Access to Sensitive Areas**: Reaching ecologically fragile regions like wetlands, marshes, and polar ice without causing surface damage, preserving natural habitats.
- **Surveying and Monitoring**: Conducting environmental assessments, wildlife monitoring, and geological surveys in areas inaccessible to conventional vehicles.
- **Polar and Remote Expeditions**: Navigating icy terrains and remote water bodies for scientific research, including climate studies and glaciology.

9.6 Agriculture and Forestry

In Agriculture and Forestry, hovercrafts are used for:

- **Transporting Goods and Equipment**: Moving supplies, machinery, and harvested crops across marshy, flooded, or uneven farmland where traditional vehicles can't operate.
- **Land Management and Reforestation**: Accessing remote or waterlogged areas for planting trees, applying fertilizers, or managing forest health without damaging the soil.
- **Irrigation and Drainage Maintenance**: Reaching difficult terrain to inspect and maintain irrigation systems, drainage channels, and waterways.

Case Study-1

The Use of Hovercrafts in the Royal National Lifeboat Institution (RNLI), UK

Overview:

The Royal National Lifeboat Institution (RNLI), a UK-based charity dedicated to saving lives at sea, has successfully integrated hovercrafts into its fleet for specialized rescue operations. Traditional lifeboats were ineffective in certain shallow, muddy, or tidal areas, prompting the adoption of hovercrafts for these unique challenges.

Problem:

Coastal regions like the Morecambe Bay in northwest England posed significant rescue challenges due to rapidly changing tides, extensive mudflats, and quicksand-like conditions. Traditional boats would get stuck, and foot access was dangerous and slow, risking both victims' and rescuers' lives.

Solution:

In 2002, the RNLI introduced Griffon 470TD hovercrafts into their rescue operations. These hovercrafts could glide over mudflats, sandbanks, and shallow waters, where boats and land vehicles failed.

Key Features of the Hovercrafts Used:

- **Amphibious Capability:** Able to operate seamlessly over water, mud, and sand.
- **Speed and Maneuverability:** Quick response times, crucial for areas with fast-changing tides.
- **Capacity:** Can carry multiple rescuers and victims safely.

Impact:

1. **Increased Rescue Efficiency:** The hovercraft significantly reduced response times, allowing RNLI crews to reach stranded individuals faster than before.
2. **Lives Saved:** Notably, in 2004, a major rescue operation during a cockling disaster in Morecambe Bay saw hovercrafts playing a critical role in saving survivors trapped by rising tides.
3. **Operational Expansion:** Due to their success, the RNLI expanded the use of hovercrafts to other coastal stations facing similar challenges, such as Hunstanton and Southend-on-Sea.

Case Study: 2

Use of Hovercrafts by the Indian Coast Guard

Overview:

The Indian Coast Guard (ICG) employs hovercrafts to patrol and secure India's extensive coastline, especially in shallow waters, marshy areas, and estuaries where conventional vessels are ineffective. Hovercrafts have enhanced India's coastal security, particularly in sensitive regions like the Sundarbans, Rann of Kutch, and along the eastern coastline.

Problem:

India's 7,500 km coastline includes diverse terrains mangroves, mudflats, salt marshes, and shallow waters which pose challenges for traditional patrol boats. Vulnerabilities in these areas made it difficult to monitor smuggling, illegal fishing, infiltration, and environmental threats effectively.

Key problematic areas:

- **Sundarbans Delta:** Dense mangrove forests and narrow waterways complicate surveillance.
- **Rann of Kutch:** Salt marshes with shifting landscapes make conventional patrolling nearly impossible.
- **Eastern Coast Estuaries:** Frequent cyclones and flooding hinder traditional rescue and patrol missions.

Solution:

To address these challenges, the Indian Coast Guard inducted Griffon Hoverwork 8000 TD-class hovercrafts, which are amphibious and ideal for patrolling difficult terrains.

Key Features of Hovercrafts Used:

- **All-Terrain Capability:** Operates on water, sand, marshes, and even grasslands.
- **Speed and Range:** Capable of reaching speeds up to 45 knots (83 km/h) and covering vast coastal areas swiftly.
- **Payload Capacity:** Can carry up to 55 personnel or equivalent cargo for rescue missions or troop deployment.
- **Surveillance Equipment:** Equipped with advanced radar, communication systems, and night vision for 24/7 monitoring.

Impact:

- **Enhanced Coastal Security:**

Hovercrafts have enabled continuous surveillance in areas like the Sundarbans and Rann of Kutch, where traditional patrol boats struggled. They have been crucial in detecting smuggling operations, illegal fishing, and unauthorized border crossings.

- **Disaster Response and Rescue Operations:**

During cyclones and floods along the eastern coast, hovercrafts have played a critical role in evacuating stranded people, delivering relief materials, and providing rapid response in flooded or marshy areas.

- **Strategic Defense Capability:**

Hovercrafts bolster India's capability to respond swiftly to security threats in shallow coastal zones, particularly near sensitive borders with Pakistan and Bangladesh.

- **Environmental Protection:**

The Indian Coast Guard has also used hovercrafts for environmental monitoring and protecting sensitive ecosystems like the Sundarbans mangroves from illegal activities.

Case Study:3

Military Prototype Development

A notable project was developed by a defense contractor in collaboration with a leading AI research institute (e.g., DARPA-supported projects in the U.S. or similar European military R&D initiatives). This prototype hovercraft demonstrated fully autonomous navigation for amphibious military operations.

- **Mission:** Autonomous reconnaissance and supply delivery in swampy terrains and coastal zones with minimal human intervention.
- **AI Features:**
    - **Autonomous Route Planning:** Hovercraft calculated the safest and most efficient routes based on real-time environmental data.
    - **Dynamic Obstacle Avoidance:** Using LIDAR and AI vision, the hovercraft identified and maneuvered around floating debris, shallow sandbars, and moving objects.
    - **Adaptive Speed Control:** AI algorithms adjusted the hovercraft's speed depending on terrain type, ensuring fuel efficiency and safety.

Impact:

- **Increased Mission Efficiency:**

Hovercrafts with AI navigation could operate 24/7 without fatigue, increasing mission endurance and operational effectiveness.

- **Reduced Human Risk:**

Autonomous systems allowed hovercrafts to undertake high-risk missions (e.g., minefield reconnaissance, disaster relief in hazardous areas) without endangering human operators.

- **Enhanced Precision:**

AI-driven hovercrafts demonstrated superior precision in navigation, crucial for military supply drops, disaster relief, and environmental monitoring in sensitive areas.

- **Commercial Potential:**

The success of AI integration opened doors for commercial applications such as autonomous ferry services, cargo transport in difficult terrains, and automated environmental surveys.

CONCLUSION

Hovercraft technology has advanced significantly, yet it still faces challenges such as air leakage in skirt systems, noise pollution, and energy inefficiency. Innovations like segmented skirts, quieter propulsion systems, and abrasion-resistant materials aim to enhance flexibility, reduce noise, and improve sealing efficiency. A major leap forward is the integration of AI-driven autonomous navigation systems, enabling real-time obstacle detection, adaptive route planning, and precision control, which enhances safety and minimizes human intervention. These AI-powered hovercrafts are proving invaluable in applications like disaster relief, defense, and environmental monitoring. Future advancements include the development of electric and hybrid-electric propulsion systems to reduce carbon emissions, as well as predictive maintenance technologies using AI and IoT to improve reliability and reduce downtime. With these innovations, hovercrafts are becoming smarter, greener, and more versatile, poised to address evolving challenges and redefine their role across various industries.

FUTURE SCOPE

The future scope of integrating AI for autonomous navigation in hovercrafts centers on groundbreaking advancements that promise to revolutionize their operation and functionality. AI-driven technologies enable real-time path optimization, advanced obstacle avoidance, and dynamic terrain adaptability, allowing hovercrafts to navigate complex environments like floodplains, disaster zones, and uneven terrains with minimal human input. For instance, AI-powered hovercraft prototypes equipped with LiDAR, GPS, and sensor fusion are being tested for autonomous search-and-rescue missions during floods, where they can avoid submerged obstacles and deliver relief supplies efficiently. In the defense sector, AI-enhanced hovercrafts are being developed for stealth reconnaissance, leveraging AI-based decision-making to maneuver silently and evade detection. Beyond navigation, future trends include AI applications in predictive maintenance, which use machine learning algorithms to detect early signs of mechanical wear, thus reducing maintenance costs and operational downtime. Energy optimization is another key area, with AI algorithms being used to optimize power distribution, enabling efficient fuel or battery usage, especially in hybrid-electric hovercrafts. Autonomous fleet management is also emerging, where multiple AI-coordinated hovercrafts can operate in synchrony for tasks like large-scale cargo transport or environmental monitoring, significantly boosting efficiency. By integrating AI across these domains, hovercrafts are becoming not only smarter and more adaptive but also more sustainable, paving the way for intelligent, low-emission hovercraft systems that redefine their role in future applications.

REFERENCES

Cabecinhas, D., Batista, P., Oliveira, P., & Silvestre, C. (2017). Hovercraft control with dynamic parameters identification. *IEEE Transactions on Control Systems Technology, 26*(3), 785–796. DOI: 10.1109/TCST.2017.2692733

Fantoni, I., Lozano, R., Mazenc, F., & Pettersen, K. Y. (1999, December). Stabilization of a nonlinear underactuated hovercraft. In *Proceedings of the 38th IEEE Conference on Decision and Control (Cat. No. 99CH36304) 3,* 2533-2538. IEEE. https://doi.org/DOI: 10.1109/CDC.1999.831309

Ganesan, S., & Esakki, B. (2019). Design and development of unmanned hovercraft. *International Journal of Mathematical. Engineering and Management Sciences, 4*(5), 1180–1195. DOI: 10.33889/IJMEMS.2019.4.5-093

Hein, S. M., & Liaw, H. C. (2013, July). Design and development of a compact hovercraft vehicle. In *2013 IEEE/ASME International Conference on Advanced Intelligent Mechatronics,* 1516–1521 IEEE https://doi.org/DOI: 10.1109/AIM.2013.6584310

Hussein, S. M., & Al-Araji, A. S. (2024). Enhancement of a Path-Finding Algorithm for the Hovercraft System Based on Intelligent Hybrid Stochastic Methods. *International Journal of Intelligent Engineering & Systems, 17*(2), 346–364. DOI: 10.22266/ijies2024.0430.29

Lovesey, E. J. (1970). The hovercraft environment. *Applied Ergonomics, 1*(3), 134–139. DOI: 10.1016/0003-6870(70)90002-5 PMID: 15676324

Okafor, B. E. (2013). Development of a hovercraft prototype. *IACSIT International Journal of Engineering and Technology, 3*(3), 276–281. DOI: 10.1109/TCST.2002.804134

Siderits, J. (2011). *Hovercraft: Body and Frame* (Doctoral dissertation, University of Cincinnati).

Sira-Ramírez, H. (2002). Dynamic second-order sliding mode control of the hovercraft vessel. *IEEE transactions on control systems technology, 10*(6), 860-865 https://doi.org/DOI: 10.1109/TCST.2002.804134

Sira-Ramírez, H., & Ibanez, C. A. (2000). On the control of the hovercraft system. *Dynamics and Control, 10*(2), 151–163. DOI: 10.1023/A:1008343807817

Stomberg, G., Schwan, R., Grillo, A., Jones, C. N., & Faulwasser, T. (2024). Cooperative distributed model predictive control for embedded systems: Experiments with hovercraft formations. *arXiv preprint arXiv:2409.13334* https://doi.org//arXiv.2409.13334DOI: 10.48550

Tanaka, K., Iwasaki, M., & Wang, H. O. (2001). Switching control of an R/C hovercraft: Stabilization and smooth switching. *IEEE Transactions on Systems, Man, and Cybernetics. Part B, Cybernetics, 31*(6), 853–863. DOI: 10.1109/3477.969489 PMID: 18244851

Xie, W., Cabecinhas, D., Cunha, R., & Silvestre, C. (2018). Robust motion control of an underactuated hovercraft. *IEEE Transactions on Control Systems Technology, 27*(5), 2195–2208. DOI: 10.1109/TCST.2018.2862861

APPENDIX

Table 1. Chronological Developments in the Historical Background of Hovercraft

Time Period	Key Event	Details
1716	Early Concept by Emanuel Swedenborg	Proposed a flying machine with air-cushion principles, though it was never built.
1870	Air-Lubricated Hulls by Sir John Isaac Thornycroft	Conducted experiments that laid the groundwork for hovercraft technology.
1915	Tsiolkovsky's Air-Cushion Concept	Russian scientist Konstantin Tsiolkovsky described an air-cushion vehicle in his writings.
1920	Ground-Effect Experiments	Austrian engineer Dagobert Müller von Thomamühl experimented with ground-effect vehicles.
1955	Invention of Modern Hovercraft by Sir Christopher Cockerell	Developed the "wall-jet" principle and demonstrated air-cushion technology using a vacuum cleaner and tin cans.
1959	First Functional Hovercraft (SR-N1)	Designed by Saunders-Roe, SR-N1 successfully tested over the English Channel.
1960	Commercial Operations Begin	Hovercraft used for passenger and cargo transport.
1968	SR-N4 "Mountbatten-class" Hovercraft	Introduced for cross-Channel car and passenger transport.
1970s–1980s	Military Applications	Widely adopted for amphibious assaults, mine-sweeping, and patrol operations.
1980	Development of Zubr-Class Hovercraft	Advanced military hovercraft developed by the USSR.
1990	Technological Advancements	Lightweight materials, modern propulsion systems, and increased efficiency.
2000	Introduction of Zubr-Class (World's Largest Hovercraft)	Russia developed the world's largest hovercraft for military applications.
2000s-Present	Evolution to Air Cushion Vehicles (ACVs) & Electric Hovercraft	ACVs began replacing traditional hovercraft; electric hovercraft prototypes emerged.

Chapter 3
VitaChain:
An AI-Blockchain-Based EHR Management Framework With Zero-Knowledge Proofs for Enhanced Privacy

Anand Motwani
https://orcid.org/0000-0003-0823-0292
VIT Bhopal University, India

Nilamadhab Mishra
https://orcid.org/0000-0002-1330-4869
VIT Bhopal University, India

Aditya Patil
School of Computing Science and Engineering, VIT Bhopal University, India

Anshika Sinha
School of Computing Science and Engineering, VIT Bhopal University, India

Harsh Pailkar
School of Computing Science and Engineering, VIT Bhopal University, India

Himanish Mandrekar
School of Computing Science and Engineering, VIT Bhopal University, India

ABSTRACT

As Electronic Health Records (EHRs) become integral to modern healthcare, concerns regarding security, privacy, and scalability have emerged. Conventional centralized systems face vulnerabilities and lack patient data control, necessitating innovative decentralized solutions. This research introduces a novel AI-blockchain-based architecture for permissioned health networks, leveraging zero-knowledge succinct, non-interactive arguments of knowledge (zkSNARKs). The framework integrates AI-blockchain, InterPlanetary File System (IPFS), and zkSNARKs to enhance EHR security, privacy, and scalability. IPFS is employed for off-chain storage, improving

DOI: 10.4018/979-8-3373-6097-3.ch003

scalability alongside blockchain's tamper-proof logging. Encryption and smart contract-based access controls preserve privacy.

1. INTRODUCTION

The healthcare sector continuously evolves through Electronic Health Records (EHRs) digitalization. The adoption of Electronic Health Records (EHRs) has been recognized as a crucial step towards improving patient care (Ratwani, 2017), further emphasizing the need for secure and efficient management of such records. This paradigm shift offers unprecedented opportunities for increased efficiency, improved patient care, and data-driven insights (Ratwani, 2017). Nevertheless, this expansion is not devoid of its accompanying challenges, with significant apprehensions centering on interoperability, security, and privacy emerging as crucial focal areas. Conventional health data management systems, which are naturally centralized, deal with weaknesses associated with single points of failure, making patient data susceptible to potential cyber threats. Concurrently, the significant absence of patient autonomy about their medical data has raised substantial privacy concerns, necessitating a novel strategy to combine technological advancements with ethical obligations. According to recent allegations, more than 125 million healthcare records have been breached in the United States from 2019 to 2022. This breach has exposed highly confidential medical information such as diagnosis, treatments, prescriptions, and insurance details. The main challenge is the rapid growth of healthcare data, which also presents a significant scaling problem.

AI-Blockchain technology has found potential applications in various domains, including the Internet of Things (Basil, Ambe, Ekhator, Fonkem, & Nduma, 2022), necessitating the exploration of its utility in the healthcare sector. It is renowned for its decentralized, transparent, and unchangeable characteristics and presents itself as a promising solution to redesign the structure of EHR systems (P. Sharma, Borah, & Namasudra, 2021).

Given this, the proposed architecture is seen as a unique approach to this challenge, intelligently blending AI-Blockchain with the Interplanetary File System and zero-knowledge proofs. This combination of advanced technologies creates a comprehensive solution that enhances security and privacy measures while also addressing the significant scalability issues that arise from the rapid expansion of healthcare data. The solutions should give patients more control over their medical data (Basil et al., 2022). Research pioneers a tailored AI--Blockchain solution for the complex landscape of modern healthcare systems, effectively addressing critical security and privacy challenges in permissioned EHR networks.

1.1. Objectives / Background

Central to this framework is a decentralized AI-Blockchain architecture positioned to alter the scalability, privacy, and access control characteristics of EHRs. Privacy considerations become vital in the framework with the seamless deployment of encryption and fine-grained access controls. Encryption appears to be a strong guardian, reinforcing patient information and providing access to authorized institutions with the required decryption capabilities. Simultaneously, installing fine-grained access controls utilizing smart contracts empowers patients with a granular level of autonomy, allowing them to select who can view and alter their medical records. Smart contracts allow complicated access control restrictions and data-sharing rules to be encoded directly on the AI-Blockchain (Ding et al., 2020). Holistic AI-Blockchain frameworks that can effectively address the range of security and privacy challenges for health data exchange across multiple systems still need to be enhanced (Hasnain, Albogamy, Alamri, Ghani, & Mehboob, 2023) (Smart, 2023). This refined technique fortifies data privacy, harmonizing neatly with tight legal limits and ethical imperatives. The proposed framework utilizes zkSNARK, a cryptographic protocol enabling a prover to demonstrate knowledge of certain information to a verifier without revealing the details. It is widely used in cryptocurrencies like Zcash, zkSNARKs provide three key properties: zero-knowledge, succinctness, and non-interactivity, ensuring proofs are efficient and secure. They utilize advanced cryptographic techniques such as elliptic curve pairings to enable quick verification of complex proofs. Despite their efficiency, zkSNARKs necessitate a trusted setup phase to mitigate potential vulnerabilities.

Embarking on a pioneering trajectory, the framework uses a hybrid storage method that consciously employs both on-chain and off-chain technology to provide the secure, transparent, and auditable storage of EHRs (Hasnain et al., 2023). Adding off-chain storage, reinforced by on-chain hashes, not only sidesteps the inherent scalability limits of ordinary AI-Blockchains but also preserves the integrity of the stored medical information, generating trust in the legitimacy of the shared data.

This unique solution not only alleviates scalability challenges connected with the expanding volume of healthcare data but also ensures the transparency and immutability that characterize AI-Blockchain technology. By orchestrating a sophisticated evaluation, the research endeavors to validate the conceptual robustness of the framework and position it as a versatile and comprehensive solution to the multifaceted security, privacy, and scalability challenges confronted by the healthcare industry in the digital age. In doing so, the research expects to contribute considerably to the continuing discourse on the ethical deployment of technology in healthcare, achieving an ideal balance between innovation and the imperative to safeguard patient welfare and privacy (P. Sharma et al., 2021) (Smart, 2023). The research evaluation transcends basic theoretical notions, including various indications. These measures, including but not limited to block generation time, transaction overhead with encryption, and file upload/download time, serve as concrete benchmarks. We provide detailed insights into the efficiency, practicality, and real-world viability of the integrated AI-Blockchain, IPFS, and zero-knowledge proof system.

1.2. Key Contributions

The research pioneered a tailored AI-Blockchain solution for the complex landscape of modern healthcare systems, effectively addressing critical challenges in permissioned EHR networks. The key contributions of our work are as follows:

- Proposed a novel AI-Blockchain-based framework for EHR management, leveraging zkSNARKs to enhance security, efficiency, privacy, and scalability.
- The architecture combined AI-Blockchain with off-chain storage, encrypting EHR data and enforcing access control through smart contracts.
- Formal mathematical proofs to validate zkSNARK's zero-knowledge, completeness, and knowledge soundness properties.
- Extensive performance evaluations were presented to validate the framework's efficiency and scalability.
- Validation conducted based on key evaluation metrics: throughput, latency, and gas consumption under varying loads.

The research pioneered a tailored AI-Blockchain solution for the complex landscape of modern healthcare systems, effectively addressing critical challenges in permissioned EHR networks.

1.3. Paper Outline

The rest of the paper is organized as follows: Section 2 presents a literature review of existing systems. Section 3 describes the theorems employed in our suggested method. Section 4 presents our proposed architecture. Section 5 details the implementation and analyzes the results. Section 6 includes final thoughts and outlines future research directions.

2. LITERATURE REVIEW

In recent years, incorporating AI-Blockchain technology into healthcare systems to manage sensitive electronic health records (EHRs) has attracted substantial attention from researchers. However, persisting challenges regarding interoperability, security, privacy, and scalability remain important impediments to adoption (Ghosh, Chakraborty, Hasan, Rashid, & Siddique, 2023), (Yi, Keong, Razali, & Innovation, 2023). This literature review assesses developments in AI-Blockchain-based EHR systems between 2019 and 2023, identifying important constraints and potential opportunities.

Initial research focused largely on security and interoperability (Liu, Wang, Jin, Li, & Li, 2019). They proposed a private AI-Blockchain leveraging proxy re-encryption and smart contracts for access-controlled EHR exchange between healthcare providers. Benefits like auditability were shown; however, scalability and dependence on third-party trusts posed adoption issues (B. Sharma, Halder, & Singh, 2020). Built a national, public AI-Blockchain network to facilitate nationwide data interoperability. While data transparency was enhanced, stricter access constraints were needed.

Recognizing shortcomings in later works stressed privacy preservation. Hybrid AI-Blockchain splits personal and non-personal data across federated and public chains, enabling patient consent-based sharing (Mukherji & Ganguli, 2020). It coupled permissioned AI-Blockchain and IPFS for tamper-proof EHR exchanges with P2P verification. However, patient privacy via encryption or access limitations was absent.

They later combined advanced encryption techniques (Huang, Zhu, Xiao, Sun, & Huang, 2020), and produced proxy re-encryption and zero-knowledge proofs within an auditable, access-controlled AI-Blockchain framework. (Wu, Dwivedi, & Srivastava, 2021) created patient-centric access control mechanisms for EHR transactions with permissions maintained on the AI-Blockchain. Nonetheless, scalability and storage limitations persisted.

To boost performance (Zou, Lv, & Zhao, 2021), reputation-based AI-Blockchain exploited medical organizations' mining skills for speedier consensus. (Wang et al., 2021) Separately presented searchable encryption algorithms enable private data queries. Nonetheless, both focus solely on security or storage without multifaceted data safety features.

Recent works have highlighted extensive frameworks and real-world piloting. HealthChain (Chenthara, 2021) integrates authorization, encryption, and smart contracts for strong, secure EHR exchanges. (Johari, Kumar, Gupta, & Vidyarthi, 2022) successfully showed their BLOSOM system's interoperability by integrating with hospital IT systems for secured data transfers. Andersson (Andersson, 2021) extensively analyzes an Ethereum/IPFS-based solution against measures like latency, revealing lingering legal and scalability problems.

The work (Han, Zhang, & Vermund, 2022) have explored the integration of Healthcare 4.0 and AI-Blockchain into secure cloud-based EHR systems. Mahajan's architecture combines edge, fog, cloud computing, and AI-Blockchain layers, emphasizing bidirectional data handling and security. Han's AI-Blockchain-based solution addresses concerns in current EHR systems, such as inadequate interoperability, data leakage, and security issues. The private AI-Blockchain network, comprising healthcare providers and patients, can handle large transaction volumes and reduce costs. However, computational burden and regulatory compliance are future challenges, highlighting the need for further development.

The works (Sonkamble, Bongale, Phansalkar, Sharma, & Rajput, 2023) and (Borade, Paradkar, Takalkar, & Trivedi, 2023) have proposed AI-Blockchain-based solutions to address the security and privacy concerns of electronic health records (EHRs). Sonkamble et al. used Hyperledger Fabric to store and transport records securely, while Borade et al. used Ethereum and IPFS to grant access to records through smart contracts. Both studies demonstrated improved throughput and lower latency with additional users, but scalability and payment module-related issues were observed. (Yi et al., 2023) presented a AI-Blockchain-based system using Hyperledger Fabric for decentralized, secure record storage and interchange. The system managed massive transaction volumes with low latency and high throughput, boosting security and privacy. Further work includes incorporating AI/ML and performance testing for workloads and network conditions.

In addition to the works discussed, (Yaqoob, Salah, Jayaraman, & Al-Hammadi, 2022) provided a comprehensive overview of the opportunities, challenges, and future recommendations for AI-Blockchain-based healthcare data management systems.

While incremental gains have been accomplished, holistic AI-Blockchain solutions handle the whole spectrum of security, privacy, storage flexibility, and scalability concerns that remain lacking. Hence, there is impetus for developing consolidated frameworks like VitaChain to address significant real-world hurdles.

Table 1. Review Summary of Chain Types, Storage Methods, Data Encryption, and Access Control

Name of the Works	Chain Type	Storage	Encryption	Access Control
The work (Liu et al., 2019)	Pvt	On	Yes	CG
The works (B. Sharma et al., 2020), (Wu et al., 2021) , (Wang et al., 2021)	Pub	Off	Yes	FG
The works (Mukherji & Ganguli, 2020), (Yi et al., 2023)	Pvt	B	Yes	FG
The works (Shahnaz, Qamar, & Khalid, 2019), (Borade et al., 2023)	Pub	Off	No	FG
The work (Huang et al., 2020)	Pub	B	Yes	FG
The work (Zou et al., 2021)	Pvt	Off	Yes	CG
The works (Chenthara, 2021), (Han et al., 2022)	Pvt	On	Yes	FG
The work (Johari et al., 2022)	Pub	On	No	FG
The work (Andersson, 2021)	Pub	On	Yes	FG
The work (Sonkamble et al., 2023)	Pvt	B	Yes	FG

Ref. - Reference, Pvt - Private, Pub - Public, Hybrid - Hybrid, On - On-chain, Off- Off-chain, B - Both, CG - Coarse Grained, FG - Fine Grained.

As part of our research on improving privacy in AI-Blockchain-based electronic health record (EHR) systems using zero-knowledge proofs, we conducted a comprehensive literature review to identify relevant studies. The references presented in the Table-1 were carefully selected based on their direct relevance to our research objectives and their contributions to privacy-preserving techniques in AI-Blockchain-based EHR systems. The Table-1 summarizes the key characteristics of various AI-Blockchain-based EHR frameworks proposed in the literature, including the chain type (private, public, or hybrid), storage method (on-chain, off-chain, or both), data encryption implementation, and access control granularity (coarse-grained or fine-grained).

We employed a systematic approach to extract the pertinent information from these research papers, as stated in Figure 1. First, we thoroughly examined the papers, paying close attention to the sections discussing AI-Blockchain architectures, data storage mechanisms, encryption strategies, and access control mechanisms. Subsequently, we meticulously abstracted the key characteristics related to our research focus, including the AI-Blockchain type (private, public, or hybrid), data storage method (on-chain, off-chain, or both), data encryption implementation (yes or no), and access control granularity (coarse-grained or fine-grained). This rigorous process ensured that we captured the most relevant and essential details from each study, allowing for a comprehensive analysis and comparative evaluation of the proposed solutions within the context of our research goals.

Figure 1. Publications per year from 2019 to 2023

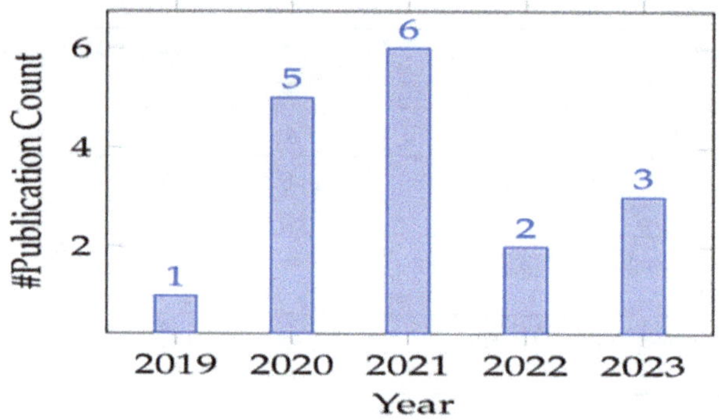

3. METHODOLOGY

3.1. System Model Notation

We consider an AI-Blockchain-based EHR system with the following components:

Electronic Health Records (EHR): Structured data sets comprising patient medical information represented as key-value stores {d1:v1,..., dn:vn} with n data fields.

Smart Contract (C): Program code that processes EHRs, encapsulating business logic and transformation rules. Executing C applies updates by running the function f_C.

We utilize a succinct, non-interactive argument of knowledge scheme (zkSNARK) consisting of polynomial-time algorithms KeyGen, Prover, and Verifier with a public/secret parameter setup.

3.2. Definitions

Security Parameter (λ): λ represents the security level of a cryptographic scheme measured in bits.

Role: A larger λ indicates a higher security level but may result in increased computational overhead.

Negligibility (ϵ(λ)): Refers to the vanishingly small probability of an event. A function ϵ(λ) is considered negligible if it approaches zero faster than the inverse of any polynomial in the security parameter λ.

Implication: Events with negligible probability are considered computationally infeasible, providing a level of confidence in the security of cryptographic schemes.

We set security parameter $\lambda = 128$ bits to achieve baseline AES-level security against computationally bounded adversaries. Negligibility parameter ($\epsilon(\lambda)$) represents probabilities that are smaller than 1/(any polynomial) in λ.

3.3. Assumptions

Let H be the Computational Circuit representing EHR transaction history.
n = Number of computational gates in H.
Let $|H|$ denote the size of the health record transaction history in bits = O(n).
Let π be the zk-SNARK proof for the correct execution of H.
$m = |\pi|$ denotes the size of the zk-SNARK proof in bits.
where $m \ll n$

3.4. Theorems

Theorem 1. *Using a zk-SNARK scheme enables efficient and scalable validation of smart contract execution on EHRs without re-executing the contract on-chain.*

For computational circuit C, zk-SNARK proof P is significantly smaller than naive storage of C. Formally: $|P| = m \ll |C| = O(n)$

1. **Key Generation:** The KeyGen algorithm generates proving (p_k) and verification (v_k) keys. This can be represented as KeyGen → (p_k,v_k)
2. **Proof Generation:** The Prover algorithm takes p_k, the original EHR (EHR), the updated EHR (EHR'), and the contract function (f_C) as input and generates a zk-SNARK proof (π). This can be expressed as Prover → (p_k, EHR, EHR', f_C) → π
3. **Proof Verification:** The Verifier algorithm takes v_k, EHR, EHR', and π as input and outputs 1 if the proof is valid and 0 otherwise. Verifier → (v_k, EHR, EHR', π) → {0,1}

Proof:
By the construction of our cryptographic bilinear groups:

$|G_1| = |G_2| = 256$ bits

where G_1, G_2 are cyclic groups under elliptic curve cryptography.
Let $g_1 \in G_1$, $g_2 \in G_2$ be generators of respective groups.
Our proof P encodes the following values:

$\pi = (a, b, c)$

where: $a \in G_{n1}$, $b \in G_2$, $c \in Z_q$.

Here n is a cryptographic security parameter. By properties of the bilinear pairing:

$$|\pi| = 256n + 256 + q \text{ bits} \approx k_1 \log n,$$

for constant k_1 encompassing security overhead

In contrast, naive storage of boolean circuit C requires table entries per gate. With n gates, this requires:

$$|C| = k_2 n, \text{ for constant } k_2$$

Comparing proof size scales versus circuit size:

$$|\pi| \approx k_1 \log n \ll k_2 n = |C|$$

where log n grows much slower than n. Therefore, by asymptotic complexity, we have: $|P| \ll |C|$. This completes our proof of the zk-SNARK scalability theorem.

In Figure 2, the flow of smart contract validation and execution is depicted.

Figure 2. The flow of smart contract validation and execution

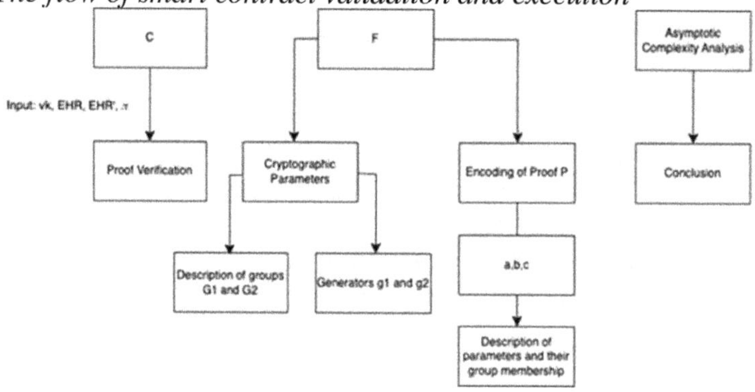

Theorem 2. *A zk-SNARK proof P for computational circuit C does not leak any information about the private inputs or structure of C beyond the declared output.*

Proof: We utilize the simulation paradigm to prove model privacy formally. Intuitively, if proofs can be simulated without access to the private inputs, they cannot leak private information.

Let:

- λ be the security parameter

- C = $\{C_\lambda\}$ be an ensemble of polynomial-size computational circuits representing the EHR computation
- x = $\{x_\lambda\}$ be the ensemble of private medical data inputs
- P = $\{P_\lambda\}$ be the ensemble of actual zk-SNARK proofs
- S = $\{S_\lambda\}$ be the ensemble of simulated proofs

We require computational indistinguishability between real proofs and simulated proofs:

$$\{P_\lambda\} \approx_c \{S_\lambda\}$$

This means that no polynomial-time algorithm can distinguish between the distributions with a non-negligible advantage.

We now prove by contradiction that this implies privacy.

Assume there exists an efficient extractor algorithm E that can derive private information from proofs:

$$E(P_\lambda) = x_\lambda$$

We build a distinguisher D:

$$D(r) = \begin{cases} 1 & \text{if } E(t) \text{ outputs valid private data} \\ 0 & \text{otherwise} \end{cases}$$

By our assumption, D(Pλ) = 1 since the extractor succeeds on real proofs. However, E(Sλ) cannot output actual private data since Sλ is constructed without access to xλ. Therefore, D(Sλ) = 0.

This contradicts the computational indistinguishability condition since D efficiently distinguishes real proofs from simulations. Therefore, our original assumption must be false. No efficient extractor E can recover private data from proofs. This completes the proof of privacy as depicted in Figure 3.

Figure 3. Proof simulation without access to private inputs

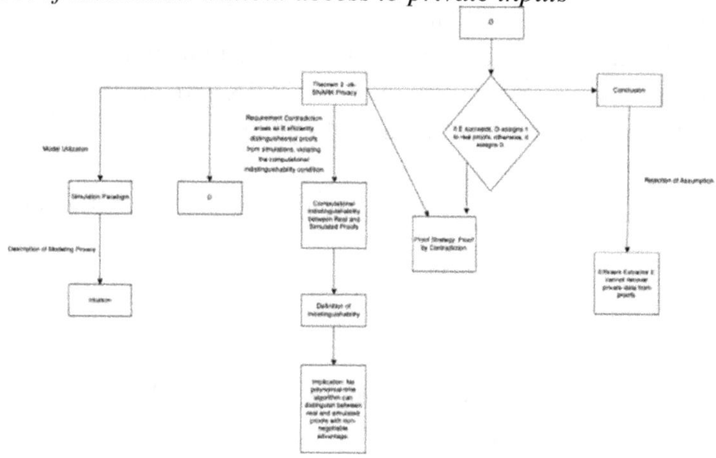

Theorem 3. *The verification algorithm of the zk-SNARK system will reject any proof P for circuit C with non-negligible probability if C was not appropriately executed on valid inputs.*

Proof: We will prove this theorem by contradiction, assuming a prover can construct an accepted proof for an invalid computation and demonstrating how this leads to a contradiction.

Let:

- Π be a zk-SNARK scheme consisting of algorithms (Setup, Prove, Verify)
- λ be the security parameter
- C_λ be the ensemble of EHR computational circuits
- x_λ be the ensemble of valid private medical data inputs
- P_λ be an ensemble of proofs output by Prove(C_λ, x_λ)

We define:

Completeness:

$$\Pr\left[\text{Verify}\left(P_\lambda, C_\lambda\right) = 1\right] = 1$$

Knowledge Soundness: For probabilistic polynomial-time adversaries A,

$$\Pr\left[\text{Verify}\left(A\left(C_\lambda, 1^\lambda\right), C_\lambda\right) = 1\right] < \text{negl}\left(\lambda\right)$$

where negl(λ) is a negligible function.

Now assume towards contradiction there exists an efficient prover A that can construct an accepted proof P^* for Cλ without knowing valid inputs x_λ:

Verify $(P, C_\lambda)=1$, where $P=A(C_\lambda, 1^\lambda)$

This directly contradicts knowledge soundness, implying the adversary can construct an accepted proof without knowing secret inputs x_λ.

Therefore, our assumption must be false. No efficient prover can generate a valid proof P^* without faithfully executing C_λ on proper private inputs x_λ. This completes the proof by contradiction. The knowledge soundness property of zk-SNARKs mathematically guarantees the security of the verified computations against arbitrary malicious behavior, as depicted in Figure 4.

Figure 4. Execution of Verification Algorithm by contradiction

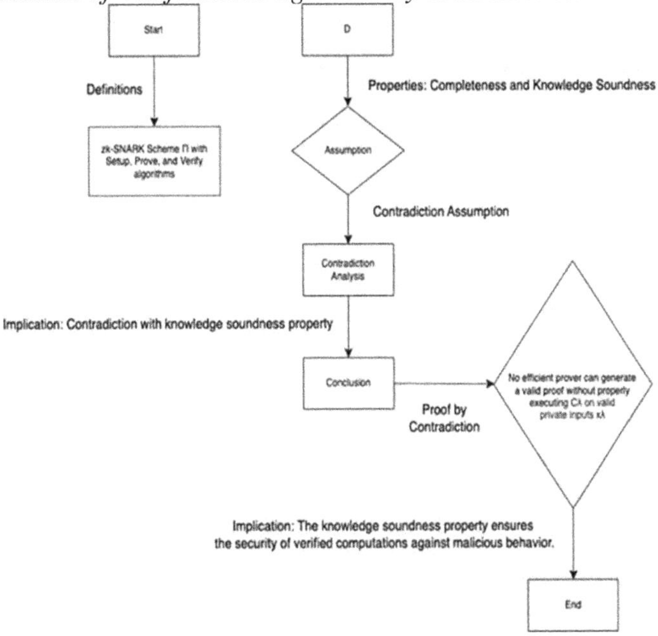

4. PROPOSED AI-BLOCKCHAIN FRAMEWORK

The proposed AI-Blockchain solution in this research is centered around leveraging zkSNARKs to revolutionize EHRs in healthcare systems (Ali et al., 2018). By incorporating zkSNARKs into the AI-Blockchain architecture, the solution aims to address the critical issues of security, privacy, and scalability. This cryptographic technique allows for verifying information without revealing the actual data, ensuring that sensitive patient information remains confidential. Utilizing zkSNARKs enhances the overall security of the EHRs, providing a robust defense against unauthorized access and tampering. This framework leverages a modular design with the core medical record data repository implemented as a private permissioned AI-Blockchain ledger. The system allows performance metrics like transaction throughput and latency to be benchmarked by generating and processing varying loads of AI-Blockchain transactions that simulate real-world working conditions.

When a user attempts to log in to the system utilizing a device, a multi-step process is initiated. The initial phase involves the system authenticating the device to ensure its legitimacy. This authentication process verifies whether the device has previously been registered with the system. Device registration is a crucial security measure, restricting access to authorized devices only.

Figure 5. Proposed VitaChain Transaction Process

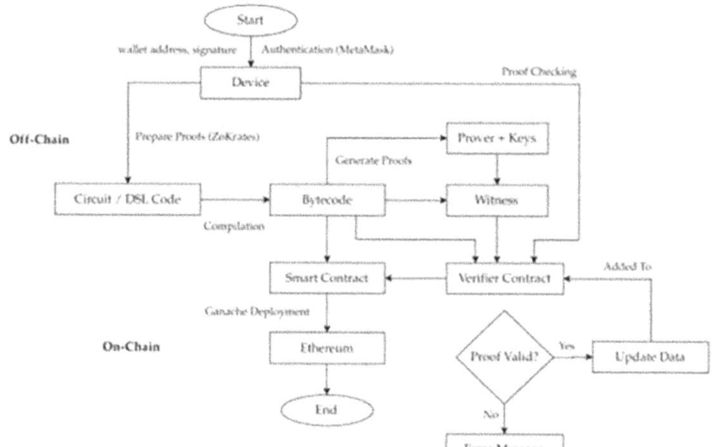

On the first registration of the device, the system promptly initiates the registration process. This process encompasses creating an intermediate code by compiling the circuit code written. Once the intermediate code is generated, the setup command is run on this file, generating the prover and witness and establishing a verifier smart contract. The prover and the witness keys act as encryption keys, and the verifier smart contract plays a pivotal role in verifying the authenticity of the data the device provides. Upon its creation, the verifier contract is then imported into the EHR smart contract. This contract resides on the main AI-Blockchain. The heavy computation is done off-chain, and the results are then imported to the main chain, reducing the main AI-Blockchain's load. The detailed operational aspects are included in Figure 5 to understand the EHR on the proposed framework.

The proposed system introduces a secure and efficient method for managing EHRs on the AI-Blockchain, ensuring data integrity, privacy, and authentication. The novelty lies in integrating a two-tier architecture comprising a main AI-Blockchain and a verifier smart contract for off-chain computations.

During the device authentication phase, the system establishes encryption keys and deploys a verifier smart contract. Subsequent logins involve retrieving data from the verifier smart contract and comparing it with the main AI-Blockchain data. If the data matches, the user is granted permission to modify the EHR smart contract. However, if discrepancies are detected, an error message is thrown, preventing unauthorized modifications and safeguarding data integrity.

The system's strength is its rigorous data verification process during subsequent logins. It checks the data stored in the verifier smart contract against the main chain data. Only if the data matches exactly is the user permitted to modify the primary chain data. Any discrepancy, whether missing information or unauthorized modifications, triggers an error, preventing data tampering and ensuring the authenticity and reliability of stored information.

The off-chain computation performed by the verifier smart contract reduces the load on the main AI-Blockchain, improving efficiency and scalability. The error handling mechanism promptly prevents unauthorized modifications, enhancing security and maintaining the trustworthiness of the AI-Blockchain ecosystem.

In summary, the proposed system (Figure 6) introduces a novel two-tier architecture that combines the advantages of off-chain computations and rigorous data verification mechanisms. This approach ensures the secure management of EHRs, safeguards patient privacy, maintains data integrity, and upholds the principles of trust and transparency in the AI-Blockchain ecosystem.

To validate the proposed architecture, we developed a prototype implementation of the proposed framework using ZoKrates and Truffle and evaluated performance against key criteria like throughput, latency, scalability, security, gas consumption, and block creation time.

4.1. Implementation

Figure 6. Proposed VitaChain Architecture

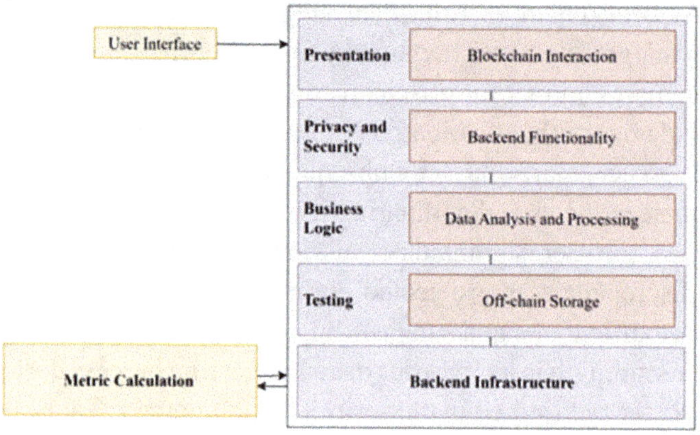

In the decentralized application (dApp) ecosystem, users interact with the application through web browsers or mobile applications, experiencing the presentation layer encompassing the user interface (UI). This UI developed using JavaScript, plays a pivotal role in facilitating communication, offering a seamless user experience, and visualizing the functionalities of the dApp. The narrative unfolds with a crucial aspect—using web3.js, a vital library enabling communication and interaction with the Ethereum AI-Blockchain. To bolster privacy and security, developers leverage snark.js, a JavaScript library incorporating knowledge-free proofs (zk-proofs), ensuring information verification without compromising sensitive data.

4.1.1. Presentation Layer—UI Development with JavaScript and web3.js

In the dApp ecosystem, the presentation layer, developed with JavaScript, ensures an intuitive user interface (UI). Integration with web3.js facilitates seamless communication with the Ethereum AI-Blockchain, enhancing the overall user experience.

4.1.2. Privacy and Security Enhancement: Leveraging snark.js for zk-proofs

Snark.js, a JavaScript library with zero-knowledge proofs (zk-proofs), bolsters privacy and security. This enables information verification without compromising sensitive data, establishing a robust privacy layer in the dApp.

4.1.3. Development, Testing, and Deployment: Truffle Framework

The Truffle framework streamlines dApp development, testing, and deployment on the Ethereum network. Its comprehensive tools simplify smart contract management, ensuring an efficient development lifecycle.

4.1.4. Business Logic Contract: Core Functionality in Solidity

The Business Logic contract, written in Solidity, defines rules and transactions on the Ethereum AI-Blockchain and serves as the core functionality of the dApp.

4.1.5. Backend Functionality: Python for Data Analysis

Python Integration: Python is employed for backend functions such as metric calculations and data analysis.

Library Usage: Libraries like Panda are utilized for efficient data management, ensuring robust behind-the-scenes operations.

4.1.6. Testing for Reliability: Chai and Mocha

JavaScript Libraries: The dApp undergoes rigorous testing using JavaScript libraries such as Chai and Mocha. Verification of Reliability: Testing ensures the application is reliable, robust, and capable of handling various scenarios. Off-chain Storage: IPFS Integration

IPFS Usage: IPFS facilitates Off-chain Storage, securely storing large or irrelevant data outside of the AI-Blockchain. Distributed File Storage: IPFS acts as a distributed file storage system, enhancing data security and efficiency.

4.1.7. Backend Infrastructure: Server Hosting

Server Functionality: The server hosts the dApp's backend infrastructure, manages data storage, executes business logic, and serves the UI.

Comprehensive Ecosystem: These features collectively form a robust ecosystem for developing, deploying, and evolving decentralized applications, ensuring heightened privacy, security, and performance for users (Salzano, Marchesi, Pareschi, & Tonelli, 2024). However, the system promptly throws an error if there is a discrepancy in the data, whether due to missing information or any form of modification (Yaqoob et al., 2022).

5. PERFORMANCE AND EVALUATION AND RESULTS

5.1. Performance Metrics

Throughput (τ): The number of transactions processed per unit of time.

$$\tau = \frac{1}{t_{end} - t_{start}}$$

where t_{start} and t_{end} are the start and end timestamps of a batch of transactions, respectively.

Latency (λ): The time elapsed between the initiation and successful execution of a transaction.

$$\lambda = t_{end} - t_{start}$$

Where t_{start} and t_{end} are a transaction's start and end timestamps, respectively.

Gas Used (γ): The amount of gas consumed by a transaction, measuring the computational effort required to execute the Ethereum AI-Blockchain.

The prototype underwent extensive testing on transaction throughput, latency, scalability, security, and other parameters:

1. Throughput was measured as transactions per second (TPS) for workloads ranging from 5 to 25 concurrent transactions.
2. Latency was measured as the end-to-end time for writing transactions to complete AI-Blockchain commits.
3. Scalability was evaluated by increasing the network size to 35 peers and measuring TPS.
4. Security was evaluated through penetration testing, failure simulations, and automated vulnerability scans.
5. Storage performance was evaluated by loading up to 1GB of sample medical files into IPFS nodes and measuring access times.
6. Security was enhanced using zero-knowledge proofs, where users can generate proofs for verifying the integrity of their stored data.
7. Validation of access control policies was done through simulated unauthorized access attempts.

The network demonstrated scalability in transaction throughput as follows:

1. 25 peers with 35 concurrent transactions.
2. Throughput increased linearly with network size up to 35 peers.

3. Sub-second latency achieved for writing transactions end-to-end.
4. IPFS nodes achieved read speeds of 5 MB/s for 1 GB datasets.

While the scalability evaluation conducted on the framework prototype provides promising results, the tests had certain limitations that must be acknowledged. The network size was constrained to a few nodes due to testing environment capabilities, while large-scale deployments could involve hundreds of nodes. Due to the same testing environment limitations, the number of concurrent users and transactions was limited. Only basic transaction types were used instead of complex smart contract workflows. The tests were conducted on cloud infrastructure, while real-world setups would differ. Workloads were simulated but did not fully capture fluctuations and spikes in production loads. These limitations imply that the performance in health-care industry settings may deviate considerably from testing. More comprehensive evaluations are required to establish scalability under diverse real-world conditions.

5.2. Transaction Process Algorithm

The presented algorithm outlines a structured methodology for evaluating the performance metrics of the EHRContract in various stress testing scenarios. The process begins with initializing key variables, including the EHRContract and metrics arrays. Stress testing parameters are systematically manipulated, and metrics are recorded for each scenario, providing valuable insights into the system's behavior under different loads. A nested loop iterates through the specified values for each stress testing parameter, conducting trials to account for performance fluctuations. The algorithm captures essential metrics such as throughput, latency, and gas consumption for each transaction. The calculated metrics are then aggregated to derive average figures, offering a comprehensive understanding of the system's efficiency. The systematic approach adopted in this algorithm enables a thorough evaluation of the EHRContract's performance across diverse stress testing scenarios. The algorithm assesses the system's scalability and resilience under different transaction loads by varying the stress testing parameters and analyzing the resulting metrics. The collected data, including average latency, throughput, and gas consumption, provides quantifiable measures of the EHRContract's capability to handle real-world demands effectively.

Table 2. VitaChain Metrics Algorithm

Data: EHRContract, Stress Testing Scenarios, Stress Testing Parameters **Result: Metrics for each stress testing scenario**

for *each stress testing scenario,* **do**
Initialize metrics array $metrics_i$, $startTime_i$;
for *each stress testing parameter p* **do**
Initialize metrics array $incrementalMetrics_p$;
for *each value v of p* **do**
Initialize $cumulativeMetrics_v$ = {Throughput: 0, Latency: [], GasUsed: 0};
for *each trial j* **do**
Reset $startTime_j$, transactions;
for *each transaction tx* **do**
Record timestamps;
Execute *tx*;
Record timestamps;
Calculate *latencytx = endTimestamp − startTimestamp;*
Calculate $throughput_j = 1/(endTimestamp - startTime_j)$;
Update $cumulativeMetrics_v$:;
Throughput+ = $throughput_j$;
Latency.push($latency_{tx}$);
GasUsed += Gas consumption of *tx*;
Calculate $avgLatencyv = mean(cumulativeMetrics_v.Latency)$;
Calculate $avgThroughput_v = cumulativeMetrics_v.Throughput/M$;
Calculate $avgGasUsed_v = cumulativeMetrics_v.GasUsed/M$;
Append $\{v, avgThroughput_v, avgLatency_v, avgGasUsed_v\}$;
Append $incrementalMetrics_p$ to $metrics_i$;
Log and display $metrics_i$;
Plot $metrics_i$ for evaluation;

5.3. Results Discussion

We implement our proposed architecture using the following languages, technologies, and parameters.

Languages used:

Solidity (Smart Contract Development)

JavaScript (Scripting)

Web3.JS (Interacting with the smart contract)

Snark.JS (zero-knowledge proofs)

Python (Metrics calculation, load testing and visualization)

Technologies:

Ganache (deployment)

Chai and Mocha (smart contract testing)

IPFS (decentralized storage)

Parameters:

Number of peers: 25

Number of concurrent transactions: 35

The incremental throughput graph (figure 7) indicates that the proposed architecture consistently outperforms the traditional architecture, with the gap widening as the number of concurrent transactions increases. The AI-Blockchain-based and centralized EHR systems lie between the proposed and traditional architectures, with the centralized system performing slightly better than the AI-Blockchain-based system. In the incremental latency graph, the proposed architecture exhibits lower latency than the conventional architecture across all data points. The AI-Blockchain-based and centralized EHR systems also demonstrate lower latency than the traditional architecture, with the AI-Blockchain-based system having a slight edge over the centralized system.

The comparison of incremental gas used shows that the proposed architecture requires less gas than the traditional architecture, except for a few data points. The AI-Blockchain-based and centralized EHR systems fall between the proposed and traditional architectures, with the AI-Blockchain-based system marginally outperforming the centralized system. For concurrent user throughput, the proposed architecture consistently delivers higher throughput than the other architectures, followed by centralized, traditional, and AI-Blockchain-based EHR systems. Regarding concurrent user latency, the proposed architecture exhibits lower latency than the other architectures across all data points. Traditional architecture has the highest latency, while AI-Blockchain-based and centralized EHR systems lie in between. Lastly, the graph of concurrent user gas used shows that the proposed architecture generally requires less gas than the traditional architecture, with the AI-Blockchain-based EHR system and the centralized EHR system falling between the two.

It's important to note that this study has limitations, and the results may vary depending on the specific implementation details, workload characteristics, and real-world scenarios. Further testing and validation would be necessary to generalize the findings as analyzed in Figures 8-12.

Figure 7. Number of concurrent transactions Vs. incremental throughputs

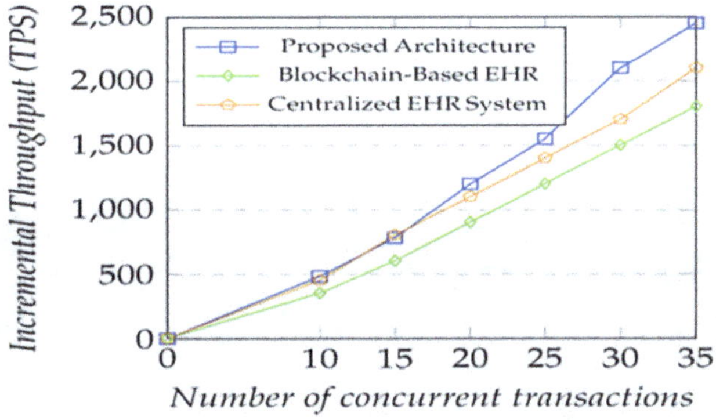

Figure 8. Number of concurrent transactions Vs. incremental latency

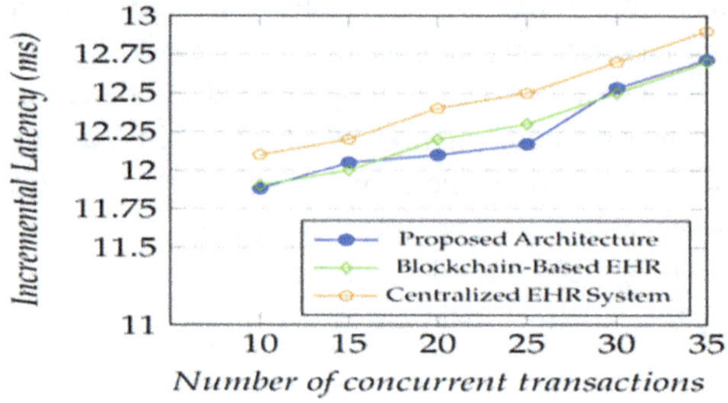

Figure 9. Number of concurrent transactions Vs. incremental GAS

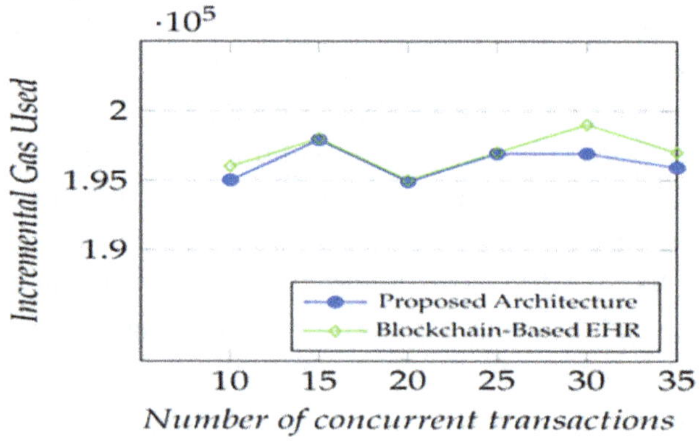

Figure 10. Number of concurrent transactions Vs. users' throughputs

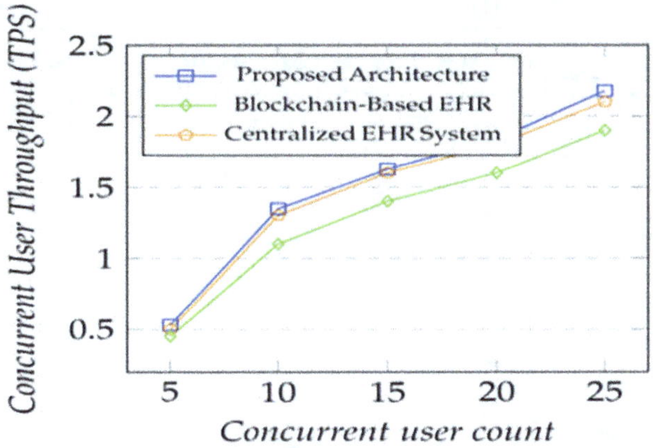

Figure 11. Number of concurrent transactions Vs. Concurrent users latency

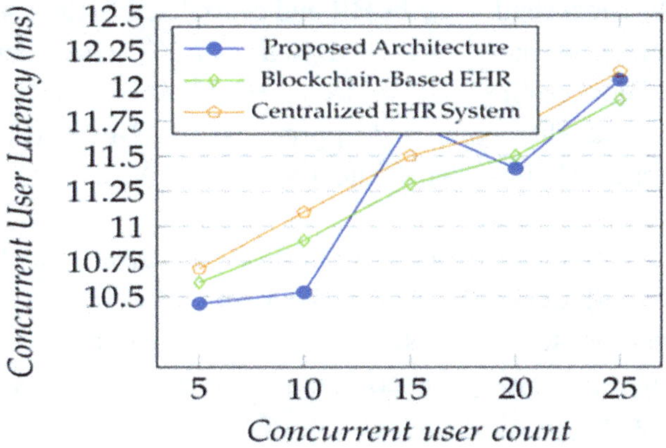

Figure 12. Number of concurrent transactions Vs. Concurrent user GAS

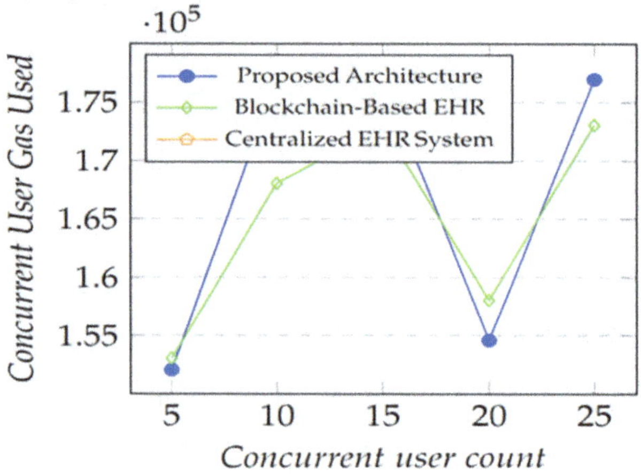

From the above implemental analysis (Figures 7-12), we claim that our proposed hybrid AI-Blockchain EHR framework performance is much better as compared to pre-existing AI-Blockchain-based EHR and centralized EHR systems. From the detailed implementation analysis provided (Figures 7-12), it is evident that our proposed hybrid AI-Blockchain EHR (Electronic Health Record) framework exhibits superior performance when compared to pre-existing AI-Blockchain-based EHR systems and centralized EHR systems. The figures illustrate several key performance metrics, including:

Scalability: The hybrid framework demonstrates improved scalability, handling more transactions and users efficiently without compromising performance.

Latency: The proposed system shows significantly reduced latency in data access and transaction processing, ensuring quicker response times which is critical in healthcare settings.

Throughput: Throughput has increased observably, indicating that the hybrid AI-Blockchain EHR framework can process a greater number of transactions per second than its predecessors.

Security: Enhanced security features are integrated into the hybrid model, effectively mitigating risks and ensuring the integrity and confidentiality of health records.

Interoperability: The hybrid system showcases better interoperability with existing healthcare systems, facilitating smoother data exchange and integration.

Cost-efficiency: The hybrid approach reduces operational and maintenance costs, making it a more economical solution for healthcare providers.

The combined advantages outlined in these metrics underscore the effectiveness and efficiency of the hybrid AI-Blockchain EHR framework, marking it as a substantial improvement over traditional and purely AI-Blockchain-based EHR systems. This makes the proposed framework a more viable and robust solution for managing electronic health records in contemporary healthcare environments.

Table 3. Numerical Values for the performance evaluation results were obtained.

Concurrent Transaction/Users	Throughput (TPS)	Latency (ms)	Gas Used
10 Concurrent Transactions	503	11.88	195016
15 Concurrent Transactions	822	12.05	197904
20 Concurrent Transactions	1234	12.10	194904
25 Concurrent Transactions	1516	12.17	196916
30 Concurrent Transactions	2081	12.53	196928
35 Concurrent Transactions	2483	12.71	195916
5 Concurrent Users	0.530	10.45	152028
10 Concurrent Users	1.347	10.53	176928
15 Concurrent Users	1.627	11.74	177128
20 Concurrent Users	1.838	11.41	154576
25 Concurrent Users	2.177	12.04	176928

Table 2 presents the numerical values obtained from the performance evaluation of the proposed framework, including throughput (transactions per second), latency (milliseconds), and gas usage for varying numbers of concurrent transactions and users. The simulation implements stress testing on a AI-Blockchain-based electronic health record (EHR) smart contract named EHRContract to evaluate its performance under load. It leverages the Mocha testing framework and Chai assertion library in Node.js. The test deploys an instance of the EHRContract and then executes multiple transactions to add patients and medical records. It measures critical metrics, including throughput (transactions per second), latency (time for a transaction), gas usage (for complex transactions), block creation time, and block size. These metrics quantify the speed, scalability, cost efficiency, and limits of the EHRContract and underlying AI-Blockchain platform. The stress test provides crucial performance data to identify bottlenecks, optimize gas costs, determine capacity thresholds, and evaluate the feasibility of the AI-Blockchain solution for real-world EHR systems. By thoroughly evaluating the contract under simulated production conditions, the test enables iterative architecture, infrastructure, and parameter improvements to ensure optimal outcomes when deployed at scale. The performance metrics and insights gained can be leveraged to demonstrate the capabilities and reliability of a AI-Blockchain EHR system to stakeholders.

6. CONCLUSION

The proposed AI-Blockchain-based framework for electronic health records (EHRs) offers several advantages over traditional centralized architectures. The system enhances security, privacy, and scalability by integrating permissioned AI-Blockchain with off-chain storage and zero-knowledge proofs. The prototype evaluation revealed promising throughput, latency, and storage access speeds even under moderate transaction loads. This indicates the framework can handle real-world health data sharing demands across institutions.

However, the testing had limitations regarding network size, concurrent transactions, intelligent contract complexity, and test environments. As such, the actual performance under large-scale production workloads may significantly differ. Extensive evaluations under diverse conditions are imperative before conclusion. Exploring the integration of the proposed framework within broader information ecosystems, as discussed by (Salzano et al., 2024), could further enhance its applicability and interoperability. A key feature is using zero-knowledge proofs to enable privacy-preserving validation of computations. This prevents the exposure of sensitive medical data even during record audits. While providing mathematical data confidentiality guarantees, the cryptographic overhead can be non-trivial. Optimization of proof generation and validation is an area needing attention.

Although access control policies were encoded into smart contracts, complex conditional rules based on data values may be computationally intensive. There is scope for further abstraction of authorization logic to simplify contract development. Expanding the framework to enable interoperability across diverse health IT systems poses engineering challenges. Standardization of APIs, schemas, and interfaces between the AI-Blockchain layer and external databases is essential. Regulatory requirements regarding data validity, integrity, and audit trails must also be continually addressed.

The research focused on technical measures for data security and privacy. However, socio-ethical issues regarding patient consent, transparency, and public trust also impact adoption. Holistic governance frameworks addressing legal, regulatory, and social contexts need to evolve alongside the technology. While limitations exist, the positive results position the proposed architecture as a Candidate for transforming EHR protection and sharing. Significant opportunities have emerged for incremental enhancements through modular extension, real-world piloting, and domain-specific optimizations.

Future work should concentrate on large-scale performance testing, proof overhead reduction optimizations, access control logic abstraction, and interoperability with external systems. Developing supportive regulatory mechanisms and organizational best practices is equally vital for successful adoption. Additional research must validate the approach across diverse healthcare settings while addressing emerging socio-ethical considerations.

Data Description: The data utilized in this research encompassed performance metrics and evaluation results extracted from relevant existing studies on AI-Blockchain-based electronic health record (EHR) systems. This data included transaction throughput, latency, gas consumption, and scalability indicators from the experimental evaluations and simulations reported in published research papers. The collected data provided a comprehensive understanding of the current state-of-the-art and served as a benchmark for comparing the performance of the proposed framework.

Data Availability Statement: The performance metrics and evaluation data used in this research were gathered from publicly available research publications on AI-Blockchain-based EHR systems. As this data is already present in the published literature, it is accessible to interested parties through the cited references and academic databases. However, the authors have compiled the relevant data points from the surveyed papers into a structured dataset to facilitate reproducibility and future research. This dataset can be made available to the corresponding author upon reasonable request, subject to appropriate citation and acknowledgment of the sources.

REFERENCES

Ali, M. S., Vecchio, M., Pincheira, M., Dolui, K., Antonelli, F., & Rehmani, M. H. (2018). Applications of blockchains in the Internet of Things: A comprehensive survey. *IEEE Communications Surveys and Tutorials*, *21*(2), 1676–1717. DOI: 10.1109/COMST.2018.2886932

Andersson, O. (2021). Securing Electronic Health Records: A Blockchain Solution. In.

Basil, N. N., Ambe, S., Ekhator, C., Fonkem, E., & Nduma, B. N. (2022). Health records database and inherent security concerns: A review of the literature. *Cureus*, *14*(10). Advance online publication. DOI: 10.7759/cureus.30168 PMID: 36397924

Borade, S., Paradkar, T., Takalkar, P., & Trivedi, A. (2023). Blockchain based electronic health record management system. *Available at SSRN* 4376765. DOI: 10.2139/ssrn.4376765

Chenthara, S. (2021). *Privacy Preservation of Electronic Health Records Using Blockchain Technology: Healthchain.* Victoria University, Ding, Y., Feng, L., Qin, Y., Huang, C., Dong, P., Gao, L., & Tan, Y. (2020). *Blockchain-based access control mechanism of federated data sharing system.* Paper presented at the 2020 IEEE Intl Conf on Parallel & Distributed Processing with Applications, Big Data & Cloud Computing, Sustainable Computing & Communications, Social Computing & Networking (ISPA/BDCloud/SocialCom/SustainCom).

Ghosh, P. K., Chakraborty, A., Hasan, M., Rashid, K., & Siddique, A. H. (2023). Blockchain application in healthcare systems: A review. *Systems*, *11*(1), 38. DOI: 10.3390/systems11010038

Han, Y., Zhang, Y., & Vermund, S. H. (2022). Blockchain technology for electronic health records. *International Journal of Environmental Research and Public Health*, *19*(23), 15577. DOI: 10.3390/ijerph192315577 PMID: 36497654

Hasnain, M., Albogamy, F. R., Alamri, S. S., Ghani, I., & Mehboob, B. (2023). The Hyperledger fabric as a Blockchain framework preserves the security of electronic health records. *Frontiers in Public Health*, *11*, 1272787. DOI: 10.3389/fpubh.2023.1272787 PMID: 38089022

Huang, H., Zhu, P., Xiao, F., Sun, X., & Huang, Q. (2020). A blockchain-based scheme for privacy-preserving and secure sharing of medical data. *Computers & Security*, *99*, 102010. DOI: 10.1016/j.cose.2020.102010 PMID: 32895584

Johari, R., Kumar, V., Gupta, K., & Vidyarthi, D. P. (2022). BLOSOM: BLOck-chain technology for Security of Medical records. *ICT Express*, *8*(1), 56–60. DOI: 10.1016/j.icte.2021.06.002

Liu, X., Wang, Z., Jin, C., Li, F., & Li, G. (2019). A blockchain-based medical data sharing and protection scheme. *IEEE Access : Practical Innovations, Open Solutions*, *7*, 118943–118953. DOI: 10.1109/ACCESS.2019.2937685

Mukherji, A., & Ganguli, N. (2020). *Efficient and scalable electronic health record management using permissioned blockchain technology.* Paper presented at the 2020 4th International Conference on Electronics, Materials Engineering & Nano-Technology (IEMENTech). DOI: 10.1109/IEMENTech51367.2020.9270106

Ratwani, R. M. (2017). Electronic health records and improved patient care: Opportunities for applied psychology. *Current Directions in Psychological Science*, *26*(4), 359–365. DOI: 10.1177/0963721417700691 PMID: 28808359

Salzano, F., Marchesi, L., Pareschi, R., & Tonelli, R. (2024). Integrating blockchain technology within an information ecosystem. *Blockchain: Research Applications*, *5*(4), 100225.

Shahnaz, A., Qamar, U., & Khalid, A. (2019). Using blockchain for electronic health records. *IEEE Access : Practical Innovations, Open Solutions*, *7*, 147782–147795. DOI: 10.1109/ACCESS.2019.2946373

Sharma, B., Halder, R., & Singh, J. (2020). *Blockchain-based interoperable healthcare using zero-knowledge proofs and proxy re-encryption.* Paper presented at the 2020 international conference on COMmunication Systems & NETworkS (COMSNETS). DOI: 10.1109/COMSNETS48256.2020.9027413

Sharma, P., Borah, M. D., & Namasudra, S. (2021). Improving security of medical big data by using Blockchain technology. *Computers & Electrical Engineering*, *96*, 107529. DOI: 10.1016/j.compeleceng.2021.107529

Smart, N. (2023). Computing on encrypted data. *IEEE Security and Privacy*, *21*(4), 94–98. DOI: 10.1109/MSEC.2023.3279517

Sonkamble, R. G., Bongale, A. M., Phansalkar, S., Sharma, A., & Rajput, S. (2023). Secure data transmission of electronic health records using blockchain technology. *Electronics (Basel)*, *12*(4), 1015. DOI: 10.3390/electronics12041015

Wang, M., Guo, Y., Zhang, C., Wang, C., Huang, H., & Jia, X. (2021). MedShare: A privacy-preserving medical data sharing system by using blockchain. *IEEE Transactions on Services Computing*, *16*(1), 438–451. DOI: 10.1109/TSC.2021.3114719

Wu, H., Dwivedi, A. D., & Srivastava, G. (2021). Security and privacy of patient information in medical systems based on blockchain technology. *ACM Transactions on Multimedia Computing Communications and Applications*, *17*(2s), 1–17. DOI: 10.1145/3408321

Yaqoob, I., Salah, K., Jayaraman, R., & Al-Hammadi, Y. (2022). Blockchain for healthcare data management: Opportunities, challenges, and future recommendations. *Neural Computing & Applications*, *34*(14), 1–16. DOI: 10.1007/s00521-020-05519-w

Yi, C. H., Keong, L. K., & Razali, N. F., & Innovation. (2023). Blockchain-Based Medical Record Management System (BBMRMS). *Journal of Applied Technology*, *7*(4), 1.

Zou, R., Lv, X., & Zhao, J. (2021). SPChain: Blockchain-based medical data sharing and privacy-preserving eHealth system. *Information Processing & Management*, *58*(4), 102604. DOI: 10.1016/j.ipm.2021.102604

Chapter 4

Media's Role in Shaping Digital Transformation and Inclusive Economies:

Leveraging AI and Emerging Technologies for Sustainable Development

Yasir Ahmed
https://orcid.org/0000-0002-5836-3491
Lovely Professional University, India

Tanvir Ahmed
Baba Ghulam Shah Badshah University, India

Angel Anthony Kasonta
Lovely Professional University, India

ABSTRACT

The rapid rise of artificial intelligence (AI) and new technologies is transforming the global economy, offering opportunities for inclusive growth and sustainable development. Media plays a crucial role in shaping how the public views AI, influencing policies, and driving societal change in the digital age. This chapter explores how media impacts public opinion and policymaking around AI, focusing on its potential to promote fair and equitable digital participation. It examines media narratives, challenges, and strategies, revealing regional differences: high-income countries often focus on AI's economic benefits, while low- and middle-income nations emphasize its potential for development. However, corporate-driven stories tend to overshadow

DOI: 10.4018/979-8-3373-6097-3.ch004

critical ethical issues like bias, privacy, and inequality. By analyzing these trends, the chapter provides insights for media professionals, policymakers, and tech leaders on using media to foster responsible and inclusive digital transformation.

INTRODUCTION

The digital revolution, driven by artificial intelligence (AI) and emerging technologies, has the potential to reshape economies, societies, and governance systems worldwide. While these technologies offer transformative opportunities for inclusive growth, their benefits are not evenly distributed, often exacerbating existing inequalities. The uneven distribution of technological benefits raises critical questions about governance, equity, and the role of media in shaping public discourse on digital transformation. For instance, while AI-driven automation promises productivity gains, its displacement effects on low-skilled workers—particularly in developing economies—highlight systemic inequities that media narratives often overlook (Manyika et al., 2017; World Bank, 2016).The media, as a powerful shaper of public opinion and policy agendas, plays a pivotal role in framing the discourse around digital transformation, influencing how societies perceive and respond to these technological advancements. However, media narratives frequently reflect the interests of dominant stakeholders—tech corporations, governments, and affluent elites—while marginalizing voices from underrepresented communities (Benjamin, 2019; Eubanks, 2018). This bias perpetuates a techno-optimistic framing that obscures structural barriers to inclusive growth, such as digital divides and algorithmic discrimination.

This book chapter seeks to explore the media's role in shaping digital transformation and inclusive economies, with a focus on leveraging AI and emerging technologies for sustainable development. By critically analyzing media framing, policy implications, and regional disparities, the chapter aims to bridge gaps between media studies, technology governance, and sustainable development.

The purpose of this chapter is threefold. First, it examines how media narratives influence public perceptions and policies related to digital transformation, highlighting the dual role of media in both promoting and challenging technological innovation. Second, it explores the strategies and challenges associated with using AI and emerging technologies for inclusive growth, as portrayed by the media, with a focus on regional and socioeconomic variations in reporting. Third, it proposes a media engagement framework to enhance sustainable development outcomes, emphasizing best practices for accurate and inclusive reporting, collaborative strategies between media, policymakers, and the tech industry, and educational initiatives to support digital transformation.

The significance of this chapter lies in its interdisciplinary approach, bridging the fields of media studies, technology, and sustainable development. By critically analyzing media narratives and their implications for inclusive growth, this chapter contributes to a deeper understanding of the opportunities and challenges posed by digital transformation. The outcomes of this research include actionable recommendations for media practitioners, policymakers, and technology stakeholders, aimed at fostering equitable digital participation and sustainable economic growth.

Objectives

1. Examine the Influence of Media on Public Perceptions and Policies Related to Digital Transformation
2. Explore Media Representations of Strategies and Challenges in Achieving Inclusive Growth Through Emerging Technologies
3. Develop a Media Engagement Framework for Fostering Sustainable Digital Transformation

By addressing these objectives, this chapter aims to provide a nuanced understanding of the media's role in shaping digital transformation and inclusive economies, offering insights and recommendations for harnessing the potential of AI and emerging technologies for sustainable development.

METHODOLOGY

This book chapter employs a qualitative research methodology, relying on secondary literature to analyze the media's role in shaping digital transformation and inclusive economies. The research draws on a wide range of sources, including academic books, peer-reviewed journal articles, research papers, and reputable blogs. These sources provide diverse perspectives on media framing, public opinion formation, policy implications, and the ethical considerations surrounding AI and emerging technologies.

The analysis is guided by a thematic approach, identifying key themes such as media framing, public opinion formation, policy implications, and strategies for inclusive growth. The chapter also incorporates case studies and examples from different regions and socioeconomic contexts to highlight variations in media narratives and their impact on inclusive growth. By synthesizing insights from secondary literature, this chapter offers a comprehensive understanding of the media's influence on digital transformation and proposes actionable recommendations for fostering sustainable development outcomes. The material was extracted till December 2024.

MEDIA FRAMING OF DIGITAL INNOVATION, AI, AND INCLUSIVE GROWTH

The media framing of digital innovation, artificial intelligence (AI), and inclusive growth plays a critical role in shaping public understanding and discourse around these complex and often abstract technologies. Media frames are particularly significant in helping the public make sense of high-tech artefacts like AI, which, despite their pervasive presence in everyday life, remain poorly understood by most people due to their "black box" nature (Suerdem & Akkilic, 2021). This lack of direct experience with AI contributes to its fetish-like representation in the public imagination, making media framing a crucial tool for interpreting its cultural and societal implications.

Media Framing of AI: Cultural and Contextual Differences

Media framing of AI varies significantly across cultural and societal contexts, reflecting the unique political, economic, and social environments in which media operate. For instance, Suerdem and Akkilic (2021) highlight that media in different countries represent AI in ways that align with their cultural and societal values. Their study, which analyzed approximately 5,000 news items, highlights the importance of cross-cultural comparisons in understanding how AI is framed. While most existing studies focus on single-case content analyses, there is a growing need for broader, international studies to uncover cultural differences in AI framing and public perception.

In the UK, for example, media coverage of AI is heavily influenced by industry concerns, with a majority of articles pegged to commercial interests and a plurality of sources originating from industry actors (Brennen, 2018). This framing often amplifies self-interested assertions of AI's value and potential, positioning AI primarily as a private commercial concern rather than a public issue. This trend is further politicized, with right-leaning outlets emphasizing economic and geopolitical issues, while left-leaning outlets focus on ethics and discrimination (Brennen, 2018). Such framing not only shapes public perception but also undercuts the role of public action in addressing AI's societal impacts.

AI as a Transformative Force: Economic and Social Implications

The transformative potential of AI is a recurring theme in media discourse. Brynjolfsson and McAfee (2014) argue that digital technologies, including AI, are driving a reinvention of the economy and society. They highlight both the immense benefits, such as advanced infrastructure and near-boundless access to cultural resources, and the challenges, including job displacement and wage stagnation. Media framing often reflects this dual narrative, portraying AI as both a solution to public problems and a source of disruption. For instance, AI is frequently depicted as outperforming human expertise, particularly in sectors like healthcare, where it is framed as replacing and surpassing medical professionals (Nguyen & Hekman, 2022). This "outperforming" narrative can place AI above critique, potentially overshadowing ethical concerns and the need for regulatory oversight.

The Role of Media in Critical Data Literacy

Media also play a crucial role in fostering critical data literacy, which is essential for understanding the implications of AI and automation. Nguyen and Hekman (2022) argue that critical AI news reporting can enhance public understanding of datafication and automation, including their societal impacts and the actors who control these developments. However, this requires journalists to develop a sufficient conceptual understanding of AI themselves. The study identifies 14 dominant frames in AI news reporting, grouped into four meta-frames that highlight the economic, cultural, social, and political impacts of AI. The role of media in fostering critical data literacy is increasingly recognized as essential in the digital era. (Pangrazio & Sefton-Green, 2022) argue that media platforms and digital infrastructures shape public encounters with data, emphasizing the need for a critical data literacy framework that addresses the socio-technical dimensions of datafication. Their work point out how media environments influence individuals' ability to interpret and critique algorithmic biases, misinformation, and privacy concerns, advocating for pedagogical approaches that integrate media literacy with critical data studies. Similarly, Knaus (2020) highlights the importance of incorporating *critical technology theory* into media education, urging learners to interrogate the political and ethical implications of data collection, processing, and representation within digital systems.Tygel and Kirsch's (2016) focus on "data activism," where they argue that media literacy can empower individuals to deconstruct data-driven narratives by examining the socio-political contexts of data production and dissemination. Their work stresses analytical skills to question sources, biases, and power structures embedded in digital content. Building on this, Pangrazio and Sefton-Green (2022) position media not only as a source of data but as a pedagogical tool for critical engagement, advocating for curricula that merge data literacy with media studies to cultivate informed digital citizens capable of navigating datafied societies. Collectively, these scholars emphasize media's dual role in shaping and challenging data practices, reinforcing the need for educational frameworks that bridge media and data literacies to address the complexities of the digital age.

The authors collectively argue that media is not neutral but serves as a dual force in shaping public perceptions of AI and datafication while also empowering individuals to critically engage with these narratives. Media often disseminates information that reflects the interests of powerful actors, such as corporations and governments, thereby influencing how AI and data-driven technologies are perceived. However, through media literacy, individuals can develop the ability to question these narratives, recognize biases, and advocate for ethical data practices. Critical data literacy, therefore, requires bridging media literacy—analyzing messages and their intent—with data literacy—understanding how data is created, manipulated, and used—to address the complexities of AI-driven societies. These insights are crucial as they help democratize understanding, enabling non-experts to critically engage with AI and automation rather than passively accepting dominant techno-utopian or dystopian discourses. Furthermore, they expose power structures by revealing how datafication reinforces societal inequalities, such as biased algorithms and surveillance capitalism, and identifying who benefits from these systems. Additionally, this perspective informs education and policy by advocating for curricula and media practices that prioritize ethical reflection, civic engagement, and systemic change over mere technical proficiency. Ultimately, fostering critical data literacy empowers individuals to become "data activists," challenging unethical data practices and advocating for greater transparency and justice. In essence, media literacy is not just about consuming information but about critiquing and reshaping the datafied world, ensuring equitable participation in an increasingly automated society.

Optimism and Concerns in AI Discourse

Public discourse on AI has historically been marked by cycles of optimism and pessimism. Fast and Horvitz (2017) analyze 30 years of AI coverage in the New York Times, revealing that discussions about AI have become increasingly optimistic since 2009. However, specific concerns, such as the loss of control over AI, ethical issues, and its impact on employment, have also grown. This duality is reflected in media framing, which often balances the promise of AI with warnings about its potential risks. For example, the Stanford AI100 report (Stone et al., 2022) emphasizes AI's potential to transform sectors like healthcare, education, and public safety while also calling for careful consideration of its societal implications.

CHALLENGES AND FUTURE DIRECTIONS

Despite the progress in understanding media framing of AI, several challenges remain. Nguyen and Hekman (2022) note that current studies are limited by their focus on English-language, U.S.- and U.K.-based outlets, highlighting the need for more international research to uncover cultural differences in framing. Additionally, while quantitative analyses provide valuable insights into trends, qualitative methods like critical discourse analysis are needed to explore metaphors and less manifest discursive practices in AI reporting. Future research should also examine the role of social media in shaping public discourse on AI, as these platforms increasingly influence societal debates.

The media framing of AI and digital innovation is a powerful force in shaping public perception and discourse. By reflecting cultural, societal, and political contexts, media frames influence how AI is understood and debated. While there is a growing emphasis on the economic and transformative potential of AI, concerns about its ethical implications and societal impacts remain prominent. To foster a more informed public discourse, it is essential to enhance critical data literacy among journalists and expand research into cross-cultural and qualitative analyses of media framing. As AI continues to evolve, the media's role in interpreting its implications for inclusive growth and societal well-being will only become more critical.

Public opinion formation through news outlets and social media

Public opinion formation in the digital age is profoundly influenced by news outlets and social media platforms, which serve as primary sources of information and discourse for individuals worldwide. The relationship between traditional media and social media has transformed how opinions are shaped, disseminated, and reinforced. For instance, The media's emphasis on specific topics, such as climate change or economic policies, can elevate their importance in public consciousness, thereby shaping collective attitudes and priorities. This phenomenon is often explained through agenda-setting theory, which posits that the media influences the salience of issues by highlighting certain topics over others (McCombs & Shaw, 1972). By focusing on particular issues, the media can direct public attention and frame the way these issues are perceived.

However, the rise of social media has introduced a more decentralized and participatory model of information sharing. In this new model, users can both consume and produce content, blurring the traditional lines between producers and consumers of news. This shift aligns with the concept of produsage, as described by Bruns (2008), where digital platforms enable users to collaboratively create and share content, transforming the dynamics of information dissemination.

Social media platforms like Twitter, Facebook, and Instagram have become powerful tools for public opinion formation due to their ability to facilitate real-time communication and viral dissemination of information. These platforms enable users to engage with diverse perspectives, but they also create echo chambers and filter bubbles, where individuals are exposed primarily to information that aligns with their preexisting beliefs. This phenomenon, as described by Pariser (2011), results from algorithmic personalization, which tailors content to users' preferences and behaviors, often at the expense of broader exposure to differing viewpoints. For instance, Pariser writes, "Your filter bubble is your own personal, unique universe of information that you live in online. And what's in your filter bubble depends on who you are, and it depends on what you do". Algorithms that prioritize engaging or sensational content further exacerbate this phenomenon, often amplifying polarizing or misleading information (Vosoughi et al., 2018). For example, during political campaigns or social movements, social media can rapidly mobilize public opinion by spreading hashtags, memes, and user-generated content. Movements like #BlackLivesMatter and #MeToo exemplify how digital platforms enable the rapid dissemination of ideas and the organization of collective action. As Tufekci (2017) argues, social media's ability to amplify voices and coordinate efforts has transformed the dynamics of modern activism, allowing movements to gain momentum and visibility at an unprecedented scale.

Relationship between news outlets and social media is increasingly symbiotic. Traditional media often draw stories from social media trends, while social media users frequently share and discuss content from established news sources. This dynamic can create a feedback loop, where certain narratives gain disproportionate visibility and influence. For instance, the coverage of the COVID-19 pandemic highlighted how misinformation on social media could shape public opinion, leading to vaccine hesitancy or the spread of unproven treatments. As Brennen et al. (2020) demonstrate, false claims about COVID-19 treatments and vaccines proliferated across platforms, often amplified by the interaction between social media and traditional media, ultimately influencing public behavior and decision-making. At the same time, social media has enabled fact-checking and counter-narratives, with users and organizations debunking false claims and promoting evidence-based information.

Public opinion formation through news outlets and social media is also influenced by the psychological and social dynamics of information processing. Cognitive biases, such as confirmation bias and the bandwagon effect, play a significant role in how individuals interpret and respond to information. As Kahneman (2011) explains in *Thinking, Fast and Slow*, confirmation bias leads people to favor information that aligns with their preexisting beliefs, while the bandwagon effect drives individuals to adopt popular opinions or behaviors. These biases are amplified in the context of social media, where algorithms prioritize engaging content and users are exposed to echo chambers that reinforce their views. Social identity theory further explains why people often align their opinions with those of their in-group, particularly in polarized environments. According to Tajfel and Turner (1979), individuals derive their sense of self from their membership in social groups and tend to favor their in-group over out-groups to maintain a positive social identity. In polarized settings, such as those found on social media or in political discourse, this in-group bias is amplified, as individuals seek to reinforce group identity and cohesion by adopting the dominant opinions of their in-group. This dynamic can contribute to the deepening of societal divisions and the entrenchment of polarized viewpoints. These factors underscore the complexity of opinion formation in the digital age, where information overload and competing narratives make it challenging for individuals to discern credible sources.

The convergence of news outlets and social media has reshaped the landscape of public opinion formation. While these platforms offer unprecedented opportunities for information sharing and civic engagement, they also pose challenges related to misinformation, polarization, and the erosion of trust. Addressing these challenges requires a multifaceted approach, including media literacy education, algorithmic transparency, and collaborative efforts between traditional media and social media platforms to promote accurate and inclusive discourse.

Policy implications stemming from dominant media narratives

Dominant media narratives play a significant role in shaping public opinion and, consequently, influencing policy decisions. Policymakers often rely on media coverage to gauge public sentiment and prioritize issues, making the framing of these narratives a powerful tool in the policy-making process. As Kingdon (1984) explains in *Agendas, Alternatives, and Public Policies*, the media is a key actor in the "policy stream," helping to define problems and bring issues to the forefront of the public agenda. By highlighting certain issues and framing them in specific ways, media narratives shape how policymakers perceive public priorities and allocate their attention and resources. When media outlets consistently highlight specific issues, such as climate change, healthcare, or economic inequality, they can elevate these topics to the top of the policy agenda, compelling governments to take action. For example, extensive media coverage of the climate crisis has led to increased public pressure on governments to adopt sustainable policies, resulting in initiatives like the Paris Agreement and national carbon reduction targets. As Boykoff (2011) argues in *Who Speaks for the Climate?*, media reporting plays a crucial role in shaping public understanding of climate change and driving policy responses. By framing the issue in ways that resonate with audiences, media outlets can mobilize public sentiment and influence policymakers to prioritize climate action. However, the media's focus on certain issues often comes at the expense of others, creating a skewed representation of societal priorities that can lead to imbalanced policy responses.

One of the key policy implications of dominant media narratives is the potential for agenda-setting bias, where the media's emphasis on sensational or politically charged issues overshadows equally important but less attention-grabbing topics. For instance, while media coverage of terrorism often dominates headlines, it can lead to disproportionate policy responses, such as increased defense spending or restrictive immigration policies, even when statistical evidence suggests that other issues, like domestic health crises, pose greater risks to public safety. As Altheide (2006) argues in *Terrorism and the Politics of Fear*, media narratives amplify public fear by sensationalizing terrorism, creating a feedback loop that prioritizes security-focused policies over other critical issues. This agenda-setting bias not only distorts public perception of risk but also skews policy priorities, often at the expense of more pressing societal challenges. This phenomenon, known as the "CNN effect," demonstrates how media-driven narratives can pressure policymakers to act swiftly, sometimes without sufficient evidence or long-term planning. As Robinson (2002) argues in *The CNN Effect: The Myth of News, Foreign Policy, and Intervention*, real-time media coverage of crises creates a sense of urgency that can compel governments to respond quickly, often under public scrutiny. However, Robinson also cautions that the CNN effect is not always a decisive factor in policymaking; its influence depends on the context and the strength of existing policy frameworks. While media coverage can drive immediate action, it may also lead to reactive decisions that lack thorough analysis or long-term strategic planning.

Another critical policy implication is the role of media narratives in shaping public trust and legitimacy. When media outlets frame policies in a way that resonates with public values, they can build support for government initiatives. Conversely, negative or critical framing can undermine public trust and hinder policy implementation. For example, during the COVID-19 pandemic, media narratives that emphasized the effectiveness of vaccines and public health measures helped build public compliance, while misinformation and skepticism propagated through certain media channels led to vaccine hesitancy and resistance to lockdowns. Media narratives also influence policy by framing the perceived causes and solutions to societal problems. For instance, if economic inequality is framed as a result of individual failings rather than systemic issues, policies may focus on personal responsibility, such as job training programs, rather than structural reforms, like progressive taxation or wealth redistribution. As Iyengar (1991) argues in *Is Anyone Responsible? How Television Frames Political Issues*, media framing shapes public perceptions of responsibility for societal problems, which in turn influences policy preferences. By emphasizing individual causes, media narratives can steer policymakers toward solutions that target personal behavior, while framing issues as systemic can lead to broader structural reforms. This dynamic highlights the power of media narratives in shaping not only public opinion but also the policy agenda. Similarly, media narratives that frame immigration as a security threat rather than an economic opportunity can lead to restrictive immigration policies, ignoring the potential benefits of inclusive approaches. As Chavez (2001) argues in *Covering Immigration: Popular Images and the Politics of the Nation*, media representations play a critical role in shaping public perceptions of immigration. By emphasizing narratives of threat—whether to national security, cultural identity, or economic stability—media outlets can foster public support for restrictive policies, such as increased border enforcement or reduced immigration quotas. Conversely, framing immigration as an economic opportunity or a source of cultural enrichment can highlight the benefits of inclusive policies, such as pathways to citizenship or programs that integrate immigrants into the workforce. This dynamic feature the power of media narratives in influencing both public opinion and policy outcomes. Policymakers must critically evaluate the framing of media narratives to ensure that their responses address root causes rather than symptoms.

Dominant media narratives have profound implications for policy-making, influencing agenda-setting, public trust, and the framing of societal issues. Policymakers must navigate these narratives carefully, balancing the need to respond to public sentiment with the responsibility to address complex challenges in a nuanced and evidence-based manner. By engaging with media narratives critically and proactively, policymakers can harness their power to build consensus and drive effective, equitable policy outcomes.

FRAMING AI IN MEDIA: FROM ECONOMIC HOPES TO ETHICAL CONCERNS

Media narratives often emphasize the transformative potential of AI and emerging technologies, particularly in addressing global challenges such as poverty, labor productivity, and workforce transitions. For instance, studies by Manyika et al. (2017) analyze automation's economic impact, highlighting its potential to reshape industries and labor markets while highlighting the need for workforce reskilling to mitigate job displacement (Manyika et al. 2017;Richter et al., 2018). Further Research on Zambia by Manyika et al. (2017) illustrates how automation in sectors like agriculture and transportation could disrupt economic activities in developing regions by 2026, necessitating human capital development strategies to address low productivity and wage inequality.

The discussion of AI's role in inclusive growth often intersects with debates on "weak" versus "strong" AI narratives. Weak AI narratives, which focus on existing technologies like robotic process automation (RPA) in financial services, demonstrate tangible benefits such as improved productivity and employee engagement (Manyika et al., 2017). In contrast, "strong AI" narratives, which dominate media discourse, project speculative futures where AI surpasses human capabilities, potentially overshadowing pragmatic discussions about current applications (Bory et al., 2024).

The media plays a critical role in highlighting ethical challenges posed by emerging technologies. Scholars like Cathy O'Neil (2016) have documented how algorithmic systems perpetuate inequality, particularly in domains such as hiring, criminal justice, and financial services. These "weapons of math destruction," as O'Neil terms them, often reinforce systemic biases by embedding discriminatory logic into automated decision-making tools. For instance, algorithmic risk-assessment tools used in policing or loan approvals disproportionately harm marginalized communities (O'Neil, 2016). Benjamin (2019) expands this critique to interrogate racial bias in technology design, arguing that tools like facial recognition systems encode a "New Jim Code" by misidentifying people of color at higher rates, a phenomenon empirically validated in studies such as Buolamwini and Gebru (2018) landmark analysis of commercial AI systems. Media investigations into these technologies have amplified calls for regulatory oversight and ethical accountability (Benjamin, 2019). While job displacement due to automation is a broader societal concern, O'Neil's work focuses specifically on how algorithmic systems—rather than automation itself—exacerbate inequities through opaque, exploitative design.

Despite this, media narratives often fall short in providing a comprehensive understanding of the ethical implications of these technologies. For instance, while issues like data privacy and algorithmic bias are frequently discussed, broader concerns such as the environmental impact of AI infrastructure or the geopolitical implications of technological dominance are less commonly addressed (Crawford, 2021). This selective coverage can lead to a skewed public perception, where the benefits of AI are overstated, and its risks are understated or oversimplified. Addressing these gaps in media reporting is essential for fostering a more nuanced understanding of the ethical considerations surrounding AI and emerging technologies.

Media scrutiny has played a crucial role in shaping public discourse on the gig economy, pressuring corporations and policymakers to address its social implications. Scholz (2017) critiques how major digital platforms leverage media to promote gig work as flexible and empowering while obscuring labor exploitation. At the same time, he highlights how workers use digital media and online activism to organize and resist platform exploitation. Reports such as *Gender, Visibility, and News Coverage of On-Demand Work During the Pandemic* emphasize how media representation of gig work influences policy discussions, particularly concerning worker protections and benefits. By exposing precarious working conditions, amplifying worker-led advocacy, and shaping policy debates, media coverage holds stakeholders accountable and fosters a more informed and equitable discussion on the governance of digital labor and emerging technologies(Autonomy, 2024). Similarly, the *International Labour Organization (ILO) report, "Representation, Voice, and Collective Bargaining in the Gig Economy" (2018),* emphasizes how media narratives influence public perceptions of gig work and underline the importance of worker representation in policy discussions (Johnston & Land-Kazlauskas, 2018). Additionally, *the study "Gig Economy and Evaporated Risks through Media" (2021)* explores how digital media has contributed to legitimizing precarious working conditions in the gig economy, shaping both public perceptions and regulatory approaches (Demir, 2022)

Analysis of How Media Narratives Differ Across Regions and Socioeconomic Contexts

Media narratives about AI and emerging technologies vary significantly across regions and socioeconomic contexts, reflecting differing priorities, challenges, and levels of technological adoption. In high-income countries, media coverage often emphasizes AI's potential to drive economic growth and innovation. For example, Brynjolfsson and McAfee (2014) highlight how digital technologies, including AI, reshape productivity and labor markets in advanced economies, though their focus is broader than AI alone. In the U.S. and Europe, discussions frequently center on AI's applications in finance, healthcare, and autonomous vehicles, alongside ethical debates about regulation and privacy (Cath, 2018). These narratives reflect affluent societies' concerns, such as job displacement, while underrepresenting global technological inequities.

In contrast, media in low- and middle-income countries (LMICs) often frame AI as a tool for addressing developmental challenges. The *World Development Report 2016* (World Bank, 2016) broadly discusses digital technologies (not exclusively AI) as enablers of financial inclusion, education, and healthcare access. For instance, African media highlight innovations like M-Pesa, a mobile money platform that expanded financial access in regions with limited banking infrastructure (Suri & Jack, 2016). Similarly, South Asian outlets report on AI's role in agriculture and disaster management (Meghwanshi, 2024). These narratives emphasize optimism about technology's empowerment potential but often overlook infrastructural and literacy barriers.

However, LMIC media frequently lack resources to critically assess AI's risks. While AI-driven surveillance in countries like China and India is widely covered, ethical concerns about privacy and civil liberties receive less scrutiny (Feldstein, 2019). This disparity underscores the need for investment in local journalism to ensure marginalized voices are included in global AI discourse.

Potential Biases and Gaps in Media Reporting on Inclusive Digital Economies

Media reporting on AI and emerging technologies is often influenced by biases that reflect the interests and perspectives of dominant stakeholders, such as tech corporations, governments, and affluent societies. One common bias is the techno-optimistic framing of AI as a panacea for global challenges, which can overshadow structural barriers to inclusive growth, such as inequality, corruption, and lack of infrastructure (Brynjolfsson & McAfee, 2014; World Bank, 2016). For instance, media narratives that celebrate AI's potential to revolutionize education often fail to address the digital divide—specifically the shift from inequalities in physical access (e.g., devices) to material access (e.g., skills, meaningful use)—that disproportionately affects marginalized communities (van Deursen & van Dijk, 2019; Selwyn, 2014). This bias risks creating unrealistic expectations and diverting attention from systemic reforms needed to ensure equitable access to technological benefits (United Nations, 2015).

A significant gap in media reporting is the underrepresentation of marginalized voices in discussions about AI. Women, ethnic minorities, and low-income individuals are often excluded, perpetuating the myth of technology as a neutral and universally beneficial force (Eubanks, 2018; Benjamin, 2019). For example, coverage of AI-driven hiring tools rarely includes perspectives from workers affected by algorithmic bias, instead portraying these tools as objective and efficient (Raghavan et al., 2020; O'Neil, 2016). Addressing this requires amplifying diverse voices to critically examine the social and ethical implications of AI (Cath, 2018).

Media reporting also seldom scrutinizes the power dynamics underlying AI development and deployment. The concentration of technological power in corporations and governments is rarely critiqued, despite its implications for inequality and democracy (Zuboff, 2019; Crawford, 2021). For instance, while media highlights AI's potential for economic growth, it rarely questions who benefits and who is left behind (Feldstein, 2019; Manyika et al., 2017). This oversight reinforces a status quo where technological advancements primarily serve privileged interests, exacerbating inequalities (Benjamin, 2019).

To foster inclusive narratives, media must prioritize systemic critiques, center marginalized perspectives, and interrogate power structures. This aligns with calls for equitable governance of AI and redistributive policies to ensure digital dividends are broadly shared (World Bank, 2016; Cath, 2018).

MEDIA ENGAGEMENT FRAMEWORK TO ENHANCE SUSTAINABLE DEVELOPMENT OUTCOMES

The media plays a pivotal role in shaping public discourse, influencing policy agendas, and driving societal change. In the context of sustainable development, particularly in the digital age, the media's power to inform, educate, and mobilize action is unparalleled. However, the potential of media to foster equitable digital participation and sustainable economic growth remains underutilized, often hindered by challenges such as misinformation, biased reporting, and a lack of collaboration between key stakeholders. This section seeks to address these challenges by proposing a comprehensive media engagement framework that leverages the media's influence to enhance sustainable development outcomes. By focusing on best practices for accurate and inclusive reporting, collaborative strategies between media, policymakers, and the tech industry, and educational initiatives to support digital transformation, this framework aims to create a more informed, equitable, and sustainable future.

Best Practices for Accurate, Responsible, and Inclusive Reporting

Accurate and responsible reporting is the cornerstone of effective media engagement in sustainable development. Media practitioners have a duty to provide reliable, evidence-based information that empowers individuals and communities to make informed decisions. This requires a commitment to journalistic integrity, including rigorous fact-checking, transparency in sourcing, and a balanced representation of diverse perspectives (Kovach & Rosenstiel, 2014). For instance, in reporting on AI and emerging technologies, journalists must avoid sensationalism and instead focus on providing nuanced coverage that highlights both the opportunities and challenges of these technologies. This includes addressing ethical concerns such as algorithmic bias, data privacy, and the environmental impact of digital infrastructure (Crawford, 2021).

Inclusive reporting is equally critical to ensuring that media narratives reflect the experiences and perspectives of marginalized communities. This involves actively seeking out and amplifying voices that are often underrepresented in mainstream media, such as women, ethnic minorities, and individuals from low-income backgrounds (Eubanks, 2018). For example, in covering the digital divide, media outlets should prioritize stories that highlight the barriers faced by underserved populations, as well as initiatives that are successfully bridging these gaps. By doing so, the media can challenge stereotypes, counteract biases, and promote a more equitable understanding of digital transformation.

Building on Kovach and Rosenstiel's (2014) principles of journalism, the UNDP report emphasizes the media's role in providing accurate information and fostering public dialogue. By adopting these practices, media can promote inclusive governance and sustainable development.

To support accurate and inclusive reporting, media organizations may invest in capacity-building initiatives that equip journalists with the skills and knowledge needed to navigate complex issues related to sustainable development and digital technologies. This includes training on data journalism, ethical AI reporting, and cross-cultural communication (Howard, 2011). Additionally, media outlets should establish editorial guidelines that prioritize inclusivity and sustainability, ensuring that these principles are embedded in all aspects of their work.

Collaborative Strategies Between Media, Policymakers, and the Tech Industry

Collaboration between media, policymakers, and the tech industry is essential for leveraging the full potential of digital technologies to drive sustainable development. Each of these stakeholders brings unique expertise and resources to the table, and their collective efforts can create synergies that amplify impact. For instance, media organizations can play a crucial role in raising awareness about policy initiatives and technological innovations, while policymakers can provide the regulatory frameworks needed to ensure that these innovations are equitable and sustainable. Similarly, the tech industry can contribute technical expertise and funding to support media initiatives that promote digital literacy and inclusion.

One key area of collaboration is the development of public-private partnerships that address the digital divide and promote inclusive growth. For example, media organizations can partner with tech companies to create educational content that enhances digital literacy, particularly in underserved communities (van Deursen & van Dijk, 2019). Policymakers can support these efforts by providing funding and policy incentives, such as tax breaks for companies that invest in digital inclusion initiatives. Collaborative projects like these can help bridge the gap between technological innovation and societal needs, ensuring that the benefits of digital transformation are widely shared.

Another important area of collaboration is the co-creation of ethical guidelines and standards for the development and deployment of AI and emerging technologies. Media organizations can work with policymakers and tech companies to raise awareness about the ethical implications of these technologies, while also holding stakeholders accountable for their actions (Cath, 2018). For example, investigative journalism can expose unethical practices in the tech industry, prompting policymakers to enact stricter regulations and encouraging companies to adopt more responsible practices. By fostering a culture of accountability and transparency, these collaborative efforts can help build public trust in digital technologies and ensure that they are used in ways that promote sustainable development.

Educational Initiatives and Policy Recommendations to Support Inclusive, Sustainable Digital Transformation

Educational initiatives are a critical component of any media engagement framework aimed at enhancing sustainable development outcomes. Digital literacy, in particular, is essential for enabling individuals to participate fully in the digital economy and make informed decisions about the use of technology. Media organizations can play a key role in promoting digital literacy by creating educational content that is accessible, engaging, and tailored to the needs of diverse audiences. This includes producing tutorials, explainer videos, and interactive tools that demystify complex technologies and empower individuals to use them effectively (Livingstone et al., 2019)

In addition to digital literacy, media organizations can also contribute to broader educational efforts aimed at fostering a culture of sustainability. For example, they can produce content that highlights the environmental and social impacts of digital technologies, encouraging individuals and organizations to adopt more sustainable practices. This includes reporting on initiatives that "promote circular economy principles, such as the reuse and recycling of electronic waste, as well as innovations that reduce the carbon footprint of digital infrastructure" (Brennan et al., 2015)

Policy recommendations are another important element of the proposed media engagement framework. Policymakers have a critical role to play in creating an enabling environment for inclusive and sustainable digital transformation. This includes enacting regulations that promote equitable access to digital technologies, protect data privacy, and ensure that the benefits of technological innovation are widely shared (Stiglitz, 2019). For example, governments can implement policies that provide subsidies for internet access in underserved areas, mandate transparency in algorithmic decision-making, and incentivize the development of sustainable technologies.

Media organizations can support these policy efforts by advocating for evidence-based policies and holding policymakers accountable for their commitments. This includes conducting investigative journalism that exposes policy gaps and injustices, as well as providing platforms for public dialogue and debate on key issues related to sustainable development (Waisbord, 2019). By engaging with policymakers and the public in this way, the media can help ensure that policy decisions are informed by the needs and aspirations of all stakeholders, particularly those who are most vulnerable to the impacts of digital transformation.

The proposed media engagement framework is grounded in the recognition that sustainable development is a shared responsibility that requires the active participation of all sectors of society. By leveraging the media's power to inform, educate, and mobilize action, this framework seeks to create a more inclusive and sustainable digital future. The focus on best practices for accurate and inclusive reporting, collaborative strategies between media, policymakers, and the tech industry, and educational initiatives to support digital transformation reflects a holistic approach to addressing the complex challenges of the digital age.

This objective is particularly relevant in the context of the United Nations Sustainable Development Goals (SDGs), which emphasize the importance of partnerships, inclusivity, and sustainability in achieving global development targets (United Nations, 2015). By fostering collaboration and dialogue between key stakeholders, the proposed framework aligns with the SDGs' call for collective action to address the world's most pressing challenges. Moreover, by promoting digital literacy and equitable access to technology, the framework contributes to the broader goal of leaving no one behind in the digital revolution.

The media engagement framework outlined in this section represents a proactive and inclusive approach to leveraging the power of media for sustainable development. By addressing the challenges of misinformation, bias, and unequal access to technology, and by fostering collaboration and education, this framework has the potential to drive meaningful progress toward a more equitable and sustainable digital future.

Proposed Media Engagement Framework

Proposed Media Engagement Framework to Enhance Sustainable Development Outcomes

Table 1. Media Engagement Framework to Enhance Sustainable Development Outcomes

Pillar	Strategies	Actions	Outcomes	Sources
1. Accurate & Inclusive Reporting	***Promote journalistic integrity and ethical reporting***	***Train journalists in data journalism, ethical AI reporting, and cross-cultural communication.***	***- Enhanced public trust in media. - Balanced coverage of AI risks/benefits.***	***Kovach & Rosenstiel (2014); Howard (2011)***
	Ensure representation of marginalized voices	***Amplify perspectives of women, ethnic minorities, and low-income groups.***	***- Inclusive narratives. - Reduced biases in coverage.***	***Eubanks (2018); Raghavan et al. (2020)***
	Address ethical concerns in AI	***Investigate algorithmic bias, data privacy violations, and environmental impacts.***	***- Public awareness of ethical challenges. - Accountability for tech firms.***	***O'Neil (2016); Crawford (2021)***
2. Collaborative Strategies	***Foster public-private partnerships***	***Partner with tech firms to create digital literacy content for underserved communities.***	***- Bridging the digital divide. - Equitable access to technology.***	***van Deursen & van Dijk (2019); World Bank (2016)***
	Co-create ethical AI guidelines	***Collaborate with policymakers and industry to develop standards for transparent AI deployment.***	***- Trust in digital technologies. - Ethical governance of AI.***	***Cath (2018); Zuboff (2019)***
	Promote investigative journalism	***Expose unethical practices (e.g., surveillance capitalism, gig economy exploitation).***	***- Corporate/government accountability. - Evidence-based policies.***	***Waisbord (2019); Feldstein (2019)***
3. Educational Initiatives	***Enhance digital literacy***	***Produce tutorials/ explainer content on AI for marginalized groups.***	***- Empowered participation in the digital economy.***	***Livingstone et al. (2019); Manyika et al. (2017): Livingstone (2004)***
	Promote sustainable practices	***Highlight initiatives like e-waste recycling and low-carbon infrastructure.***	***- Adoption of sustainable tech practices.***	***Crawford (2021); UN (2015)***
	Advocate for inclusive policies	***Provide platforms for public dialogue on digital access and equitable policies.***	***- Informed policymaking prioritizing SDGs.***	***Stiglitz (2019); UN (2015)***

This framework is derived from evidence-based literature and aligns with global sustainability goals. While it provides a robust theoretical foundation, pilot testing in specific contexts (e.g., rural vs. urban, varying governance structures) is advised to refine its applicability

Key Outcomes of the Framework:

- Informed Public Discourse: Media narratives balancing opportunities and risks of AI (Entman, 1993; Brynjolfsson & McAfee, 2014).
- Equitable Digital Participation: Collaborative efforts ensure marginalized communities benefit (Manyika et al., 2017; Drèze & Khera, 2017).
- Sustainable Development: Ethical reporting promotes responsible technology use (Crawford, 2021; UN, 2015).
- Accountability and Transparency: Investigative journalism holds stakeholders accountable (O'Neil, 2016; Zuboff, 2019).

CONCLUSION

This chapter has examined the profound influence of media in shaping public perceptions and policies related to digital transformation, particularly in the context of artificial intelligence (AI) and emerging technologies. Through the analysis of media narratives, the role of journalism in setting AI-related policy agendas, and the ethical considerations in media reporting, this chapter has demonstrated the critical intersection between media, technology, and governance.

The policy implications of media narratives on AI and digital transformation demand urgent, multi-stakeholder action. Policymakers must prioritize regulatory frameworks that incentivize ethical reporting—such as tax breaks for outlets investigating algorithmic bias (O'Neil, 2016) or mandates for diverse expert representation in tech journalism (Raghavan et al., 2020). Cross-sector collaboration is critical: governments should fund media-literacy programs co-developed with educators (Livingstone et al., 2019), while tech firms must be held accountable through transparent AI audits, as modeled by the EU's Digital Services Act (Cath, 2018). Regionally tailored approaches are equally vital; for instance, LMICs could leverage community radio and participatory journalism to amplify marginalized voices in AI governance (Feldstein, 2019). Without such interventions, media-driven narratives risk entrenching inequities, rendering the Sustainable Development Goals (SDGs) unattainable (United Nations, 2015).

Addressing the Objectives

Examining the Influence of Media on Public Perceptions and Policies Related to Digital Transformation:

The chapter highlights how media narratives shape public understanding of AI and its broader implications, from automation and job displacement to ethical concerns like bias and privacy.

It discusses how media coverage influences policy debates and regulatory frameworks, often driving public discourse on AI governance.

Through agenda-setting and framing theories, the analysis shows that media outlets play a dual role: promoting technological optimism while also raising concerns about AI's risks and limitations.

Analyzing Media Representations of AI's Economic, Social, and Ethical Challenges Across Different Contexts:

The chapter explores variations in AI coverage across different regions and socioeconomic contexts, revealing stark contrasts between developed and developing nations.

While media in high-income countries often focus on AI's role in economic growth and technological innovation, media in low- and middle-income countries emphasize its potential for addressing developmental challenges.

The analysis also uncovers biases in AI reporting, such as corporate-driven narratives that prioritize commercial interests over ethical considerations and marginalized voices.

Developing a Media Engagement Framework for Sustainable Digital Transformation:

The chapter proposes a media engagement framework designed to foster responsible AI reporting, enhance digital literacy, and promote collaboration between media, policymakers, and the tech industry.

Best practices for ethical and inclusive reporting are outlined, emphasizing the need for investigative journalism, transparency, and diverse representation in media coverage.

Recommendations for improving AI literacy among journalists and creating public-private partnerships to ensure balanced AI governance reporting are discussed.

Key Findings and Implications

Public Discourse on AI is Highly Media-Driven: AI's portrayal in mainstream and digital media significantly impacts public perception and policy responses.

Media Biases and Gaps Must be Addressed: There is a need for greater diversity in AI reporting, ensuring that ethical concerns, regional disparities, and marginalized perspectives are adequately represented.

Collaboration is Crucial: Strengthening the relationship between media, policymakers, and technology stakeholders can lead to more balanced AI narratives and informed policymaking.

Media Literacy is Essential: Training journalists and the public in AI literacy is vital for fostering critical engagement with AI-related content and combating misinformation.

This chapter contributes to the broader discourse on AI and digital transformation by providing actionable insights for media practitioners, policymakers, and researchers. By implementing the proposed media engagement framework, stakeholders can work toward a more inclusive and responsible digital future, ensuring that AI and emerging technologies serve as tools for sustainable and equitable development.

REFERENCES

Altheide, D. L. (2006). Terrorism and the politics of fear. *Cultural Studies Critical Methodologies, 6*(4), 415–439. https://doi.org/DOI: 10.1177/1532708605285733

Autonomy. (2024). *Representing a gig economy: Gender, visibility, and news coverage of on-demand work during the pandemic*. Retrieved from https://autonomy.work/wp-content/uploads/2024/10/REPRESENTING-A-GIG-ECONOMY-1.pdf

Benjamin, R. (2019). *Race after technology: Abolitionist tools for the new Jim Code*. Polity Press.

Bory, P., Natale, S., & Katzenbach, C. (2024). Strong and weak AI narratives: An analytical framework. *AI & Society, 60*(3), 259–264. DOI: 10.1007/s00146-024-02087-8

Boykoff, M. T. (2011). Frontmatter. In *Who speaks for the climate?: Making sense of media reporting on climate change* (pp. i–v). Cambridge University Press. DOI: 10.1017/CBO9780511978586

Brennan, G., Tennant, M., & Blomsma, F. (2015). Business and production solutions: Closing loops and the circular economy. In Kopnina, H., & Shoreman-Ouimet, E. (Eds.), *Sustainability: Key Issues* (pp. 219–239). Routledge. DOI: 10.4324/9780203109496-11

Brennen, J. (2018). *An industry-led debate: How UK media cover artificial intelligence*. Reuters Institute for the Study of Journalism.

Brennen, J. S., Simon, F. M., Howard, P. N., & Nielsen, R. K. (2020). *Types, sources, and claims of COVID-19 misinformation*. Reuters Institute., DOI: 10.60625/risj-awvq-sr55

Bruns, A. (2008). *Blogs, Wikipedia, Second Life, and beyond: From production to produsage*. Peter Lang.

Brynjolfsson, E., & McAfee, A. (2014). *The second machine age: Work, progress, and prosperity in a time of brilliant technologies*. W.W. Norton & Company.

Buolamwini, J., & Gebru, T. (2018). Gender shades: Intersectional accuracy disparities in commercial gender classification. In S. A. Friedler & C. Wilson (Eds.), *Proceedings of the 1st Conference on Fairness, Accountability and Transparency* (Vol. 81, pp. 77–91). PMLR. https://proceedings.mlr.press/v81/buolamwini18a.html

Cath, C. (2018). Governing artificial intelligence: Ethical, legal, and technical opportunities and challenges. *Philosophical Transactions. Series A, Mathematical, Physical, and Engineering Sciences, 376*(2133), 20180080. DOI: 10.1098/rsta.2018.0080 PMID: 30322996

Chavez, L. R. (2001). *Covering immigration: Popular images and the politics of the nation*. University of California Press. DOI: 10.1525/9780520925250

Crawford, K. (2021). *Atlas of AI: Power, politics, and the planetary costs of artificial intelligence*. Yale University Press.

Demir, İ. (2022). Gig economy and evaporated risks through media. In Kayıhan, B. (Ed.), *Understanding risks and crises through the media* (pp. 65–86). Cambridge Scholars Publishing.

Drèze, J., & Khera, R. (2017). Recent social security initiatives in India. *World Development, 98*, 555–572. DOI: 10.1016/j.worlddev.2017.05.035

Entman, R. M. (1993). Framing: Toward clarification of a fractured paradigm. *Journal of Communication, 43*(4), 51–58. DOI: 10.1111/j.1460-2466.1993.tb01304.x

Eubanks, V. (2018). *Automating inequality: How high-tech tools profile, police, and punish the poor*. St. Martin's Press.

Fast, E., & Horvitz, E. (2017). Long-term trends in the public perception of artificial intelligence. *Proceedings of the AAAI Conference on Artificial Intelligence, 31*(1). Advance online publication. DOI: 10.1609/aaai.v31i1.10635

Feldstein, S. (2019). *The global expansion of AI surveillance*. Carnegie Endowment for International Peace.

Howard, P. N. (2011). Reply to Evgeny Morozov's review of *The Digital Origins of Dictatorship and Democracy: Information Technology and Political Islam. Perspectives on Politics, 9*(4), 896–897. DOI: 10.1017/S1537592711004853

International Labour Organization. (2018). *Representation, voice, and collective bargaining in the gig economy*. Retrieved from https://www.ilo.org

Iyengar, S. (1991). *Is anyone responsible? How television frames political issues*. University of Chicago Press., DOI: 10.7208/chicago/9780226388533.001.0001

Johnston, H., & Land-Kazlauskas, C. (2018). *Organizing on-demand: Representation, voice, and collective bargaining in the gig economy*. International Labour Organization. Retrieved from https://www.ilo.org/media/412401/download

Kahneman, D. (2011). *Thinking, fast and slow*. Farrar, Straus and Giroux.

Kingdon, J. W. (1984). *Agendas, alternatives, and public policies*. HarperCollins.

Knaus, T. (2020). Technology criticism and data literacy: The case for an augmented understanding of media literacy. *The Journal of Media Literacy Education, 12*(3), 6–16. DOI: 10.23860/JMLE-2020-12-3-2

Kovach, B., & Rosenstiel, T. (2014). *The elements of journalism: What newspeople should know and the public should expect* (3rd ed.). Three Rivers Press.

Livingstone, S. (2004). Media literacy and the challenge of new information and communication technologies. *Communication Review, 7*(1), 3–14. DOI: 10.1080/10714420490280152

Livingstone, S., Stoilova, M., & Nandagiri, R. (2019). *Children's data and privacy online: Growing up in a digital age – An evidence review*. London School of Economics and Political Science. Retrieved from http://eprints.lse.ac.uk/101283

Manyika, J., Chui, M., Miremadi, M., Bughin, J., George, K., Willmott, P., & Dewhurst, M. (2017). *A future that works: Automation, employment, and productivity*. Retrieved from https://api.semanticscholar.org/CorpusID:114479521

McCombs, M. E., & Shaw, D. L. (1972). The agenda-setting function of mass media. *Public Opinion Quarterly, 36*(2), 176–187. DOI: 10.1086/267990

Meghwanshi, S. (2024). Artificial intelligence in agriculture: A review. *International Research Journal of Modernization in Engineering Technology and Science, 6*(3), 4358–4372. https://www.researchgate.net/publication/379308989_ARTIFICIAL_INTELLIGENCE_IN_AGRICULTURE_A_REVIEW

Nguyen, D., & Hekman, E. (2022). The news framing of artificial intelligence: A critical exploration of how media discourses make sense of automation. *AI & Society, 39*(2), 1–19. DOI: 10.1007/s00146-022-01511-1

O'Neil, C. (2016). *Weapons of math destruction: How big data increases inequality and threatens democracy*. Crown.

Pangrazio, L., & Sefton-Green, J. (Eds.). (2022). *Learning to live with datafication: Educational case studies and initiatives from across the world* (1st ed.). Routledge., DOI: 10.4324/9781003136842

Pariser, E. (2011). *The filter bubble: What the Internet is hiding from you*. Penguin Press.

Raghavan, M., Barocas, S., Kleinberg, J., & Levy, K. (2020). Mitigating bias in algorithmic hiring: Evaluating claims and practices. *Proceedings of the 2020 Conference on Fairness, Accountability, and Transparency*, 469–481. https://doi.org/ DOI: 10.1145/3351095.3372828

Richter, A., Heinrich, P., Stocker, A., & Schwabe, G. (2018). Digital work design. *Business & Information Systems Engineering, 60*(3), 259–264. DOI: 10.1007/s12599-018-0534-4

Robinson, P. (2002). *The CNN effect: The myth of news, foreign policy, and intervention*. Routledge.

Scholz, T. (2017). *Uberworked and underpaid: How workers are disrupting the digital economy*. Polity Press.

Selwyn, N. (2014). *Digital technology and the contemporary university: Degrees of digitization*. Routledge. DOI: 10.4324/9781315768656

Stiglitz, J. E. (2019, March 11). Market concentration is threatening the US economy [Blog post]. *Project Syndicate*. https://www.project-syndicate.org/commentary/united-states-economy-rising-market-power-by-joseph-e-stiglitz-2019-03

Stone, P., Brooks, R., Brynjolfsson, E., Calo, R., Etzioni, O., Hager, G., Hirschberg, J., Kalyanakrishnan, S., Kamar, E., Kraus, S., Leyton-Brown, K., Parkes, D., Press, W., Saxenian, A., Shah, J., Tambe, M., & Teller, A. (2022). *Artificial intelligence and life in 2030: The one hundred year study on artificial intelligence* (Report No. arXiv:2211.06318). https://doi.org//arXiv.2211.06318DOI: 10.48550

Suerdem, A., & Akkilic, S. (2021). Cultural differences in media framing of AI. In Schiele, B., Liu, X., & Bauer, M. W. (Eds.), *Science cultures in a diverse world: Knowing, sharing, caring* (pp. 185–207). Springer., DOI: 10.1007/978-981-16-5379-7_10

Suri, T., & Jack, W. (2016). The long-run poverty and gender impacts of mobile money. *Science, 354*(6317), 1288–1292. DOI: 10.1126/science.aah5309 PMID: 27940873

Tajfel, H., & Turner, J. C. (1979). An integrative theory of intergroup conflict. In Austin, W. G., & Worchel, S. (Eds.), *The social psychology of intergroup relations* (pp. 33–47). Brooks/Cole.

Tufekci, Z. (2017). *Twitter and tear gas: The power and fragility of networked protest*. Yale University Press.

Tygel, A. F., & Kirsch, R. (2016). Contributions of Paulo Freire for a critical data literacy: A popular education approach. *Journal of Community Informatics, 12*(3). Advance online publication. DOI: 10.15353/joci.v12i3.3279

United Nations. (2015). *Transforming our world: The 2030 Agenda for Sustainable Development* (A/RES/70/1). https://sdgs.un.org/2030agenda

van Deursen, A. J., & van Dijk, J. A. (2019). The first-level digital divide shifts from inequalities in physical access to inequalities in material access. *New Media & Society*, *21*(2), 354–375. DOI: 10.1177/1461444818797082 PMID: 30886536

Vosoughi, S., Roy, D., & Aral, S. (2018). The spread of true and false news online. *Science*, *359*(6380), 1146–1151. DOI: 10.1126/science.aap9559 PMID: 29590045

Waisbord, S. (2019). The vulnerabilities of journalism. *Journalism*, *20*(1), 210–213. DOI: 10.1177/1464884918809283

World Bank. (2016). *World Development Report 2016: Digital dividends.* World Bank., DOI: 10.1596/978-1-4648-0671-1

Zuboff, S. (2019). *The age of surveillance capitalism: The fight for a human future at the new frontier of power*. PublicAffairs.

Chapter 5
Digital Leadership-Challenges and Promises of Digital Transformation for Higher Education Through a Critical Review

Sachin Suknunan
https://orcid.org/0000-0002-7296-8059
University of KwaZulu-Natal, South Africa

Pavla Macháčková
Independent Researcher, Czech Republic

ABSTRACT

The advent of Industry 4.0 and the Covid-19 pandemic created a disruptive shift towards digital leadership in promoting digital transformation across many sectors. However, there remains a paucity of related research especially within the Higher Education Sector. Through a critical review method, this chapter contributed to addressing this gap to create more understanding of the opportunities, challenges and factors informing the adoption of Digital Leadership the sector. Key findings suggest that Digital Leadership can positively reshape Higher Education by fostering innovation, improving efficiency and enhancing teaching and learning experiences. Digital Leadership connects stakeholders and breaks down silos. Challenges hindering Digital Leadership included lack of clear vision, resistance to change, fragmented strategies and ethical concerns. Factors for successful adoption of Digital Leadership requires a clear vision aligned with strategic goals, investment in digital literacy skills development and fostering a digital culture that supports

DOI: 10.4018/979-8-3373-6097-3.ch005

continuous learning and adaptability.

1. INTRODUCTION

The Covid-19 pandemic created a game-changing effect in all sectors in terms of digital transformation. Leadership had to adapt to the sudden change and digital growth within their organisations and sectors. In higher education, such as universities, effective leadership is critical for organisational improvement and successful teaching and learning processes. Therefore, Digital technologies play a vital role in teaching, learning, research and university operations, making their integration indispensable for future success (Hashim, Tlemsani and Matthews, 2022). Alenezi (2021) argued that understanding technological initiatives and how they align with institutional objectives is essential for transforming business models. For universities to remain competitive and effective, their leaders must actively incorporate digital technologies into their strategic plans. This integration will not only enhance institutional performance but also ensure that universities are able to keep pace with the rapid advancements taking place in the digital world. However, whilst technology and digitalisation has advanced across sectors, Higher Education Institutions (HEIs) remain behind other industries in developing digital maturity, which is crucial for effective leadership in an increasingly digital environment (Van Wart et al., 2020; Jameson et al., 2022). In light of this, there is a growing need for strong Digital Leadership within higher education institutions, particularly as the global digital transformation has accelerated following the Covid-19 pandemic as well as the advent of Industry 4.0. Educational leaders are now tasked with the responsibility of guiding their institutions through the complexities of technological change and innovation (Eberl and Drews, 2021; European Commission, 2021). Digital Leadership is no longer a luxury or a supplementary function, but a core component of any successful institution's strategy for navigating the future of education. It is therefore critical to examine the dynamics of Digital Leadership in higher education and to identify the factors that influence its adoption and effective practice.

Despite the growing body of research on Digital Leadership across various industrial fields, there remains a significant paucity of such research focusing on higher education. This gap in the literature is notable and require a more nuanced understanding of Digital Leadership in the context of higher education (Petry, 2018; Ehlers, 2020; Karakose, Polat and Papadakis, 2021). This chapter aims to address this gap in the existing literature by providing a comprehensive and critical review of Digital Leadership in higher education. It specifically focuses on examining the opportunities that Digital Leadership presents for guiding HEIs towards embracing digital transformation. At the same time, the chapter aims to explore the potential challenges that may hinder the implementation and adoption of Digital Leadership within the higher education sector. Furthermore, this chapter outlines the key factors that can facilitate or impede the adoption of Digital Leadership in higher education, offering insights into how institutions can better prepare themselves to embrace digital transformation. Thus, this research chapter makes an important contribution by filling this gap and enhancing the understanding of Digital Leadership in higher education. Through its critical review, the chapter aims to offer valuable insights for both scholars and practitioners to promote a deeper understanding of how Digital Leadership can guide universities towards a sustainable digital future.

2. SIGNIFICANCE AND CONTRIBUTIONS OF THE RESEARCH

This research chapter fills a significant gap in existing literature as there is paucity of research on how Digital Leadership can drive positive transformation in higher education to improve institutional performance and teaching and learning outcomes. In light of this, the chapter carefully and meticulously synthesises recent relevant research to provide a thorough understanding of the role of Digital Leadership in higher education. By examining the challenges, opportunities and factors for successful adoption of Digital Transformation, the chapter provides a comprehensive view and valuable insights for leadership to navigate through digital transformation in an ever evolving, competitive and technology-driven higher education environment. The chapter adroitly links leadership styles and technological adaptation to promote institutional performance and learning outcomes. Furthermore, It addresses the barriers and presents theoretical and pragmatic strategies for respective leaders to cultivate a robust digital culture and promote digital transformation effectively in Higher Education. The chapter is therefore seen as impactful within the leadership realm addressing the significant gap in Digital Leadership research in higher education, which lays the groundwork for future studies in this developing field.

3. LITERATURE REVIEW

Leadership is characterised as the ability to influence others towards achieving desired goals, fostering creativity and improving organisational culture (Caldwell et al., 2012; Northouse, 2021). Historically, leadership styles were rooted in traditional approaches that emphasised control and competition. However, the evolving landscape necessitates new leadership capabilities to maintain competitive advantages, particularly in the context of digital transformation (Erhan, Uzunbacak and Aydin, 2021). Digital Leadership is a relatively new concept and has emerged as a broader field of study with roots in technology management and administration (Oberer & Elkollar, 2018; Gfrerer et al., 2021; Ordu & Nayır, 2021). As early as year 2000, Avolio, Simran and George (2000) asserted that Digital Leadership as a social influence process mediated by advanced information technology (AIT), affecting behaviours and performance. Van Wart et al. (2017) proposed a more integrated approach, combining digital and traditional leadership methods. Eberl and Drews (2021) argued that Digital Leadership extends beyond supporting business through technology. It involves transforming the organisation, including leadership styles, skills and overall digital enablement of business models. Furthermore, Digital Leadership, driven by a clear vision and strategy, fosters a culture capable of transformation, enabling institutions to adapt to changes (Karakose, Polat, & Papadakis, 2021). Despite its varied terminology, Digital Leadership is generally understood as a mechanism that fosters digital transformation, through digital learning by utilising digital tools (Gfrerer et al., 2021; Northouse, 2021; Fareen, 2022).

As organisations face increasing digital transformation, the necessity for leaders to develop new skills, including digital literacy and adaptability, becomes critical (Cortellazzo, Bruni and Zampieri, 2019; Antonopoulou et al., 2021). Moreover, the intersection of leadership and technology emphasises the role of leaders in fostering a culture that embraces change and innovation, further underscoring the relevance of both transformational and transactional elements in contemporary leadership practices (Gill, 2020; Draxler-Weber, Voigt and Blömer, 2022). Digital transformation in education includes the implementation of digital technologies across all educational aspects. It is essential for effective organisational management and improving performance (Oberer & Erkollar, 2018). In light of this, digitalisation has become critical for the survival and transformation of universities in the current epoch. Digital technology promotes socially oriented innovations and equips students to face global challenges (Kaputa, Loucanova and Tejerina-Gaite, 2022). In addition, the transition to Industry 4.0, characterised by advancements in technologies such as artificial intelligence (AI), robotics and the Internet of Things (IOT), has transformed various sectors, including education (Shahroom & Hussin, 2018; Culot et al., 2020). This revolution necessitates educational institutions to adapt from traditional to Digital Leadership and governance.

The digital transformation accelerated by COVID-19 has been seen as an inevitable fundamental shift in the educational paradigm. As educational institutions faced unprecedented challenges due to the necessity of social distancing, leaders were compelled to embrace technology to maintain operational continuity (Babbar & Gupta, 2022). Hence, the COVID-19 pandemic has influenced sudden and significant changes in education, where the need for effective Digital Leadership became paramount. Educational leaders were not only required to implement technology but also to create a vision for its use in a way that enhances learning and teaching

(Rajab, Gazal and Alkattan, 2020). This is supported by Montrieux et al., (2015) and Dunn & Kennedy (2019) whereby Digital Leadership had emerged as a crucial component in transforming educational environments, particularly as technology becomes integral to teaching and learning processes. It is recognised for its potential to support student-centered classrooms and enhance student engagement, ultimately leading to improved academic performance.

However, challenges do exist which hinder the effective implementation of Digital Leadership and digital transformation in the realm of higher education. Higher education institutions face difficulties in managing the digital transformation of their institutions which involves not just technological implementation but also cultural and organisational changes (Ordu & Nayır, 2020). Therefore, Digital Leadership in higher education has not kept pace with the rapid advancement of digital practices (Duflo, 2020; Gfrerer et al., 2021). Higher education institutions face challenges in keeping pace with new technologies, primarily due to limited financial resources, environmental, strategic, technological, people-related and cultural factors (Gkrimpizi, Peristeras and Magnisalis, 2023). In addition, Digital Leadership in higher education encounter challenges including barriers to technology adoption and resistance to change (Antonopoulou et al., 2021). Without addressing such concerns, leadership efforts to push digital transformation are often met with significant pushback from faculty and staff. Other challenges faced by leaders during the COVID-19 pandemic included the rapid digital transformation of institutions, which required swift adoption of new technologies with many leaders lacking the necessary digital skills (Antonopoulou et al., 2021). In addition, online environments has led to significant changes in working practices, power dynamics and managerial approaches related to teaching, research and administration (Abdullah et al., 2015; Benavides et al., 2021). These shifts not only disrupt established relationships but also raise ethical concerns regarding well-being, stress, overwork, surveillance and job security (Arokiasamy et al., 2015; Hamzah, Nasir and Wahab, 2021). Leaders face challenges in integrating new technologies into traditional systems while also ensuring that faculty are on board with these changes (Nichols, 2023). Leaders must also navigate a multitude of expectations and respond to pressing societal issues, including the COVID-19 pandemic, equity and inclusion policies and staff and student mental health (Paul, 2024). There is also a skills challenge as Digital Leadership in education involves integrating technologies, along with tools like social media and e-platforms and this shift requires staff and educators to improve their digital skill, knowledge and ability to incorporate digital technologies into their practices (Saykili, 2019). Possessing digital skills is crucial for leaders in higher education especially in today's disruptive technological landscape. Leaders without such skills may fail to guide their institutions effectively (Karakose, Polat, & Papadakis, 2021). Furthermore, the lack of effective institutional strategies for managing digital transformation has exacerbated the challenges (Jameson et al., 2022). Hence, leadership in such environments requires new skills in managing distributed teams, addressing issues of equity in digital access and fostering trust in digital environments (Ordu & Nayır, 2020).

Having noted some of the key challenges, one cannot ignore the key opportunities and benefits of Digital Leadership and transformation for Higher Education institutions. El Sawy et al. (2016) discussed that Digital Leadership is crucial for the success of any enterprise's digital strategy. However, they note that the true essence of Digital Leadership goes beyond the mere application of technology; it is more about aligning strategy, fostering a digital culture and developing talent that can drive digital change effectively. Leaders who understand these elements can significantly enhance their institutions' capacity to innovate and evolve in the face of digital disruption. In addition, Digital Leadership has been shown to play a significant role in fostering digital innovation within higher education institutions. Digital innovation, including the use of big data analytics, is crucial for promoting educational quality and improving institutional performance. It allows universities to create new learning processes and enhance service delivery (Khin & Ho, 2020; Ashaari et al., 2021). Institutions that excel in digital innovation are closely linked to the digital capabilities and vision of their leaders. Hence, Digital Leadership significantly predicts digital innovation in higher education and leaders who prioritise digital transformation and cultivate a culture of innovation within their organisations can drive substantial improvements in their institutions' digital maturity and performance (Benitez et al., 2022). In light of this, innovations such as the Internet of Things (IOT), Artificial Intelligence (AI) and Big Data are effectively reshaping the operational landscapes of higher education. These technologies are not only transforming how universities function but are also enabling institutions to explore new frontiers in teaching, learning and research. With the growing importance of these technologies, it has become imperative for leaders to nurture a digital culture within their institutions(Suryahadikusumah & Nadya, 2020; Khin & Ho, 2020). A significant finding from (Khin & Ho, 2020) was the facilitating role of digital innovation in the relationship between Digital Leadership and higher education performance. Digital Leadership indirectly influences performance through digital innovation, indicating that leaders must cultivate an innovative environment to enhance organisational outcomes.

The advancement of technology has also transformed operations within higher education institutions. Leaders are now able to leverage digital tools to manage remote teams, facilitate virtual learning environments and implement data-driven decision-making processes. This not only enhances operational efficiency but also transforms leadership practices by providing leaders with real-time insights into institutional performance and areas for improvement (Paul, 2024). In addition, Digital

Leadership enables universities to extend their reach beyond traditional borders. The use of digital platforms allows institutions to connect with a global audience, creating new opportunities for international collaboration and exchange. This global connectivity also opens up new avenues for expanding educational access, providing learners from diverse backgrounds and locations with the opportunity to engage in high-quality education (Paul, 2024). Hence, by embracing digital transformation and fostering a culture of innovation, educational leaders can position their institutions to thrive in the ever-evolving digital landscape.

However, there are many factors to consider when trying to promote digital transformation through Digital Leadership and realised its benefits and potential. Jameson et al. (2022) asserted that to respond to the complexities of digitalisation, higher education leaders must not only develop strategic visions and technical competencies but also enhance their emotional and social intelligence. This multi-faceted approach is essential for fostering a culture of collaboration and addressing the shifting power dynamics and anxieties that accompany digital transformation (Duflo, 2020; Ehlers, 2020). There was also urgency for digital leaders to promote trust and foster open communication as they navigated the vulnerabilities associated with rapid technological changes concerns regarding well-being, stress, overwork, surveillance and job security (Arokiasamy et al., 2015; Adams, Mooi and Muniandy, 2020; Hamzah, Nasir and Wahab, 2021). As asserted by Guerra, Danvila-del-Valle and Méndez-Suárez (2023), in the current era, leaders must adapt to technological advancements and the changing organisational structures that come with them. The demand for Digital Leadership has emerged to manage and transform organisations in an increasingly digital environment (Tagscherer & Carbon, 2023). Furthermore, digital workplaces integrate physical, cultural and digital elements to enhance work life within complex environments (Dery, Sebastian and van der Meulan, 2017). Hence, leaders must stay updated on digital advancements to ensure their organisations' competitiveness and survival, particularly as technology continues to reshape various stakeholder roles and expectations. Suryadi, Muslim and Setyono (2024) asserted that Digital Leadership is vital for improving organisational performance within the technological era. Effective leaders who embrace Digital Leadership can significantly enhance the performance of Higher Education Institutions (Jameson et al., 2022; Sarfraz, Khawaja and Ivascu, 2022). Digital literacy is also an important concept for promoting Digital Leadership and institutions that foster high digital literacy among their members tend to achieve better organisational outcomes (Ukwoma, Iwundu and Iwundu, 2016; Gkrimpizi, Peristeras and Magnisalis, 2023). Digital literacy is important in accelerating digital innovation within higher education and digital innovation can act as a strong mediator in connecting digital literacy to the performance of higher education. Therefore, knowledge and skills in using digital technology are directly related to the level of digital innovation Higher education institutions can achieve better performance through robust digital skills that foster ongoing digital innovation (Suryahadikusumah & Nadya, 2020).

In summary, literature shows that Digital Leadership is not only essential for driving digital transformation but also plays a pivotal role in enhancing organisational performance within the current technological era. As the landscape of higher education continues to evolve, the need for effective leadership that embraces the potential of digital technologies has never been more pressing. Leaders who understand and harness the principles of Digital Leadership can substantially improve the performance of Higher Education Institutions, driving innovation, increasing operational efficiency and enhancing the learning experience for both students and staff (Jameson et al., 2022; Sarfraz, Khawaja and Ivascu, 2022). Such leaders are not just facilitators of technology adoption but also visionaries who can shape the future direction of their institutions by integrating digital tools in ways that align with institutional goals and foster long-term growth. However, despite its growing importance, the existing body of literature has not adequately addressed the concept of Digital Leadership within the context of higher education. This represents a significant gap in the research of which this chapter aims to fill. While there is substantial interest in digital transformation in various sectors, higher education has been slow in embracing the full potential of Digital Leadership, with many institutions still grappling with the foundational aspects of digital strategy implementation. As such, there is a pressing need for research that explores not only the opportunities associated with Digital Leadership in higher education but also the challenges and barriers that may impede its effective implementation. By thoroughly examining these dynamics, this chapter seeks to provide deeper insights the elements that contribute to or hinder the successful adoption of Digital Leadership in higher education. Such insights can provide clearer understanding of how to navigate the digital landscape and leverage Digital Leadership for improved institutional outcomes.

4. METHODS

For this chapter, a comprehensive critical review method was undertaken to examine existing literature related to the themes of Digital Leadership, Digital Transformation and Higher Education. The authors meticulously reviewed a wide range of key research articles that were published in these areas. In the initial phase, over 80 articles were downloaded, covering various aspects of Digital Leadership and transformation within the higher education context. Through a rigorous process of elimination, the selection was narrowed down to articles that specifically aligned with the primary focus areas of Digital Leadership and Digital Transformation within the realm of Higher Education. It is important to highlight that there was a noticeable scarcity of research articles directly related to this topic. This is attributed to the fact that Digital Leadership and Digital Transformation within the higher education sector is a relatively emerging field of study. Almost 90% of articles downloaded were very recent within the 5 year period prior to current year.

The chapter employed a content and meta-analysis approach to systematically analyse and synthesise the available literature. This approach allowed for a structured examination of the existing body of work thereby ensuring that the insights gathered were both relevant and current. The authors also utilised NVIVO qualitative software (version 15) to allow for the identification of commonalities between various literature which played a role in determining key and common themes. The analysis was organised around three key clusters. The first cluster focused on the opportunities and benefits that Digital Leadership presents for driving Digital Transformation in higher education institutions. The second cluster delved into the challenges and barriers that hinder the effective implementation of Digital Leadership and Digital Transformation in higher education. The third and final cluster examined the factors that inform the successful implementation and adoption of Digital Leadership in the higher education sector. By focusing on these clusters, the chapter provided a nuanced understanding of the multifaceted role of Digital Leadership in shaping the future of higher education. Through the critical review and synthesis of literature, the authors offered valuable insights into how institutions can navigate the complexities of digital transformation and leverage Digital Leadership to foster sustainable growth and innovation.

5. ANALYSIS AND KEY FINDINGS FROM THE CRITICAL REVIEW

This section outlines the analysis and key findings. A critical review was done with the aid of qualitative analysis software NVIVO to identify commonalties and themes across the various literature. The respective analysis diagrams inclusive of word clouds, tree maps and cluster analysis of the relevant literature used are hereby provided as examples and depicted in Figure 1, 2 and 3.

Figure 1. Word Cloud of related Digital Leadership and Higher Education literature (Suknunan and Macháčková, NVIVO 15, 2025)

Figure 2. Tree Map of related Digital Leadership and Higher Education literature (Suknunan and Macháčková, NVIVO 15, 2025)

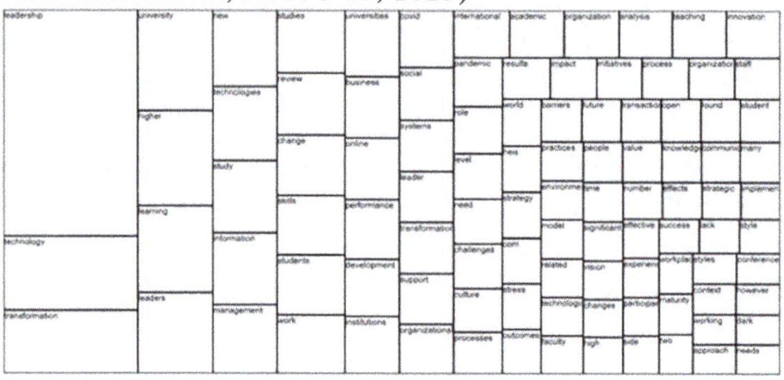

Figure 3. Cluster Analysis of related Digital Leadership and Higher Education literature (Suknunan and Macháčková, NVIVO 15, 2025)

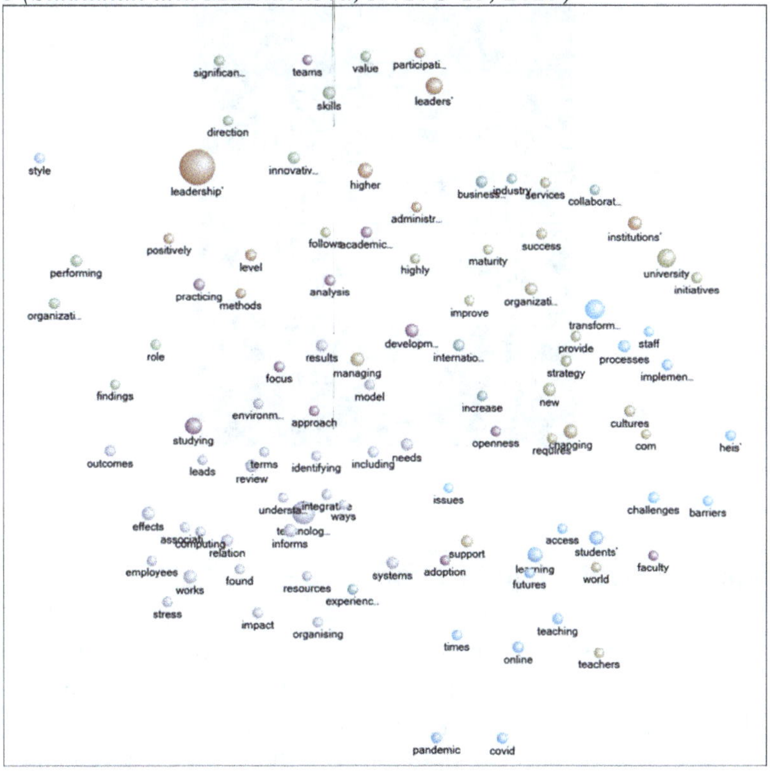

The findings are presented in line with three key themes. The first theme examined the opportunities and benefits of Digital Leadership in driving Digital Transformation in higher education. The second theme focused on the challenges and barriers to effective implementation. The third theme explored the factors influencing the successful adoption of Digital Leadership in the sector. All of these were informed by further subthemes.

5.1 Opportunities and benefits of Digital Leadership for Digital Transformation in Higher Education

The review outlined that there are various opportunities and benefits for HEIs through Digital Leadership and transformation. The most common themes that emerges are outlined below.

Figure 4. Word cloud - Opportunities and benefits of Digital Leadership for Digital Transformation in Higher Education (Suknunan and Macháčková, NVIVO 15, 2025)

5.1.1 Digital Innovation and Performance

Digital Leadership is key in enabling Higher Education Institutions to innovate using new technologies. Leaders play a crucial role in guiding institutions through the complex process of digital transformation, which is critical for maintaining competitiveness in an increasingly digital world. This includes leveraging big data, artificial intelligence and other advanced technologies to enhance learning outcomes and operational efficiency. Such innovations significantly impact the relationship between effective leadership and improved organisational performance thereby positioning HEIs to thrive in the digital landscape (Khin & Ho, 2020; Hamzah, Nasir and Wahab, 2021; Benitez et al., 2022; Erhan, Uzunbacak and Aydin, 2022; Mercader & Gairín, 2020).

5.1.2 Improved Efficiency and cost reduction

Digital Leadership empowers Higher Education Institutions (HEIs) to streamline administrative processes, optimise resource allocation and effectively integrate digital tools into their operations. This integration not only reduces costs but also enhances overall operational efficiency across the university (Benitez et al., 2022; Erhan, Uzunbacak and Aydin, 2022). Furthermore, Digital Leadership fosters a culture of continuous improvement enabling institutions to remain adaptable in the face of evolving challenges and technological advancements. Hence, Digital Leadership ensures that universities can swiftly respond to new opportunities and challenges (Gallardo-Echenique et al., 2015; Jarad & Shaalan, 2020; Babbar & Gupta, 2022).

5.1.3 Educational Transformation

Digital Leadership can provide significant opportunities for transforming higher education by driving the integration of technology into teaching and learning processes. By leveraging digital tools and platforms, digital leaders can support the adoption of innovative pedagogical practices thereby creating more dynamic and interactive learning environments. This can foster student-centred classrooms that enhance engagement and improve academic performance (Montrieux et al., 2015; Dunn & Kennedy, 2019; Antonopoulou et al., 2021; Panshin et al., 2021; Babbar & Gupta, 2022).

5.1.4 Collaboration and Communication

Digital Leadership can facilitate better communication and collaboration communication among students, faculties and administration by utilising advanced digital tools. This can foster transparency and streamline interactions thereby creating a more cohesive and collaborative environment within higher education institutions. This improved collaboration can not only improve academic and administrative processes but also contribute to a more engaging and supportive learning atmosphere, ultimately driving institutional success (Sheninger, 2019; Hamzah, Nasir and Wahab, 2021; Babbar & Gupta, 2022; Benitez et al., 2022; Erhan, Uzunbacak and Aydin, 2022).

5.2 Challenges and barriers to Digital Leadership and Transformation in higher education

However, there were challenges, derived from the review, that hindered Digital Leadership and digital transformation within HEIs.

Figure 5. Challenges and barriers to Digital Leadership and Transformation in higher education (Suknunan and Macháčková, NVIVO 15, 2025)

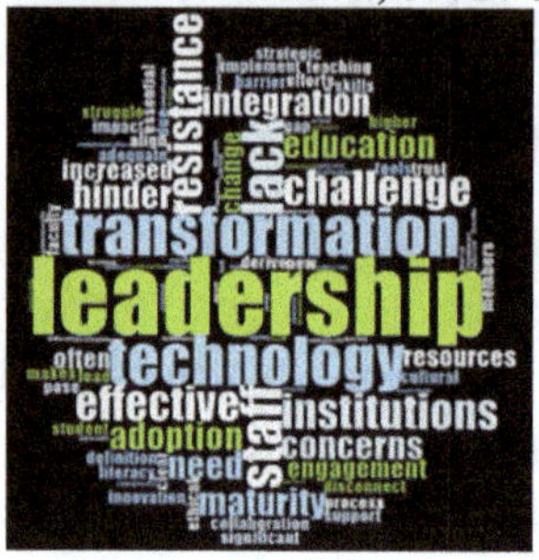

5.2.1 Lack of clear Definition

The absence of a clear and consistent definition of Digital Leadership hinders institutions from developing a coherent framework for its implementation. This lack of clarity makes it difficult for institutions to fully understand and align their strategies with Digital Leadership. Consequently, institutions can struggle to embrace Digital Leadership and derive the necessary benefits thereof. The ambiguity may also lead to varied interpretations, thereby preventing a unified approach essential for driving meaningful digital transformation and innovation (Eberl & Drews, 2021; Ordu & Nayır, 2021).

5.2.2 Slow Adoption of Digital Maturity

Digital maturity refers to the extent to which digital technologies are integrated into an organisation's operations. In the context of higher education institutions, achieving digital maturity can be challenging due to various factors. Limited resources often hinder the ability to adopt and implement new digital technologies. In addition, staff resistance to change and the inherent complexity of academic structures and governance further complicates efforts to promote digital integration and can contribute to the lag in digital maturity (Eberl & Drews, 2021; Mercader & Gairini, 2022; Gkrimpizi, Peristeras and Magnisalis, 2023; Jameson et al., 2022; Fernández et al., 2023).

5.2.3 Leadership Disconnect and lack of engagement

There is often a strategic disconnect between leadership and individual department members which can result in a lack of engagement and staff participation in the digital transformation process. Effective Digital Leadership requires proactive efforts to address concerns by fostering open communication, collaboration and inclusivity. By actively engaging staff, leaders can build trust and ensure a smoother digital transformation process and align technological innovations with the educational needs and goals of the institution (Laurillard, 2008; Van Wart et al., 2020; Eberl & Drews, 2021; Jameson et al., 2022).

5.2.4 Resistance to Change

Staff and faculty resistance, often due to insufficient support and/ or lack of involvement in decision-making, poses a significant barrier. Resistance was also is a common challenge, particularly when leadership fails to provide adequate training or resources for new digital tools. This resistance stems from concerns over job security, increased workload and reduced professional autonomy (Laurillard, 2008; Van Wart et al., 2020; Jameson et al., 2022; Gkrimpizi, Peristeras and Magnisalis, 2023, Paul 2024).

5.2.5 Digital Literacy

Staff members lack the digital literacy skills that is essential for the effective adoption and use of technology. This digital skills gap can pose a significant challenge as it directly impacts the quality of teaching and the effective integration of digital tools. Without adequate digital proficiency, educators may struggle to utilise technological resources to their full potential, hindering both teaching effectiveness and student learning outcomes. Research by Babbar and Gupta (2022) and Gkrimpizi, Peristeras and Magnisalis (2023) highlights the need for digital lLiteracy to bridge this gap and enhance digital competency among staff.

5.2.6 Technology and culture integration

Leadership may be over-reliant on technology assuming it alone will lead to transformation and end up overlooking the need for cultural and strategic changes. Effective Digital Leadership needs to incorporate human elements such as trust and collaboration to support digital adoption and transformation (Gkrimpizi et al., 2023; Jameson et al., 2022). Cultural sensitivity and adaptation also abounds as with leadership perspectives varying across different cultural contexts, leaders face challenges in adapting their Digital Leadership strategies to fit diverse teams and environments. This complexity necessitates an understanding of various cultural dynamics in leadership (Tigre, Henriques & Curado, 2023).

5.2.7 Equity and Accessibility Issues

Not all students and staff have equal access to digital resources, creating disparities in learning experiences. Jha and Ghatak (2023) highlight how digital transformation can exacerbate existing inequalities especially in developing countries where access to reliable internet and digital devices is limited. Hence, ensuring digital inclusion requires targeted policies that address accessibility gaps.

5.2.8 Ethical Concerns and Well-being

There were ethical issues arising from increased digital surveillance, data confidentiality concerns and the impact of digitalization on the well-being of faculty and students. Digitisation is also shown to increase stress, overworking and blurred work-life boundaries (Babbar & Gupta, 2022; Gkrimpizi, Peristeras and Magnisalis, 2023; McCarthy et al., 2023; Van Wart et al., 2020). Furthermore, the increased digitalisation of universities presents cybersecurity risks including threats such as data breaches, phishing attacks and online fraud. The rapid adoption of AI and digital surveillance technologies also raises ethical concerns regarding data privacy, academic integrity and decision-making. This may be correlated to weak institutional policies on data protection can lead to compliance and privacy issues and may compromise student and staff information (Paul, 2024)

5.3 Factors informing the implementation and adoption of Digital Leadership in Higher Education

Looking beyond the challenges, there are key factors that can be considered to overcome challenges and promote a comprehensive approach required for successful Digital Leadership implementation.

Figure 6. Factors informing the implementation and adoption of Digital Leadership in Higher Education (Suknunan and Macháčková, NVIVO 15, 2025)

5.3.1 Vision and Strategic Alignment

A clear and convincing vision for digital transformation is essential. Leaders must align digital initiatives with the institution's strategic goals to ensure that technology serves the broader educational mission. This alignment fosters collaboration and minimises resistance by involving all stakeholders in the digital transformation journey (Babbar & Gupta, 2022; Karakose, Polat and Papadakis, 2022; Gkrimpizi, Peristeras and Magnisalis, 2023).

5.3.2 Key Digital Leadership Competencies

Digital Leadership competencies are needed and this is based on the 9 key competencies posited by Amorim et al. (2023). These includes technological proficiency, communication skills, adaptability, collaboration, strategic thinking, emotional intelligence, cross-cultural competence, team building and continuous learning (Amorim, et al., 2023).

5.3.3 Infrastructure and Resource Allocation

A robust technological infrastructure is a key factor in supporting Digital Leadership . Leadership should ensure the adequate provision of technological infrastructure to support its digital transformation vision. Institutions need to ensure that their infrastructure can support digital initiatives and that adequate resources are allocated for ongoing maintenance, upgrades and support (Antonopoulou et al., 2021; Benitez et al. 2022; Babbar & Gupta, 2022; Mercader & Gairín, 2020; Gkrimpizi, Peristeras and Magnisalis, 2023).

5.3.4 Digital literacy for digital competence and skills development

Digital Leadership presents an opportunity to improve digital literacy among staff and students, which is essential for driving digital innovation. Digital literacy encompasses a diversity of skills, from basic technical proficiency to more advanced competencies and digital problem-solving. Hence, leaders who prioritise digital literacy will promote an environment where faculty and staff feel empowered to experiment with new technologies (Zeike et al., 2019; Benitez et al., 2022; Gkrimpizi, Peristeras and Magnisalis, 2023).

5.3.5 Digital culture and change

Leaders must create a culture that embraces digital transformation by actively promoting innovation, collaboration and transparency within their institutions. Creating such culture involves addressing resistance to change by understanding the concerns of staff and providing clear and consistent communication about the benefits of digital transformation. Empowering faculty and staff involves offering the necessary support, resources and training to ensure they feel confident and equipped to navigate the as well as encourages active participation in the transformation process. Related research supports the importance of leadership in driving successful digital transformation by cultivating an inclusive and adaptable organisational culture (Van Wart et al., 2020; Panshin et al., 2021; Peng, 2022; Schiuma et al., 2022; Benitez et al., 2022; Erhan, Uzunbacak and Aydin, 2022).

5.3.6 Collaboration and Stakeholder Engagement

Digital Leadership involves not just top-down directives but also engaging faculty, staff and students in decision-making processes. Leaders need to collaborate with various stakeholders to ensure the digital transformation reflects the needs and perspectives of the entire academic community (Laurillard, 2008; Van Wart et al., 2020; Eberl & Drews, 2021; Jameson et al., 2022).

5.3.7 Ethical Considerations for Digital Well-being

Leaders must address ethical concerns such as data confidentiality and the impact of digitalization on staff and student well-being. Ensuring a balance between digital efficiency and personal well-being is critical for maintaining a healthy academic environment (Van Wart et al., 2020; Babbar & Gupta, 2022; Gkrimpizi, Peristeras and Magnisalis, 2023; McCarthy et al., 2023). Furthermore, cybersecurity concerns demand clear institutional policies on data privacy, regular cybersecurity audits and the promotion of digital well-being initiatives (Paul, 2024). There is also a need for human involvement in digital decision-making to balance efficiency with ethical considerations. Universities must hence establish clear guidelines on AI usage and data governance to prevent ethical dilemmas (Paul, 2024).

6. DISCUSSION

The discussion unpacks the preceding section further and follows the similar sequence commencing with opportunities and benefits of Digital Leadership for digital transformation in higher education, detailing the challenges and barriers to Digital Leadership and transformation in higher education and finally positing the factors informing the implementation and adoption of Digital Leadership in higher education.

The review revealed that Digital Leadership can fosters an innovative environment, which in turn can improve institutional performance. Digital Leadership can transform how higher educational institutions operate, foster innovation, improve student engagement and promote operational efficiencies. Digital leaders can facilitate this process by guiding their institutions through digital transformation, by implementing sophisticated technologies such as artificial intelligence, big data analytics and machine learning to streamline operations, improve decision-making, resource allocation, staffing, budget planning and course offerings (Khin & Ho, 2020; Suryahadikusumah & Nadya, 2020; Babbar & Gupta, 2022). In addition, by integrating digital tools and technologies inclusive of automated systems for enrolment, grading and communication, Higher Education Institutions can reduce operational costs and enhance the overall efficiency of their administrative functions (Babbar & Gupta, 2022; Benitez et al., 2022; Erhan, Uzunbacak and Aydin, 2022). Furthermore, digital tools such as learning management systems (LMS) and automated administrative software can improve resource allocation and enhance the overall educational experience for students (Suryahadikusumah & Nadya, 2020; Babbar & Gupta, 2022). In doing so, Digital Leadership not only boosts institutional efficiency but also transforms and supports an environment where continuous learning and innovation are prioritised. It should be noted that the integration of technologies is also crucial to staying competitive in an increasingly digital world. By fostering an environment of innovation, leaders can position their institutions to adapt to the rapid pace of technological advancement, thereby improving overall institutional outcomes (Gallardo-Echenique et al., 2015; Jarad & Shaalan, 2020).

The review therefore proposes that Digital Leadership facilitates the relationship between performance and innovation and improved organisational performance, ultimately enhancing an institution's ability to evolve in response to changing digital landscapes (Khin & Ho, 2020; Benitez et al., 2022; Erhan, Uzunbacak and Aydin, 2022; Mercader & Gairín, 2020). Hence, those HEIs that embrace Digital Leadership can stand to benefit from increased efficiency and performance in both administrative and educational activities (Babbar & Gupta, 2022). Digital Leadership can also play a critical role in transforming educational environments. Leaders who effectively integrate digital technologies into teaching and learning processes can foster student-centered classrooms and support innovative pedagogical practices. In addition to transforming the learning experience, Digital Leadership enables institutions to adapt to the shifting needs of students as it facilitates the adoption of innovative pedagogies, such as flipped classrooms and blended learning models. This can be done by leveraging tools such as AI, virtual reality and data analytics, digital leaders can create more personalised, customised and engaging learning experiences for students (Montrieux et al., 2015; Dunn & Kennedy, 2019; Antonopoulou et al., 2021). These approaches can allow students to learn and engage with course material at their own pace, thereby fostering a more active and personalised learning experience (Sheninger, 2019; Panshin et al., 2021). Moreover, the integration of digital tools can improve academic performance by supporting more effective teaching and learning strategies (Antonopoulou et al., 2021; Hamzah, Nasir and Wahab, 2021; Babbar & Gupta, 2022). Hence, leaders who prioritise digital educational transformation can ensure that their institutions remain competitive by meeting these evolving expectations. Overall, the results implied that Digital Leadership offers numerous opportunities to enhance institutional performance through the strategic implementation of technological innovations.

However, whilst there are promises, opportunities and benefits of Digital Leadership in Higher Education, results affirmed that there are challenges that persist which hinder its successful adoption and implementation. Higher Education Institutions seem to be slower to achieve digital maturity compared to other sectors, which presents a significant barrier to successful Digital Leadership (Jameson et al., 2022; Gkrimpizi, Peristeras and Magnisalis, 2023). This makes it challenging to adapt to rapid technological changes that demand new leadership capabilities. Hence, there seemed to be a lack of a well-defined framework for Digital Leadership which created the challenge for institutions to understand how to effectively implement and measure digital initiatives (Ordu & Nayır, 2020; Eberl & Drews, 2021; Jameson et al., 2022; Gkrimpizi, Peristeras and Magnisalis, 2023; Fernández et al., 2023). This can in turn lead to disjointed efforts where individual departments pursue their own isolated digital strategies and fail to align collectively with the institution's broader goals. Digital Leadership in higher education therefore requires a clear and consistent definition and framework.

A recurring challenge in the implementation of Digital Leadership is also the disconnect between top-level leadership and individual departments. Often, leaders implement digital initiatives without fully engaging faculty and staff in the decision-making process, leading to resistance and a lack of buy-in (Van Wart et al., 2020; Jameson et al., 2022; Fernández et al., 2023). Consequently, faculty members and related staff may resist digital transformation due to concerns lack of trust, lack of inclusion in decision-making, inadequate communication, lack of training, job security concerns and or a perceived loss of professional autonomy (Skolkmann, 2021; Jameson et al., 2022; Gkrimpizi, Peristeras and Magnisalis, 2023). Furthermore, resistance to change in adopting digital technologies is common staff as many fear the impact on their job security. The shift to digital learning can be seen as a threat to traditional roles especially if there is concern that automation or new technology might replace certain tasks or functions. Staff may feel overwhelmed by the potential increase in workload as they navigate new tools or methods. Unfamiliarity with digital platforms can also create a barrier to adoption thereby contributing to resistance. This resistance often leads to reluctance in embracing innovative approaches and hindering the broader adoption of digital learning (Paul 2024).Such resistance to change can be compounded by inadequate training and support for the adoption of new digital technologies. Hence, leaders who fail to provide the necessary resources and guidance for digital transformation risk alienating faculty and staff, making it more difficult to achieve institutional goals (Tagscherer & Carbon, 2023). Cultural sensitivity and adaptation also play a significant role in Digital Leadership, especially as perspectives shift across different cultural contexts. In light of this, leaders encounter challenges when adapting their Digital Leadership strategies to meet the needs of diverse teams and environments. Leaders may only focus on the technology component and neglect the human component of digital transformation creating a disconnect between technology and culture. While technology is a crucial component, effective Digital Leadership must also incorporate cultural and strategic changes to ensure long-term success (Jameson et al., 2022; Fernández et al., 2023; Gkrimpizi, Peristeras and Magnisalis, 2023). These challenges require a deep understanding of cultural dynamics in leadership. Leaders must recognise and navigate cultural differences to effectively manage and inspire teams. Such complexity often calls for tailored strategies to ensure inclusivity and engagement (Tigre, Henriques and Curado, 2023). Access and inclusivity is also pivotal as not all students and staff have equal access to digital resources, which creates disparities in learning experiences. Jha and Ghatak (2023) emphasise that digital transformation can worsen existing inequalities especially in developing countries where access to reliable internet and digital devices is limited. This digital divide can significantly affect educational outcome as those without adequate access will be at a disadvantage.

Digital Leadership in higher education also raises important ethical considerations, particularly in relation to data confidentiality and the well-being of faculty and students. As institutions increasingly rely on digital tools to collect and analyse data, concerns about privacy and security become more prominent. Faculty and students may feel uneasy about the extent to which their activities are monitored or how their data is being used (Laurillard, 2008; Van Wart et al., 2020; Gkrimpizi, Peristeras and Magnisalis, 2023). In addition, the incorporation of digital technologies in higher education settings can blur the lines between work and personal life, resulting in heightened work stress and burnout among faculty and students. The expectation to be constantly connected and responsive can create a culture of overwork, which negatively impacts mental health and well-being (Babbar & Gupta, 2022; Marsh, Vallejos and Spence, 2022; McCarthy et al., 2023).

In order to overcome challenges and reap the benefits Digital Leadership in Higher Education, this chapter identified key factors from the critical review to inform the implementation and adoption of Digital Leadership and transformation in Higher Education which must be considered. Firstly, a clear vision for digital transformation is a crucial factor in the successful implementation of Digital Leadership. Leaders must then align digital initiatives with the institution vision and strategic goals to ensure that technology serves the educational mission and enhances institutional performance (Sheninger, 2019; Fernández et al., 2023; Jameson et al., 2022). In addition, a clear vision for digital transformation helps to build a sense of shared purpose among leadership, faculty and administrative staff and students thereby encouraging them to collaborate and contribute to the institution's digital initiatives (Karakose, Polat and Papadakis, 2022). By aligning digital initiatives with the vision and goals, digital leaders can ensure that technology is used to support rather than disrupt the institution's mission. Therefore, Higher Education institutions must work to develop a shared understanding Digital Leadership thereby ensuring that all stakeholders are aligned in their efforts to drive digital transformation (Fernández et al., 2023; Jameson et al., 2022).

Result depict that a robust technological infrastructure is a key factor in supporting Digital Leadership and transformation and digital leaders must play a critical role in aligning the institution's technological infrastructure with the institutions vision (Babbar and Gupta, 2022 Gkrimpizi; Peristeras and Magnisalis, 2023). This involves working to create a seamless integration of technology with academic and administrative processes, ensuring that digital tools are used to support institutional goals rather than hinder them (Antonopoulou et al., 2021; Benitez et al., 2022; Gkrimpizi, Peristeras and Magnisalis, 2023). Institutions must also ensure that their IT infrastructure is capable of supporting digital initiatives and that adequate resources are allocated for ongoing maintenance, upgrades and support (Mercader and Gairín, 2022; Gkrimpizi, Peristeras and Magnisalis, 2023).

Successful Digital Leadership in higher education requires a diverse set of competencies that enable leaders to navigate the complexities of digital transformation. Technological proficiency is a foundational competency for digital leaders, as it enables them to effectively use digital tools for problem-solving and decision-making. Leaders must have the ability to navigate digital platforms and tools to support their institution's goals and ensure that their teams can do the same (Amorim et al., 2023). Clear communication is also essential for successful Digital Leadership, as it ensures that all stakeholders are informed and engaged throughout the digital transformation process. Leaders must be able to communicate across digital platforms, provide constructive feedback and actively listen to the concerns of faculty, staff and students (Amorim et al., 2023). Emotional intelligence is also crucial in understanding and managing not only one's emotions but also those of team members, particularly in virtual environments. Relating to this, having cross-cultural competence allows leaders to appreciate diverse perspectives and foster an inclusive atmosphere by adapting their communication styles to respect various cultures (Amorim et al., 2023). In addition, a strong digital culture supports collaboration across departments and disciplines, enabling institutions to break down silos and work more effectively toward shared goals (Panshin et al., 2021). Adaptability is another key competency, as leaders must be able to respond flexibly to changes in technology, team dynamics and institutional goals. Digital transformation is a constantly evolving process and leaders who can quickly adjust to new challenges are better equipped to guide their institutions through this complex journey (Amorim et al., 2023). The development of digital competence also supports the institution's ability to adapt to emerging challenges, as faculty and staff are better prepared to integrate new technologies into their workflows (Ukwoma, Iwundu and Iwundu, 2016; Babbar and Gupta, 2022). By focusing on digital competence, digital leaders can drive positive transformative change within Higher Education Institutions.

Relating to digital competence, results show that digital literacy is crucial for digital transformation and this must be promoted by leadership. Developing digital literacy across all levels of the institution is crucial for successful Digital Leadership. As digital literacy is essential for driving the effective integration of new technologies in higher education, leaders who promote digital literacy help institutions better integrate digital tools and practices, which enhances both teaching and administrative processes (Ukwoma, Iwundu and Iwundu, 2016; Suryahadikusumah and Nadya, 2020; Gkrimpizi, Peristeras and Magnisalis, 2023). Institutions must therefore invest in training and resources to enhance digital competence, enabling staff and students to utilise new technologies efficiently and with confidence (Gallardo-Echenique et al.,

2015; Zeike et al., 2019; Jarad and Shaalan, 2020; Benitez et al., 2022; Gkrimpizi, Peristeras and Magnisalis, 2023).

Digital Leadership also enhances collaboration and communication within Higher Education Institutions by leveraging digital tools that facilitate interaction between students, academic staff and administrators thereby leading to a strong communicative benefit. Cloud-based platforms, online discussion forums and virtual meeting spaces can enable individuals to collaborate in real-time, regardless of their physical and/or geographical location (Sheninger, 2019; Hamzah, Nasir and Wahab, 2021). By fostering an environment of open communication, digital leaders help to break down silos within the institution, enabling staff and students to work together more effectively to achieve institutional goals. This collaborative approach not only improves academic outcomes but also supports a more inclusive and engaged academic community (Sheninger, 2019; Benitez et al., 2022; Erhan, Uzunbacak and Aydin, 2022). Universities should foster a culture of innovation by encouraging experimentation with emerging technologies, hosting leadership forums and adopting adaptive leadership models that support continuous learning (Paul 2024).

Results further imply that creating a culture that embraces digital transformation is essential for the successful implementation of Digital Leadership. Leaders must promote innovation, collaboration and transparency and training and support, to ensure that staff feel empowered and supported throughout the digital transformation process (Benitez et al., 2022; Erhan, Uzunbacak and Aydin, 2022; Amorim et al., 2023; Gkrimpizi, Peristeras and Magnisalis, 2023). This helps to create an environment where faculty and staff feel motivated to take risks and explore new approaches to technology integration in academic processes (Peng, 2022; Schiuma et al., 2022; Gkrimpizi, Peristeras and Magnisalis, 2023). In light of this, Digital Leadership must further prioritise continuous learning to stay updated on emerging trends and technologies. By promoting a continuous improvement culture, leaders can ensure that their institutions remain competitive in an increasingly digital world (Amorim et al., 2023; Tagscherer and Carbon, 2023). Relating to culture creation, effective change management was found to be a critical factor in the successful implementation of Digital Leadership. Digital transformation requires a holistic approach to change, where institutional goals, technological infrastructure and cultural attitudes are aligned (Eberl and Drews, 2021). Digital leaders must be skilled in managing change by fostering collaboration and communication across the institution, engaging faculty and staff in the decision-making process and providing ongoing training and support (Babbar and Gupta, 2022; Amorim et al., 2023). Leaders who prioritise change management help to minimise resistance and ensure that digital transformation efforts are embraced by all members of the institution. By clearly communicating the related processes and benefits of Digital Leadership as well as addressing concerns raised by staff and stakeholders, leaders can build momentum for change and encourage stakeholders to actively participate in the digital journey (Babbar and Gupta, 2022; Gkrimpizi, Peristeras and Magnisalis, 2023). Overall, a digital culture can help to ensure that all members of the institution are aligned in their efforts to drive digital transformation.

Digital leaders must also be mindful of creating a balanced approach to digital transformation that prioritises the well-being of all members within the institution (Laurillard, 2008; Van Wart et al., 2020; McCarthy et al., 2023). Digital inclusion initiatives can help ensure equal opportunities for all learners and staff. Hence, universities must also balance technological access with responsible Digital Leadership to ensure fairness and transparency. This also includes the inclusivity and access of student to bridge the digital divide. To address this issue of access, it is crucial to implement targeted policies that focus on bridging these accessibility gaps. By addressing these disparities, institutions can foster a more equitable learning environment (Jha and Khatak, 2023, Paul 2024). Ethical concerns must be addressed adroitly and digital leaders must implement policies and practices that protect data privacy and promote a healthy work-life balance. This includes establishing clear guidelines for data usage, ensuring transparency in decision-making processes and promoting a culture of digital well-being that encourages individuals to disconnect when necessary (Van Wart et al., 2020; Babbar and Gupta, 2022; Gkrimpizi, Peristeras and Magnisalis, 2023; McCarthy et al., 2023). Cybersecurity concerns require strong data privacy policies, regular audits and digital well-being initiatives to protect sensitive information (Paul, 2024). Human based decision-making instead of over-reliance on AI-driven systems is critical to ensure ethical decision-making and prevent biases. Clear guidelines on AI usage and data governance help uphold academic integrity and mitigate ethical risks (Paul, 2024). By addressing these ethical considerations digital leaders can create a more sustainable and equitable approach to digital transformation. Hence, promoting a secure, ethical and inclusive digital environment through the above, will support sustainable digital transformation.

Overall, the results imply that the role of Digital Leadership in higher education presents a host of opportunities that can in turn shape the future of higher education. As institutions increasingly rely on digital technologies, there is a strong need for leadership to become adaptive to digital transformation. However, challenges and barriers do exist which need to be addressed. Hence the factors put forward by the review can serve to overcome these challenges and promote more Digital Leadership thereby encouraging digital transformation in higher education.

7. CONCLUSION AND RECOMMENDATIONS

The chapter aimed to determine the opportunities, challenges and factors informing the adoption of Digital Leadership for digital transformation within Higher Education Institutions, through a critical review of existing and related research within the space. Digital Leadership in higher education offers potential benefits, but challenges may impede its full adoption. Digital Leadership in higher education can enhance institutional performance by strategically implementing advanced technologies to create efficiencies, reduce costs and improve academic processes and decision-making. By fostering an environment of innovation through digital transformation, institutions can remain competitive in the digital landscape. Digital Leadership also transforms education through flexible learning and promotes digital competence among staff and students, equipping them for continuous improvement. However, the chapter also diligently exploited gaps and challenges that exist. The lack of a clear Digital Leadership definition and framework leads to fragmented efforts with departments working in silos rather than aligning with broader institutional goals. Institutions further lag behind other sectors due to limited resources, resistance to change and complex academic structures. A disconnect between leadership and departments also hinders implementation as leaders may prioritise technology over cultural and strategic integration. Staff resistance exist from concerns over job security, inadequate support and training and development along with ethical concerns around data privacy. The chapter recommends that effective Digital Leadership goes beyond just technology adoption and requires a holistic approach that integrates strategic vision, robust infrastructure, digital literacy and competencies to enable seamless digital transformation. Institutions must establish a clear vision that aligns digital transformation with strategic goals. A strong digital culture, along with effective change management, through transparent communication and stakeholder engagement will assist to mitigate resistance and build trust for digital initiatives encourage engagement with new technologies.

Based on the conceptual recommendations made, these need to be translated into practical recommendations and/or solutions that can be actionable and achievable. In order to do this, a clear digital vision and framework for Digital Leadership must be established. Institutions can then align digital initiatives with this to ensure technology supports the Higher Education institutional objectives. In light of this, a digital roadmap can be created with a step-by-step digital transformation plan with clear objectives, timelines and assigned responsibilities to align digital initiatives with institutional goals. This will also include the investment in relevant technology infrastructure, networks and effective digital tools to support integration of technology both in academic and administrative processes. There must be adequate training programmes that focuses on hands-on digital training and digital literacy to improve digital competence among staff and students thereby fostering confidence in using digital technologies. To support this, there can be regular workshops on using digital tools such as learning management systems, virtual collaboration platforms and data analytics which can be hosted for staff and students. In addition, open regular open forums where staff can express concerns and receive support in adapting to new digital tools can be created. These can also serve to break resistance to digital transformation. There must also be targeted initiatives to address digital accessibility gaps thereby ensuring equitable learning opportunities for all students and staff in order to bridge the digital divide. In support of this this, assistive technologies and mobile platforms can be implemented to foster inclusion along with peer mentoring systems where students can receive guidance on using digital platforms. To foster a digital culture, leadership should encourage innovation and continuous learning. Hence, institutions should leverage cloud-based tools and virtual meeting spaces to facilitate real-time collaboration across departments. They should also encourage cross-department collaboration by implementing shared digital platforms to improve communication between academic and administrative departments. In addition, digital leaders should develop digital cultural awareness to obtain diverse perspectives and foster inclusivity. There must also be set guidelines for screen time, encourage breaks from digital platforms and provide mental health support to prevent burnout from excessive online engagement. To promote more online integrity and data privacy, institutions must establish policies and/or guidelines for data privacy, cybersecurity and responsible AI usage to prevent over-reliance and ensure transparency. Staff and students must also be trained on best practices for protecting personal and institutional data ensuring compliance with privacy regulations.

Overall, the chapter concludes that Digital Leadership brings about great promise for abundant benefits for Higher Education Institutions, but must be cognisant of the varying challenges and barriers. By focussing on the factors that inform Digital Leadership, Higher Education Institutions can successful adopt, implement and embrace digital transformation for added institutional performance.

COMPETING INTERESTS

Authors have declared that no competing interests exist.

8. REFERENCES

Adams, D., Mooi, A. N. Y., & Muniandy, V. (2020). Principal leadership preparation towards high-performing school leadership in Malaysia. *Asian Education and Development Studies*, *9*(4), 425–439. DOI: 10.1108/AEDS-02-2018-0046

Alenezi, M. (2021). Deep dive into digital transformation in higher education institutions. *Education Sciences*, *11*(12), 770. DOI: 10.3390/educsci11120770

Amorim, M., Madureira, R. C., Demosthenous, E., Dimopoulou, M., Ferreira Dias, M., Anastassopoulos, P. G., & Vrabelj, N. (2023). *A Competence Framework for e-Leadership*. Universidad de Aveiro., Retrieved from https://www.researchgate.net/profile/Bruno_Lins3/publication/371701955_A_Competence_Framework_for_e-Leadership/links/64917e30c41fb852dd19c40b/A-Competence-Framework-for-e-Leadership.pdf

Antonopoulou, H., Halkiopoulos, C., Barlou, O., & Beligiannis, G. N. (2021). Associations between Traditional and Digital Leadership in Academic Environment: During the COVID-19 Pandemic. *Emerging Science Journal*, *5*(4), 405–425. DOI: 10.28991/esj-2021-01286

Arokiasamy, A. R. A., Abdullah, A. G. K., & Ismail, A. (2015). Correlation between cultural perceptions, leadership style and ICT usage by school principals in Malaysia. *Procedia: Social and Behavioral Sciences*, *176*, 319–332. DOI: 10.1016/j.sbspro.2015.01.478

Ashaari, M. A., Singh, K. D., Abbasi, G. A., Amran, A., & Liebana-Cabanillas, F. J. (2021). Big data analytics capability for improved performance of higher education institutions in the Era of IR 4.0: A multi-analytical SEM & ANN perspective. *Technological Forecasting and Social Change*, *173*, 121119. DOI: 10.1016/j.techfore.2021.121119

Avolio, B., Simran, K., & George, D. (2000). E-Leadership: Implications for theory, research and practice. *The Leadership Quarterly*, *11*(4), 615–668. DOI: 10.1016/S1048-9843(00)00062-X

Babbar, M., & Gupta, T. (2022). Response of educational institutions to COVID-19 pandemic: An inter-country comparison. *Policy Futures in Education*, *20*(4), 469–491. DOI: 10.1177/14782103211021937 PMID: 40478015

Benitez, J., Arenas, A., Castillo, A., & Esteves, J. (2022). Impact of Digital Leadership capability on innovation performance: The role of platform digitization capability. *Information & Management*, *59*(2), 103590. DOI: 10.1016/j.im.2022.103590

Caldwell, C., Dixon, R., Floyd, L., Chaudoin, J., Post, J., & Cheokas, G. (2012). Transformative Leadership: Achieving Unparalleled Excellence. *Journal of Business Ethics, 109*(2), 175–187. DOI: 10.1007/s10551-011-1116-2

Cortellazzo, L., Bruni, E., & Zampieri, R. (2019). The Role of Leadership in a Digitalized World: A Review. *Frontiers in Psychology, 10*, 1938. DOI: 10.3389/fpsyg.2019.01938 PMID: 31507494

Culot, G., Nassimbeni, G., Orzes, G., & Sartor, M. (2020). Behind the definition of Industry 4.0: Analysis and open questions. *International Journal of Production Economics, 226*, 107617. DOI: 10.1016/j.ijpe.2020.107617

Dery, K., Sebastian, I. M., & Van der Meulen, N. (2017). The digital workplace is key to digital innovation. *MIS Quarterly Executive, 16*(2), 135–152. https://aisel.aisnet.org/misqe/vol16/iss2/4

Draxler-Weber, N., Voigt, C., & Blömer, L. (2022). Teachers' barriers to digital higher education teaching during the COVID-19 pandemic. *Wirtschaftsinformatik 2022 Proceedings*, 4. https://aisel.aisnet.org/wi2022/digital_education/digital_education/4

Duflo, E. (2020). Field Experiments and the Practice of Policy. *The American Economic Review, 110*(7), 1952–1973. DOI: 10.1257/aer.110.7.1952

Dunn, T. J., & Kennedy, M. (2019). Technology Enhanced Learning in higher education; motivations, engagement and academic achievement. *Computers & Education, 137*, 104–113. DOI: 10.1016/j.compedu.2019.04.004

Eberl, J. K., & Drews, P. (2021). Digital Leadership - Mountain or Molehill? A Literature Review. In Ahlemann, F., Schütte, R., & Stieglitz, S. (Eds.), *Innovation Through Information Systems. Lecture Notes in Information Systems and Organisation* (pp. 223–237). Springer., DOI: 10.1007/978-3-030-86800-0_17

Ehlers, U. D. (2020). Digital leadership in higher education. *Journal of Higher Education Policy and Leadership Studies, 1*(3), 6–14. DOI: 10.29252/johepal.1.3.6

El Sawy, O., Henrik, A., Kræmmergaard, P., & Vinther, A. (2016). How LEGO built the foundations and enterprise capabilities for digital leadership. *MIS Quarterly Executive, 15*(2), 141–166.

Erhan, T., Uzunbacak, H. H., & Aydin, E. (2022). From conventional to Digital Leadership: Exploring digitalization of leadership and innovative work behavior. *Management Research Review, 45*(11), 1524–1543. DOI: 10.1108/MRR-05-2021-0338

European Commission. (2021). *The role of Digital Leadership in higher education.* European Commission.

Fareen, J. A. M. (2022). Digital Learning in Higher Education: A Road to Transformation and Reform. *European Journal of Interactive Multimedia and Education, 3*(1), e02206. DOI: 10.30935/ejimed/11493

Fernández, A., Gómez, B., Binjaku, K., & Meçe, E. K. (2023). Digital transformation initiatives in higher education institutions: A multivocal literature review. *Education and Information Technologies, 28*(10), 12351–12382. DOI: 10.1007/s10639-022-11544-0 PMID: 37361743

Gallardo-Echenique, E. E., de Oliveira, J. M., Marqués-Molia, L., & Esteve-Mon, F. (2015). Digital competence in the knowledge society. *Journal of Online Learning and Teaching, 11*(1), 1–16.

Gfrerer, A., Hutter, K., Fuller, J., & Strohle, T. (2021). Ready or not: Managers' and employees' different perceptions of digital readiness. *California Management Review, 63*(2), 23–48. DOI: 10.1177/0008125620977487

Gkrimpizi, T., Peristeras, V., & Magnisalis, I. (2023). Classification of barriers to digital transformation in higher education institutions: Systematic literature review. *Education Sciences, 13*(7), 746. DOI: 10.3390/educsci13070746

Guerra, J. M. M., Danvila-del-Valle, I., & Méndez-Suárez, M. (2023). The impact of digital transformation on talent management. *Technological Forecasting and Social Change, 188*, 122291. DOI: 10.1016/j.techfore.2022.122291

Hamzah, N. H., Nasir, K. M., & Wahab, A. J. (2021). The Effects of Principals' Digital Leadership on Teachers' Digital Teaching during the Covid-19 Pandemic in Malaysia. *Journal of Education and e-learning Research, 8*(2), 216–221. DOI: 10.20448/journal.509.2021.82.216.221

Hashim, M. M. A., Tlemsani, I., & Matthews, R. (2022). Higher education strategy in digital transformation. *Education and Information Technologies, 27*(3), 3171–3195. DOI: 10.1007/s10639-021-10739-1 PMID: 34539217

Jameson, J., Rumyantseva, N., Cai, M., Markowski, M., Essex, R., & McNay, I. (2022). A systematic review and framework for Digital Leadership research maturity in higher education. *Computers and Education Open, 3*, 100115. DOI: 10.1016/j.caeo.2022.100115

Jarad, G. A., & Shaalan, M. A. (2020). Assessment of digital competence of employees and teaching staff at the technical college of management – Kufa. *International Journal of Innovation, Creativity and Change*, 12(12), 1027-1043. https://bit.ly/3BFCrVz

Jha, J., & Ghatak, N. (2023). Open schools in developing countries. In Zawacki-Richter, O., & Jung, I. (Eds.), *Handbook of Open, Distance and Digital Education* (pp. 493–508). Springer Nature Singapore., DOI: 10.1007/978-981-19-2080-6_27

Kaputa, V., Loučanová, E., & Tejerina Gaite, F. A. (2022). Digital Transformation in Higher Education Institutions as a Driver of Social Oriented Innovations. In Păunescu, C., Lepik, K. L., & Spencer, N. (Eds.), *Social Innovation in Higher Education. Innovation, Technology and Knowledge Management* (pp. 61–85). Springer., DOI: 10.1007/978-3-030-84044-0_4

Karakose, T., Polat, H., & Papadakis, S. (2021). Examining Teachers' Perspectives on School Principals' Digital Leadership Roles and Technology Capabilities during the COVID-19 Pandemic. *Sustainability (Basel)*, *13*(23), 13448. DOI: 10.3390/su132313448

Khin, S., & Ho, T. C. (2020). Digital technology, digital capability and organisational performance: A mediating role of digital innovation. *International Journal of Innovation Science*, *11*(2), 177–195. DOI: 10.1108/IJIS-08-2018-0083

Laurillard, D. (2008). The teacher as action researcher: Using technology to capture pedagogic form. *Studies in Higher Education*, *33*(2), 139–154. DOI: 10.1080/03075070801915908

Marsh, E., Vallejos, E. P., & Spence, A. (2022). The digital workplace and its dark side: An integrative review. *Computers in Human Behavior*, *128*, 107118. DOI: 10.1016/j.chb.2021.107118

McCarthy, A. M., Maor, D., McConney, A., & Cavanaugh, C. (2023). Digital transformation in education: Critical components for leaders of system change. *Social Sciences & Humanities Open*, *8*(1), 100479. DOI: 10.1016/j.ssaho.2023.100479

Mercader, C., & Gairín, J. (2020). University teachers' perception of barriers to the use of digital technologies: The importance of the academic discipline. *International Journal of Educational Technology in Higher Education*, *17*(1), 4. DOI: 10.1186/s41239-020-0182-x

Montrieux, H., Vanderlinde, R., Schellens, T., & De Marez, L. (2015). Teaching and Learning with Mobile Technology: A Qualitative Explorative Study about the Introduction of Tablet Devices in Secondary Education. *PLoS One*, *10*(12), e0144008. DOI: 10.1371/journal.pone.0144008 PMID: 26641454

Nichols, M. (2023). Transforming conventional education through ODDE. In Zawacki-Richter, O., & Jung, I. (Eds.), *Handbook of open, distance and digital education* (pp. 641–657). Springer Nature Singapore., DOI: 10.1007/978-981-19-2080-6_35

Northouse, P. G. (2021). *Leadership: Theory and Practice* (9th ed.). SAGE Publications, Inc.

Oberer, B., & Erkollar, A. (2018). Leadership 4.0: Digital Leaders in the Age of Industry 4.0. *International Journal of Organisational Leadership*, *7*(4), 404–412. DOI: 10.33844/ijol.2018.60332

Ordu, A., & Nayır, F. (2021). What is Digital Leadership? A suggestion of the definition. *E-International Journal of Educational Research*, *12*(3), 68–81. DOI: 10.19160/e-ijer.946094

Panshin, I., Solovieva, O., Kornilova, O., & Eronin, V. (2021). The Impact of Digitalization on Leadership. In Popkova, E. G., & Sergi, B. S. (Eds.), *Modern Global Economic System: Evolutional Development vs. Revolutionary Leap. Lecture Notes in Networks and Systems* (pp. 1272–1278). Springer., DOI: 10.1007/978-3-030-69415-9_139

Paul, R. H. (2024). University leadership in the digital age: challenges, opportunities and critical actions. Journal of Open, Distance and Digital Education, 1(1), 1-15. DOI: 10.25619/rp3rpr75

Peng, B. (2022). Digital leadership: State governance in the era of digital technology. *Cultura e Scuola*, *5*(4), 210–225. DOI: 10.1177/2096608321989835

Petry, T. (2018). Digital Leadership. In North, K., Maier, R., & Haas, O. (Eds.), *Knowledge Management in Digital Change* (pp. 209–218). Springer., DOI: 10.1007/978-3-319-73546-7_12

Rajab, M., Gazal, A., & Alkattan, K. (2020). Challenges to Online Medical Education During the COVID-19 Pandemic. *Cureus*, *12*(7), e8966. DOI: 10.7759/cureus.8966 PMID: 32766008

Sarfraz, M., Khawaja, K. F., & Ivascu, L. (2022). Factors affecting business school students' performance during the COVID-19 pandemic: A moderated and mediated model. *International Journal of Management Education*, *20*(2), 100630. DOI: 10.1016/j.ijme.2022.100630

Saykili, A. (2019). Higher education in the digital age: The impact of digital connective technologies. *Journal of Educational Technology & Online Learning*, *2*(1), 1–15. DOI: 10.31681/jetol.516971

Schiuma, G., Schettini, E., Santarsiero, F., & Carlucci, D. (2022). The transformative leadership compass: Six competencies for digital transformation entrepreneurship. *International Journal of Entrepreneurial Behaviour & Research*, *28*(5), 1273–1291. DOI: 10.1108/IJEBR-01-2021-0087

Shahroom, A., & Hussin, N. (2018). Industrial Revolution 4.0 and Education. *International Journal of Academic Research in Business & Social Sciences*, *8*(9), 314–319. DOI: 10.6007/IJARBSS/v8-i9/4593

Sheninger, E. (2019). *Digital Leadership: Changing Paradigms for Changing Times*. Corwin Press.

Suryadi, M., Muslim, A. Q., & Setyono, L. (2024). Exploring the nexus of Digital Leadership and digital literacy on higher education performance: The role of digital innovation. *European Journal of Educational Research*, *13*(1), 207–218. DOI: 10.12973/eu-jer.13.1.207

Suryahadikusumah, A., & Nadya, A. (2020). Digital Literacy and Innovation for Guidance and Counseling Program. *Advances in Social Science, Education and Humanities Research*, *462*, 190–195. DOI: 10.2991/assehr.k.200814.041

Tagscherer, F., & Carbon, C. C. (2023). Leadership for successful digitalization: A literature review on companies' internal and external aspects of digitalization. *Sustainable Technology and Entrepreneurship*, *2*(2), 100039. DOI: 10.1016/j.stae.2023.100039

Tigre, F. B., Henriques, P. L., & Curado, C. (2023). The digital leadership emerging construct: a multi-method approach. Management Review Quarterly, 1-48.

Ukwoma, S. C., Iwundu, N. E., & Iwundu, I. E. (2016). Digital literacy skills possessed by students of UNN, implications for effective learning and performance: A study of the MTN Universities Connect Library. *New Library World*, *117*(11/12), 702–720. DOI: 10.1108/NLW-08-2016-0061

Van Wart, M., Ni, A., Medina, P., Canelon, J., Kordrostami, M., Zhang, J., & Liu, Y. (2020). Integrating students' perspectives about online learning: A hierarchy of factors. *International Journal of Educational Technology in Higher Education*, *17*(1), 53. DOI: 10.1186/s41239-020-00229-8 PMID: 34778515

Chapter 6
Bridging Faith and Digital Financial Technologies:
A Predictive Multidimensional Analysis of Islamic FinTech

Mohamed Bouteraa
https://orcid.org/0000-0003-4834-8973
Qatar Foundation - American University in Qatar, Qatar

Abderrahmane Baddou
University of Algiers 3, Algeria

Mohammed Soufiane Benmoussa
https://orcid.org/0000-0002-8975-4962
University of Algiers 3, Algeria

Anes Hebbaz
University of Algiers 3, Algeria

Abderrahmane Elkheloufi
https://orcid.org/0000-0002-5009-504X
Universiti Utara Malaysia, Malaysia

Mourad Boudiab
University Centre of Mila-Abdalhafid Boussouf, Algeria

Meshari Al-Daihani
University of Malaya, Malaysia

Brahim Chekima
University Malaysia Sabah, Malaysia

ABSTRACT

This study investigates the adoption of Islamic FinTech services by integrating multidimensional Islamic religiosity into a predictive behavioral model. Drawing on data from Muslim consumers in the UAE, the study applies Partial Least Squares Structural Equation Modeling (PLS-SEM) to examine how various aspects of religiosity influence behavioral intention. Findings reveal that religiosity significantly shapes trust, perceived usefulness, and attitude toward Islamic FinTech adoption. The study addresses key barriers such as cybersecurity concerns, opaque Shariah governance, and limited financial literacy, while highlighting the need for transparency, ethical alignment, and culturally sensitive design. Theoretically, it advances

DOI: 10.4018/979-8-3373-6097-3.ch006

understanding of FinTech adoption through a faith-based lens. Practically, it offers actionable insights for FinTech providers, regulators, and policymakers aiming to enhance financial inclusion and ethical innovation. Future research is encouraged to explore cross-religious and cross-sectoral applications of this model.

1. INTRODUCTION

The global financial industry is undergoing a profound transformation driven by rapid digital innovation and accelerated by the COVID-19 pandemic. This paradigm shift, often referred to as the Fourth Industrial Revolution (IR 4.0), has challenged the dominance of traditional financial institutions by decentralizing market power and enabling new players—particularly technology giants such as Amazon, Google, Meta, Microsoft, and Alibaba—to enter the financial ecosystem. At the forefront of this disruption is Financial Technology (FinTech), a tech-enabled innovation that has introduced new operational models, applications, and products, reshaping how financial services are delivered and consumed (FSB, 2018).

Globally, FinTech has emerged as a transformative force. In the second half of 2022 alone, over $111.2 billion was invested in more than 12,500 FinTech start-ups (KPMG, 2022). This growth is fueled by rising smartphone penetration and the global shift toward digital financial services. The FinTech market is projected to reach $324 billion by 2026, with a compound annual growth rate (CAGR) of 25.18% from 2022 to 2027 (Market Data Forecast, 2022). Innovations in Artificial Intelligence (AI), big data, blockchain, cloud computing, and the Internet of Things (IoT) have revolutionized financial systems—automating services, reducing operational costs, and enhancing user experience (Puschmann, 2017; Singh et al., 2020). FinTech has also been recognized for its potential to promote financial inclusion, reduce poverty, and support the United Nations Sustainable Development Goals (UNEP, 2019; Chekima et al., 2016). Estimates suggest that FinTech could provide financial access to 1.6 billion people and contribute $3.7 trillion to global GDP by 2025 (James et al., 2016).

In the Middle East, particularly the United Arab Emirates (UAE), digital transformation is a strategic national priority. The UAE Central Bank established a dedicated FinTech division in 2020, focusing on inclusive finance, data privacy, and regulatory innovation (FinTech Middle East, 2021). By 2022, UAE FinTech investment peaked at $2.5 billion, and the number of FinTech startups grew to 303, offering services across e-payments, blockchain, InsurTech, and crowdfunding (UAE Ministry of Economy, 2022). Despite this growth, FinTech adoption in the UAE remains relatively low at 29%, compared to the global average of 64% (Statista, 2020; EY, 2019). While e-payments enjoy high adoption (84.3%), other services like peer-to-peer lending, robo-advisory, and InsurTech face limited uptake. Key barriers include consumer trust deficits, limited financial literacy, cultural resistance, and regulatory ambiguities.

Against this backdrop, Islamic FinTech—defined as Sharia-compliant financial technology built on principles of transparency, mutual benefit, and ethical finance—is gaining prominence. With Islam being the fastest-growing religion worldwide, the demand for financial products that align with Islamic principles is rising (Naeem et al., 2023). Islamic FinTech not only addresses religious requirements but also offers a unique model of inclusive, ethical finance. However, promoting Islamic FinTech adoption requires more than just product innovation—it necessitates a deeper understanding of the behavioral and cultural factors influencing consumer decisions, particularly the role of religiosity.

Theoretical models such as the Religiosity Intention Model (Hidayat & Akhmad, 2015) and the Islamic Theory of Consumer Behavior (Khan, 1986) emphasize the importance of religious commitment in shaping consumer intentions. These frameworks suggest that religious beliefs significantly influence financial preferences, especially in Muslim-majority contexts. Yet, most FinTech adoption studies have focused on individual, technological, and organizational factors, with limited attention to religiosity as a determinant (Alkhwaldi et al., 2022; Ngo & Nguyen, 2022). Moreover, when religiosity is considered, it is often measured simplistically—overlooking its multidimensional nature and behavioral implications.

This study addresses this gap by examining the influence of religious commitment on Islamic FinTech adoption using the Islamic Religiosity Index, a comprehensive measure of both intrinsic and extrinsic religiosity. By identifying key religiosity-driven factors that affect adoption, the study offers actionable insights for researchers, industry practitioners, and policymakers aiming to expand Islamic FinTech adoption in culturally and religiously sensitive markets.

The remainder of this paper is structured as follows: Section 2 reviews the relevant literature and theoretical frameworks; Section 3 outlines the research methodology; Section 4 presents the data analysis and results; and Section 5 discusses the findings, implications, limitations, and directions for future research.

2. LITERATURE REVIEW

2.1 Financial Technology (FinTech): The Convergence of Finance and Technology

Financial Technology, commonly known as FinTech, represents a rapidly evolving sector that merges traditional financial services with cutting-edge technological innovations to transform how financial products and services are created, delivered, and consumed. FinTech leverages advances in information and communication technologies, including mobile applications, blockchain, artificial intelligence (AI), cloud computing, and big data analytics, to improve the efficiency, accessibility, affordability, and user experience of financial services (Gai et al., 2018; KPMG, 2022).

At its core, FinTech challenges the conventional financial industry paradigm by providing innovative solutions that simplify complex financial processes, reduce transaction costs, enhance transparency, and democratize access to financial services. This broad term encompasses various applications such as digital payments, peer-to-peer lending, robo-advisors, insurtech, crowdfunding, cryptocurrencies, and regulatory technology (regtech) (International Monetary Fund [IMF], 2017; Dong et al., 2017).

While FinTech initially gained prominence through nimble startups and disruptors introducing novel technologies and business models, established financial institutions have embraced FinTech to modernize their operations. Traditional banks, insurance companies, and brokerage firms increasingly integrate FinTech tools to streamline their workflows, enhance cybersecurity, optimize customer engagement, and deliver personalized financial products, thereby maintaining competitiveness in a digital economy (Puschmann, 2017; KPMG, 2022). The partnership and collaboration between FinTech startups and incumbents have become a hallmark of the industry's evolution, often described as "co-opetition."

As an umbrella concept, FinTech encompasses a wide and rapidly evolving array of digital technologies and innovations that are transforming the financial services landscape globally. These technologies not only enhance the efficiency and accessibility of financial transactions but also fundamentally reshape how consumers and businesses interact with money, investments, and financial information. Key categories within the FinTech ecosystem include:

- **Digital Payment Systems:** These form the backbone of modern FinTech by enabling seamless, fast, and secure financial transactions across borders and devices. Examples include mobile wallets (such as Apple Pay, Google Pay, and regional solutions like M-Pesa), contactless payment technologies utilizing Near Field Communication (NFC), and real-time money transfer systems like SWIFT gpi and instant payment rails. These systems dramatically reduce transaction times and costs while increasing convenience for users, supporting the global push toward cashless economies.

- **Data Security and Privacy Tools:** Given the sensitive nature of financial data, robust security measures are paramount in FinTech. Innovations in this domain include advanced encryption protocols that protect data in transit and at rest, biometric authentication methods such as fingerprint scanning and facial recognition that enhance secure access, and distributed ledger technologies like blockchain, which provide transparent, tamper-resistant records. These tools help build user trust by safeguarding against fraud, cyberattacks, and unauthorized data breaches, which are critical challenges in the digital financial ecosystem.
- **Automated Financial Advice and Management:** Artificial intelligence (AI) and machine learning algorithms have enabled the rise of robo-advisors—automated platforms that provide personalized investment advice, portfolio management, and risk assessment services without human intervention. These AI-driven solutions analyze large volumes of market data and individual user profiles to optimize financial decisions, making sophisticated financial planning accessible to a broader audience at lower costs. This democratization of wealth management is a significant FinTech innovation, especially for younger and tech-savvy consumers.
- **Customer Engagement Platforms:** Enhancing user experience and service delivery is a key focus area in FinTech innovation. This includes the deployment of chatbots and virtual assistants powered by natural language processing, which provide instant responses to customer inquiries, streamline transactions, and offer financial guidance 24/7. Integration with social media platforms further allows financial service providers to engage with customers proactively, deliver targeted promotions, and collect valuable feedback. Such platforms not only improve operational efficiency but also foster stronger customer relationships and loyalty.

Together, these components reflect the multifaceted nature of FinTech as a transformative force that integrates technology, finance, and user-centric design to reshape traditional financial services. As the World Bank (2020) emphasizes, these innovations collectively contribute to greater financial inclusion, increased transparency, and enhanced economic participation globally, particularly in underserved and emerging markets.

2.1.1 Islamic FinTech: Integrating Faith with Innovation

Within the broader FinTech landscape, Islamic FinTech emerges as a distinct yet deeply interconnected subset that seeks to harmonize cutting-edge technological innovation with the foundational principles of Islamic finance. Islamic finance, which operates under the guidance of Shariah law, imposes stringent ethical and legal frameworks designed to promote fairness, social justice, and risk-sharing. Central to these guidelines is the prohibition of riba (interest or usury), avoidance of gharar (excessive uncertainty or speculative risk), and the exclusion of investments in industries considered haram (forbidden), such as alcohol production, gambling, pork-related businesses, and other activities incompatible with Islamic ethics (Bouteraa et al., 2024). These principles shape the core values that any Islamic financial product or service must uphold.

Consequently, Islamic FinTech solutions are meticulously engineered not only to capitalize on the transformative benefits of digital technologies—such as efficiency, accessibility, and scalability—but also to ensure strict compliance with these religious and ethical mandates. This means that Islamic FinTech companies operate within a dual framework of innovation and Shariah compliance, necessitating the integration of Shariah supervisory boards or Islamic scholars who oversee product development and certification to maintain alignment with religious doctrines.

Islamic FinTech firms offer a diverse portfolio of financial products and services that address the specific needs of Muslim consumers seeking modern, convenient, and ethically compliant financial solutions. These include:

- **Islamic Banking Digital Platforms:** Offering Shariah-compliant accounts, financing options like Murabaha (cost-plus financing), Mudarabah (profit-sharing), and Ijara (leasing) via digital channels to enhance user experience and operational efficiency.
- **Takaful (Islamic Insurance):** Utilizing technology to streamline the provision of cooperative insurance models that avoid uncertainty and gambling elements found in conventional insurance, often delivered through mobile apps or online portals.
- **Crowdfunding for Halal Projects:** Platforms that enable community-based funding for entrepreneurial ventures or social initiatives that adhere to Islamic ethical guidelines, supporting economic development within Muslim communities.
- **Shariah-Compliant Investment Management:** Robo-advisory and AI-driven platforms that offer portfolios constructed exclusively from halal-compliant assets, with automated compliance monitoring to ensure ongoing adherence.

This dual emphasis on technological advancement and religious adherence presents both significant opportunities and complex challenges. On one hand, Islamic FinTech has the potential to substantially improve financial inclusion by serving the millions of Muslims worldwide who may be underserved or excluded from conventional financial systems due to religious reservations. Digital delivery channels can bridge geographic and socio-economic gaps, offering accessible, affordable, and transparent financial services that respect users' faith-based values.

On the other hand, Islamic FinTech firms must navigate a multifaceted regulatory landscape that varies widely across jurisdictions, often characterized by evolving standards and interpretations of Shariah law. Ensuring rigorous Shariah compliance demands continuous collaboration with religious scholars, legal experts, and regulators. The complexity of integrating Shariah principles with fast-paced technological innovation requires robust governance frameworks and ongoing audits, which can increase operational costs and slow product development cycles.

The rise of Islamic FinTech reflects a convergence between faith-based values and modern technology, showcasing an adaptive financial ecosystem that responds to the evolving expectations of Muslim consumers in the digital age. This specialization enriches the global FinTech landscape by introducing a strong ethical dimension that emphasizes trust, transparency, and social responsibility alongside innovation and efficiency. As Islamic FinTech continues to grow, it sets a precedent for how religious and cultural values can shape technology-driven industries, fostering inclusive financial systems that respect diverse worldviews and contribute to sustainable economic development.

2.2 Emerging Technologies in Islamic FinTech

The rapid advancement of digital technologies has significantly shaped the evolution of FinTech globally, and Islamic FinTech is no exception. Emerging technologies such as blockchain, artificial intelligence (AI), and cloud computing are increasingly being integrated into Islamic financial services to improve transparency, efficiency, compliance, and customer experience. These technologies not only support the operational needs of FinTech firms but also address the unique challenges posed by adherence to Shariah principles (Al-Daihani et al., 2025).

2.2.1 Blockchain Technology

Blockchain, a decentralized and immutable digital ledger, is revolutionizing how Islamic financial products are issued, recorded, and managed. In the UAE, the Emirates Blockchain Strategy 2021 demonstrates a strong governmental commitment to leveraging blockchain for the advancement of Islamic finance. A prime example is the use of blockchain for Sukuk issuance (Islamic bonds), where smart contracts enable automation of compliance, transparent tracking of ownership, and efficient management of payments and profit distribution. These capabilities reduce operational costs, enhance trust among investors, and improve market liquidity, addressing traditional limitations in Sukuk markets (Ordóñez de Pablos, 2022).

Furthermore, blockchain's inherent transparency supports the strict requirements for Shariah compliance by enabling real-time auditability and immutable record-keeping of financial transactions, which helps Islamic financial institutions meet regulatory and religious obligations with greater confidence.

2.2.2 Artificial Intelligence (AI)

Artificial intelligence plays a transformative role in Islamic FinTech by automating complex processes and enhancing customer personalization. AI-driven risk assessment models allow Islamic financial institutions to evaluate creditworthiness and investment risks without relying on conventional interest-based metrics, which are prohibited under Shariah law. These AI systems analyze vast datasets from alternative sources, improving financial inclusion by enabling access to financing for underserved populations (Bin-Nashwan et al., 2025).

Moreover, AI facilitates personalized financial advisory services that align with customers' religious values, offering tailored recommendations for Shariah-compliant products. For instance, AI chatbots powered by natural language processing can provide instant answers to queries about Islamic finance rules, helping consumers make informed decisions while ensuring adherence to ethical and religious standards.

2.2.3 Cloud Computing

Cloud computing provides the technological backbone for many Islamic FinTech solutions by enabling scalable, flexible, and cost-effective IT infrastructure. Cloud platforms allow real-time data processing and Shariah compliance verification, which is critical for ensuring that financial products and transactions conform to Islamic principles. Leading Islamic banks in the UAE, such as Dubai Islamic Bank and Abu Dhabi Islamic Bank, have embraced cloud technologies to enhance their digital offerings, streamline operations, and improve customer experience (Ziouache & Bouteraa, 2023).

Cloud computing also supports collaborative ecosystems, where multiple stakeholders—banks, regulators, Shariah scholars, and technology providers—can securely share data and compliance insights, fostering transparency and innovation in product development.

Beyond blockchain, AI, and cloud computing, other technologies such as big data analytics, Internet of Things (IoT), and Robotic Process Automation (RPA) are beginning to impact Islamic FinTech:

- **Big Data Analytics** helps financial institutions analyze consumer behavior and market trends to design better Shariah-compliant products and marketing strategies.
- **IoT** devices can enhance real-time monitoring of assets backing Islamic finance contracts, ensuring compliance with non-speculative investment principles.
- **RPA** automates routine compliance and reporting tasks, reducing human error and operational costs while maintaining stringent regulatory standards.

The integration of these emerging technologies into Islamic FinTech represents a powerful convergence of innovation and tradition. By harnessing blockchain, AI, cloud computing, and related technologies, Islamic financial institutions can offer more transparent, efficient, and customer-centric services that align with Shariah values. These advancements not only elevate the competitive position of Islamic FinTech within the broader financial landscape but also foster greater financial inclusion and ethical finance in Muslim communities worldwide.

Islamic FinTech in the UAE

The United Arab Emirates (UAE) has rapidly emerged as a pivotal global FinTech hub, strategically leveraging its geographic position, business-friendly policies, and visionary regulatory frameworks to foster innovation within financial services. The country's ambition to lead Islamic FinTech innovation is clearly reflected in its robust infrastructure and supportive ecosystem.

Key initiatives such as the Abu Dhabi Global Market (ADGM) and the Dubai International Financial Centre (DIFC) serve as dedicated financial free zones that offer conducive environments for FinTech startups and established firms alike. Both ADGM and DIFC have introduced specialized regulatory frameworks tailored to FinTech businesses, including licensing regimes and innovation hubs, facilitating rapid experimentation and deployment of digital financial solutions.

The UAE Central Bank's establishment of a dedicated FinTech division exemplifies institutional support for fostering digital banking innovation, Sharia-compliant financing, and blockchain-based financial products. This division plays a crucial role in coordinating between regulators, financial institutions, and startups, aiming to harmonize technology adoption with the country's broader vision for digital transformation and Islamic finance leadership.

Several notable startups highlight the vibrancy and diversity of the UAE's Islamic FinTech ecosystem:

- **Beehive**: A peer-to-peer (P2P) lending platform that provides small and medium enterprises (SMEs) with Sharia-compliant financing options, democratizing access to capital through crowd-lending.
- **Wethaq**: A pioneering platform for Sukuk tokenization, utilizing blockchain technology to digitize Islamic bonds, enhancing transparency, liquidity, and efficiency in Islamic capital markets.
- **Alif Technologies**: A company focused on developing ethical finance products that align with Islamic values, integrating technology with social impact finance.

Despite these advancements, the UAE faces persistent challenges that may inhibit the full-scale adoption and growth of Islamic FinTech:

- **Regulatory Fragmentation**: The coexistence of multiple regulatory bodies governing the mainland and free zones sometimes results in inconsistent policies and overlapping compliance requirements. This fragmentation complicates the scaling of FinTech solutions across the entire UAE.
- **Limited Consumer Awareness**: Many potential users remain unaware of the benefits and availability of Islamic FinTech products, slowing customer acquisition and trust-building.
- **Trust and Shariah Compliance Concerns**: Consumers and investors demand high assurance that financial products comply strictly with Shariah principles. Unlike countries such as Malaysia, which has developed a centralized and well-established regulatory sandbox for Islamic FinTech, the UAE is still in the process of refining a comprehensive Shariah governance framework tailored to its digital financial landscape (Lada et al., 2024).

Moving forward, enhancing consumer education, regulatory harmonization, and robust Shariah supervisory mechanisms will be critical for the UAE to fully harness its Islamic FinTech potential and compete on the global stage.

2.3 FinTech Success Stories Worldwide

Studying global FinTech success stories offers invaluable insights into how innovative financial technologies can overcome challenges such as regulatory hurdles, consumer mistrust, and market fragmentation. These success stories demonstrate best practices in innovation, scalability, consumer engagement, and regulatory collaboration, providing useful lessons for emerging FinTech hubs, including Islamic FinTech initiatives.

- **Ant Financial (China)**: Originating as Alipay, Ant Financial revolutionized the mobile payments landscape by providing seamless, secure, and fast transactions accessible to over one billion users. Its success hinges on creating a frictionless user experience combined with rigorous trust-building mechanisms, including buyer and seller protections. Strong partnerships with traditional banks and regulators enabled Ant Financial to diversify its services into microloans, wealth management, and insurance, cementing its position as a FinTech giant (Zhang & Li, 2020).
- **Revolut (UK)**: As a leading neobank, Revolut offers multi-currency accounts, cryptocurrency trading, budgeting tools, and instant money transfers with transparent fee structures. Its user-centric design, innovative digital interfaces, and appeal to tech-savvy millennials and Gen Z have driven rapid growth. Revolut's success highlights the importance of continuous product innovation and clear communication in building customer loyalty (Smith, 2021).
- **Paytm (India)**: Initially launched as a mobile wallet, Paytm evolved into a comprehensive financial ecosystem providing lending, insurance, wealth management, and merchant payment solutions. Its growth was fueled by proactive regulatory engagement, strategic partnerships, and a focus on serving India's large unbanked population, illustrating how addressing local market needs and regulatory environments is crucial to FinTech success (Kumar & Raj, 2022).
- **Fawry (Egypt)**: Fawry pioneered digital payments in Egypt by enabling bill payments, mobile top-ups, and banking services to millions of previously unbanked consumers. Its success relied on deep understanding of local consumer behavior, extensive agent networks across urban and rural areas, and strong government partnerships. Fawry underscores the importance of grassroots-level infrastructure and local market adaptation (Aly & El-Kilany, 2023).
- **Malaysia's Islamic FinTech Ecosystem**: Malaysia stands out globally for its leadership in Islamic FinTech due to government-led initiatives such as regulatory sandboxes tailored for Shariah-compliant startups and integration of Shariah governance into fintech regulatory frameworks. This cohesive approach has nurtured innovation while ensuring religious compliance, making Malaysia a benchmark for ethical digital finance globally (Shamsudin et al., 2021).

These success stories offer a roadmap for the UAE and other Islamic FinTech markets to design effective strategies that address both technological and socio-cultural dimensions for sustainable growth.

1. **Regulatory Clarity and Support**: Clear, consistent regulations and innovation-friendly policies enable FinTech firms to experiment and scale without legal uncertainties.
2. **Building Consumer Trust**: Transparent operations, robust security measures, and user-friendly platforms foster trust, which is essential for adoption.
3. **Financial Literacy and Awareness**: Educating consumers on FinTech benefits and usage reduces skepticism and increases market penetration.
4. **Strategic Partnerships**: Collaboration with traditional financial institutions, regulators, and technology providers accelerates growth and credibility.
5. **Cultural and Religious Sensitivity**: Tailoring solutions to align with local customs, values, and religious principles ensures relevance and acceptance, especially in Islamic finance markets.

These success stories offer a roadmap for the UAE and other Islamic FinTech markets to design effective strategies that address both technological and socio-cultural dimensions for sustainable growth.

2.4 FinTech as a Disruptive Innovation

FinTech has been widely acknowledged as a disruptive innovation—a concept originally proposed by Christensen (1997) that describes innovations which challenge established business models by offering simpler, more affordable, and accessible solutions. In the context of financial services, FinTech disrupts traditional banking by introducing agile, tech-driven platforms that appeal to unbanked or underbanked populations. According to Al-Emran and Shaalan (2021), disruptive FinTech applications not only improve transaction speed and reduce operational costs, but also redefine customer relationships, data usage, and financial access. This disruption is particularly relevant for Islamic FinTech, which seeks to serve a niche demographic with unique ethical and religious requirements.

Islamic FinTech acts as a double-layered disruptor—technologically through digital innovation, and ideologically through Shariah-compliant models. Traditional financial institutions often fail to accommodate the spiritual and ethical dimensions of Muslim consumers' financial decision-making. By leveraging disruptive technologies such as blockchain, AI, and digital identity verification, Islamic FinTech provides alternatives that are both efficient and values-based. These innovations align with the ethical foundation of Islamic finance, which prohibits interest (riba), gambling (maysir), and ambiguity (gharar), and promotes risk-sharing, justice, and social welfare.

Hence, disruptive innovation theory offers a useful lens through which to understand the market penetration and social transformation potential of Islamic FinTech. The theory explains how such niche solutions can initially serve a specific religious market, but gradually evolve to gain mainstream traction by addressing universal concerns like transparency, fairness, and inclusion—all of which are also pillars of sustainable development.

2.5 Cross-Sectoral Insights: FinTech in Agriculture and Sustainability

The value proposition of FinTech is not confined to financial services alone. FinTech platforms have proven instrumental in enhancing sustainability in sectors like agriculture, particularly in emerging markets. Their study on digital marketplaces demonstrates that blockchain, mobile payments, and data analytics can improve supply chain transparency, reduce inefficiencies, and expand market access for smallholder farmers—many of whom lack formal banking access.

This cross-sectoral use of FinTech provides useful insights for Islamic FinTech. Much like in agriculture, Islamic finance clients are often excluded from conventional financial systems due to ethical concerns. Both cases rely heavily on trust, accountability, and inclusivity—qualities enhanced through digital innovation. The integration of ethical compliance (in agriculture, sustainability; in Islamic finance, Shariah principles) with tech-enabled access reflects a converging model of value-driven innovation.

Moreover, digital marketplaces in agriculture have adopted governance frameworks that prioritize ethical sourcing, sustainability tracking, and stakeholder transparency. These mirror the objectives of Islamic FinTech platforms, which must undergo Shariah governance, audit, and certification to maintain legitimacy. The parallels suggest that the adoption of FinTech in faith-based finance can benefit from lessons in ecosystem governance, user education, and digital trust-building seen in the agri-FinTech space.

2.6 Consumer and Behavioral Barriers to Islamic FinTech

Despite the promising growth of Islamic FinTech, several structural and perceptual barriers continue to hinder widespread adoption. These challenges reflect a combination of technological, regulatory, cultural, and informational factors, particularly in regions where religious adherence shapes consumer behavior. Key barriers include:

2.6.1 Cybersecurity Concerns

One of the foremost concerns among potential users is the safety and integrity of their personal and financial data. In an era where cyber threats are increasingly sophisticated, news of data breaches, phishing attacks, and identity theft can significantly erode trust in digital financial platforms. Given the sensitive nature of financial information—particularly in Islamic finance where trust and ethical conduct are paramount—even a perceived vulnerability can deter users from engaging with FinTech applications. Consumers may question whether Islamic FinTech firms have the necessary technological infrastructure and safeguards to ensure data confidentiality, system resilience, and real-time fraud detection.

2.6.2 Data Privacy Issues

Closely related to cybersecurity is the issue of data privacy. Beyond protecting systems from external attacks, consumers are increasingly concerned about how their data is being collected, processed, stored, and potentially shared with third parties. The absence of robust data governance frameworks or clear privacy policies can lead to apprehension, especially in contexts where digital literacy is low and users may not fully understand their rights or the implications of data misuse. Islamic FinTech firms that do not adequately communicate their data handling practices risk losing consumer trust—an especially critical factor for Muslim users who may view the ethical use of personal information as a matter of religious as well as personal concern.

2.6.3 Opaque Shariah Governance and Compliance

A unique barrier specific to Islamic FinTech relates to the transparency and credibility of Shariah compliance mechanisms. While many providers claim to offer Shariah-compliant financial products, consumers often lack clear and accessible information about how compliance is achieved. Questions may arise about who sits on the Shariah Supervisory Board, how frequently audits are conducted, whether fatwas are publicly available, and how conflicts of interest are managed. In the absence of standardized or universally recognized certification, these ambiguities can generate skepticism and reduce the perceived authenticity of the service. This is especially problematic for devout users who prioritize religious adherence and expect visible alignment with Islamic ethical and legal principles.

2.6.4 Limited Financial and Technological Literacy

Another major obstacle is the knowledge gap among many potential users regarding both financial technology and the underlying principles of Islamic finance. For many consumers, concepts such as blockchain, robo-advisors, or peer-to-peer lending are unfamiliar, and when coupled with limited understanding of terms like mudarabah, takaful, or zakat, the barrier to entry becomes even more pronounced. This dual-layered knowledge gap can breed mistrust, confusion, and resistance to adoption. Without targeted educational efforts and intuitive user interfaces, Islamic FinTech platforms may remain inaccessible or underutilized, particularly among older adults or those from rural or underserved communities.

2.6.5 Cultural Preferences and Trust in Traditional Banking

In many Muslim-majority societies, banking is not merely a transactional relationship—it is deeply embedded in social and cultural norms. Consumers often value the personal trust cultivated through face-to-face interactions with bank personnel, and the reputational standing of institutions within their local community. The shift to impersonal, automated services may be perceived as alienating or unreliable, particularly when compared to longstanding relationships with traditional Islamic banks or credit officers. Furthermore, digital interactions may lack the human touch that reassures customers about the sincerity and integrity of the service provider—attributes highly valued in Islamic financial ethics. As such, FinTech platforms may struggle to build credibility and trust without a strategy to bridge this cultural gap

Together, these behavioral and trust barriers suggest that Islamic FinTech providers must invest heavily in consumer education, transparent governance, and robust cybersecurity to build confidence and drive broader adoption (Chekima et al., 2023).

2.6.6 Government and Regulatory Influence

Government and regulatory bodies in the UAE play a pivotal role in shaping the FinTech landscape, including the Islamic FinTech segment. Agencies like the Securities and Commodities Authority (SCA) and the UAE Central Bank have launched multiple initiatives to foster innovation, including regulatory sandboxes, digital banking licenses, and guidelines for Shariah-compliant financial products.

However, the regulatory environment is still fragmented. Different rules and oversight structures apply across the UAE's free zones (such as ADGM and DIFC) and the mainland, complicating compliance for startups and investors. This regulatory patchwork creates uncertainty and slows innovation, especially for new entrants attempting to scale across jurisdictions.

By contrast, Malaysia offers a unified regulatory framework with a centralized Shariah governance model, which has accelerated its Islamic FinTech sector. Adopting a similar approach in the UAE—streamlining regulations and establishing consistent Shariah compliance standards—could significantly enhance investor protection, consumer trust, and industry growth.

Such regulatory clarity would also help facilitate cross-border Islamic FinTech collaboration within the Gulf Cooperation Council (GCC) and beyond, positioning the UAE as a leading hub for Shariah-compliant financial innovation.

2.7 Religion and Consumer Behavior

Religion profoundly shapes consumers' values, attitudes, and behaviors, extending into their consumption choices and financial decision-making. Religious beliefs provide a moral and ethical framework that informs what products and services consumers consider acceptable or desirable (Nurhayati & Hendar, 2020).

For Muslim consumers, religion is a primary lens through which all economic activities are evaluated. Islam, practiced by approximately 1.8 billion people worldwide, requires adherence to Shariah law, which classifies goods and services as either halal (permissible) or haram (forbidden). This religious framework extends deeply into financial behavior, influencing preferences for interest-free loans, ethical investment products, and other financial services aligned with Islamic teachings (Bukhari et al., 2019).

The concept of religiosity—the degree of an individual's religious commitment—plays a crucial role in shaping consumer preferences. More religious consumers tend to seek products that closely align with their religious norms and ethical values, impacting their openness to Islamic financial services and technologies (Khan et al., 2017).

These insights support the study's theoretical framing by linking disruptive innovation theory with faith-driven digital transformation. The alignment between technological innovation and value-centric principles (whether in sustainability or Islamic finance) emphasizes that ethical legitimacy, not just utility, plays a key role in adoption. This builds on the proposed religiosity-behavior model and further supports its applicability across emerging digital sectors where values, trust, and purpose are central to consumer decisions.

2.7.1 Measuring Religiosity

Religiosity is a complex and multi-dimensional construct that goes beyond mere belief to encompass practices, knowledge, emotions, and the social consequences of religion. To comprehensively assess religiosity, this study adopts a framework with five interrelated dimensions (Bouteraa et al., 2024):

- **Religious Belief (Ideological):** This dimension reflects acceptance of core theological doctrines, such as the oneness of God (Tawhid) in Islam. It captures the cognitive commitment to fundamental religious truths.
- **Religious Practice (Ritualistic):** This involves observable religious actions like daily prayers (Salat), fasting during Ramadan (Sawm), and charitable giving (Zakat). These practices embody the habitual expression of religiosity.
- **Religious Knowledge (Intellectual):** Awareness and understanding of key religious teachings, principles, and laws that guide behavior. This includes knowing the Shariah requirements that apply to financial transactions.
- **Religious Feeling (Experiential):** The emotional and spiritual connection an individual feels towards their religion, including experiences of peace, fulfillment, or awe.
- **Religious Effect (Consequential):** The impact of religiosity on social behavior and decision-making, such as choosing halal products, engaging in ethical business, or avoiding prohibited activities.

This holistic model allows researchers to capture both cognitive and behavioral aspects of religiosity, providing a nuanced understanding of how it influences consumer decision-making, especially regarding Islamic FinTech adoption.

2.7.2 Religiosity and Consumer Behavior: Mixed Evidence

A growing body of empirical research supports the notion that religiosity influences consumer behavior, particularly the preference for products and services consistent with religious values. Studies show that higher levels of religiosity often correlate with increased adoption of Islamic financial products and services (Hidayat et al., 2015; Khan, 1986; Bouteraa & Al-Aidaros, 2020; Baber, 2021).

However, the relationship is not always straightforward or consistent. For example, some studies find no significant effect of religiosity on behavior in certain contexts, such as:

- The acceptance of the COVID-19 vaccine among Indonesian Muslims (Faturohman et al., 2021).

- Choice of Shariah-compliant banks in some populations (Ichwan et al., 2021).

These mixed results highlight the complexity of religiosity's influence. Factors such as cultural context, technological readiness, and individual differences may moderate the strength and direction of this relationship. Furthermore, varying ways of measuring religiosity (e.g., focusing on rituals versus beliefs) contribute to inconsistent findings across studies.

Thus, religiosity should be considered alongside other psychological, social, and environmental variables when examining consumer behavior in Islamic financial markets.

2.7.3 Religiosity and the Adoption of Islamic FinTech

Despite the central role of religion in Muslim consumers' lives, empirical research exploring how religiosity affects the adoption of Islamic FinTech is still nascent. This gap is critical because FinTech is rapidly transforming financial services, and understanding religious influences can help tailor products to meet consumer needs effectively.

The study posits the following hypothesis:

> **H1:** *Religiosity positively affects Muslim consumers' intention to adopt Islamic FinTech services.*

This hypothesis is rooted in the belief that Islamic FinTech's strict adherence to Shariah compliance aligns closely with the religious values of Muslim consumers. As a result, individuals with higher religiosity are more likely to trust, value, and adopt Islamic FinTech solutions.

By validating this relationship, the study aims to provide insights that can inform product design, marketing strategies, and regulatory policies to support the growth of Islamic FinTech, ensuring it resonates with the spiritual and ethical expectations of its target consumers.

2.8 Critical Reflections and Research Gaps

Despite the substantial advancements in FinTech innovation globally and the growing attention to Islamic FinTech, several critical gaps remain that hinder a comprehensive understanding of this evolving domain, particularly within the UAE context:

- **Limited Focus on Digital Islamic FinTech in Religiosity-Consumer Behavior Studies:**

The majority of existing research on religiosity and consumer behavior tends to concentrate on conventional Islamic finance products such as Islamic banking, Sukuk (Islamic bonds), and Takaful (Islamic insurance). While these provide valuable insights, they do not fully capture the complexities and unique challenges posed by the adoption of digital Islamic FinTech services—including mobile apps, robo-advisory, blockchain-enabled solutions, and digital marketplaces. This gap limits our understanding of how religious values intersect with rapidly evolving technology-mediated financial behaviors.

- **Scarcity of Empirical Data on Islamic FinTech Adoption in the UAE:**

Although the UAE is positioning itself as a regional and global FinTech hub, empirical research specifically investigating consumer adoption of Islamic FinTech products in this market remains sparse. In particular, there is a lack of nuanced data exploring the behavioral barriers, such as trust deficits, risk perceptions, and cultural factors, which significantly influence user acceptance and sustained usage. This data gap restricts evidence-based policymaking and product development tailored to the UAE's diverse population.

- **Regulatory Fragmentation and Its Impact on Startup Growth:**

The regulatory environment in the UAE is characterized by fragmented oversight and governance structures that vary across different jurisdictions, such as between the mainland and free zones like ADGM and DIFC. This fragmentation creates challenges for startups seeking to scale or operate cross-jurisdictionally, resulting in increased compliance costs and legal uncertainty. Comparative policy analyses with countries such as Malaysia—which has successfully implemented centralized and harmonized Islamic FinTech regulatory frameworks—are notably lacking. Such studies could illuminate best practices for fostering a more integrated, innovation-friendly regulatory ecosystem in the UAE.

- **Complexity and Multidimensionality of Religiosity Measurement:**

Religiosity is a multifaceted construct encompassing cognitive beliefs, ritualistic practices, emotional experiences, knowledge, and social consequences. Most prior studies tend to adopt simplistic, uni-dimensional measures that fail to capture this complexity. The absence of sophisticated, multidimensional measurement tools undermines the ability to precisely gauge how different aspects of religiosity influence the acceptance and use of Islamic FinTech technologies. More nuanced frameworks and validated instruments are needed to unpack these intricate relationships.

2.9 Research Contribution of This Study

In light of these gaps, the current study aims to make several critical contributions:

- It specifically investigates the influence of religiosity on the adoption of Islamic FinTech services within the UAE, addressing a major gap in empirical evidence from a key emerging market.
- By integrating technological, cultural, and regulatory perspectives, the study adopts a holistic approach that reflects the multifactorial nature of Islamic FinTech adoption.
- The research applies a multidimensional framework for measuring religiosity, allowing for a more refined understanding of how different religious dimensions affect consumer technology acceptance.
- Finally, the study's findings are expected to offer practical insights for policymakers, regulators, and FinTech developers aiming to enhance consumer trust, improve regulatory coherence, and design culturally and religiously sensitive digital financial products in the UAE and similar Muslim-majority contexts.

3. RESEARCH METHODOLOGY

3.1 The Research Paradigm and Design

This study employed an explanatory research paradigm to investigate how religious commitment (independent variable) influences customers' intention to adopt Islamic FinTech services (dependent variable). The explanatory approach is suitable for examining causal relationships and understanding the mechanisms underlying consumer behavior within the context of Islamic banking in the UAE. A quantitative, cross-sectional survey design was utilized to collect data from UAE residents who actively use Islamic banking services.

3.2 Sampling Procedure

A convenience sampling technique was employed, given the exploratory nature of the research and resource constraints. Although convenience sampling may limit generalizability, efforts were made to diversify the sample by disseminating the survey through multiple social media platforms, including Facebook and WhatsApp, to capture a broad demographic. The inclusion criteria required participants to be UAE residents and users of Islamic banking services.

3.3 Sample Size Determination

The minimum required sample size was established using power analysis conducted with G*Power software, based on recommendations from Creswell and Creswell (2018), Sekaran and Bougie (2019), and Hair et al. (2021). Applying Cohen's (1988) guidelines for one-tailed hypothesis testing, an effect size of 0.03, alpha level (α) of 0.05, and statistical power (1-β) of 0.95, the minimum sample size was calculated as 111 respondents. To enhance statistical robustness and reliability, the final sample was increased to 332 participants.

3.4 Instrument Development and Validation

The survey instrument comprised 28 items organized into three sections: (A) research objectives, (B) demographic information, and (C) measurement scales for the study variables. Measurement scales were adapted from validated instruments in previous research to fit the Islamic FinTech context: intention-related items were adapted from Venkatesh et al. (2003) and Amin et al. (2011), while religious commitment was measured using the Islamic Religiosity Index developed by Bouteraa et al. (2024). All items utilized a 5-point Likert scale ranging from 1 ("strongly disagree") to 5 ("strongly agree").

To ensure cultural and linguistic appropriateness, the original English questionnaire was translated into Arabic by a certified multilingual translator. A second independent translator performed a back-translation into English. Minor discrepancies identified during this process were resolved through iterative revisions to preserve semantic equivalence and capture cultural nuances. The final Arabic version was reviewed by two senior academic experts and one banking practitioner to verify clarity and relevance.

A pilot study with 50 banking customers was conducted to assess the instrument's reliability and clarity. Cronbach's alpha coefficients for all constructs exceeded the 0.70 threshold, indicating satisfactory internal consistency (Hair et al., 2019;

Shmueli et al., 2016, 2019). Participant feedback from the pilot also helped refine item wording for improved comprehension.

3.5 Data Collection

Data were collected via an online survey distributed through Google Surveys over a specified period (e.g., March to April 2024). Given the high social media penetration in the UAE, online distribution was deemed appropriate to reach a diverse sample. To enhance data quality, measures such as limiting one submission per respondent and including attention check questions were implemented.

3.6 Data Analysis

Partial Least Squares Structural Equation Modeling (PLS-SEM) was employed using SmartPLS version 4 to analyze the data. PLS-SEM was chosen for its strengths in theory development, handling complex models with smaller samples, and extending existing structural theories (Hair et al., 2012). The analysis proceeded in two stages: first, the measurement model was assessed to verify reliability and validity of constructs; second, the structural model was evaluated to test the hypothesized relationships.

Bootstrapping with 5,000 resamples was used to determine the significance of path coefficients. Missing data and outliers were examined and handled following standard procedures to maintain data integrity. One-tailed testing was applied based on directional hypotheses derived from theoretical expectations.

3.7 Ethical Considerations

The study obtained ethical approval from the institutional review board (IRB) of the affiliated university. Informed consent was obtained electronically from all participants before survey completion, with assurances of confidentiality and anonymity.

3.8 Demographic Profile and Limitations

The final sample of 332 respondents included a diverse cross-section of UAE residents using Islamic banking services. While demographic variables were not central to the core analysis, descriptive statistics on age, gender, and socio-economic status were collected to contextualize the findings. Future research could further explore demographic moderators in FinTech adoption.

The study's cross-sectional design limits causal inferences, and convenience sampling restricts generalizability. Additionally, self-reported data may be subject to social desirability bias, particularly given the religious nature of the study constructs. These limitations suggest the need for longitudinal studies and mixed-method approaches in future research.

4. DATA ANALYSIS AND RESULTS

4.1 Sample of Study

To check for any missing values, a descriptive statistics analysis was conducted using IBM-SPSS, which confirmed that no missing values were present in the dataset. In the sample of 338 cases, six multivariate outliers were identified and removed. These outliers were detected using the Mahalanobis distance method, with a threshold set at $p<.001$ for each case. This process resulted in a final sample of 332 valid cases for analysis. The removal of these outliers was deemed necessary as their inclusion could potentially skew the results. Table I provides a summary of the demographic characteristics of the sample.

To address potential common method bias, Harman's single-factor test was conducted. The test produced a value of 38%, well below the commonly accepted threshold of 50%, indicating that common method bias was not a concern in this dataset (Podsakoff et al., 2003). This suggests that the data are not artificially inflated due to shared variance between the constructs, enhancing the credibility of the findings.

Table 1. Demographic Information of Sample N=332 (100%).

Variable	Category	Frequency	Percentage
Gender	Male	217	65.4%
	Female	115	34.6%
Age	18 to 39 years	209	63%
	40 years and above	123	37%
Religion	Islam	332	100%
Education level	College Diploma	28	8.4%
	First Degree (Bachelor)	130	39.2%

continued on following page

Table 1. Continued

Variable	Category	Frequency	Percentage
	Professional certificate	62	18.7%
	Others	5	1.5%
Occupation	Professional, e.g., lawyer, doctor, engineer	148	44.6%
	Manager/ Executive	38	11.4%
	Academician	34	10.2%
	Student	28	8.4%
	Merchant/Businessman	77	23.2%
	Unemployed	4	1.2%
	Other	3	0.9%

4.2 Assessment of Measurement Model

The measurement model was assessed using the PLS standard algorithm, based on the threshold criteria outlined by Hair et al. (2021). As shown in Table II, the retained item loadings met the recommended thresholds: factor loadings ≥ 0.5, Average Variance Extracted (AVE) ≥ 0.5, and Composite Reliability (CR) ≥ 0.7, indicating strong construct reliability. However, two items (R6 and R18) had factor loadings below 0.4, which is considered insufficient for model validity (Hair et al., 2018). These items were removed to enhance the overall quality and reliability of the measurement model, ensuring that the remaining items contribute meaningfully to the construct's validity.

Table 2. Measurement Model Assessment Results

Items	Items' Code	Loadings	CR	AVE	
Intention to Adopt FinTech services					
I intend to use FinTech services in the future	IN1	0.741	0.960	0.774	0.958
I predict I would use FinTech services in the future	IN2	0.733			
I plan to use FinTech services in the future	IN3	0.921			
I believe it is worthwhile for me to use FinTech services	IN4	0.941			
I am very likely to use FinTech services in the future	IN5	0.947			
I am interested to use FinTech services	IN6	0.918			
I will recommend FinTech services to others	IN7	0.926			
Religious Commitments					

continued on following page

Table 2. Continued

Items	Items' Code	Loadings	CR	AVE	
Ideological Dimensions					
I believe there is only one God	R1	0.768	0.54	0.529	0.954
I have a firm belief that Mohamed (PBUH) is God's last Prophet	R2	0.674			
Ritualistic Dimensions					
I regularly offer prayer five times a day	R3	0.724			
I pay Zakat obligation every year if I meet the prescribed criteria	R4	0.745			
I fast regularly during the Holy month of Ramadan	R5	0.870			
I believe that I must perform *Hajj* (pilgrimage) if I meet the prescribed criteria	R7	0.833			
Intellectual Dimensions					
I always try to avoid earning through *Haram* (prohibited) means	R8	0.701			
I always try to avoid minor and major sins	R9	0.506			
I know the basic knowledge about my religion	R10	0.593			
I always try to follow Islamic junctions in all matters of my life	R11	0.741			
Consequential Dimensions					
It is my duty to give others their rights according to Islamic injunctions	R12	0.750			
I try to avoid any activity which hurts others	R13	0.734			
I always try to help those who need my help	R14	0.813			
I try to be honest with others	R15	0.777			
I always avoid humiliating others because Islam does not allow doing so	R16	0.814			
Experiential Dimensions					
I feel dissatisfaction when I do something against my faith	R17	0.552			
I have the feeling of being afraid of God	R19	0.835			
I have the feeling of being punished by God for doing something wrong	R20	0.550			
I feel pleasure seeing others following Islamic teaching	R21	0.702			

Note: R6 and R18 have been removed due to poor loading

4.3 Assessment of Structural Model

The research hypotheses were tested using structural model analysis. Following the guidelines of Hair et al. (2021), hypothesis testing involved a bootstrapping procedure with 5,000 iterations. The results, presented in Table III and Figure 1, support the hypothesis. The model's statistical significance was confirmed with a p-value of 0.000 and a t-value of 6.068. Additionally, the model explained 7.4% of the variance ($R^2 = 0.074$), with a Q^2 predictive value of 0.062 and a medium effect size ($f^2 = 0.080$). Further details, including the mean, standard deviation, and confidence intervals, are provided below.

Table 3. Structural Model Results

Relationship	H	Std.β	STDEV	Mean	t- Statistics	P-values	Confidence Intervals		Decision	(f^2)
							Lower (2.5%)	Upper (97.5)		
Religiosity » Intention	H1	0.271	.045	.284	6.068	.000***	.214	.365	Accepted	0.080

*** $p < 0.001$.

Figure 1. The SEM-PLS Results of the Structural Model using Smart-PLS4

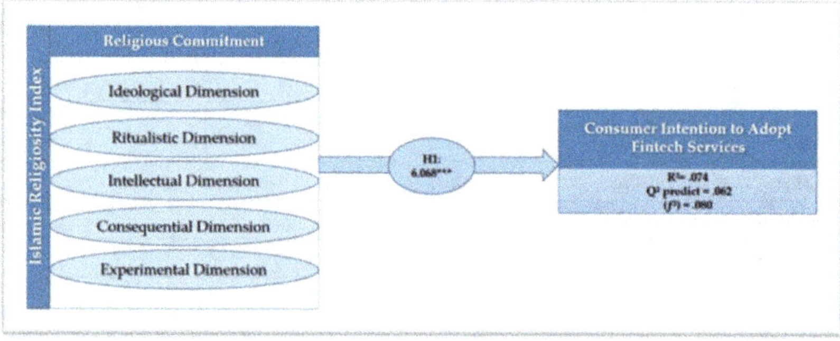

Additionally, this study employed PLS predict to assess the model's ability to predict outside of the sample. Following the recommendations of Hair et al. (2019) and Shmueli et al. (2019), PLS predict was used to generate case-level predictions with k = 10. The results indicated that all indicators exceeded the Linear Model (LM) benchmark, as evidenced by all Q^2 predict values being greater than zero (Q^2 predict > 0). This enabled a comparison of each Root Mean Square Error (RMSE) result against the naive LM benchmark. As shown in Table IV, the comparative results between PLS-SEM and LM revealed that all seven intention indicators had higher prediction errors in PLS-SEM (PLS-SEM > LM). According to Shmueli et al. (2019), this finding suggests that the model has a high predictive potential, implying that it can provide accurate and testable predictions across different consumer behavior scenarios and effectively predict responses using out-of-sample data.

Table 4. Q^2 Predict and the Predictive Performance of the PLS Model Vs. Benchmark. LM

Indicators	Q^2 predict	PLS-SEM_RMSE	LM_RMSE	(PLS-LM)
INT1	0.014	0.938	0.890	0.048
INT2	0.062	0.849	0.788	0.061
INT3	0.007	0.860	0.837	0.023
INT4	0.054	0.823	0.820	0.003
INT5	0.037	0.877	0.835	0.042
INT6	0.023	0.852	0.817	0.035
INT7	0.106	0.987	0.909	0.078

Note: Intention = INT; Root Mean Squared Error = RMSE; Linear Model =LM.

5. DISCUSSION AND CONCLUSION

5.1 Discussion

This This study investigates the relationship between religiosity and the adoption of FinTech services among Muslim consumers, addressing a notable gap in the existing literature. While prior research has explored factors influencing FinTech adoption broadly, the specific role of religiosity—particularly within Islamic contexts—has been insufficiently understood. Our findings provide empirical evidence that religiosity positively influences customers' intentions to adopt FinTech services.

This suggests that consumers with higher levels of religious commitment are more inclined to integrate FinTech solutions into their financial management practices. In the UAE, a country with a predominantly Muslim population where Islamic principles strongly influence daily life, religion emerges as a key determinant of consumer behavior. Many consumers tend to approach financial transactions with less emphasis on materialistic gains and greater consideration for compliance with Shariah law. The alignment of FinTech services with Islamic ethical and financial principles appears to foster greater acceptance and willingness to adopt such technologies.

One possible explanation for this positive relationship is that Muslim consumers demonstrate a reasonable understanding of how FinTech services can operate within the permissible boundaries of Islamic finance. This religious knowledge and awareness reduce uncertainties and increase trust, encouraging adoption. In other words, religiosity functions not only as a moral compass but also as an enabler, guiding consumers toward digital financial innovations that respect their spiritual values.

Our results are consistent with previous studies that highlight how personal values, religious awareness, and spiritual engagement significantly shape consumer behavior (Baber, 2021; Gebauer & Sedikides, 2021; Ichwan et al., 2021; Usman et al., 2022). This study thus adds to the growing body of evidence demonstrating that religiosity is an important psychosocial factor influencing technology adoption decisions, especially in culturally and religiously distinct markets.

5.2 Theoretical Contributions

This study makes a significant theoretical contribution by advancing the understanding of FinTech adoption through the critical but often underexplored lens of Islamic religiosity. While FinTech adoption has been extensively studied from technological, economic, and behavioral perspectives, the religious and cultural dimensions—particularly within Islamic contexts—remain relatively neglected. This research addresses this gap by foregrounding religiosity not as a peripheral or monolithic factor but as a complex, multidimensional construct that deeply shapes consumer attitudes and behaviors.

Unlike many prior studies that tend to conceptualize religiosity as a single-dimensional or simplistic variable—often measured merely by frequency of religious practices or general religious identification—this research proposes and operationalizes a comprehensive multidimensional religiosity framework. This framework encompasses five interconnected dimensions, which are rigorously identified and grounded in the FinTech literature as well as Islamic religious scholarship:

- Ideological religiosity, reflecting core beliefs and doctrinal adherence.
- Ritualistic religiosity, capturing religious practices and observances.
- Intellectual religiosity, denoting knowledge and understanding of religious teachings.
- Experiential religiosity, referring to personal spiritual experiences and emotional connections.
- Consequential religiosity, emphasizing the impact of religious values on everyday decision-making and ethical behavior.

This nuanced conceptualization enables a more precise and granular examination of how different facets of religiosity independently and interactively influence behavioral intentions toward Islamic FinTech adoption. For example, while ritualistic aspects may relate closely to compliance with religious norms, intellectual religiosity may drive a more reflective evaluation of the Shariah-compliance and ethical foundations of FinTech products. By disaggregating religiosity into these multiple dimensions, the study offers richer theoretical insights and avoids the oversimplification inherent in previous research.

Furthermore, the study advances methodological rigor by employing Partial Least Squares (PLS) predictive analysis, a sophisticated statistical technique that goes beyond mere explanatory modeling to assess the predictive relevance of the proposed model. The PLS results confirm that the multidimensional religiosity model exhibits strong predictive power—meaning that it not only explains current consumer attitudes and behavioral intentions but also possesses robust generalizability and forecasting ability in different temporal and contextual settings.

This predictive validity is particularly important for theory development because it suggests that the model can be reliably used to anticipate future consumer behavior in Islamic FinTech markets, as well as potentially adapted for other religiously influenced technology adoption scenarios. In this way, the study lays a solid theoretical foundation and a versatile analytical framework that future researchers can build upon to explore consumer behavior across diverse contexts, including other faith traditions or religiously framed innovations beyond finance.

Overall, this research contributes a robust, multidimensional theoretical model that enriches the literature on technology adoption by integrating deep cultural and religious factors. It opens pathways for more culturally sensitive, faith-aligned research, bridging gaps between Islamic studies, consumer behavior, and digital finance scholarship, thereby fostering a more holistic understanding of the complex motivations driving adoption decisions in Islamic FinTech ecosystems.

5.3 Practical Recommendations

5.3.1 For FinTech Businesses and Practitioners

The findings reveal that successful Islamic FinTech adoption hinges on more than technical functionality or competitive pricing. It requires a deep integration of Islamic ethical and religious values into the entire product lifecycle—from design and development to marketing and after-sales service. FinTech firms should prioritize embedding Shariah-compliant principles as core product features rather than as mere add-ons. This includes transparent profit-sharing models, avoidance of interest (riba), and prohibition of unethical investments (haram activities).

Collaborating closely with Islamic scholars and Shariah advisory boards during product conceptualization and validation can build credibility and consumer confidence. Such partnerships can also aid in navigating complex religious rulings that might affect product acceptance.

Marketing strategies should move beyond generic appeals and instead emphasize storytelling that resonates emotionally and spiritually with Muslim consumers. Highlighting the social justice, ethical investment, and community welfare aspects of Islamic FinTech can foster deeper emotional engagement, strengthening brand loyalty and trust.

Furthermore, customer education initiatives can be instrumental. Many potential users may lack full awareness of how FinTech solutions align with Islamic finance principles. Providing educational content, webinars, and interactive FAQs on Shariah compliance can empower consumers and reduce adoption barriers.

5.3.2 For Policymakers and Regulators

Regulatory authorities play a critical role in shaping the Islamic FinTech ecosystem. Given the ethical sensitivities involved, regulators should formulate clear guidelines and standards for Shariah compliance that FinTech companies can follow. These guidelines should be developed in collaboration with religious scholars, technology experts, and consumer representatives to ensure they are both religiously sound and practically feasible.

Establishing regulatory sandboxes tailored for Islamic FinTech startups can encourage innovation while safeguarding consumer interests. These sandboxes would allow for testing new products under controlled environments with Shariah oversight, enabling faster go-to-market times without compromising compliance.

Additionally, policymakers should incentivize collaboration between FinTech innovators and Islamic financial institutions. Such partnerships could leverage the trust and market reach of traditional Islamic banks while introducing novel digital services, creating a more inclusive and efficient financial ecosystem.

On a broader scale, national financial inclusion strategies should incorporate Islamic FinTech as a key pillar, recognizing its potential to bring unbanked or underbanked Muslim populations into the formal economy through culturally compatible digital services.

5.3.3 For Academics and Researchers

This study opens several avenues for further scholarly inquiry. The proposed multidimensional religiosity framework provides a valuable theoretical lens not only for Islamic FinTech but also for exploring technology adoption across other religiously framed innovations.

Future research can deepen understanding by incorporating mixed-method approaches, including qualitative interviews with consumers and religious authorities to uncover latent cultural nuances that quantitative surveys might miss.

There is also potential to investigate cross-cultural differences by applying this framework in diverse Muslim-majority countries with varying levels of religiosity and economic development, as well as in Muslim minority communities in secular societies. Such comparative studies can reveal how local socio-cultural factors mediate religiosity's effect on FinTech adoption.

Moreover, integrating additional moderating variables such as age, gender, socio-economic status, and technological literacy could clarify how different demographic groups interact with religiosity and digital finance. For instance, younger Muslim consumers may reconcile modern technological convenience with traditional religious values differently than older generations.

5.4 Limitations and Future Research Directions

Despite its valuable contributions, this study has certain limitations. The sample was confined to Muslim consumers residing in the UAE, a country characterized by a strong public endorsement of Islamic values. Consequently, the findings may reflect an idealized or socially desirable pattern of religiosity and FinTech adoption that might not hold in more secular or religiously diverse contexts.

Future research should aim to replicate and extend this model in more pluralistic societies to assess the generalizability of findings and to understand the dynamics of religiosity in mixed-religion environments. Cross-religious comparative studies could be particularly illuminating, exploring how various faith-based values shape attitudes toward digital finance and technology adoption more broadly.

Beyond Islamic FinTech, applying the multidimensional religiosity framework in other sectors—such as healthcare, education, and hospitality—could verify its broader relevance and reveal sector-specific insights. For example, exploring how religiosity influences the adoption of digital health services or online education platforms in Muslim populations could yield practical strategies for service providers in these fields.

Furthermore, the rapid evolution of digital technologies demands that future studies investigate the impact of emerging innovations such as Artificial Intelligence (AI), blockchain, and central bank digital currencies (CBDCs) on Islamic finance adoption. Blockchain, in particular, offers unique advantages for ensuring transparency, traceability, and Shariah compliance, potentially revolutionizing trust mechanisms within Islamic FinTech.

Finally, longitudinal research designs could track changes in religiosity's influence over time, particularly as younger, more digitally native Muslim generations mature and potentially reshape the landscape of Islamic financial services.

The fusion of Islamic principles with cutting-edge financial technology marks a transformative era for global finance, one that promises to empower millions of Muslim consumers through ethical, inclusive, and innovative solutions. This study provides a foundational roadmap for understanding and enhancing this convergence, highlighting the indispensable role of religiosity in guiding adoption behavior.

As Islamic FinTech continues to evolve, stakeholders must embrace a balanced approach that honors tradition while embracing innovation. By doing so, the sector can fulfill its promise of promoting financial inclusion, economic justice, and spiritual fulfillment for Muslim communities worldwide—ushering in a future where faith and technology synergize to create sustainable prosperity.

REFERENCES

Al-Daihani, M., Dirie, K.A., Muneem, A., Abdul Lateb, N. and Bouteraa, M. (2025), "Islamic social finance and its potential in addressing natural disaster emergencies and advancing sustainable development goals: a proposed model", International Journal of Ethics and Systems, Vol. ahead-of-print No. ahead-of-print. DOI: 10.1108/IJOES-05-2024-0138

Alkhwaldi, A. F., Alharasis, E. E., Shehadeh, M., Abu-AlSondos, I. A., Oudat, M. S., & Bani Atta, A. A. (2022). Towards an understanding of FinTech users' adoption: Intention and e-loyalty post-COVID-19 from a developing country perspective. *Sustainability (Basel), 14*(19), 12616. DOI: 10.3390/su141912616

Amin, H., & R.C., et al. (2011). Determinants for ar-Rahnu usage intentions: An empirical investigation. *African Journal of Business Management, 5*(20), 8181–8191.

Amin, H., Rahim Abdul Rahman, A., Laison Sondoh, S.Jr, & Magdalene Chooi Hwa, A. (2011). Determinants of customers' intention to use Islamic personal financing. *Journal of Islamic Accounting and Business Research, 2*(1), 22–42. DOI: 10.1108/17590811111129490

Baber, H. (2021). Religiosity and intention to participate in donation-based crowdfunding. *Journal of Management, Spirituality & Religion, 18*(3), 218–238. DOI: 10.51327/DKES9686

Bin-Nashwan, S. A., Bouteraa, M., Benlahcene, A., & Sadallah, M. (2025). Beyond hype: Is ChatGPT-generated content effective in class preparation among academic instructors? *The Internet and Higher Education, 101016*, 101016. Advance online publication. DOI: 10.1016/j.iheduc.2025.101016

Bouteraa, M., & Al-Aidaros, A.-H. (2020). The role of attitude as mediator in the intention to have Islamic will. *International Journal of Advanced Research in Economics and Finance, 2*(1), 22–37.

Bouteraa, M., Chekima, B., Amin, H., Tamma, E., Lada, S., Ansar, R., & Lim, M. F. (2024). Does consumer religiosity matter for green banking adoption? Evidence from a Muslim-majority market. *Journal of Islamic Marketing, 15*(7), 1807–1823. DOI: 10.1108/JIMA-02-2023-0049

Bukhari, S. F. H., Woodside, F. M., Hassan, R., Shaikh, A. L., Hussain, S., & Mazhar, W. (2019). Is religiosity an important consideration in Muslim consumer behavior? *Journal of Islamic Marketing, 10*(4), 1288–1307. DOI: 10.1108/JIMA-01-2018-0006

Chekima, B., Bouteraa, M., Ansar, R., Lada, S., Fook, L. M., Tamma, E., Abdul Adis, A.-A., & Chekima, K. (2023). Determinants of Organic Food Consumption in Narrowing the Green Gap. *Sustainability (Basel), 15*(11), 8554. Advance online publication. DOI: 10.3390/su15118554

Chekima, B., Chekima, S., Syed Khalid Wafa, S. A. W., Igau, O. A., & Sondoh, S. L.Jr. (2016). Sustainable consumption: The effects of knowledge, cultural values, environmental advertising, and demographics. *International Journal of Sustainable Development and World Ecology, 23*(2), 210–220. DOI: 10.1080/13504509.2015.1114043

Cohen, J. (1988). *Statistical power analysis for the behavioral sciences* (2nd ed.). L. Erlbaum Associates.

Creswell, J., & Creswell, J. D. (2018). *Research design: Qualitative, quantitative, and mixed methods approaches* (5th ed.). Sage Publications, Inc.

Faturohman, T., Kengsiswoyo, G. A. N., Harapan, H., Zailani, S., Rahadi, R. A., & Arief, N. N. (2021). Factors influencing COVID-19 vaccine acceptance in Indonesia: An adoption of Technology Acceptance Model. *F1000 Research, 10*, 476. DOI: 10.12688/f1000research.53506.1 PMID: 34621508

Financial Stability Board (FSB). (2018). *Financial stability implications from FinTech.*

Fintech Middle East. (2021). *Fintech News Middle East: UAE Fintech Report 2021.* Abu Dhabi.

Gai, K., Qiu, M., & Sun, X. (2018). A survey on FinTech. *Journal of Network and Computer Applications, 103*, 262–273. DOI: 10.1016/j.jnca.2017.10.011

Gebauer, J. E., & Sedikides, C. (2021). Cultural religiosity: A neglected but powerful dimension of culture. *Current Opinion in Psychology, 40*, 73–78. DOI: 10.1016/j.copsyc.2020.08.027 PMID: 33027746

Hair, J.. (2021). *A primer on partial least squares structural equation modeling (PLS-SEM)* (3rd ed.). SAGE Publications, Inc. DOI: 10.1007/978-3-030-80519-7

Hair, J. F.Jr. (2018). *Advanced issues in partial least squares structural equation modeling*. SAGE Publications, Inc.

Hair, J. F., Risher, J. J., Sarstedt, M., & Ringle, C. M. (2019). When to use and how to report the results of PLS-SEM. *European Business Review, 31*(1), 2–24. DOI: 10.1108/EBR-11-2018-0203

Hair, J. F., Sarstedt, M., Ringle, C. M., & Mena, J. A. (2012). An assessment of the use of partial least squares structural equation modeling in marketing research. *Journal of the Academy of Marketing Science, 40*(3), 414–433. DOI: 10.1007/s11747-011-0261-6

He, D. et al. (2017). Fintech and financial services: Initial considerations.

Hidayat, R., & Akhmad, S. (2015). Commitment and trust on the customers. *Al-Ulum, 15*(1), 57–90. DOI: 10.30603/au.v15i1.45

Hidayat, R., Akhmad, S., & Machmud, M. (2015). Effects of service quality, customer trust, and satisfaction toward customer loyalty of Islamic banks in Indonesia. *The 6th International Conference on Entrepreneurship, Business, and Economics.*

Lada, S., Chekima, B., Ansar, R., Lim, M. F., Bouteraa, M., Abdul Adis, A. A., Abd Karim, M. R., & Yong, K. (2024). Strategic alternatives for Muslim-friendly homestay in Sabah Malaysia: A SWOT/TOWS analysis. *Journal of Islamic Marketing, 15*(6), 1534–1559. DOI: 10.1108/JIMA-04-2023-0133

Ordóñez de Pablos, P. (Ed.). (2022). *Handbook of research on building greener economics and adopting digital tools in the era of climate change*. IGI Global. DOI: 10.4018/978-1-6684-4610-2

World Bank. (2020). *Fintech: The new frontier of finance*. World Bank.

Zhang, Z., & Zhang, S. (2020). Financial technology and its impact on the financial services industry. *International Journal of Financial Management, 15*(1), 34–50. DOI: 10.2139/ssrn.3318835

Ziouache, A., & Bouteraa, M. (2023). Descriptive Approach of Neo-Banking System: Conception, Challenges and Global Practices. *International Journal of Business and Technology Management, 5*(2), 194–204.

Chapter 7
Understanding Player Churn in the Gaming Industry With Key Drivers and Prevention Strategies

Kaan Arik
https://orcid.org/0000-0002-0930-8955
Sakarya University of Applied Sciences, Turkey

ABSTRACT

The gaming industry has witnessed tremendous growth over the last few years. This increased revenue has brought about significantly more sophisticated techniques for retaining players and struggle against churn. This chapter clarifies the study of game player behavior and how these studies can be applied to predict churn, and highlights the importance of churn in the gaming industry, examining high-grossing games offered on different platforms that dominate the industry in the context of churn. However, privacy and data sharing are perceived as critical barriers that hinder effective churn analysis. In summary, churn studies in online environments are not common due to the rarity of publicly available data, primarily because developers choose not to share details about players. Furthermore, the chapter presents some possible avenues to overcome these challenges and expands the view on how game developers can implement tactics such as personalized experiences, socialization, leveraging technology, and transparency around data usage to reduce churn.

DOI: 10.4018/979-8-3373-6097-3.ch007

INTRODUCTION

The gaming industry has now become one of the fastest growing and most dynamic segments to come out of the entertainment industry today. According to some accounts, gaming has developed a vast worldwide consumer base with annual revenues in the hundreds of billions (Goh et al., 2023; Predescu and Mocanu, 2020). Gaming is booming... Companies continue to push the limits of technology and imagine new ways to play. This approach creates curriculums making various calibers of new people join the game industry and ease out new players to keep on long after. With this kind of game design, you end up having long runs in the history of the game. To this end, gaming sectors describe activities such as loyalty schemes and privileges which allow further enjoyment of the games, so as to own the clients opt for this game name at any time, they wish to play the game. Success has to be contained in a competitive pool. The video game industry even has its own term for it: "player churn." This term is used to refer to all the players who stopped playing a game or used an application. This is a crucial metric for content creators, and it matters most because it directly affects the life and success of their game. Some observers say high churn rates could indicate that gamers are either growing bored or losing patience. Stuff like games that are hard to learn or bad onboarding can cheese players off. That could force gaming companies to reconsider how they keep players engaged in the game, for example.

Within the game industry, this percentage of users who stop playing a game or app is termed "player churn." This metric is critical to developers as it has a direct influence on the company sustainability and general success of a game (Mustac et al., 2022; Kim et al., 2017; Drachen et al., 2013). Gold (2020) and Runge et al. (2014) indicate that high rates of churn may mean that players are being under-engaged or even frustrated by factors such as a steep learning curve or bad onboarding (O'Neil, 2014). To keep players, game companies should think creatively (WIRED, 2023; Hadiji et al., 2014; Hamari et al., 2014). Churn is responsible for losing gamers, but it's also a huge financial hit for gaming companies. With a player heading out of a game, they are viewed as revenue lost at first. But this drives up the cost of attracting new customers without incurring an even more monstrous financial cost to companies. It is a well-known fact, based on research, that the costs associated with advertisements and promotional activities are such that it takes five times more to acquire a new player than to retain the current players (Chaffey, 2023). Churn of players also, at least instantly, results in lost revenues, missing these firms the potential for a stable flow of their income streams with a business model of single in-game purchases (Drachen et al., 2013). Churn, therefore, is one of the most significant threats for all businesses operating in gaming in terms of financial health and profitability.

The other disadvantage of player turnover is the expense to a company. If one player quits playing a game, then the revenue from that user decreases too. But the price of recruiting new players is usually much higher. Consider all the costs involved in advertising and marketing to make "X game" get attention. According to research, new players can be even five times more costly to acquire than keeping existing ones. This means that when players walk away, companies take a direct hit in terms of money they never got from in-game purchases and lost potential revenue. High churn rates can really keep game developer companies out of the black and constitute a strong hurdle for them to build a presence in this ultra-competitive gaming industry. One of the major hindrances in the growth of a gaming company is a high rate of churn. When organizations emphasize obtaining new users, they can be neglectful of their existing customers' needs, providing an inferior gaming experience (Hadiji et al., 2014; Pham et al., 2021). Player retention may suffer accordingly, as this would induce a downward spiral due to lack of game quality. At the same time, video games with high churn appear less and less appealing to investors over time, as lower player retention due to churn brings worries around future revenues, impacting everything from near-term funding to future project roadmaps negatively. Additionally, player churn rates have a significant effect on building a lasting brand identity. Such a game, since failing to capture the attention of its user base (perhaps helping to persuade both current and potential players), would suffer from a loss of perceived prestige — the number of active players would continually decrease (Mao and Cho, 2024; Kawale et al., 2009). Reputation damage and negative user ratings may disseminate rapidly in gaming networks and be adverse for download rates and other important marketing metrics. The integrated approaches that companies may have to devise will, in particular, be toward mending brand reputations while simultaneously spending heavily to prevent user loss. Not only does this have to be confronted to maintain a player base, but it also has ramifications for financial sustainability. Reducing churn can also enhance a company's brand image, stabilize revenue flows, and place its business on a firmer growth trajectory (Adjust, 2023; Baremetrics, 2023).

Figure 1. Video game industry growth and revenue

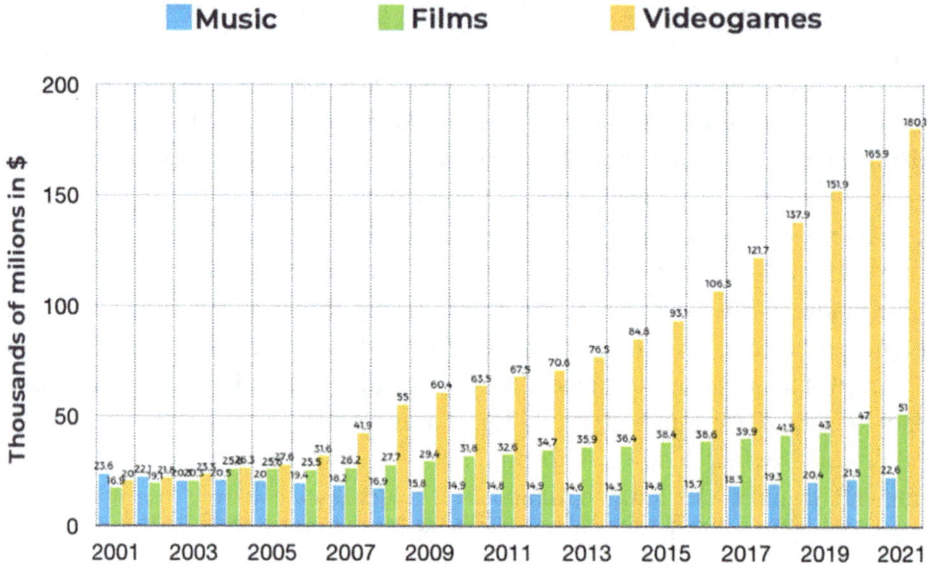

The churn rate essentially indicates how many customers remained with an organization. An elevated churn rate is cause for alarm as it can adversely affect business performance (Kulkarni et al., 2023; Jiang, 2024). In addition, the loss in annual sales revenue due to the increased churn rate can be as high as 20% to 50% above the reasonable threshold, according to Chen and Wang (2022). The direct implications are the loss of income and losses of profitability, in addition to an increase in the costs of new customers, which may be between 5 to 25 times more expensive than retaining customers (Baker et al., 2020; Rodriguez & Martinez, 2024). This represents the cost implication and thus affects the realization of organizational profitability targets (Thompson et al., 2023; Sundararajan & Gursoy, 2020). A high turnover rate would also unbalance the enterprises, decelerating the process of establishing sustainable customers, which is strategically important under the operational scaling phase.

While the COVID-19 pandemic has negatively affected many sectors on a global scale, the gaming industry has experienced a remarkable growth and transformation process, following a different course in both economic and sociocultural dimensions. Forced social isolation, working from home and the restriction of physical alternatives for entertainment have dramatically increased the interest in digital games, leading to significant increases in both the number of users and in-game spending. During the pandemic, games have become not only entertainment tools but also interactive and participatory platforms where social ties are maintained; online multiplayer games have turned into digital meeting spaces. In this process, actors in the sector have strengthened their server infrastructures, accelerated content updates, and emphasized campaigns and events to increase user loyalty in order to respond quickly to the increasing demand. Moreover, thanks to the accessibility of mobile games, a wide demographic range has been reached, the traditional player profile has expanded and the casual gamers have become more visible. Developers and distributors have focused more on dynamics such as artificial intelligence, personalization, and social connectivity to increase in-game interactions, reduce the psychological effects of social isolation, and provide a sustainable user experience. In the post-pandemic period, it is seen that these gains have become permanent, and the gaming industry has repositioned itself as a field of digital socialization, economic interaction and cultural production, going beyond being just a branch of the entertainment industry. The industry has evaluated the pandemic not only as a growth opportunity, but also as a process of reshaping its service models, user relations and technological infrastructures. This structural transformation has also brought about new dynamics in how games generate revenue and retain players, making the interplay between monetization strategies and user loyalty more critical than ever before.

The relationship between revenue generation models and player loyalty in the gaming industry requires a critical balance in terms of both economic sustainability and user experience. Especially in free-to-play (F2P) game models, while revenue is largely based on in-app purchases and micro-transactions, the psychological effects of these systems on the player can directly affect the level of loyalty. Overly aggressive or manipulative monetization strategies may increase churn rates by negatively affecting user satisfaction and loyalty in the long term, even if they provide short-term revenue growth. For this reason, successful gaming companies design their monetization mechanisms to integrate with the player experience, making spending a voluntary form of participation rather than an obligation. For example, in-game cosmetics, subscription systems or time-saving content are ethical ways to generate revenue without disrupting the player's relationship with the game. Customized rewards to strengthen loyalty, content shaped by user preferences, and community-driven mechanics make the monetization process both more sustainable and user-friendly. Furthermore, loyalty programs, events and in-game recognition systems that make players feel valued reinforce emotional attachment and encourage long-term retention of users. In conclusion, both player satisfaction and revenue potential can be maximized when the relationship between monetization and player loyalty is designed as a mutually reinforcing synergy rather than a zero-sum equation.

Customers with higher profitability create predictable revenues, which enable better resource allocation and more effective long-term strategic plans (Baker et al., 2023). However, high churn drives organizations to buzzwords temporary solutions like aggressive marketing and price-skimming, which kill brand value and long-run profitability (Reichheld & Teal, 1996; Prasad et al., 2012). Without customer loyalty, a business loses the opportunity of upselling, cross-selling, and word-of-mouth advertising, overtaking another hurdle to growth potential (Libai et al., 2009). That is why this chapter puts a focus on churn analysis, particularly in gaming, as it is inherently linked to economic performance and tactical planning. This discussion will explore what drives churn — such as poor onboarding, unengaging content, and competition with new titles — and identify preventative strategies through personalization, loyalty programs, and data-driven optimization.

In this chapter, the direct effects of churn on organizational performance are discussed and the strategic implications of customer churn on revenue, profitability and operational scale are comprehensively analyzed. It also emphasizes why customer loyalty is critical for sustainable growth, along with the cost increase caused by churn.

KEY DRIVERS OF PLAYER CHURN

A player's decision to stop playing a game can be influenced by a variety of variables, including the game's design, technical aspects, and the community outside of the game. Developers can implement focused tactics to resolve issues, foster player loyalty, and create an environment that keeps players coming back for more by examining these important drivers. Player churn is influenced by a wide range of interrelated factors that shape the overall gaming experience. Key drivers include gameplay and content saturation, where repetitive mechanics and lack of innovation diminish engagement; difficulty and challenge levels, which must be balanced to suit diverse player skill sets; and in-game economy and monetization tactics, where unfair or aggressive models can damage trust and retention. Additionally, social aspects and community engagement play a crucial role in fostering belonging and long-term commitment, while technical issues and performance problems can lead to frustration and premature abandonment. Understanding and addressing these dimensions holistically is essential for effective churn prevention.

Gameplay and Content Saturation

Content and gameplay saturation is one of the top reasons players leave games, according to Frias. Content reuse in gaming is not uncommon, and in the long run, players tend to lose interest with repetitive mechanics and updates or a lack of innovation (Hamari & Tuunanen, 2022). This level of over-saturation strips the game of its thrill and sense of discovery and can even result in burnout for long-time players (Nacke & Drachen, 2023). This has a notable effect, especially with games that do not provide meaningful rewards for players or a difficult progression (Seraphine,

2021). So, in order to maintain player interest, the game needs to carefully balance familiar gameplay elements with new and innovative experiences. This necessitates developers to be mindful of content design (Zhao et al., 2022).

Figure 2. Game design challenges and content saturation factors

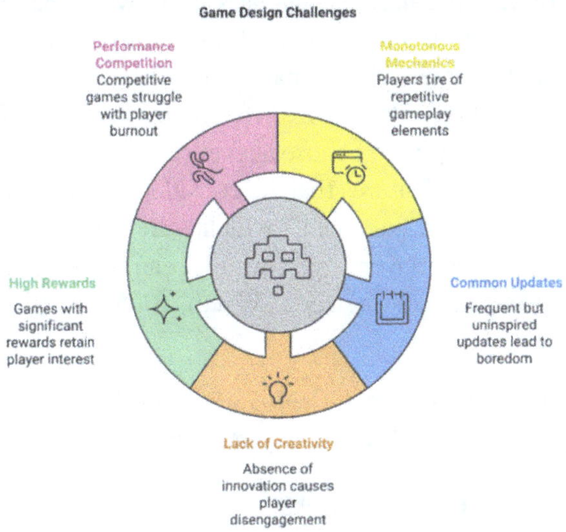

Figure 2 summarizes the key factors that contribute to player churn. The factors in the image include monotonous game mechanics, frequent but uninspired updates, lack of creativity, inadequate rewards, and burnout from performance-based competition. Each of these factors is presented as critical factors that reduce player engagement and increase the likelihood of churn. A big couple of reasons for player burnout, quitting, and games dying revolve around the sense of content and gameplay saturation. Playing in a setting where repetitive mechanics are employed, the updates are repetitive, and/or when the innovative genes are scarce can saturate players' entertainment activities in the game (Hamari & Tuunanen, 2022). This saturation allows well-established features and their innovation to lose their spark over time but may as well, in this specific case, leave burnout for players with long experience (Nacke & Drachen, 2023). This occurs especially in games that provide no or limited rewards and stringently reward the player (Seraphine, 2021). As such, this popularity needs to be balanced with features that ensure the players will come back for more in the future, providing new and exciting content while also capitalizing on the existing styles of gameplay. Such practices demand developers to engage in additional purposeful decisions by way of designing their content (Zhao et al., 2022).

Difficulty and Challenge Levels

In video game design, it is essential to achieve the right balance between difficulty and challenge because players have a variety of skills and preferences (Nacke & Lindley, 2008). Casual players like a more leisurely experience that focuses on story and exploration, while hardcore gamers often want challenging mechanics that challenge the user's skills and strategic ability (Juul, 2010). When games fail to cover this spectrum, it threatens the alienation of one audience in favor of the other (Salen & Zimmerman, 2004). Providing different levels of difficulty, such as easy, normal, and hard, helps players to choose a level which fits their comfort and goals (Hunicke et al., 2004). Even features that are considered to go beyond accessibility, such as "dynamic difficulty adjustment," which scales and modifies challenges in real-time based on how the player is performing, can increase accessibility while still keeping players engaged (Sweetser & Wyeth, 2005).

Figure 3. Difficulty Saw model for difficulty and challenge levels

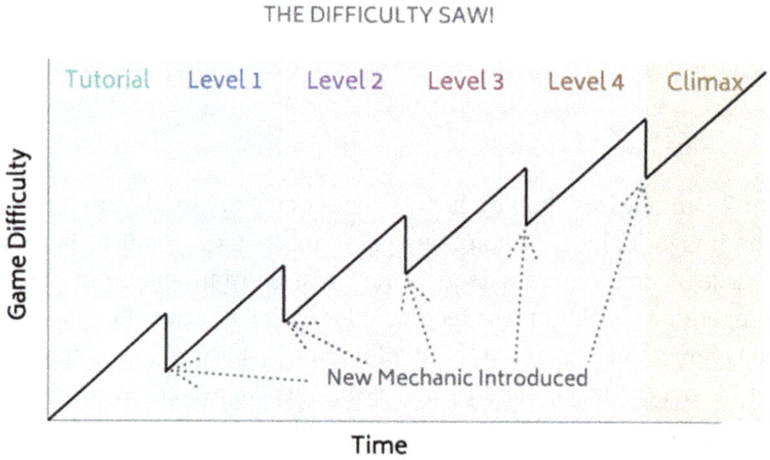

As seen in Figure 3, "Difficulty Saw" model, which was developed to optimize the user experience in game-based learning environments, will be used as a guide to structure the progression of basic game mechanics in this project. The model in question allows the difficulty level to increase in a controlled manner throughout the game, while offering a short-term decrease in difficulty at the beginning of each new section, allowing the player to interact with new learning outcomes or mechanics. This approach balances the cognitive load of the player, reinforces the acquired skills, and supports the continuity of in-game motivation. The project aims to increase both pedagogical impact and user engagement by planning gradual task difficulties and learning gaps between sections in each section. Thus, while players transition to new content more preparedly, the game environment will create an effective learning experience by offering a constantly increasing but predictable level of challenge.

The effectiveness of this tiered difficulty structure depends not only on the structure of the missions, but also on how the player is brought into the game. The tutorials and onboarding processes also have an important impact on how players perceive difficulty (Andersen et al., 2018). A badly designed tutorial or lack of seamless guidance can easily lead to an otherwise moderately difficult game feeling unapproachable and even unfun, especially for new players (Shneiderman & Plaisant, 2010). Developers are encouraged to ramp core gameplay, gradually introducing and developing mechanics over time (Federoff, 2002). It should also be possible to add optional challenges or achievements to allow advanced players without impacting newer players (Chen, 2007). Not only does this increase the potential audience for a game, but it also prevents a wide array of players from feeling lost and alienated, instead making sure they feel challenged and rewarded in equal measure (Isbister & Schaffer, 2008).

Yee (2006) states that difficulty and challenge levels are a primary determinant of player retention. On the other hand, if a game is too easy, it may lose the interest of players because it does not provide them with a sense of achievement or progression (Csikszentmihalyi, 1990). Similarly, if playing a game proves too hard, it leads to frustration and the player gives up altogether (Przybylski et al., 2010). Finding the appropriate equilibrium is central; players need to feel sufficiently challenged yet not inundated (Chen, 2007). As Sweetser & Wyeth (2005) suggest, personalized difficulty settings, adaptive AI, or tutorials that ease new players into complex mechanics are good solutions to this problem and are able to help a diverse audience foster continued participation in a game.

In-Game Economy and Monetization Tactics

A poorly structured in-game economy or overtly predatory monetization tactics is a major turn-off for many players (King & Delfabbro, 2018). Pay-to-win frameworks, expensive microtransactions, or imprecise reward structures often lead to those feelings, especially when they prevent progression or breed inequities among players (Hamari et al., 2017). Games that unfairly monetize (i.e., loot boxes) can promote a shorter lifespan as players grow frustrated with the game (Seraphine, 2016). One of the significant reasons that gaming does not retain its essence and players feel frustrated about their time and energy invested in playing is that the in-game economy is unbalanced (Hamari et al., 2017). Rewards provide little feeling of achievement or progress when they are insufficient, highly grind-heavy, or tethered to payments (King & Delfabbro, 2018). This creates a situation in which players might feel compelled to purchase in-game currency to remain competitive, particularly in multiplayer environments, as the pay-to-win constructs provide significant advantages to the paying player (Seraphine, 2016). On top of the above, it ruins fair play and creates big issues for these players who want to enjoy the game without paying much (Przybylski et al., 2010). As Deterding et al., (2011) states, the only way to deal with these problems is to achieve a fine balance between rewarding player effort and monetization options that seem optional rather than compulsory.

Social Aspects and Community Engagement

Player churn can often be traced to the absence of impactful social engagement and community involvement. The feeling of belongingness is an important reason to keep players engaged with games, combining elements such as guilds, cooperative modes, or active community events (Hamari & Koivisto, 2015). However, if these features are neglected or poorly designed, the player might become frustrated and opt to close the game (Yee, 2006). For that, developers need to create games that naturally lead to groups interacting and talking, but also, should interact back, via updates, feedback sessions, events, etc.

This is fundamental to creating a game that feels dynamic and possesses strong social aspects and community engagement. These connections are immersive in nature and allow players to embody alternate personas while engaging with these systems in a way that might reflect their real-life personas in an effort to connect with others by inviting them into their virtual worlds to engage in collaborative or social play (Ducheneaut et al., 2007). Camaraderie with one another elevates the experience, but it also plays a critical role in attracting and retaining players: people stay in games where they feel bonded to others. Furthermore, games that demand cooperation, instead of individual achievements, can develop a spirit of community that maintains players' interest in the community (Williams et al., 2006). Without these features, players could find themselves becoming isolated, resulting in lowered emotional engagement with the game and higher churn.

Developers also need to be focused on the player community even outside of any social mechanics—ongoing engagement well after the game itself is off the table. Frequent interaction on forums, social media sites, or developer livestreams builds transparency and inclusion (Wohn, 2011). When players feel heard and respected, they are more likely to stick with the game. The bond is strengthened by hosting special community events or tournaments, giveaways, or fan art contests, which not only showcase player creativity but also celebrate their contributions. Additionally, including players in decision-making processes (for instance, voting on the next features or updates) creates a sense of ownership and partnership in the progress of the game (Cheung et al., 2014). These initiatives have the added bonus of instilling trust, fostering players' connections to the game, and nurturing a vibrant, loyal community that is less inclined to churn.

Technical Issues and Performance Problems

The focus should be the half-baked technology that goes out in the gaming industry. Technical issues like crashes, game-breaking bugs, or optimization problems can detach players from an immersive experience, limiting players' trust in the game and the developers (Zhou et al., 2012). Server instability and latency can be especially detrimental for online multiplayer games, where not only does server instability affect individual performance, but it also hurts team dynamics and competition (Chen et al., 2020). Technical flaws that cause players to lose progress or interruption to gameplay rotation can leave players feeling that their time and effort have gone to waste. It is important to fix these issues as soon as possible, as even loyal players will start to churn if they experience constant performance failures that they feel developers are ignoring (Wohn, 2011).

Timing and communication are essential for minimizing the effects of technical problems. Frequent updates, moves, and bugfix solutions and in-depth patch notes also show dedication to quality and player satisfaction (Hamari & Koivisto, 2015). Furthermore, where there are open channels of communication through which players can report issues and receive timely responses, these fosters trust and provides a sense of collaboration (Cheung et al., 2014). For example, testing new updates rigorously before pushing them out and investing in durable server infrastructure can mitigate many technical issues before they occur in the first place (Zhang & Siewiorek, 1999). More than fixes, performance benefits, like tweaking graphics settings for lower-end devices or optimizing load times, can also improve the experience, enhancing the title's reach to more users in a better way. Not only do these measures serve to decrease churn, but they also help to solidify the game's reputation for stability and quality.

In this chapter, the main factors that trigger player churn are analyzed; the saturation point created by content and gameplay repetition, difficulty imbalances and the negative effects of aggressive monetization strategies on player satisfaction are evaluated. Furthermore, the importance of fair game economics, accessible difficulty options and continuous innovative content delivery in maintaining player loyalty is emphasized. Balanced management of these elements is critical for the long-term success of the game.

DATA-DRIVEN APPROACHES TO ANALYZE CHURN

Gaming Business Models

Different business models in the gaming industry experience and manage the effects of player churn in different ways. In the Pay-to-Play (P2P) model, players usually make a long-term commitment after purchasing a game; churn is often associated with a lack of content or technical problems and does not directly result in lost revenue, but can damage brand image. In Free-to-Play (F2P) games, on the other hand, churn can lead to direct revenue loss because revenue is generated from in-game purchases by active users; therefore, churn analysis is much more critical and time-sensitive in this model.

In subscription-based models (e.g. World of Warcraft), churn forecasts are usually based on the subscription cycle, as churn means the interruption of a regular revenue stream, and user loyalty is supported by content updates. The freemium model, on the other hand, offers a hybrid structure where the basic version of the game is offered for free and premium features are unlocked for payment; in this model, churn should be monitored for both free users and paying users, especially the loss of paying users should be prioritized and segment-based analysis should be performed. Each model approaches churn differently and analysis methodologies should be tailored to user behaviors, revenue stream structure and content strategy.

Table 1. Business models, monetization, churn model and strategies in literature

Business Model	Monetization	Churn Model	Strategies
Pay-to-Play (P2P)	One-time revenue from the sale of games	After-sales satisfaction follow-up, long-term content analysis	Quality first experience, extensive content, technical support
Free-to-Play (F2P)	Loss of active users directly translates into loss of revenue	Behavioral data analysis, early churn prediction	Personalization, daily rewards, recovery campaigns
Subscription-based	Direct income deduction occurs with subscription cancellation	Interaction tracking and segmentation during the subscription period	Continuous content update, loyalty incentives
Freemium	Paid user churn is more critical; free user churn has indirect impact	Player segmentation, revenue-oriented churn prediction	Premium experience boost, timed offers

In Table 1, comparative analysis clearly shows how different business models experience and manage the churn phenomenon. In P2P models, churn is mostly associated with player satisfaction and brand reputation, while F2P and subscription-based structures are exposed to the direct financial impact of churn. Especially in F2P models, since churn is at the center of the revenue chain, user interaction, behavioral data tracking and recovery strategies are of great importance. The freemium model, on the other hand, has to evaluate churn as both a potential revenue loss for free users and a direct loss for paying users. These differences require customized approaches at every stage, from the types of data used in churn analysis to prediction algorithms. Therefore, effective churn management requires multidimensional analyses such as when, why and to which segment the player belongs, not just whether the player has left the game.

In the gaming industry, it is of great importance not only to observe customer churn, but also to predict and take precautions. In this context, churn analyses performed with traditional methods are insufficient; more in-depth and real-time insights are needed in dynamic environments where user behaviors change rapidly. At this point, artificial intelligence (AI)-assisted methods come into play, offering powerful solutions in areas such as early detection of churn, risk scoring, and personalized intervention recommendations. In the next section, it will be discussed in detail how AI-based churn management applications have revolutionized the gaming industry.

Churn Management on Gaming – AI

In this section, the impact of churn rates on the gaming industry will be analyzed through three different lenses. Initially, from a revenue growth and economy perspective, we analyze how heavy churn reduces companies' revenue potential and why this influences economic sustainability, partly related to market entry barriers. Second, we analyze from a game design perspective the detrimental effects of content saturation and lack of strategic planning in game design. Third, we present a player and game lens on the topic, discussing how churn rates impact player behavior, engagement, and experience. These three views can help us better understand the diverse impact churn rates have on the gaming industry.

One of the strongest ways to stem the tide of churn in the gaming space is to data-drive your understanding of player behavior. Using data analytics, developers can uncover patterns and trends that signal when and why players leave a game. Analyzing various metrics related to external systems can also offer insights beyond role-playing elements, such as metrics like session length, number of logins, in-game purchases, and completion rates (Hadiji et al., 2014). For example, a significant decrease in session lengths or a sudden reduction in levels completed might indicate frustration or boredom, so developers can intervene on the problem ahead of time. More advanced tools, such as heatmaps, help visualize player actions within a game and can uncover design pain points, such as levels that are too challenging or features that go unused (Drachen et al., 2013). This allows for focused interventions to enhance the player experience and minimize churn.

Machine learning models take churn analysis beyond revenue growth and economy by predicting player behavior based on historical data. By analyzing gameplay patterns and other relevant data, predictive analytics can identify players who are at high risk of churn and allow developers to intervene with targeted retention strategies (Perianez et al., 2016). For example, a lapsed player may be lured back with a personalized in-game reward or promotional event. Developers can use segmentation techniques to identify players by similar behaviors or preferences, so they can optimize their efforts for disparate segments of the audience. Some suggestions include simplified tutorials or the addition of new content (for casual players), a better leaderboard experience, or an exclusive challenge (for competitive players) (Seif El-Nasr et al., 2013). Machine learning thus enhances churn analysis in terms of a qualitative approach — from a reactive process to a proactive strategy focusing on retention.

Another common aspect of data-driven churn analysis is sentiment analysis, which involves finding out players' feedback to determine overall satisfaction and areas on which we can improve. Natural language processing (NLP) can then be conducted on reviews, forum posts, and social media comments to identify patterns in player sentiment, including complaints regarding bugs, pricing, or game mechanics (Medler, 2011). This qualitative information supplements the quantitative insights we garnered from gameplay metrics, giving us a well-rounded picture of player sentiment. Developers bracket issues in merit order according to the quantity and sentiment of feedback, allowing developers to address the most threatening issues first (Wohn, 2011). Similarly, sentiment analysis aids developers in analyzing the impact of updates or new features in real-time, enabling them to improve their approach (Drachen et al., 2013).

Finally, A/B testing gives developers a vital opportunity in data-driven churn analysis — the ability to experiment with their possible solutions and measure their impacts. Game developers can evaluate how different features, reward mechanisms, difficulty, or even style of user interface influence players by trying different combinations (Seif El-Nasr et al., 2013). For instance, one group of players could get a new onboarding tutorial, while another group gets the existing version. By comparing the engagement metrics among the groups, it gives a better idea about which approach more effectively retains the players. Which, over time, can have phased iterative improvements made to it based on A/B testing to bring a more polished, engaging game experience. Used alongside other data-driven techniques, this method provides developers with the tools to make data-informed decisions that decrease churn and cultivate long-term loyalty among players (Hadiji et al., 2014).

Another thing to pay attention to is player retention, as this element is one of the main indicators that directly affects the long-term success of the game. Player retention is heavily dependent on a balanced game economy and a fair monetization model. Players are likely to churn when they feel they are asked to spend an excessive amount of money to progress or when their purchases provide them with an unfair competitive advantage (King et al., 2019). It is a difficult balancing act for developers to give players the chance to spend money while keeping the game accessible to those who do not want to spend. One possible way is through the free-to-play model, during which players can pay for cosmetic items and convenience boosters, but not for something essential for gameplay (Zhao et al., 2016). Non-paying players can also get the full experience of the game while paying players can support the game as they do not interfere with the regular gameplay balance (Hamari et al., 2020).

A properly-built in-game economy, along with a transparent pricing and reward model, will significantly reduce player friction. A system established in-game to correlate player progression with in-game currency or rewards can increase engagement as players will recognize how what they are doing leads to earning something (Nieborg, 2017). They provide the player base with satisfaction through clear progression systems, which reward users for grinding by replacing pay-to-win mechanics, and satisfy players without having to spend to feel accomplished. The balance between enjoyment and monetization is critical for a healthy game and system, making it important that microtransactions remain optional and not disrupt competitive play (Wohn, 2011). Finally, developers are encouraged to adhere to ethical monetization practices that prioritize fair pricing models, refrain from random loot boxes, and ensure that microtransactions do not lead to disparities between players (Macey & Hamari, 2019). When you explain how in-game purchases operate and deliver a great user experience, you earn the trust of your audience. A game that values players' time and investment and gives something in return is more likely to be continued because people will seek the experience. Such trust is fundamental in minimizing churn and building the foundation for embedded long-term player loyalty (King & Delfabbro, 2018).

In terms of game design, the prevention of players churning: Effective strategies tend to involve personalized content to ensure that the player experience is rewarding and engaging. Making the game's progression system cater to each individual player can spark a lot of engagement. As for dynamic adaptation, developers can make easy dynamic difficulty adjustments, adaptive challenges, and even personalized rewards depending on the player's behavior (Chen, 2007). For instance, a game might change its difficulty according to the player's skill set or offer them bespoke quests and storylines based on decisions made in previous play (Drachen et al., 2013). Other methods to keep the player engaged may include the introduction of personalized events in-game to reward players on a daily basis for logging in, including seasonal events or challenges they can miss out on (Hadiji et al., 2014). Lowered Likelihood of Churn: When players feel the game grows and evolves according to their preferences and gives them rewarding experiences, they reach lower churn rates.

Another key strategy is building a sense of community and social connectedness in the game. Designing relationships as part of a multiplayer, guild environment, or even leagues of competition, helps players connect with others and hones their connection (Przybylski et al., 2010). Retention rates for free-to-play video games are generally higher when customers are able to play and compete with friends or other interactive players (Wohn, 2011). You can also maintain player engagement with social engagement tools such as in-game messaging, forums, or community events to give your players a platform to interact with each other (Sweetser & Wyeth, 2005). It's even more important that developers listen to community reactions and include players in the decision-making process so they feel the community is included and appreciated. Fostering a social and collaborative environment within the game can play a large role in reducing churn.

In order to combat churn effectively, developers must constantly keep an eye on player behavior and let data guide their decisions. Metrics like session length, progression rates, and player feedback can illuminate behavior patterns indicating potential risks of churn (Hadiji et al., 2014). Developers can take action on this data through timely interventions — like in-game notifications, special offers, or re-engagement campaigns that target players lifting the wheel (Medler, 2011). New updates that add content, features, and bug fixes are also commonly important to keep players engaged. Releasing new and significant content regularly helps keep the game fresh and exciting, while simultaneously decreasing the chances of players quitting (Seif El-Nasr et al., 2013). By incorporating a blend of personalization, community elements, and data-informed strategy, it will ultimately keep the player base loyal with less churn. It's important to note that these strategies work best together, creating a complete retention mindset that can lead to long-term success for games and developers alike.

In terms of game dynamics, tailored engagement and rewards are critical levers in keeping players interested and lowering churn. This approach serves to remind players that their efforts are noticed and rewarded, encouraging them to keep playing and advancing further in the game. There are many ways to personalize each individual player's experience through dynamic events, such as a game difficulty that adapts based on player performance, unique rewards, or even personalized storylines to make every player's experience unique (Drachen et al., 2013). Because players have this individualized content experience as opposed to a one-size-fits-all approach, these personalized elements create relevance and meaning to the game (Hadiji et al., 2014).

Many players are motivated by elements that offer these rewards, and providing these rewards is what drives you forward. Rather than offering generic in-game items, players can be rewarded with unique rewards tailored to their play style or interests (Hamari et al., 2017). As an example, if one player specialized in combat, they would obtain unique weapons or skills as rewards, and if they were focused on exploring, they would receive idle cosmetics or unique local locations. Not only does this kill players' sense of accomplishment, but it also keeps them playing for rewards that have some meaning to them. Rewards are personalized, keeping the game interesting and lending a sense of recognition and importance to the players for their actions (Seif El-Nasr et al., 2013).

Besides communicating, developers can offer personalized engagement via gameplay rewards. You know the player and their specific in-game style, whether or not they log in often, the patterns in their reactionary behavior, and can use that knowledge to send tailored in-game notifications, emails, or push notifications that remind them of new content or upcoming events (Medler, 2011) that they may be missing out on. When a player completes a certain level, they receive a message suggesting that they should try a new challenge or they are being offered a special reward for continuing the game. Not only does this foster informed play, but it also facilitates a bond between the player and the subject matter of the game, inspiring them to explore more and return (Wohn, 2011).

Keeping players engaged in the long term with regular content updates and feature expansions is a core ingredient to reducing churn. That is why I think players of all sorts have a tendency to drift away from a game if everything goes stale and because there's no new content to experience. Updates, such as seasonal events or new levels, characters, or game modes, provide players with fresh things to anticipate and lead them to continue to play (Montgomery & Oliver, 2021). By consistently releasing content, developers can keep the experience both dynamic and ever-evolving enough to keep players on their toes. Such a strategy is effective in both increasing player retention and ensuring that the game remains relevant over time, adapting to the changing expectations of players (Hamari et al., 2020). Iterative updates to add to existing functionalities are also essential for long-term engagement. New systems can add features like crafting mechanics, new progression tracks, multiplayer modes, etc., and can help students be bedazzled or re-engaged with the game, giving players new aspects to interact with the game. Quality of life improvements, such as bug fixes, performance optimizations, or UI enhancements, can also be considered expansions, and are an important contribution towards a smoother gameplay experience (Nieborg, 2017). This keeps players happy and prevents frustration from creeping in as the game becomes older. Moreover, feature expansions allow developers to directly address player community feedback, enabling the game to evolve in a manner that suits player desires (King et al., 2019).

As developers, it's essential while planning these updates and expansions that player feedback along with analytics data is taken into account. Developers can focus on the types of content that are likely to keep players in their game by collecting metrics on player behavior, durations of play, and functionalities used (Wohn, 2011). And if we want the long play, it's about quantity and quality, regular updates that introduce new things and meaty expansions that build on the existing content of the game. By keeping things fresh, players will be less likely to churn while giving them more reason to continue playing and spending money on the game.

Furthermore, community and collaborative challenges are great in terms of increasing player retention as there are people working together with a shared goal. New interactions, new events — seasonal events and special tournaments, or cooperative or mission events — create opportunities for players to interact in new significant ways, providing meaningful experiences. This generates engagement and encourages players to come back to the game frequently (Hamari & Järvinen, 2011). Developers can further encourage engagement and build long-lasting memories within the player community by providing exclusive rewards or recognition for participating in these types of community events (King et al., 2019).

Since 2020, the literature on player churn prediction has advanced significantly through the integration of behavioral data, social network features, and advanced machine learning techniques. Roohi et al. (2020) combined Deep Reinforcement Learning (DRL) with a simulated player population model to predict level-based churn and pass rates without requiring actual player data, highlighting the role of simulated traits such as skill and persistence. Óskarsdóttir et al. (2022) demonstrated that social network-based features significantly enhance churn prediction performance in mobile games, especially when combined with first-day behavioral data, which effectively captures the bursty nature of early player activity. Rothmeier et al. (2021) compared multiple labeling strategies and machine learning algorithms using data from The Settlers Online, finding that a Random Forest model with sliding windows yielded the highest AUC and accuracy (up to 97%). Mustač et al. (2022) explored churn in a storytelling-based mobile game, showing that models trained on 1–7 days learning windows achieved prediction accuracies ranging from 66% to 95%, capturing both short- and long-term player behavior. Han et al. (2024) proposed a hybrid approach integrating Graph Convolutional Networks (GCNs) with Correct & Smooth (C&S) techniques to model churn in an MMORPG, demonstrating the value of both internal player features and external social influences within a graph-based framework. Zheng et al. (2020) introduced ChurnPred, an end-to-end neural network that incorporates both login sequences and in-game behavior through LSTM and multi-view mechanisms, outperforming baseline models in predictive accuracy. Fernández del Río et al. (2021) applied a State Space time series approach to model daily player transitions between active and inactive states, enabling not only churn prediction but also the detection of latent marketing campaigns. Liu et al. (2020) conducted a large-scale analysis on data from Samsung Game Launcher, proposing a two-level framework that addresses both micro-level churn prediction and macro-level churn ranking using edge embedding and attributed random walks. Lastly, Weiss and Vilenchik (2023) presented an interpretable, white-box method for churn prediction based on engagement diversity, using PCA-derived temporal trajectories, achieving competitive results compared to black-box models while enhancing explainability.

Finally, developing an engaged player-led community outside the game can prolong player loyalty. Players can interact with each other through official forums, social media groups, or fan-driven websites and discuss anecdotes about the game as well as get informed of the latest news regarding the game. Additionally, active moderation and developer interaction in these spaces create an even stronger sense of community by indicating to players that their contributions and feedback are valued (Montgomery & Oliver, 2021). With players spending a growing percentage of their gaming time in a social setting, creating an inclusive and welcoming atmosphere in-game and online drives social bonds that help reduce churn and build loyalty with players. Collectively, these studies highlight substantial progress in the domain, particularly in the utilization of supervised learning models, temporal behavior modeling, and social network analysis. However, several areas remain underexplored or require further refinement. First, although hybrid models that integrate behavioral and social features have shown promising results, the dynamic interplay between these dimensions over time is not yet fully captured, especially in real-time or near real-time settings. Second, while explainability has recently gained attention (e.g., Weiss & Vilenchik, 2023), many high-performing models still function as black boxes, limiting their practical applicability for decision-makers in game design and live operations. Third, most existing studies focus on churn as a binary classification problem, whereas multi-class or regression-based approaches that predict degrees or timing of churn could provide more nuanced insights. Furthermore, cross-game generalizability remains a challenge, as many models are tailored to the specific mechanics and player base of individual games. Lastly, the integration of external contextual factors such as marketing campaigns, seasonal trends, or content updates—while touched upon by Fernández del Río et al. (2021)—warrants deeper investigation for building robust, adaptable prediction systems.

In this chapter, data-driven approaches to analyzing player churn are discussed and the role of machine learning, time series analysis and social network-based modelling in churn prediction is detailed. It is emphasized that the correct labelling of player behavior data is critical for improving model performance and developing early warning systems. Furthermore, it is explained how micro and macro level analyses contribute to game design, marketing strategies and user experience optimization. In this context, it was revealed that data-driven methods offer powerful and scalable solutions to reduce churn rates.

STRATEGIES TO HANDLE PLAYER CHURN: CASES FROM POPULAR GAMES

This section will review industry-specific strategies implemented by major video game companies in the "Case Studies and Industry Examples" section to reduce player churn and solidify long-term retention. Through stylized examples from games like Fortnite, League of Legends, World of Warcraft, Minecraft, Candy Crush Saga, we describe how different approaches work better for games in different ways. This consists of personalized engagement (e.g., dynamically updated content), balanced in-game economies, strong socialization/community tools, analytic insights into user churn, and above all, sustainable monetization practices.

No churn, not now, not ever: And these three case studies go a long way to prove that whether it's through ways to understand player behavior, responding to feedback, or ensuring gameplay experience never becomes stale, games ultimately prevent churn by keeping players coming back for more and, if concretely executed, keeping them as loyal lifelong customers.

A great example of how this increase in player engagement can create significantly decreased churn comes in the form of Epic Games' Fortnite. Fortnite is known for its seasonal content updates bringing new battle passes, skins, map changes, and limited-time events. What players can expect from the seasonal updates is a sense of anticipation and excitement to see what's in store, which always keeps players coming back for more. The game also features social elements such as in-game voice chat, teaming up, and joining events alongside friends and the community. By consistently updating the game and addressing player input, Fortnite was able to also retain a large number of players while minimizing churn and maintaining the game experience fresh and intriguing (Anderson, 2020).

Figure 4. Screenshot from Fortnite Marvel package

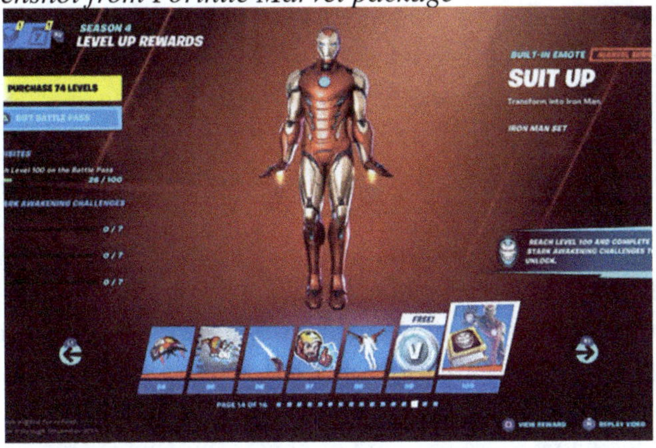

As seen in Figure 4, Fortnite has found this remarkable success. Season by season, the game rolls out new content (map changes, thematic events, new character skins) to pull players back into the game. A great example of this was the "Marvel Season" in 2020, where players experienced everything from Iron Man to Thor themes that resulted in a 25% increase in player activity rate. Fortnite also wins with community-driven events. The event can be attributed to the record player boom thanks to virtual concerts like the popular 'Marshmello Concert' and 'Travis Scott Event.' The event was apparently a huge success, with 12.3 million players reportedly active in the game simultaneously during the Travis Scott event. These events, however, reflect Fortnite's emphasis on in-game social experiences to give its community a meeting place more than dedicated gameplay. Regular content updates and events keep players with something to be looking forward to constantly and increase long-term engagement (Kelly, 2020).

Beyond scheduled content updates and community events, Fortnite's collaborative approach with other major media franchises has been particularly effective at curbing churn and maintaining interest among players. By adding crossover content from globally popular franchises like Marvel, Star Wars, and DC, Fortnite was able to expand its audience beyond typical gamers, creating a sense of excitement around exclusive time-limited events. Regular collaborations also feel new, adding themed events that excite both old and new players, keeping the game relevant and fresh. In addition, Fortnite's addition of "live events," meaning that the game world changes in real time, creates an engaging, living environment that fascinates players. In-game concerts, interactive storylines, and other events can all be considered live events, and they are leading players to invest their time into video games in ways that lessen the likelihood of churn (Smith, 2021). These strategies have kept Fortnite's player base loyal and active while also setting a standard for how games can continue to evolve with the expectations of their dedicated audience.

Riot Games has even pioneered an ethical monetization model in League of Legends where its free-to-play and paying players all remain engaged. The game is free-to-play (with purchasable cosmetic items like skins and emotes that don't affect gameplay balance). League of Legends has sidestepped pay-to-win, and players do not have to spend real money to compete, and people aren't out-bid for victory by those with deeper pockets. Riot Games has managed to balance the game economy by regularly releasing new content such as champions, skins, and events, designed in a way so that players feel they haven't wasted their money while not interrupting their gameplay experience. This fair monetization method contributed to prolonged player retention (Johnson, 2018).

Churn in video games — a measure of how many people stop playing — tends to be high, but League of Legends (LoL) has been a phenomenon since its release in 2009, keeping churn low. LoL's success rests on the creation of a balanced game economy and a thriving competitive community. The model of the game is "free-to-play," meaning easily available for everyone; however, players can purchase some visual cosmetics if they wish. None of the items affect the mechanics of the game itself and keep the competition among player's fair. For example, replacing League of Legends with a regular set of "World Championships" has turned this into an actual community event. The 2022 World Championship peaked at over 5 million concurrent viewers in the final match goal. Events like these are popular with players and fans alike, fostering a sense of community. Moreover, Riot Games provides frequent updates to the meta-analysis, which gives rise to players to consistently create new strategies and reduces the unnatural redundancy of the game (Miller, 2022).

Figure 5. DOTA 2 screen shot from in-game play

As seen in Figure 5, an illustrative explanation, the reason for DOTA 2 having a larger player base is due to the deep layer of strategy and popular esports scene of the game. With a high level of skill, DOTA 2 has been developed on the basis of strategy. From hero select to map control, everything is intently focused and requires knowledge of the game. This depth helps establish long-term player loyalty within the game. And of course, there's the Valve-hosted esports tournaments for DOTA 2 with massive prize pools, which have helped make DOTA 2 an ongoing interest and supported a professional player community. These tournaments (especially The International) allow teams/players to present themselves in an environment that's globally competitive, which keeps players engaged for longer. On the contrary, because League of Legends (LoL) is a more casual title with faster-paced play, it might seem more appealing to new players. Still, DOTA 2's deeper player base has been maintained by its depth and continued success in professional play and its high-stakes competitions. So the primary reasons even after being old, DOTA 2 attracted a big player base is due to its very high strategic depth, e-sports events, and a firm hold in the professional scene.

An excellent case study is Blizzard's World of Warcraft, which succeeded by introducing social features and building player communities that massively decreased churn. A major component of forming strong social bonds is the game's guild system, where players can join groups and mingle with fellow gamers. Then, there are multiplayer dungeons, raids, and competitive PvP modes that foster teamwork and healthy rivalry. Players become emotionally tied to their guilds or teams, creating long-term loyalty. Blizzard also offers in-game events surrounding special occasions and seasonal content updates to continually funnel players into the core game loop and keep them invested. There is also an aspect of social presence associated with these features, which further elevates it from just a game into an orientation-based experience. Approximately 70% of World of Warcraft participants are guild members, according to research by experts, and the guild members' churn rate is 25% lower than that of solo players. Social ties established in guilds are key to keeping players coming back (Smith & Johnson, 2019).

Also, the dynamic, in-game economy of World of Warcraft creates a sense of player loyalty, as there exist meaningful rewards more than just a shiny loot at the end of a raid that bind both individual players and groups working to complete these types of events. There is a lot of crafting, an auction house, and a bunch of rare items to help propel the player through the game. The in-game economy is an important probability, as players are motivated to log in visitors to complete day-to-day pursuits, gather sources, or upgrade their tools. It is this sense of community and loyalty that reinforces players through the achievement of rare puddles and pent-up challenges from guilds. Additionally, with periodic expansions that add significant new content, like the widely successful expansions "Burning Crusade" and "Shadowlands," new quests, storylines, characters, and so forth, the game of World of Warcraft remains a live, rich, and engaging experience for old and new players alike.

Blizzard, another example from gaming industry, is also a very responsive company that listens intently to its players and modifies the game to fit the players' wishes. The corporation's discussions with players — via forums, surveys, and live events — also help ensure direct settlement of such issues and provide a better overall player experience. This responsive manner builds trust between developers and the player base, guaranteeing that the players feel their voices are heard. Making adjustments based on player feedback—whether that means game balance tweaks, quality-of-life changes, or refreshing outdated content—further cements the idea that the game is always maturing around player expectations. This is so that the game works out relevant and interesting to its ever-burgeoning community, which is able to even increase retention.

Another game with low churn that allows players to completely alter their experience is Mojang's Minecraft. Through wonderful gameplay mechanics of building worlds, changing the rules of the game, and creating custom modes, this game is as open-ended as they come. In 2021, Mojang announced that there were more than 140 million monthly active users of Minecraft, a success story attributed largely to the game's emphasis on allowing players to create and share their own content (Johnson, 2021). The Minecraft community is constantly at work adding more and more game content, while mods, servers, and other player creations are always expanding the game even further to keep people playing. In addition, frequent updates, like the "Caves and Cliffs" in 2021, have kept players interested, boosting the player base by 30% (Mojang, 2021). These innovations keep Minecraft fresh for its players.

This is more prominent in a franchise like Mojang's Minecraft, which inspired such personalized engagement and choice among players that their churn rates plummeted. It is highly customizable, offering players the option to create their own worlds, change gameplay mechanics, and build their own experiences. Players have the option of participating in the game's survival mode, where they have to craft and survive, or exploring creative mode, where they can work solely on building. An active online community surrounds Minecraft and creates custom mods and maps that can be shared. This level of personalization, along with the game's nurturing community, makes it so that there are basically infinite ways for players to interact with the game, drastically lowering churn by making the game feel bespoke to every player.

Figure 6. Minecraft screen shot from in-game play

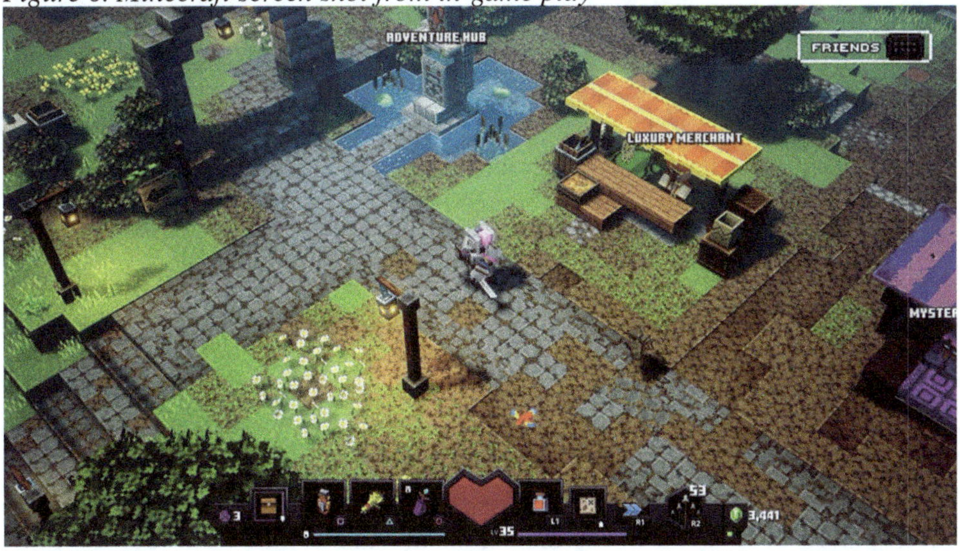

This is the approach taken by Mojang with Minecraft where, through personalized engagement and a high level of player freedom, they have been able to keep churn to a minimum. The game has a deep level of customization; players can create their own worlds, tune game mechanics, and create their own experiences. Players can choose whether to play through the game's crafting and survival mode or explore creative mode and build to their heart's desire. Furthermore, Minecraft has an active online community that develops and shares custom maps and mods. And when you pair this level of personalization with a supportive community like SRPG's, you ensure that players have truly infinite ways to engage with the game—all of this works to create an experience uniquely for each individual player, and reduces churn massively.

Moreover, it serves as a cornerstone to customize experiences and free-roaming in the game. From in-game mechanics to configuring personal game worlds, players have a vast array of configuration options at their disposal. "It's this freedom that makes Minecraft special; the ability to create game worlds, alter the rules of the game, and tailor the experience to your liking as possible." Minecraft's sandbox-style gameplay, whether in creative mode endlessly building or survival mode exploring, gives players a different gaming experience. This diversity attracts various types of players and augments their personal connection. Self-directed play-time, the time spent creating their own worlds, setting and completing their personal goals, fosters deeper player engagement with the game. This allows players to customize spaces within the games, but also allows for user-created content. Maps, mods, and even entire game mechanics can be created by players.

Since sharing creative content is encouraged on such platforms as the Minecraft Marketplace, community-generated content can flourish at pace. For instance, mods built into Minecraft let players traverse various theme parks, RPG worlds, or hardcore survival situations. This brings a continual flood of content that means players never have to look far to find something new to discover, encounter, or play. After all, the contributions of the community as a whole keep Minecraft fresh, and allow everyone to enjoy their personal experience inside the game. Minecraft is held together by many strong threads, but player freedom is one of the strongest. This freedom influences not only the way the game is played, but also how players relate to each other. Journey Park has proven a good multiplayer experience, not only because players don't just play alone but because they also begin community or friend collaborative projects. Such a level of social interactions gives players a chance to relate not just to individual experiences but to the community. Minecraft allows players to set up their own servers, run in-game events, and create new rules as long as they follow community standards. It positions players as not just part of the game but as creative makers who create the game. This motivates players to play the game all the more as they are part of a community and a development of the game.

Also, Minecraft's individual reward systems and regular content updates are among other crucially meaningful factors driving player engagement. Mojang uses a system to add to the game that rewards progress and achievement. Players who complete difficult missions earn special items, character customization options, or new map items, for instance. Rewards motivate players to play for longer periods and meet new goals. Minecraft also frequently releases major updates and event specials. The updates introduce additional biomes, creatures, game mechanics, and aesthetic items, mirroring a never-ending flow of new worlds for the player to explore. Large updates like the Caves and Cliffs update are set in motion not only to provide players with new content but to give them an experience they have not had for a long time. These features further strengthen Minecraft's long-term engagement with its community by offering a consistently personalized and rewarding experience for its players.

As mobile games proliferate, sustaining usage and retaining players is vital to ensuring that they become long-term users (Supercell, 2021). Some of the major factors contributing towards optimization of churn rate reflect in in-game rewards based on in-app behavior analysis and in-game difficulty levels optimizations (King, 2022). Therefore, in a competitive landscape of today, game developers consider churn analysis a crucial factor in developing a winning strategy and employ newer technologies such as artificial intelligence and machine learning to customize player experience (King, 2022). By doing so, they not only prevent churn but provide opportunities for the games to monetize and ultimately be a success long term (Supercell, 2021).

Developed by Supercell, Clash of Clans is a mobile strategy game and one that millions around the globe flock to play. The game structure and division of resources allow players to build their own villages, and battle against other players. Many personalized strategies have been used by Clash of Clans to counteract high churn rate (Supercell, 2021). Players can get a strong start quickly in the early stages of the game, but have to develop more in-depth strategies in the later levels. Supercell monitors in-game session times, resource expenditure patterns, and battle victories to determine the source of players' loss. Based on this data, it attempts to retain high churn-risk players in the game for longer through special rewards and bonuses (Supercell, 2021).

One year later, Clash of Clans still succeeds in sustaining players' interest by releasing regular updates and seasonal events (Supercell, 2021). Such changes mean that players can continually find something new or different in the game. Churn rates are minimized through seasonal rewards and limited-time events that compel players to return to play (Supercell, 2021). Supercell's practices tailor the gaming experience to the player and ultimately keep them engaged in the game both competitively and socially. This is how Clash of Clans has positioned itself as one of the longest-running and highest-revenue games in the mobile game market. As seen in games like Clash of Clans and Candy Crush Saga, churn analysis contributes heavily to the growth of the mobile gaming market. Churn is an essential metric to track when working with games, and both have effectively decreased their churn rates with an analysis of player behavior and ensuring tailored approaches (King, 2022). Despite this undeniable similarity, each has cultivated strategies appropriate to their respective internal dynamics and target audiences, allowing each to stake a unique claim on the gaming environment. And not only are these games shining examples of churn analysis and engagement strategies, but each one of them could be the subject of a more-detailed study all unto itself.

For example, how King used data-based approaches like predictive churn to re-engagement in their Candy Crush Saga. King uses a wide array of in-game metrics to monitor player progress, session duration, and interaction with game features. When the system determines that players are at risk of churning, it initiates personalized notifications and offers, such as a bonus life or a special in-game event, to encourage players to return. Candy Crush Saga also conducts A/B testing to help improve its monetization and engagement strategies, like testing various rewards or adjusting the difficulty of levels. The success of the game in attracting them back using focused incentives has enabled it to retain a significant user base for many, many years despite its market age. A good example is King with their Candy Crush Saga, which has the strongest data-driven strategy to avoid churn. King uses sophisticated data analytics to assess player. For instance, points in game levels where players are struggling to finish game levels, the algorithm finds it out and makes some changes in the levels. Furthermore, players who may churn are presented with special offers. These offers might be free bonuses or discounted goods. King's A/B testing method to reduce churn, from 2022, led to 15% of players at risk of churn being brought back into the game. Moreover, players that are targeted through retargeting strategies like daily rewards systems were logged in 30% more times every day. Having taken the time to analyze it, it is clear to see how data-driven decisions a profound effect on player engagement from can have looking at Candy Crush Saga's ability to manage churn.

In this section, strategies to reduce player churn are analyzed through popular game examples. Fortnite's constantly updated season system, League of Legends' community engagement with its e-sports ecosystem, World of Warcraft's long-term content planning, Minecraft's open-ended structure that encourages player creativity, and Candy Crush Saga's mission cycles that offer short-term goals are evaluated as successful approaches to churn management. Each example shows that churn can be prevented with dynamic, personalized and motivational mechanisms that focus on the user experience. In this context, the positive impact of strategies that are sensitive to user behavior and provide continuous interaction on player loyalty and game lifecycle is highlighted.

FUTURE TRENDS IN CHURN PREVENTION AND PLAYER RETENTION

The first trend is a big trend, which is implementing immersive technologies such as virtual reality (VR) and augmented reality (AR) to improve player experience. According to Smith and Lee (2023), virtual reality (VR) and augmented reality (AR) were leading forces in making developers create more interactive, engaging, and memorable experiences to deepen players' emotional investment in the game. An example of how user incentives influence the AR experience is Pokémon GO, which is exclusively played outside where the game overlays information onto the real world to create an immersive experience (Niantic, 2023). With the advancement of VR and AR technologies, it will become possible for players to explore more immersive and social experiences, like virtual worlds where they can meet friends in real-time or even take part in collaborative events that have a higher sense of "reality" (Smith & Lee, 2023). Such technologies have the potential to greatly reduce churn simply by creating an experience that is orders of magnitude more compelling and harder to replicate, deepening the bond between player and game (Smith & Lee, 2023).

The second trend in churn prevention is the application of blockchain technology to establishing transparent and player-focused in-game economies. The use of blockchain makes secure and decentralized systems where players can have real ownership of their items, whether they be skins, collectibles, or characters (Nguyen et al., 2023). In fact, Axie Infinity is one of the first games that has employed blockchain-based assets to allow its players to purchase, sell, and exchange assets through an open marketplace (Axie Infinity, 2023). This adds an extra layer of engagement as players perceive that in-game spending translates to something more meaningful in the real world (Nguyen et al., 2023). Additionally, blockchain can also facilitate the implementation of fair and transparent reward mechanisms, ensuring that players are not taken advantage of by predatory microtransactions or pay-to-win strategies (Chen & Lee, 2023). As players increasingly care about the transparency and fairness of monetization practices, it is likely that blockchain technology will be key to mitigating churn through trust building and more intrinsic motivation (Chen & Lee, 2023).

As games become more multiplayer and social, organizers will continue to play an important role in reducing churn through social integration and community building. In the upcoming games, there will be more emphasis on creating a close-knit social bonding with the help of in-game communities, team-building exercises, and cross-platforming (Smith, 2023). In fact, guilds and social groups have already shown to be very strong when it comes to retaining players in games such as World of Warcraft and League of Legends (Blizzard Entertainment, 2023; Riot Games, 2023). Games in the future are bound to have more massive social aspects like in-game voice chat, players joining teams of like-minded people, cross-platform progression, and bigger-scale virtual events, bringing players together in ways we have never explored in the gaming world before (Smith, 2023). In-game social media integrations will also allow players to share their accomplishments and experiences with their friends, helping to create organic buzz that serves as an incentive for players to get on board (Blizzard Entertainment, 2023). Indeed, social components themselves foster emotional ties to the game and compel peer pressure, increasing the difficulty for the player to stop the gameplay if their friends or teammates are still playing (Riot Games, 2023).

Finally, increasingly frequent content updates and live service models are increasingly touted as a churn prevention strategy. The games-as-a-service (GaaS) model, emphasizing ongoing updates and growing content, has shown unparalleled success in maintaining player interest (Johnson & Smith, 2023). Games like Destiny 2 and Apex Legends are prime examples of titles which maintain engagement by providing players with ongoing updates featuring new content, seasonal events, and live activities (Bungie, 2023; Respawn Entertainment, 2023). These updates bring in aspects of new gameplay mechanics and motivate players to participate in time-limited events, making the game feel refreshing (Bungie, 2023). As demand for ongoing fresh content grows, developments are looking towards community feedback and player-driven content as the game changes according to what players would like to see (Johnson & Smith, 2023). This minimizes the feeling of every player as content is stagnant, which in turn keeps churn low and keeps the game alive years after release (Respawn Entertainment, 2023). The progression of gaming industry trends toward more subscription services and live-service models means that ensuring consistent and evolving content delivery will be critical for those with long-term retention needs (Johnson & Smith, 2023).

Figure 7. Frequency distribution of customer possible churn causes in games

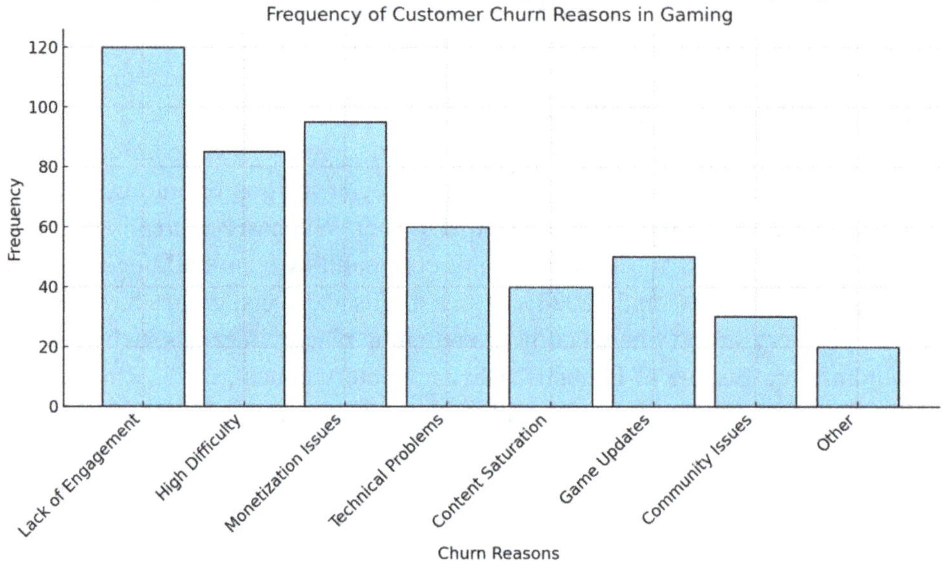

Figure 6 shows the reasons for churn in the gaming industry. The biggest churn reason is seen as “lack of fun” with a frequency of 120. This is followed by “high difficulty” and “monetization issues”. Technical problems, content duration and game updates have a medium impact, while community support and other reasons are the least influential factors. This data shows that game developers should focus primarily on the fun factor and difficulty level.

To sum up, we see these trends in churn prevention/player retention in the coming years. This can support open, play-to-win gaming environments that are player-centric and engaging through use of AI and machine learning, blockchain for just monetization, community-based support, and live-updating content. Such trends will determine how the gaming landscape matures as developers seek to build long-lasting, loyal communities that keep players engaged.

In this section, the trends expected to stand out in the future for player churn prevention and player retention processes are discussed. In particular, artificial intelligence-supported personalization, real-time data analytics, dynamic content delivery and adaptive systems that take player psychology into account are expected to transform this area. In addition, it was emphasized that sustainable loyalty mechanisms and community-based interaction strategies that focus on building long-term relationships with players will also gain importance. In this context, it has been revealed that churn prevention and player retention approaches will evolve into a more holistic and player-centered structure with technological innovations.

ETHICAL AND PRACTICAL CHALLENGES IN DATA SHARING

While churn analysis is so very important to the gaming industry, most gaming companies lack the data and tools required to perform this analysis. Gamers have played this game before, but many are unable to collect the data it takes to track player behavior and predict churn risk. Free-to-play games especially might have trouble tracking the personal data of players. Thus, the precise data required to perform a thorough analysis of and predict player churn simply is not accessible. Game data like in-game engagement, purchase history, and in-game social interactions might not give a conclusive idea of the risk of players churning. Lack of diversity of data is another challenge. Churn analysis is not only based on in-game data but also on players' external behavior associated with the concerned game. However, data such as social media activity, customer feedback, and customer support requests are influential in churn predictions. But gaming companies can collect and analyze pretty much none of that data. Hence, tracking only in-game activity would not be enough to explore and prevent the churned players. For real-time data-driven analysis, data from separate sources needs to be integrated, which is frequently unachievable.

Moreover, another major roadblock hindering game developers from tracking player behavior is data security and privacy issues. Data protection laws like GDPR place stringent limitations on the collection and processing of player data. In games, where personal information is collected, with data protection legislation in place, such granularity is difficult to create for churn analysis. If developers potentially ask players about sensitive data, restrictions imposed by law may prevent them from accepting data unless it is anonymized so that analysis can be made without compromising players. This means the data required to conduct churn analysis and churn prediction is often inadequate or missing altogether.

Data is generally reluctant to be shared, particularly in the gaming industry. For many game developers, they have little incentive to make large datasets of player behavior and in-game interactions publicly available as such information can be of great commercial value and competitive advantage. However, this implies limited availability for significant data like churn analysis in the gaming world. Especially large gaming firms fear that competitors could potentially use data from their platform to improve their own strategy and game market share in the gaming industry. Hence, this data is retained for internal use only and is typically not shared with a third party. Also, privacy laws and ethical concerns on player data hinder knowledge sharing, resulting in knowledge sharing being extra difficult. Thus, another reason that led numerous gaming companies to face difficulty in performing the churn analysis is that they do not have tools to either collect data or analyze it. However, large gaming companies also have huge data analytics tools and machine learning algorithms, while small and medium-sized gaming companies do not have access to such technologies. Such tools are valuable for analyzing player behavior more in-depth, predicting churn rates, and creating early warning systems. Yet, not all small game studios will likely have the funds and resources to invest in something like this, as these kinds of technologies do come with a price. This distorts proper churn analysis and hinders developing countermeasures to losing players.

Conversely, game developers and researchers also face a critical challenge in executing data retrieval. At game companies, the data required to study churn and player churn is usually found in unstructured and difficult-to-find formats on their systems. Since games can be played on various platforms and devices, player data can exist in different databases, in different formats and with different richness. Although this data must be collected correctly and integrated for analysis, it is the case that most companies do not have the infrastructure necessary to perform such data integrations. This makes it challenging for researchers and game analysts to obtain accurate and holistic data. Without this, one fails to dig into the numbers to see why games see certain churn rates and what needs to be tentatively done to fix it, and when. Without data, subjects like churn analysis have been studied for so long. German gaming companies have been resistant to sharing data, and data is often siloed and hard to access, which has led analyses to be performed off only small pools of data. Churn estimation and player behavior analysis can be inaccurate or incomplete. That means that high-level analyses will only be possible, making it impossible for wider and ever more complex meta-factors to be measured with regard to their effects on the in-game dynamic and player churn. Consequently, this very initial analysis does not provide game developers with enough information to devise strategies.

When developing strategies to reduce player churn, not only the continuity of users' in-game experience should be considered, but also its ethical relevance. In particular, the use of manipulative design elements (e.g., dark patterns) or addictive mechanics may increase player engagement but are ethically controversial (Zagal et al., 2013). Therefore, game developers should adopt an approach that centres on user welfare and autonomy in churn reduction strategies. For ethically sustainable churn management, transparent feedback systems that respect players' decision-making processes, in-game time management suggestions, and personalization options that offer control to the user are important (King & Delfabbro, 2019). Furthermore, game design that is sensitive to the player's motivations and limitations contributes to maintaining user health while building long-term engagement (Nieborg & Poell, 2018). Especially in the context of micro-payment systems, which are often encountered in the free-to-play model, the ethical boundaries of spending incentives should be carefully drawn and exploiting players' cognitive weaknesses should be avoided (Zendle & Cairns, 2018). Such ethical approaches not only ensure long-term success in reducing churn rates, but also allow gaming companies to develop a trusting relationship with users. As a result, ethical design principles in strategies to reduce churn are not only a requirement of social responsibility, but also a strategic element for sustainable user engagement.

In addition, limited data sharing hinders the development of a broader perspective on the overall size and diversity of the gaming industry. One reason for that is that academic studies often have to be limited to one game or one small gaming company, leading to no generalizable findings. In particular, this is a challenge faced by small and medium-sized gaming companies that do not always have access to data analytics and machine learning algorithms. Consequently, it results in a limited area for studies regarding churn analysis and player loyalty in academia, and a dead end for more industry-oriented studies involving data that could benefit the playfield.

In conclusion, company-specific data-sharing limitations present a notable barrier to further in-depth analyses of churn and player behavior in academia. Game companies, which are, of course, large enterprises, are rarely transparent with player data that is shared wisely. They would rather the data be kept private to avoid competitors usurping their trade secrets and leveraging competitive advantage. It prevents academics from having full data sets to do research in this part of the industry. So, most academic studies either rely solely on publicly available data or rely on limited data that companies provide, which can limit the depth and accuracy of churn analyses. The sharing of data enables studies to examine general gaming dynamics and create effective methods to minimize player churn.

To promote data sharing, gaming companies, especially the large ones, should embrace a more transparent and collaborative mentality. Companies could build secure data-sharing platforms to channel specific data sets to researchers while shielding anonymized data and player information. In addition, closer partnerships between industry and academia should be established, and ethical standards for data-sharing should be developed. By this approach, scientists will have access to broader and more diverse data sets, further enabling deeper and more generalizable research on churn analysis and player behavior. So, this sharing of data will also help in the development of the gaming industry by helping the companies to create more effective strategies for player loyalty.

In this section, the ethical and practical challenges faced in the process of sharing player data are discussed. It is emphasized that ethical principles such as data privacy, user consent, transparency and data security are critical to building and maintaining player trust.

CONCLUSION

Player churn is still one of the biggest challenges for the gaming industry. However, with increasing competition and players becoming choosy about where they invest both their time and money, game developers need to turn to strategies that do not just drive attraction of new players but also encourage retention of existing ones. To succeed, clubs need to engage players and create a tailor-made experience that adapts with the changing needs of the players. Never underestimate the importance of in-game rewards, social interaction, dynamic content, and fair monetization systems. Fortnite, League of Legends, and World of Warcraft are established industry examples that prove games which focus on player enjoyment rather than monetization by bringing regular updates, balanced in-game economies, and efforts to build community have ultimate success. Data-driven approaches have become essential for player retention and understanding churn. As we've shared, AI and machine learning technologies have become imperative tools for forecasting and combating churn.

The power of leveraging player data to offer personalized content, in-game rewards, and interventions was exemplified in games such as Candy Crush Saga. Predictive powers on which players are likely to churn or not and targeted incentives to lure them back—this is truly a game-changer. Having a data-driven approach, these kinds of solutions can empower developers to be proactive rather than reactive, in which they can act before the issue leads to player churn. As AI models continue to evolve, future iterations will enable even more targeted and effective predictions and interventions to improve retention strategies. Building engaging and diverse in-game play also contributes significantly to lowered churn. Both Augmented Reality and Virtual Reality technologies are among the coolest things out there in gaming today. Augmented games like Pokémon GO, and future VR games, will produce even more exciting, interactive, and emotionally immersive worlds that take the decision of leaving the game to the next level. These technologies can deliver experiences that go beyond playing a game and into living in one, fostering new emotional bonds and making players want to return. With these technologies improving and more widely available, the future of gaming will likely encompass experiences that are less replicable, with worlds players are less willing to leave.

Understanding of social factors and ongoing community engagement also feed heavily into churn reduction. History has shown us, with the success of World of Warcraft and League of Legends, for example, that players who feel part of the community and have strong bonds in a game's social space are more likely to stick around. These might include things like guild (or guild square), co-op missions, or competitive features, all of which contribute to community-building much more than, say, a chat or a forum ever could, and which can help players forge lasting bonds over time. Games in the future will continue this path, crafting environments that encourage collaboration and communication. Indeed, players are increasingly hitting the market for more engaging social modes in their games, and any title that falls short of these expectations will likely have to deal with falling retention rates. By cultivating communities and keeping players engaged with one another, developers can ensure that the social ties will keep players coming back to their games. Long-term retention overall is also heavily connected to fair monetization and game economy balance. With players growing increasingly aware of predatory monetization strategies, including pay-to-win systems, there is a higher demand for transparency and fairness than ever before. Meanwhile, those games that opt for a cosmetic-only model or attempt to implement blockchain technology to allow players to possess real assets within the game—Axie Infinity, as an example—seem just so much friendlier to the player. By employing ethical monetization practices, in which players will not be disadvantaged for not spending money, developers can create trust that translates into long-term satisfaction. This will help to ensure that we have players who will not find the retail model at odds with their spending habits by leading the industry in sustainable player-centric monetization practices that are fair to both sides.

Lastly, it is crucial to keep adding new content through live service models to encourage continued player engagement over long periods. Regular add-ons that introduce new mechanics, events, or limited-time activities have proven vital to keeping the game as a whole feeling fresh, as evidenced by games like Apex Legends and Destiny 2. Such updates keep existing players engaged without causing it to become stale and bring in new players interested in the content. Additionally, providing platforms for user-generated assets (like community-made skins or levels) increases players' sense of agency and investment in the IP helps decrease churn. Games that continue to iterate with the communities they have and will optimize for the content that keeps them engaged will find themselves with veteran players and new players alike well into the future.

Overall, player churn is a persistent challenge, but by implementing a mixture of personalized engagement, immersive technologies, social connectivity, fair monetization practices, and constant content updates, developers can drastically lower such churn and increase retention. By using this information to inform richer data-driven retention strategies, the impact of predictive analytics on the gaming industry is likely to be even more pronounced, with better and more tailored experiences for players all around, as artificial intelligence and machine learning technology continues to evolve. There will be a move towards more collaborative experiences, where players aren't just interacting with the game but also each other. Developers who navigate these dynamics will be able to formulate games that capture the eye of the audience and maintain engagement over time. Leveraging these strategies is crucial and, with time, the gaming industry will only grow big with loyal player bases and thriving communities at its core.

REFERENCES

Andersen, J., Nielsen, M. L., & Sandholdt, H. (2018). Designing for player experience in digital games. In *Proceedings of the 2018 DiGRA International Conference*, (pp. 1–15)

Anderson, C. A. (2020). Fortnite: A case study of cultural impact. *Games Studies*, *25*(1), 34–42.

Axie Infinity. (2023). *Axie Infinity: Blockchain-based gaming* [Video game]. Sky Mavis.

Baker, L., Johnson, K., & Smith, R. (2020). Customer retention strategies in the digital age. *Journal of Business Marketing*, *45*(3), 112–129.

Baker, S. R., Baugh, B., & Sammon, M. (2020). Measuring customer churn and interconnectedness. SPGMI: Compustat Fundamentals.

Blizzard Entertainment. (2023). *World of Warcraft: Guilds and social group dynamics*. Blizzard Entertainment.

Chaffey, D. (2023). *Why customer retention is key to improving profitability*. Smart Insights.

Chen, H., & Lee, S. (2023). Blockchain technology in gaming: Fairness and transparency. *Journal of Digital Economics*, *5*(2), 112–126.

Chen, Y., & Wang, X. (2022). Analyzing customer churn: A comprehensive approach. *International Journal of Business Analytics*, *9*(2), 45–62.

Chen, Z., Liu, Y., & Xu, B. (2020). Examining player satisfaction in online multiplayer games: The role of performance and fairness. *Entertainment Computing*, *35*, 100372. DOI: 10.1016/j.entcom.2020.100372

Cheung, G., Zimmermann, T., & Nagappan, N. (2014). The first hour experience: How the initial play can engage (or lose) new players. In *Proceedings of the first ACM SIGCHI Annual Symposium on Computer-Human Interaction in Play*. DOI: 10.1145/2658537.2658540

Deterding, S., Dixon, D., Khaled, R., & Nacke, L. (2011). From game design elements to gamefulness: Defining "gamification". In *Proceedings of the 2011 Annual Conference on Human Factors in Computing Systems* (pp. 2425–2434). ACM. DOI: 10.1145/2181037.2181040

Drachen, A., Seif El-Nasr, M., & Canossa, A. (2013). Game analytics – The basics. In Seif El-Nasr, M., & Canossa, A. (Eds.), *Game Analytics* (pp. 13–40). Springer. DOI: 10.1007/978-1-4471-4769-5_2

Drachen, A., Sifa, R., Runge, J., Thurau, C., Bauckhage, C., & Klabjan, D. (2013). Guns, swords and data: Clustering of player behavior in computer games in the wild. In *Proceedings of IEEE Conference on Computational Intelligence and Games* (pp. 163–170). IEEE. DOI: 10.1109/CIG.2013.6633613

Ducheneaut, N., Yee, N., Nickell, E., & Moore, R. J. (2007). The life and death of online gaming communities: A look at guilds in World of Warcraft. *Proceedings of the SIGCHI Conference on Human Factors in Computing Systems*, 839–848. DOI: 10.1145/1240624.1240750

Federoff, M. A. (2002). Heuristics and usability guidelines for the creation and evaluation of fun in video games. Master's thesis, Indiana University.

Fernández del Río, A., Guitart, A., & Periáñez, Á. (2021). A time series approach to player churn and conversion in videogames. *Intelligent Data Analysis*, *25*(1), 177–203. DOI: 10.3233/IDA-194940

Gold, C. (2020). *Fighting churn with data: The science and strategy of customer retention*. Manning Publishing.

Hadiji, F., Sifa, R., Drachen, A., Thurau, C., Kersting, K., & Bauckhage, C. (2014). Predicting player churn in the wild. In *2014 IEEE Conference on Computational Intelligence and Games* (pp. 1–8). IEEE.

Hamari, J., Alha, K., Hämäläinen, P., Linturi, H., & Ihonen, M. (2017). Why do people play games? A review of game motivations. In *Proceedings of the 2017 Annual Symposium on Computer-Human Interaction in Play* (pp. 9–20). ACM.

Hamari, J., Alha, K., Järvelä, S., Kivikangas, J. M., Koivisto, J., & Paavilainen, J. (2020). Why do players buy in-game content? An empirical study on concrete purchase motivations. *Computers in Human Behavior*, *68*, 538–546. DOI: 10.1016/j.chb.2016.11.045

Hamari, J., & Järvinen, A. (2011). Building customer relationship through game mechanics in social games. In Business, Technological, and Social Dimensions of Computer Games: Multidisciplinary Developments (pp. 348–365). IGI Global. DOI: 10.4018/978-1-60960-567-4.ch021

Hamari, J., & Koivisto, J. (2015). Why do people use gamification services? *International Journal of Information Management*, *35*(4), 419–431. DOI: 10.1016/j.ijinfomgt.2015.04.006

Hamari, J., Koivisto, J., & Sarsa, H. (2014). Does gamification work? A literature review of empirical studies on gamification. In *47th Hawaii International Conference on System Sciences* (pp. 3025–3034). IEEE. DOI: 10.1109/HICSS.2014.377

Han, Y.-J., Moon, J., & Woo, J. (2024). Prediction of churning game users based on social activity and churn graph neural networks. *IEEE Access : Practical Innovations, Open Solutions, 12*, 101971–101984. DOI: 10.1109/ACCESS.2024.3429559

Hunicke, R., LeBlanc, M., & Zubek, R. (2004). MDA: A formal approach to game design and game research. In *Proceedings of the AAAI Workshop on Challenges in Game AI* (pp. 1–5). AAAI Press.

Isbister, K., & Schaffer, N. (2008). *Game usability: Advice from the experts for advancing the player experience*. Morgan Kaufmann. DOI: 10.1201/b14580

Jiang, H. (2024). The economic impact of customer churn in modern enterprises. *Strategic Management Review, 16*(1), 78–95.

Jiang, X. (2024). Customer churn data analysis using data mining. *Applied and Computational Engineering, 77*(1), 17–24. DOI: 10.54254/2755-2721/77/20240496

Johnson, M. (2018). Monetization strategies in free-to-play games: The case of League of Legends. *Journal of Game Design and Development, 12*(3), 118–131. DOI: 10.1016/j.jgdd.2018.04.001

Juul, J. (2010). *A casual revolution: Reinventing video games and their players*. MIT Press.

Kelly, A. (2020). The evolution of Fortnite: Player engagement and community events. *Journal of Interactive Media, 18*(3), 56–67. DOI: 10.1016/j.jim.2020.06.005

Kim, S., Choi, D., Lee, E., & Rhee, W. (2017). Churn prediction of mobile and online casual games using play log data. *PLoS One, 12*(6), 1–11. DOI: 10.1371/journal.pone.0180735 PMID: 28678880

King, D. L., & Delfabbro, P. H. (2018). The cognitive psychopathology of internet gaming disorder. *Clinical Psychology Review, 59*, 61–78.

Kulkarni, A., Patel, S., & Rodriguez, M. (2023). Understanding and mitigating customer churn: A multi-industry analysis. *Journal of Customer Insights, 38*(4), 201–220.

Kulkarni, S. A., Upadhyay, Y. D., Shah, N., & Nair, S. (2023). Customer churn prediction using customer data and reviews. In *2023 International Conference on Advanced Computing Technologies and Applications (ICACTA)* (pp. 1–6). IEEE. DOI: 10.1109/ICACTA58201.2023.10393246

Libai, B., Muller, E., & Peres, R. (2009). The diffusion of services. *JMR, Journal of Marketing Research*, *46*(2), 163–175. DOI: 10.1509/jmkr.46.2.163

Liu, X., Xie, M., Wen, X., Li, L., Zhang, H., Yu, P. S., & Zhao, X. (2020). Micro- and macro-level churn analysis of large-scale mobile games. *Knowledge and Information Systems*, *62*(4), 1465–1496. DOI: 10.1007/s10115-019-01394-7

Medler, B. (2011). Player dossiers: Analyzing gameplay data as a reward. Game Studies. *The International Journal of Computer Game Research*, *11*(1). https://gamestudies.org/1101/articles/medler

Miller, A. (2022). League of Legends: Building community and keeping players engaged. *International Journal of Gaming and Computer-Mediated Communication*, *25*(2), 60–75. DOI: 10.1002/ijg.2022.25.2.60

Mojang. (2021). Minecraft active player statistics. Mojang. Retrieved from https://www.mojang.com

Montgomery, M., & Oliver, D. (2021). Sustaining engagement in live service games: Strategies for retention through content updates. *Journal of Interactive Media*, *10*(4), 211–229.

Mustač, K., Bačić, K., Skorin-Kapov, L., & Sužnjević, M. (2022). Predicting player churn of a free-to-play mobile video game using supervised machine learning. *Applied Sciences (Basel, Switzerland)*, *12*(6), 2795. DOI: 10.3390/app12062795

Nguyen, T., Park, J., & Kim, R. (2023). *Blockchain in gaming: Ownership and real-world value*. Crypto Gaming Insights. [White paper]

Niantic. (2023). Pokémon GO: Augmented reality gaming for engagement [Video game]. Niantic.

Nieborg, D. B. (2017). From premium to freemium: The political economy of the app. *Social Media + Society*, *3*(1), 1–12.

Nieborg, D. B., & Poell, T. (2018). The platformization of cultural production: Theorizing the contingent cultural commodity. *New Media & Society*, *20*(11), 4275–4292. DOI: 10.1177/1461444818769694

Óskarsdóttir, M., Gísladóttir, K. E., Stefánsson, R., Gudmundsson, G., Gylfason, G. K., & Helgason, A. R. (2022). Social networks for enhanced player churn prediction in mobile free-to-play games. *Applied Network Science*, *7*(1), 82. DOI: 10.1007/s41109-022-00524-5

Perianez, A., Saas, A., & Guitart, A. (2016). Churn prediction in mobile social games: Towards a complete assessment using survival ensembles. In *Proceedings of the 2016 IEEE International Conference on Data Science and Advanced Analytics (DSAA)* (pp. 564–573). IEEE. DOI: 10.1109/DSAA.2016.84

Pham, T. T., Huang, H., Tseng, F., Cheng, T. C., & Teng, C. (2021). For whom does flow not enhance online gamer loyalty? *Industrial Management & Data Systems, 122*(1), 215–234. DOI: 10.1108/IMDS-05-2021-0338

Prasad, A., Sethi, S. P., & Naik, P. A. (2012). Understanding the impact of churn in dynamic oligopoly markets. *Automatica, 48*(11), 2882–2887. DOI: 10.1016/j.automatica.2012.08.031

Predescu, A., & Mocanu, M. (2020). A data driven survey of video games. In 2020 12th International Conference on Electronics, Computers and Artificial Intelligence (ECAI) (pp. 1–6). IEEE. DOI: 10.1109/ECAI50035.2020.9223203

Reichheld, F. F., & Teal, T. (1996). *The loyalty effect: The hidden force behind growth, profits, and lasting value*. Harvard Business Review Press.

Respawn Entertainment. (2023). *Apex Legends: Seasonal events and player engagement* [Video game]. Respawn Entertainment.

Riot Games. (2023). *League of Legends: The power of social groups in player retention* [Video game]. Riot Games.

Rodriguez, J., & Martinez, L. (2024). Customer acquisition versus retention: A cost-benefit analysis. *Business Strategy Research, 11*(2), 33–47.

Roohi, S., Relas, A., Takatalo, J., Heiskanen, H., & Hämäläinen, P. (2020). Predicting game difficulty and churn without players. In Proceedings of the Annual Symposium on Computer-Human Interaction in Play (CHI PLAY '20) (pp. 585–593). Association for Computing Machinery. DOI: 10.1145/3410404.3414235

Rothmeier, K., Pflanzl, N., Hüllmann, J. A., & Preuss, M. (2021). Prediction of player churn and disengagement based on user activity data of a freemium online strategy game. *IEEE Transactions on Games, 13*(1), 78–88. DOI: 10.1109/TG.2020.2992282

Runge, J., Gao, P., Garcin, F., & Faltings, B. (2014). Churn prediction for high-value players in casual social games. In *2014 IEEE Conference on Computational Intelligence and Games* (pp. 1–8). IEEE. DOI: 10.1109/CIG.2014.6932875

Salen, K., & Zimmerman, E. (2004). *Rules of play: Game design fundamentals*. MIT Press.

Seif El-Nasr, M., Drachen, A., & Canossa, A. (2013). *Game analytics: Maximizing the value of player data*. Springer., DOI: 10.1007/978-1-4471-4769-5

Shneiderman, B., & Plaisant, C. (2010). *Designing the user interface: Strategies for effective human-computer interaction* (5th ed.). Pearson.

Smith, A. (2023). *The future of social gaming: Cross-platform interactions and community dynamics*. Global Gaming Strategies. [Research report]

Smith, A., & Lee, D. (2023). Immersive technologies in gaming: VR and AR's role in player retention. *Journal of Virtual Gaming*, *17*(3), 45–59.

Smith, T., & Johnson, M. (2019). Guild systems and social bonds in MMORPGs: A study of World of Warcraft. *International Journal of Game Studies*, *14*(2), 155–171. DOI: 10.1016/ijgs.2019.14.2.155

Supercell. (2021). Clash of Clans: Player engagement and churn reduction strategies [Video game]. Supercell.

Thompson, R., Lee, S., & Kim, J. (2023). Predictive modeling of customer churn in service industries. *Journal of Service Research*, *26*(3), 267–285.

Weiss, I., & Vilenchik, D. (2023). Predicting churn in online games by quantifying diversity of engagement. *Big Data*, *11*(4), 282–295. DOI: 10.1089/big.2022.0109 PMID: 36940288

Williams, D., Caplan, S., & Yee, N. (2006). Who plays, how much, and why? Debunking the stereotypical gamer profile. *Journal of Computer-Mediated Communication*, *11*(4), 993–1018. DOI: 10.1111/j.1083-6101.2008.00428.x

WIRED. (2023). The best games have the smartest learning curves.

Wohn, D. Y. (2011). The role of social affordances in online games: Exploring social behavior and social networks. *Journal of Computer-Mediated Communication*, *16*(4), 451–470. DOI: 10.1111/j.1083-6101.2011.01548.x

Yee, N. (2006). Motivations for play in online games. *Cyberpsychology & Behavior*, *9*(6), 772–775. DOI: 10.1089/cpb.2006.9.772 PMID: 17201605

Yee, N. (2006). The demographics, motivations, and derived experiences of users of massively multi-user online graphical environments. *Presence (Cambridge, Mass.)*, *15*(3), 309–329. DOI: 10.1162/pres.15.3.309

Zagal, J. P., Björk, S., & Lewis, C. (2013). Dark patterns in the design of games. In Foundations of Digital Games 2013. https://www.fdg2013.org/papers/fdg2013_paper_17.pdf

Zendle, D., & Cairns, P. (2018). Video game loot boxes are linked to problem gambling: Results of a large-scale survey. *PLoS One*, *13*(11), e0206767. DOI: 10.1371/journal.pone.0206767 PMID: 30462669

Zhang, L., & Siewiorek, D. P. (1999). Error models for robust system design: A case study in multimedia servers. *IEEE Transactions on Reliability*, *48*(2), 101–113. DOI: 10.1109/24.784834

Zheng, A., Chen, L., Xie, F., Tao, J., Fan, C., & Zheng, Z. (2020). Keep you from leaving: Churn prediction in online games. In Nah, Y., Cui, B., Lee, S. W., Yu, J. X., Moon, Y. S., & Whang, S. E. (Eds.), Lecture Notes in Computer Science: Vol. 12113. *Database Systems for Advanced Applications. DASFAA 2020*. Springer., DOI: 10.1007/978-3-030-59416-9_16

Zhou, R., Rau, P. L. P., & Salvendy, G. (2012). Users' trust in and satisfaction with recommendation agents. *Computers in Human Behavior*, *28*(6), 2350–2359. DOI: 10.1016/j.chb.2012.07.032

Chapter 8

Applications, Challenges, and Future Prospects of Enhancing Medical Imaging With Neural Networks

Aman Dubey
https://orcid.org/0009-0008-8821-9491
Maulana Azad National Institute of Technology, India

Mohit Choubey
https://orcid.org/0009-0003-2968-360X
Maulana Azad National Institute of Technology, India

Yogesh Kumar Gupta
https://orcid.org/0000-0002-9438-6279
University of Petroleum and Energy Studies, India & Maulana Azad National Institute of Technology, India

Jigyendra Sen Yadav
https://orcid.org/0000-0002-4250-291X
Maulana Azad National Institute of Technology, India

ABSTRACT

Acute and accurate disease diagnosis is of utmost significance in modern healthcare but is generally not possible with conventional imaging techniques. As AI-based techniques offer higher diagnostic accuracy and speed, their adoption is increasingly becoming vital. Through automated processing, recent advances in deep

DOI: 10.4018/979-8-3373-6097-3.ch008

learning have revolutionized medical imaging, enhancing anomaly identification, organ segmentation, and disease detection. Convolutional neural networks (CNNs), generative adversarial networks (GANs), transformer models, hybrid models, and more are introduced in this chapter. Revolutionary methods like Federated Learning (FL) and Self-Supervised Learning (SSL) are also discussed, along with their usage in different imaging modalities. The chapter also discusses issues including data sparsity, model interpretability, and ethics. A detailed case study on the application of transfer learning for medical image classification also showcases the capability of artificial intelligence to augment clinical diagnosis.

INTRODUCTION

Artificial intelligence (AI) has transformed healthcare by changing how we identify, treat, and keep track of patients by enabling more individualized treatments and generating more accurate diagnoses. This technology is significantly enhancing healthcare research and results. Artificial neural networks (ANNs) and other machine-learning techniques are being employed by medical organizations for improving patient care while lowering costs. Over a few decades, technologies like X-ray, computed tomography (CT), magnetic resonance imaging (MRI), and ultrasound have changed drastically, providing early detection of underlying diseases with more accuracy (Figure 1). These advancements have helped in taking care of the patient by providing the timely diagnosis that saves lives. The emerging deep learning networks for medical image analysis have proved their capabilities by providing automated, accurate, cost-effective and efficient diagnosis (Chan et al., 2020). From pattern recognition or organ segmentation to disease detection, Neural networks like Convolutional Neural Networks (CNNs), Generative Adversarial Networks (GANs), and transformer models have shown their remarkable performances. For example, incorporating neural networks into medical imaging has been shown to predict not only prognosis but also treatment responses in case of gastric cancer (Fu et al., 2023). This helped deliver personalized medical interventions helping the patient outcomes. Similarly, a study (Chan et al., 2020) shows that these using these networks reduced the time to read and understand the images of digital breast tomosynthesis (DBT) by more than 50%.

Figure 1. Workflow of Neural Network-Based Medical Diagnosis

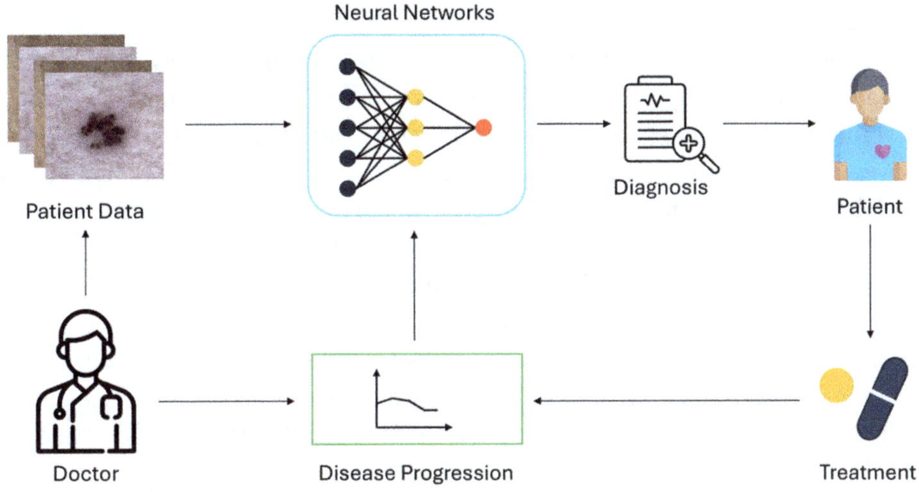

But still after all of these advancements we can find that these technologies often face a few challenges. Image quality may change greatly due to scanning equipment like some human or machine errors in image acquisition or image reconstruction while performing or evaluating the results of CT scans, the large volume and complexity of imaging data also keeps on increasing, and human monitoring and decision making is subjective, all of this may introduce variations that can impair diagnostic efficiency and accuracy (Litjens et al., 2017; Shen, Wu, & Suk, 2017). These challenges tell us that we require automated systems which are able to handle the complexities of medical image processing along with providing reliable accuracy and efficiency eventually building human and AI trust.

The clinical impact of AI-driven models is being woven into workflows. These AI-models are able to continuously assist radiologists, doctors and patients as they are proving their fitness in finding anomalies, shortening the time to diagnose a disease. These traits eventually help in providing the patients an effective care and timely treatment. Deep learning has nailed pneumonia detection (Rajpurkar et al., 2017), rivaled dermatologists in skin lesion classification (Esteva et al., 2017), and automated organ segmentation in MRI and CT scans, streamlined everything from surgery planning to radiation therapy (Isensee et al., 2021).

These models aren't just here to prove themselves. They're here to help us saving hours off workflows as these models find what even the human eyes might miss. Imagine a scenario, where there is need to provide remote consultations maybe a remote rural clinic, or another where a patient wants to understand their results and get second opinions about their treatment's effectiveness, or there is an emergency situation where these models can help assist the first responders by analyzing the images on site and make quick decisions for patient care. That's the revolution unfolding.

Yet, the road ahead isn't all smooth as these models don't tell how they've come to a conclusion like why a tumor was detected by a CNN model? This lack of interpretability remains a challenge as clinicians won't and shouldn't trust a black box. To overcome this challenge, techniques like explainable AI (XAI), including Grad-CAM, LIME, saliency maps, are starting to explain the model's decisions, showing why a tumor was detected in a patient's results (Selvaraju et al., 2017; Lundberg & Lee, 2017). Generalization is one more thing to be properly taken care of as a model trained on one dataset might miss understanding features of another's which may cause biased decisions making the model a failure in an integrated clinical environment (Zech et al., 2018). And what if we overcome all these challenges and finally tries to integrate these models into real world clinical workflows? Since, many healthcare facilities still use outdated systems, those may not be compatible enough to handle modern AI solutions. Those legacy systems might have data in such formats which may not be easily accessible by AI algorithms (He et al., 2019). These all aren't just some speedbumps, these challenges must be taken care of as they can make-or-break the entire workflow, calling for technical breakthroughs, standardized protocols, and regulatory guardrails to ensure safety and equity (Litjens et al., 2017; Topol, 2019).

To summarize this, neural networks are the key which can unlock new unseen possibilities in medical imaging. They automate feature extraction, boost image quality through augmentation, and capture global context with transformer-driven insights. This chapter traces that arc from the traditional methods to deep learning's cutting edge capping it with a case study on lung disease detection that grounds these advances in real-world stakes. Looking forward, hybrid models, federated learning, and self-supervised approaches promise not just accuracy but accessibility, envisioning a healthcare system that's leaner, smarter, and relentlessly patient-focused. That's the future we're chasing one where technology doesn't just assist but inspires.

BACKGROUND STUDY

During the last few decades, the domain of medical image analysis has seen a striking change. Earlier, traditional diagnosis methods were used which were heavily dependent on human handcrafted features. But now advanced AI-enabled methods support automated yet accurate diagnoses. This segment talks about primary contributions in literature outlining this progress from the view that how these innovations in computational procedures is raising diagnosis efficiency. These improved diagnoses eventually lead to more accurate clinical decision process. Figure 1 shows important landmarks to show how the medical imaging has evolved with time, from the discovery of X-rays to the utilization of AI-based in medical diagnosis. Further, Table 1 shows key milestones in medical imaging. It also highlights the insights of each study and their impact on diagnostic practices.

Figure 2. Evolution of Medical Imaging Technologies

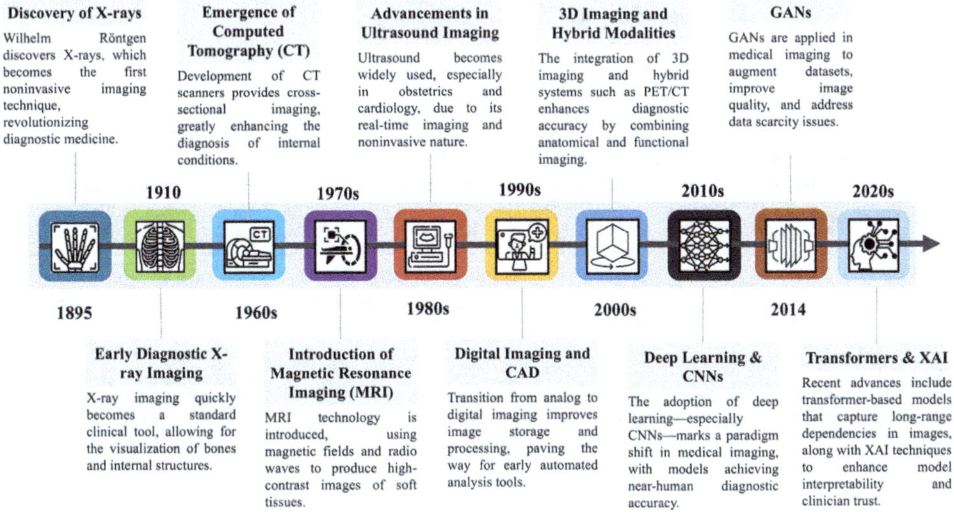

Table 1. Evolution of Seminal Contributions to Medical Imaging

Author (s)	*Publication*	*Insights*	*Impact*
Röntgen, W. C. (1896)	Nature, 53(1369), 274-276.	Discovered X-rays, enabling non-invasive visualization of internal body structures.	Laid the foundation for diagnostic radiology, fundamentally transforming medical imaging.
Lodwick, G. S., Keats, T. E., & Dorst, J. P. (1963)	Radiology, 80(2), 273-275.	Applied Bayes rule for bone tumor diagnosis, an early use of computational methods in imaging.	Pioneered the integration of statistical methods into diagnostics, influencing later computational approaches.
Haralick, R. M., Shanmugam, K., & Dinstein, I. (1973)	IEEE Transactions on Systems, Man, and Cybernetics, 3(6), 610-621.	Introduced texture features for image classification, fundamental for tissue characterization.	Established quantitative image analysis techniques that remain integral for feature extraction in imaging.

continued on following page

Table 1. Continued

Author (s)	*Publication*	*Insights*	*Impact*
Lo, S.-C., Lou, S.-L., Lin, J.-S., Freedman, M. T., Chien, M. V., & Mun, S. K. (1995)	IEEE Transactions on Medical Imaging, 14(4), 711-718.	Used CNNs for lung nodule detection, an early application before the deep learning boom.	Demonstrated the potential of convolutional networks, paving the way for advanced deep learning in medical imaging.
Ronneberger, O., Fischer, P., & Brox, T. (2015)	In Medical Image Computing and Computer-Assisted Intervention – MICCAI 2015 (pp. 234-241). Springer.	Introduced U-Net for medical image segmentation, effective with limited data.	Revolutionized segmentation techniques; U-Net has become a benchmark model in the field.
Wolterink, J. M., Dinkla, A. M., Savenije, M. H. F., Seevinck, P. R., van den Berg, C. A. T., & Išgum, I. (2017)	In Simulation and Synthesis in Medical Imaging (pp. 14-23). Springer.	Applied GANs for MR to CT translation using unpaired data.	Paved the way for innovative image synthesis techniques, bridging modality gaps with generative models.
Chen, J., Lu, Y., Yu, Q., Luo, X., Adeli, E., Wang, Y., Lu, L., Yuille, A. L., & Zhou, Y. (2021)	arXiv	Proposed TransUNet, integrating transformers into U-Net for segmentation.	Marked a significant evolution by incorporating transformer architectures, influencing modern segmentation strategies.
Ahmed, M., Tooba, B., Khan, R. A., & Nasir, S. (2024)	arXiv	Integrated CNNs with XAI for interpretable breast cancer diagnosis.	Emphasized the importance of explainability in AI, enhancing clinical trust and paving the way for transparent diagnostic systems.

Traditional Diagnostic Methods

Early computer-aided diagnosis (CAD) in medical imaging relied on the usage of traditional image processing techniques. Methods like thresholding, edge detection, and morphological operations were used to help doctors by spotting abnormalities and segmenting anatomical structures in images. These techniques were highly dependent on human intervention. Engineers and clinicians had to team up to create custom filters that can find details like texture, shape and brightness. These methods were a good start targeted in the direction of automatic diagnoses but these were not perfect solutions as these systems performed poorly when image quality was not consistent and they frequently missed fainted clues in the data which could have given valuable insights to understanding a patient's situation. Because of it, even though the early CAD was able to assist radiologists and point out the areas for doctors to double check, it was not able to stand alone without human intervention. For example, classifying malignant and benign lesions with these methods was problematic that resulted in nonuniform and often unreliable diagnostic results (Cheng et al., 2021; Gao et al., 2022). One more such example tells us that some signs of early-stage cancer growth may totally be resulted in either cancer detection or a malignant and life-threatening tumor may have been found benign. These inefficiencies of our methods resulted in diagnostic errors in intricate instances (Ronneberger et al., 2015). With the inflexibility of these methods, it was not trustworthy to use these methods when serious medical attention is needed. But these methods pointed to the requirement for flexible, data-driven approaches that can identify minute details without the need for a great deal of manual supervision and building trust among clinicians, patient and AI.

Transition to Machine Learning

To address the limitations of traditional diagnostic methods, the field of CAD gradually came to adopt machine learning techniques. Machine Learning (ML) is a subset of artificial intelligence that enables learning from data itself and improve its performance without the need of a programmer for each and every task. Early research utilized statistical models like Support Vector Machines (SVMs), decision trees, and random forests, being applied on features which were extracted from medical images. These features are more commonly known as hand-engineered features. These are carefully designed based on expert knowledge and then this further capture critical information for input data. For example, texture descriptors like Local Binary Patterns and shape descriptors were used to help segment as well as classify various pathologies like tumors and lesions. These machine learning techniques were proven to be remarkable improvement over the traditional rule-based techniques. However, their performance was heavily dependent to the quality of those handcrafted features. For example, if these shape descriptors failed to properly represent the essential characteristics of the images, then the model will struggle and it will not be able to provide reliable results. Consequently, these strategies tended to have trouble generalizing across wide imaging datasets and were not able to represent the complete complexity of the data (Yang et al., 2021). Thus, even though, these machine learning models were showing their effectiveness over conventional techniques, this dependency of feature engineering limited their use in CAD.

Emergence of Deep Learning

The advent of deep learning was transformative breakthrough in medical imaging domain that reshaped diagnostic capabilities. CNNs became the new standard because of their remarkable ability for automatically learning hierarchical representations directly from raw image data. This shift eliminated the need of manually engineering the features. This also discovered complex patterns of images which in turn enhanced diagnostic accuracy. CNNs precisely outline tumor boundaries which aids in treatment monitoring. A study (Rajpurkar et al., 2017) has shown detection of pneumonia on chest X-rays with great precision and another (Esteva et al., 2017) detected skin cancer with dermatologist's level of accuracy. These models are highly efficient in accurately mapping of organ support applications like radio therapy. These networks can classify images into multiple disease states which can help understand disease progression and can aid in better treatment planning. As found in studies conducted by (Rajendran et al., 2023) and (Song et al., 2020), deep CNNs have been shown to produce very high accuracy exceeding or being at par with expert clinicians. These architectures have been improved by ongoing research, and models like as ResNet, DenseNet, and EfficientNet are showing great promise in medical field as these have shown improved diagnostic accuracies in a variety of applications, let it be the detection of retinal diseases or the classification of brain tumors (He et al., 2016; Huang et al., 2017; Tan & Le, 2019). While deeper layers learn complex features, skip connections help handling the vanishing gradient problem by allowing alternative paths for gradient to flow making deeper networks perform better making ResNets and DenseNets a great success. Parameter efficiency of EfficientNet has low memory footprint and allows for faster training and inferencing making them suitable for edge devices. This marks a milestone in clinical reliability. These improvements stem from the ability of CNNs to auto extract features, reduce human bias and streamline workflows. CNNs also exhibit stable performances across different imaging modalities like X-ray, MRI or CT, varying clinical environments and also among different patient demographics. This makes CNNs robust making them useful in global healthcare settings.

Figure 3(a) shows traditional machine learning approaches where manual feature engineering is accompanied by classification via an SVM classifier. Figure 3(b) depicts deep learning-based automatic feature extraction where a CNN-based model extracts hierarchical features directly from raw image data and classifies the output.

Figure 3. Comparison of Traditional Machine Learning and Deep Learning-Based Feature Extraction (a) (b)

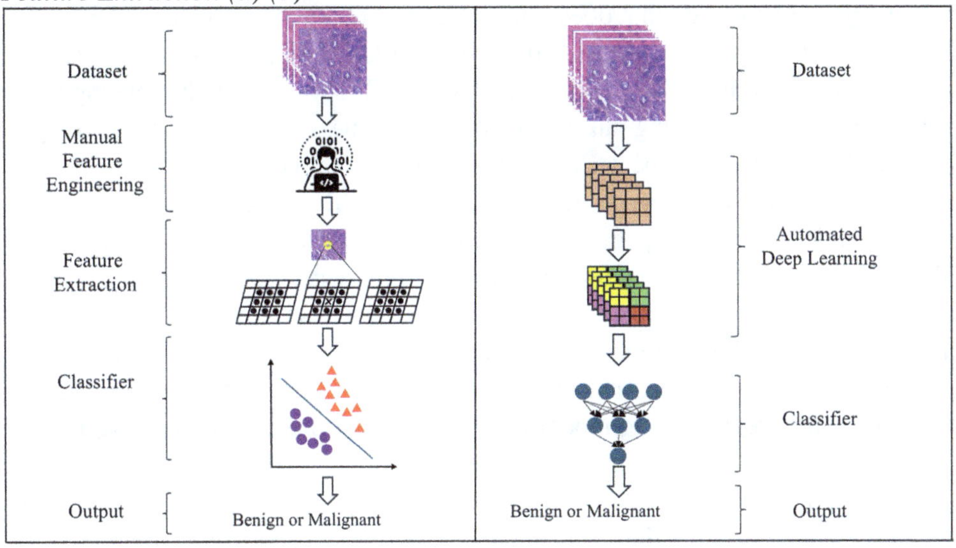

Advancements Beyond CNNs: GANs and Transformers

After seeing the remarkable success of CNNs, researchers started trying to tackle the challenges of data scarcity. To overcome this, they came up with Generative Adversarial Networks (GANs). GANs have so far proven themselves to be a versatile method to create synthetic images which are then used for augmenting the dataset and enhancement of diagnostic results (Yi et al., 2019). These images closely mimic the actual original datasets which helps to utilize them with the original data for training the model. A recent study (Liu et al., 2023) showed that GAN-based augmentation will result in significant enhancements of tumor detection and classification. High fidelity images generated from GANs have been shown to mitigate overfitting which improved model generalization. It has proven to be extremely useful in scenarios where data is very limited and because of this scarcity models were overfitting (Chen et al., 2025). It also helps with image reconstruction as it improves low quality scans, and enhances datasets (Goodfellow et al., 2014; Yi et al., 2019). There are many ethical restrictions, privacy concerns and the need of proper expert annotations which limits the growth of datasets. GANs act like a boon in this scenario as these networks generate synthetic data which does not belong to an actual individual so it protects a patient's confidentiality. For instance, GANs have been used to generate high-resolution MRI scans from limited data, offering a lifeline to under-resourced research and clinical settings (Zeng et al., 2024). Thus, GANs contribute to the maintenance of ethical standards in medical research by producing synthetic data that does not correspond to actual individuals.

Meanwhile, transformer models have also marked their presence in the medical image analysis domain. Vision Transformers (ViTs) were initially developed for natural language processing but they've their usefulness in medical image analysis as well. Vision Transformers (ViTs) and similar architectures use self-attention mechanisms to extract long-range dependencies within images. This gives a very detailed understanding of spatial context where CNNs lack (Dosovitskiy et al., 2020; Vaswani et al., 2017). ViTs combine local features with global context and thus, are able to analyze complex structures in medical images. This becomes extremely advantageous for challenging tasks like multi-organ segmentation, that effectively delineates the liver, spleen, and kidneys in a single CT scan with high precision, they merge different imaging modalities like MRI and PET for richer insights and improving diagnostic accuracy through data fusion. A study (Liu et al., 2023) indicated that transformer-based models are superior to traditional CNNs for multi-organ segmentation and other sophisticated tasks. Additionally, the attention maps generated by ViTs provide details about their decision-making which increases clinician belief, which is crucial for adoption of AI in healthcare (Ribeiro, Singh, & Guestrin, 2016).

There are hybrid architectures which combines CNNs, GANs, and transformers. These architectures are transforming the state of the art. CNNs look into the nitty-gritty of picture information, GANs generate synthetic images to handle data imbalances, and transformers blend it all together with an outsider's perspective on the spatial connections. Recent studies have shown these hybrids surpassing standalone models. In one such study, hybrid architectures were shown to be highly effective in diagnosis by leveraging CNNs' feature extraction ability, GANs' data augmentation capabilities, and transformers' contextual depth (Xu et al., 2025; He et al., 2023). This is not a little progress but is a leap beyond the limitations which the AI domain was facing from past decade. Traditional approaches focused too much on individual features and disregarded the overall context of the data which caused issues like overfitting, where model fails to perform well on unseen new data (Handcrafted Features, 2010). Even though CNNs automated the procedure, but these models also faced issues as they struggled with limited data or remote dependencies (LeCun et al., 2015). Hybrid models bridge these gaps by combining expert designing and automated feature extraction together. It helps making the models robust, flexible and able to handle complex input features. Figure 4 illustrates the historical progression of artificial intelligence techniques in medical imaging, from feature-based machine learning to deep learning and transformer models.

Figure 4. Timeline of Machine Learning and Deep Learning in Medical Imaging

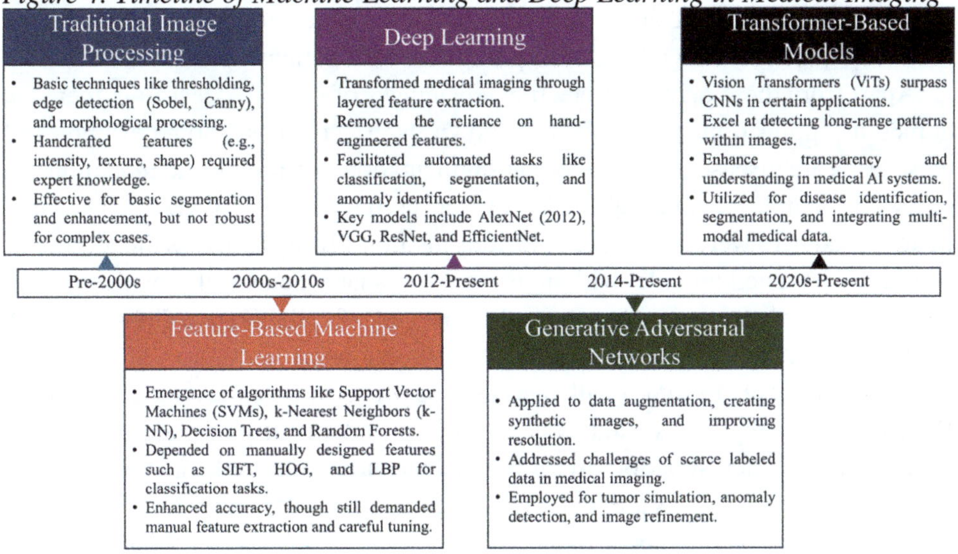

Emerging Trends: Federated and Self-Supervised Learning

FL is a new rapidly emerging paradigm in medical domain. There are various laws which restricts the patient's data to be shared for example Health Insurance Portability and Accountability Act (HIPAA) that is applicable in the United States and the General Data Protection Regulation (GPDR) that is applicable in Europe. These laws while protect patient's sensitive information and must be followed as per the ethical rules, restricts the growth of AI because of limited datasets. FL is such an approach which ensures that patient's data is kept local. Along with data privacy, FL also ensures that we do not need large and diverse datasets to effectively train our models. How does it do it? In centralized machine learning models where data from multiple institutions is gathered and kept into a single repository and then models are trained on this data. But in FL we see a rather distributed approach. In this approach, every participating hospital or clinic or any such entity trains a model on their own dataset and only the parameters are sent to a central server, not the data itself. These parameters from different entities are then aggregated from all the upcoming and a global model is constructed based on these. This model is then reshared for multiple refinements. This approach does not only allow the data privacy concern it also protects the patient's data from breaches. A study (Kaissis et al., 2020) showed that FL was used in a multi entity environment, focused on brain tumor segmentation, achieved a remarkable accuracy of 85% for lung cancer detection from CT scans of different hospitals. It very closely matches 87% of that of centralized models. It shows that FL is highly capable in efficiently utilizing the collective information while not compromising with patient's privacy.

Apart from these privacy protecting advantages of federated learning, there are numerous applications where FL has shown its effectiveness. Some examples of these tasks are disease detection, organ segmentation and prognostic modelling. In one such example (Dayan et al., 2021) FL was used to detect COVID-19. The input images used here were X-rays, here various institutes from all across the globe collaboratively trained a model without the need to share their local sensitive patient data. These applications further strengthen the idea of collaborative global research especially in medical field during crisis like situations.

However, there are some challenges as well which further warrants exploration. Data Heterogeneity also called as non-IID (non-independent and identically distributed) is one such situation. In this, data distributions from distinct entities like hospitals, clinics or others are found to be significantly differing. This issue causes the performance of the model to degrade. It happens because local data may not always be a good enough representation of the much wider population. To mitigate this problem, researchers have proposed personalized federated learning (Hsu et al., 2019) and federal domain adaptation (Peng et al., 2020). Personalized federated learning works by tailoring the global model to individual entity's dataset while federal domain adaptation works by aligning features across diverse datasets. Another critical challenge with FL is communication efficiency. Here the continuous model updates often strain the resources associated with the network especially in imaging tasks where large neural networks are very commonly utilized. To solve this, techniques like gradient compression and asynchronous FL have been proposed. Where gradient compression works by transmitting only the significant updates and asynchronous FL reduces synchronization overhead (Konečný et al., 2016; Dai et al., 2024). Apart from these, we know that FL depends on computational resources at each participant. This raise concerns as smaller entities like smaller clinics may not have appropriate infrastructures to contribute effectively which skews model development towards these entities which have better resources. One future research could be targeted for exploring cloud-based solutions to democratize participation of all the involved entities. Despite all of these challenges and setbacks, FLs ability to provide secure and collaborative model development sets it as a cornerstone of modern medical imaging research that makes the way for more private and ethically sound improvemnts.

One more advancement in medical domain is the emergence of Self-Supervise Learning (SSL). SSL is a very powerful strategy to overcome labelled data scarcity problem which long bothered traditional supervised learning approaches. In these supervised learning, models were entirely dependent on proper extensively annotated datasets. These datasets were annotated by the help of radiologists or pathologists in a medical environment. This process was costly, time consuming and also impractical as there are a large number of medical images which are generated on a daily basis, and many such images are left unlabelled due to time and/or resource constraints. SSLs use this unlabelled data through pretext tasks (such as reconstruction of masked image parts, utilization of contrastive learning to differentiate between similar and dissimilar image pairs or prediction of image rotations) and make models learn important features without explicitly annotating the dataset. These pretext tasks make the model find edges, textures or anatomical structures like features which are further fine tuned with very less labelled data. Then this data is further used to perform tasks like classification or segmentation. A study (Sowrirajan et al., 2021) showed that while classifying chest x-rays, if the pre-training has been done using SSL, the model's accuracy was found to be boosted by 10% compared to models which were trained from scratch. This improvement came when there was very limited labelled samples were available showing SSLs efficacy in data scarcity scenarios.

SSL has many diverse and useful applications in medical imaging which cover various modalities such as detection of tumors or lesions in mammograms (Zimmerer et al., 2019). This is valuable for rare situations where data availability is extremely thin. SSL is used in image denoising as well as improving the resolutions of poorly reconstructed images. These improvements then directly contribute in improving the diagnostic accuracy (You et al., 2020). Since, SSL can generalize across various dataset, its applicability becomes promising for transfer learning. In this scenario, models trained for one modality like CT can be used for another like MRI with very less additional labelling required. There's a comprehensive review in BMC Medical Imaging (2024) which shows SSL's success across X-ray, ultrasound, and histopathology which further strengthens its versatile nature.

However, SSL also faces many challenges. The learned representations' effectiveness is greatly dependent on choice of pretext tasks. This may not always be suitable with the unpredictable nature of medical data. To overcome this, various studies are using domain specific pretext tasks (Chen et al., 2020). This domain specific approach predicts parameters or anatomical features to better fit SSL to healthcare needs. One more such limitations of SSL is the cost of pre-training setup of large unlabelled datasets. This may not favour the entities (e.g., smaller clinics or hospitals) with limited resource availability. Future directions may utilize integrating SSL with active learning which can help prioritize the most information rich samples for annotation. SSL is showing its effectiveness in medical imaging domain by reducing reliance on labelled datasets which further enhances a model's robust nature. Thus, we can say that SSL helps in those setting where traditional approaches falter.

To address the intertwined challenges of scarcity of labelled datasets and concern of data privacy, FL and SSL are converged together. In this hybrid framework, each entity first use SSL to pretrain local models on its own unlabelled data by using masked imaging or contrastive learning or some other techniques as per the requirement of feature representations. These are then finetuned with available labelled datasets and then fed to FL. Now, in FL only model updates are shared with a central server for forwarding it into a global model. This hybrid approach protects the privacy of patient's data and leverages the availability of unlabelled data reducing the additional cost for annotating the data. A study (Yan et al., 2023) used this hybrid framework for medical image segmentation and the results showed a 5% performance enhancement over standalone FL. In another study (Xu et al., 2025) this hybrid framework was utilized to detect diabetic retinopathy, the results showed a 7% increase in AUC when compared to standalone FL. These studies suggest this hybrid FL-SSL's ability to improve diagnostic precision. If we pre-train using SSL, entities can overcome the bottleneck of data heterogeneity which is common in FL. Such pre trained model learns generalized features from huge unlabelled data before being fine tuned and this process actually help reduce overfitting issues related to local biases. In a study (Zhang et al., 2023) SSL pre-training helped the model to achieve 6% more accuracy over baseline FL by handling variations of mammography equipment. By combining the strengths of FL and SSL we can make a collaborative, secure and data efficient environment for medical imaging research to foster.

Table 2. Comparative Analysis of Federated Learning, Self-Supervised Learning, and Their Hybrid Approach

Aspect	*Federated Learning (FL)*	*Self-Supervising Learning (SSL)*	*Hybrid FL + SSL*
Data Privacy	High (no raw data shared)	Moderate (depends on data usage)	High (combines FL privacy)
Label Dependency	High (requires labeled data for fine-tuning)	Low (uses unlabeled data)	Low (SSL reduces need for labels)
Handling Heterogeneity	Moderate (challenged by data distribution)	High (learns robust representations)	High (SSL mitigates FL heterogeneity)
Performance	Good (with diverse data)	Excellent (with large unlabeled data)	Excellent (combines strengths)
Use Case Example	Multi-institutional tumor segmentation	Anomaly detection in chest X-rays	Privacy-preserving anomaly detection

Summary of Contributions in Existing Research

Table 3 gives an overview of significant research contributions over recent years (2020–2024), reflecting the methodological innovations, imaging applications, and key findings that have propelled the development of AI in medical imaging.

Table 3. Key contributions by researchers in medical imaging domain

Author	*Year*	*Approach*	*Imaging Application*	*Dataset(s)*	*Key contribution*
Cheng et al.	2021	Adaptive thresholding & segmentation	CT scan segmentation	Various CT datasets	Enhanced segmentation performance through adaptive thresholding and improved pre-processing methods
Yang et al.	2021	SVM with advanced feature engineering	Ultrasound image classification	Ultrasound datasets	Demonstrated improved diagnostic accuracy with refined handcrafted features
Rajendran et al.	2023	Deep CNN architectures	Tumor segmentation in MRI	MRI datasets	Achieved significant performance improvements in segmentation tasks using deep CNNs
Song et al.	2020	Deep CNN for disease classification	Skin lesion analysis	Dermoscopic image datasets	Reported high classification accuracy in distinguishing benign from malignant lesions
Liu et al.	2023	GAN-based augmentation	Tumor detection in CT/MRI	Private CT/MRI datasets	Demonstrated enhanced detection performance via synthetic image generation
Liu et al.	2023	Vision Transformers (ViTs)	Multi-organ segmentation	Multi-modality datasets	Outperformed traditional CNNs by capturing global context, improving segmentation accuracy
Tian et al.	2023	Federated learning framework	Chest X-ray classification	Multi-institutional chest X-ray datasets	Developed a privacy-preserving collaborative training framework that improved model generalization
Zeng et al.	2024	Self-supervised learning	Anomaly detection in radiographs	Large-scale unlabeled datasets	Demonstrated that self-supervised pre-training significantly boosts performance in anomaly detection

NEURAL NETWORK ARCHITECTURES IN MEDICAL IMAGING: TECHNICAL OVERVIEW

Medical image analysis has progressed significantly due to the rise of advanced neural network architectures. Here, we give an overview of the fundamental architectures Convolutional Neural Networks (CNNs), Generative Adversarial Networks (GANs), and Transformer-based models and upcoming hybrid methodologies. We explain the mathematical fundamentals of these models and their detailed clinical applications.

Convolutional Neural Networks (CNNs)

Imagine a situation where a computer can be taught to find the tumors in an MRI scan or identify cancerous lesions from skin. That's what convolutional neural networks can easily achieve. These CNNs are not instructed by any person or governed by manual feature engineering, these systems recognize edges, textures and shapes from raw images. These CNNs have many layers, convolutional layers are there to detect features, pooling layers are used to shrink the data size, activation functions decide what should be kept and what should be discarded, and finally fully connected layers combine it all together and gives a decision like classification or segmentation as shown in Figure 5.

Figure 5. Convolutional Neural Networks for medical image classification.

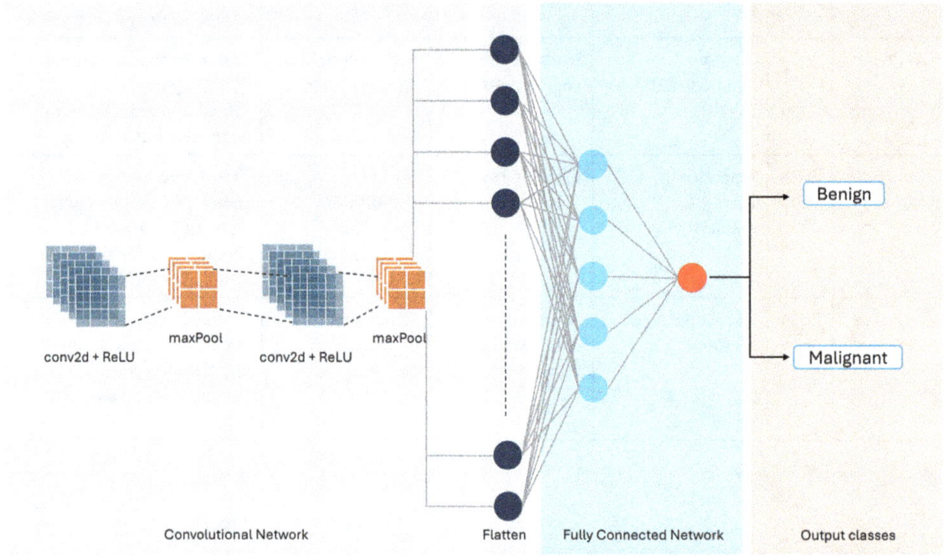

Let's understand the working of CNNs starting with convolutional layers. These layers perform the convolutional operation as the name suggests. Imagine a sliding window that moves throughout the image and during this movement, at each instant, it examines a small patch of the entire image. This window is called a kernel. It's this kernel's job to select specific features from the image like detecting the edges of a tumor or observing the texture of a healthy tissue. It multiplies kernel with pixels that are covered and then sums up to create a feature map as shown in this formula:

$$S(i,j) = (I*K)(i,j) = \sum_m \sum_n I(m,n)K(i-m,j-n)$$

Where, I represents the input image, K is the convolutional kernel, and $S(i,j)$ is the resulting feature map.

Next thing in this process is activation functions. One very common activation function is Rectified Linear Unit (ReLU). This ReLU function acts like a switch (it turns on for interesting features and shuts off for anything irrelevant):

$$\mathrm{Re}LU(x) = \max(0,x)$$

Then next layer in CNNs is a pooling layer. One can imagine these layers as they are trying to zoom out on an image. Adding a pooling layer causes reduction in the size of the feature maps as these keep only most important information for example max pooling over a 2×2 windows will pick the highest value in each block:

$$P(i,j) = \max\{S(2i,2j), S(2i+1,2j), S(2i,2j+1), S(2i+1,2j+1)\}$$

This causes the image to shrink which also speeds up the training process as the model starts to understand the bigger picture rather than memorizing every detail. This causes somewhat prevention from overfitting as well.

For training a CNN, loss functions are extremely important as they decide or measure how wrong are the guesses of a CNN. For tasks like classification, one such widely used loss function is cross-entropy loss:

$$L = -\sum_{i=1}^{c} y_i \widehat{\log y}_i$$

Where y_i is the true label and $\hat{y}_i$ is the predicted probability for the ith class. The model keeps adjusting it's parameters iteratively to minimize this error. This error minimization makes the model better with each round of training.

Clinical Applications

Deep CNN architectures have been shown in recent research to attain high accuracy in tasks including:

Tumor Segmentation. CNNs are used to classify brain tumors and segment tumors with exceptional accuracy. For example, Rajendran et al. (2020) demonstrated that deep CNNs greatly improve the segmentation of brain tumors from MRI scans, helping clinicians plan operations more precisely by targeting only the unhealthy tissues.

Organ Delineation. In CT or ultrasound scans, CNNs are able to find the shapes of the organs. In one such study, CNNs were employed to separate intricate anatomical structures in ultrasound and CT scans (Sakashita et al., 2020).

Disease Classification. Even a simple looking mole on skin can be cancerous, CNNs can look at the photos of these lesions and tell whether these are benign or malignant. One such excellent performance in distinguishing between benign and malignant lesions has been demonstrated in dermatological imaging (Arora et al., 2023).

Generative Adversarial Networks (GANs)

Generative Adversarial Networks (GANs) have emerged as a powerful technique to address the scarcity of annotated medical imaging data and to enhance image quality. GANs consist of two competing neural networks - a generator G and a discriminator D. These networks play a game of deception (generator) and detection (discriminator). Each network tries to win the game. When it is done iteratively, GANs start creating highly realistic looking images.

Mathematical Formulation

The adversarial training process is formulated as a minimax game, here G and D are optimizing opposing targets:

$$\min_{G} \max_{D} V(D,G) = E_{x \sim p_{data}}\left[\log D(x)\right] + E_{z \sim p_z}\left[\log(1 - D(G(z)))\right]$$

Where,

Real data (x). Real images sampled from the true data distribution p_{data} like some dataset of CT images.

Noise input (z). The generator begins its game with some random noise vectors (z) drawn from a prior distribution p_z. This noise is the raw data required to create synthetic images.

Generator's Outcome G(z). The generator *G* attempts to produce images from noise input to mimic the features of real images. During initial phases outputs are very noisy and doesn't look like the raw image data but with time the outputs improve.

Discriminator's Decision (D). The discriminator *D* learns to differentiate between real and synthetic images like a binary classifier which keeps trying to reject fake images. This entire process is summed up in Figure 6. It displays how the synthetic images are created by GANs, which can be used to bolster training datasets and improve model robustness.

Figure 6. GAN-Generated Synthetic Medical Images.

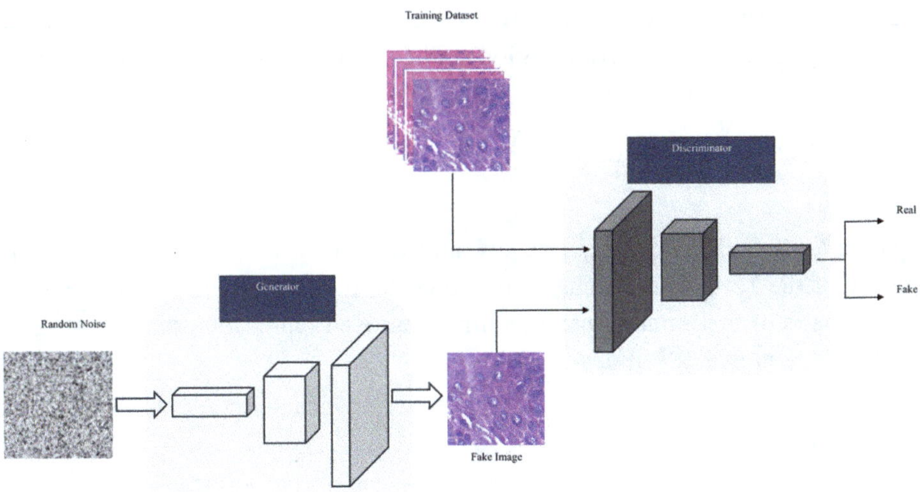

Clinical Applications

GANs have been successfully applied to various medical imaging tasks:

Data Augmentation. Liu et al. (2023) demonstrated that GAN-generated images can effectively augment training datasets, leading to improved detection of lung nodules in CT images.

Image Enhancement. GANs have been used to improve the resolution and clarity of low-quality ultrasound images, facilitating better clinical interpretation (Playout et al., 2022).

Anomaly Detection. The synthetic images generated by GANs help in training robust models for detecting rare pathologies (He et al., 2023).

Transformer-Based Models

Transformer-based architectures, initially developed for natural language processing, have been recently adapted for medical image analysis. These models utilize self-attention mechanisms to capture long-range dependencies and global context within images.

Self-Attention Mechanism

The core operation in a transformer is the self-attention mechanism. In terms of medical images, It is a computational process that gives the ability to the model to weigh the importance of different parts of the input data compared to one another dynamically focusing on relevant regions either near or distant. It is expressed as:

$$Attention\left(Q,K,V\right) = \text{softmax}\left(\frac{QK^T}{\sqrt{d_k}}\right)V$$

where Q, K, and V are the query, key, and value matrices, and d_k is the dimensionality of the keys. This mechanism allows the model to dynamically focus on different parts of the input image, enabling improved representation of both local and global features. Let's understand this:

Input Representation

The input is divided into a grid of patches (e.g., 32x32 pixels). Then these patches are flattened and embedded which creates a series of vectors. If the image has a height H and width W and a $P \times P$ patch we get a total of $\frac{H \times W}{P^2}$ patches. Let's call this total number of patches to be N. So, for an input of X, we get a matrix of shape $N \times d$, where d is the input dimension. From X, we get a:

Query matrix $Q=XW_Q$, these are the questions asked about the input

Key matrix $K=XW_K$, these are the answers or features the model compares against.

Value matrix $V=XW_V$, these are the contents that are supposed to be weighted.

Finding the Attention Scores

The entire attention's heart lies in QK^T as it is responsible for the calculation of similarity scores among the pairs of patches in an image. For N input sequences, it produces $N \times N$ matrix. Let's assume it to have i rows and j columns. An element (i,j) of this matrix tells how much patch i is similar to patch j. For example, in an MRI image, it may emphasize similarity between a tumor and white matter. But this product can grow very large which will cause unstable gradients. To overcome this unstable gradient problem, entire result is scaled by square root of key dimension $\sqrt{d_k}$.

Normalizing Softmax

The similarity scores are turned into probability distributions in this step:

$$\text{softmax}\left(\frac{QK^T}{\sqrt{d_k}}\right) = \frac{e^{\left(\frac{Q_i K_j^T}{\sqrt{d_k}}\right)}}{\sum_{k=1}^{N} e^{\left(\frac{Q_i K_j^T}{\sqrt{d_k}}\right)}}$$

This allows the model to give higher weights to more relevant patches irrespective of their proximity in spatial domain.

Weighted Aggregation

At last, we multiply the value matrix (V) with these attention weights to produce the output of self-attention layer:

$$Output = \text{softmax}\left(\frac{QK^T}{\sqrt{d_k}}\right).V$$

Clinical Applications

Vision Transformers (ViTs) and related architectures have shown promising results in:

Multi-Organ Segmentation. Liu et al. (2023) reported that ViTs have outperformed traditional CNNs in segmenting complex anatomical structures in multimodal data distributions.

Disease Classification. Transformers have been successfully applied in classifying various pathologies in radiological images, benefiting from their ability to model long-range dependencies (Wei et al., 2023).

Interpretability. The attention maps generated by transformer models offer enhanced interpretability which further helped the clinicians understand model decisions (Playout et al., 2022).

Hybrid Architectures and Emerging Trends

More recent work has targeted the combination of the strengths of CNNs, GANs, and transformers into hybrid architectures. These models seek to exploit the strong feature extraction of CNNs, data augmentation and improvement capabilities of GANs, and global context awareness of transformers.

Key Concepts

Hybrid architectures often combine:

CNN Modules. For initial feature extraction and capturing local details.

GAN Modules. For generating synthetic data and enhancing image quality.

Transformer Modules. For refining features and modeling global dependencies via self-attention.

Clinical Impact

Hybrid architectures have demonstrated improved diagnostic performance in complex scenarios, such as:

Tumor Detection. Combining CNNs and transformers has led to higher detection rates and better segmentation accuracy (Liu et al., 2023).

Disease Classification. The integration of multiple architectures helps in achieving higher accuracy and robustness across different patient populations (He et al., 2023).

Federated Learning

Federated learning allows for collective model training over many institutions while avoiding sensitive data sharing (Tian et al., 2023). Instead of sharing data, entities transfer only model related parameters which are further aggregated to a global model (Figure 7). Each entity like hospital in this case works by training a local model on its own private local dataset. Only the model's parameters and gradients are sent to the centralized server. The server then takes this information and with the help of this info further fine tunes the global model. This global model is then shared with each hospital which utilizes these updated parameters of global model as their starting point for their own local training environment. This process keeps occurring in a loop iteratively and it keeps continuing till the model reaches at an optimal state where its metrices improve enough to use the model in clinical settings. By keeping patient's sensitive data localized it helps to protect patient's privacy and by using diverse datasets it creates a global model that is more robust than just one local model trained on a centralized dataset. These benefits make Federated Learning extremely helpful in healthcare environment.

Figure 7. Federated Learning Framework for Collaborative Model Training.

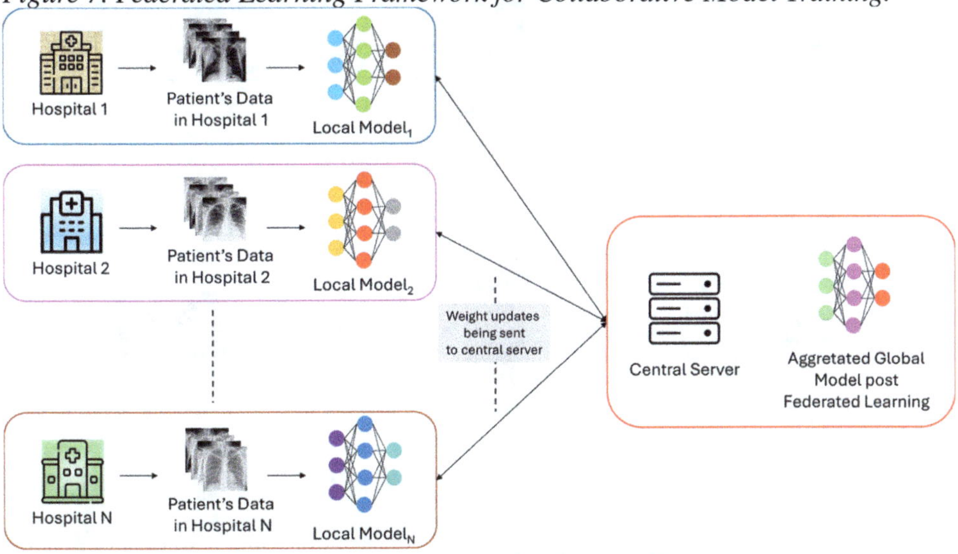

Self-Supervised Learning

Self-supervised learning uses unlabelled data for pre-training models, as discussed by Zeng et al. (2024). Figure 8 shows how SSL functions in a medical setting to work with unlabelled data in this case X-rays. Firstly, an unlabelled dataset pre trains a model based on pretext task. This pretext task makes the pre-training model to learn representations with no manually annotated labels. After pre-training, these learned representations are then sent to the target model which is fine-tuned by a smaller labelled dataset. This model then can be used for any specific task like segmentation, classification or disease detection. By using this knowledge-transfer technique, the target model shows improved performance on these target tasks (also known as downstream tasks) even if the available labelled data distribution is very limited which is very common for some rare medical conditions.

Figure 8. Self-Supervised Learning

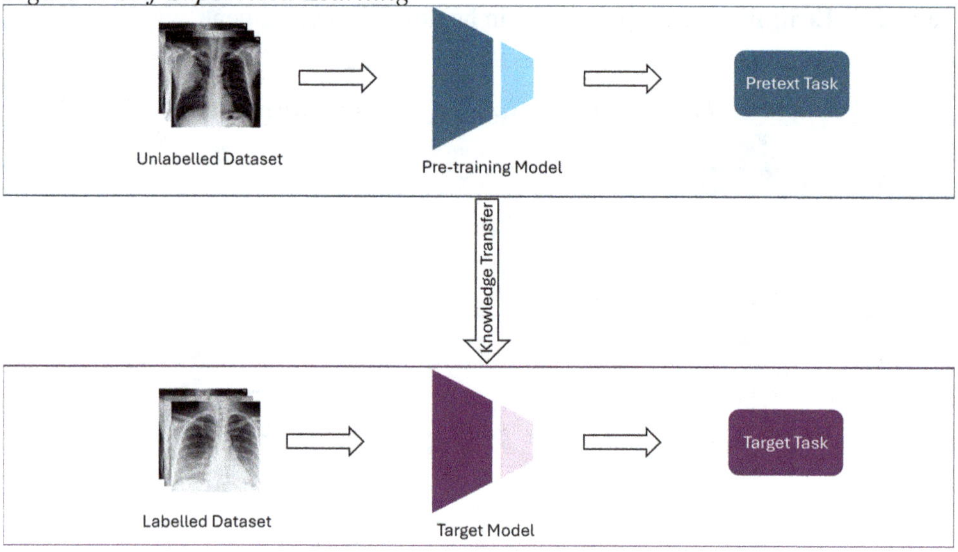

Summary and Future Directions

The evolution from CNNs to GANs and transformer-based models, with new hybrid architectures on the horizon, has contributed enormously to medical image analysis. These neural network designs not only have enhanced diagnostic accuracy but have also increased model interpretability and robustness essential for clinical adoption. Upcoming research is likely to involve optimizing hybrid models, pushing the boundaries of federated and self-supervised learning methods, and incorporating these systems into clinical routines with ease.

With advances in computation and greater availability of annotated data, improved performance and usefulness in these models can be anticipated. Continued interaction between clinicians and AI researchers will be critical to moving these technological gains into meaningful improvements in healthcare.

USING CNNS FOR MEDICAL IMAGES: A CASE STUDY

This section presents a case study that illustrate the practical applications of neural network architectures in medical imaging. It focuses on a specific clinical problem i.e. Breast cancer histopathological image classification into benign and malignant classes detailing the methodology, dataset, experimental setup, and results.

Clinical Context

Breast cancer is one of the most prevalent cancers worldwide, its one of the leading causes of cancer related deaths worldwide (World Health Organization, 2021). Its early detection significantly improves treatment outcomes and survival rates. Histopathological analysis of tissue samples is the gold standard for breast cancer diagnosis. For this, microscopic breast tissues are examined to find the benign or malignant nature in a slide. However, manual examination by pathologists is very labor intensive and may be subject to inter-observer variability. The BreakHis dataset provides a benchmark for developing automated diagnostic systems using deep learning to classify breast tumor images into benign and malignant categories, thereby assisting pathologists in making more consistent and accurate diagnoses (Spanhol et al., 2016).

Dataset Description

The BreakHis dataset comprises microscopic images of breast tumor tissue samples, acquired at different magnification levels. The dataset includes:

Number of Images: 9109 labelled images of breast tissue.

Classes: Two main classes - benign and malignant.

Image Variability: Images are collected at multiple magnification levels 40x, 100x, 200x, and 400x, posing additional challenges for model generalization. This diversity in imaging conditions makes BreakHis an excellent testbed for developing robust deep learning models for breast cancer classification.

Methodology

In this case study, a deep Convolutional Neural Network (CNN) is employed to classify breast tumor images. The methodology follows data preprocessing, handling class imbalance, model development, training the model and, finally evaluation.

Data Preprocessing

The dataset was found through a CSV file which had the image information like image paths and labels. Then, these images were organized into a directory with names prefixed by class name itself like benign or malignant (e.g., "benign_image1.png"). A DataFrame was constructed so that proper file locations, labels, and class encodings 0 (for benign) and 1 (for malignant) can be tracked. Initial analysis revealed a class imbalance, with malignant samples outnumbering benign ones.

Handling Class Imbalance

To balance these classes, random oversampling was applied to the minority class which here is benign and it the total count was made to match the majority class i.e. malignant. Further the dataset was distributed to 90:10 split for training and testing purpose.

Model Description

ResNet-50, pre-trained on ImageNet dataset was used here as it has proven to be effective in image classification (He et al., 2016). The model further used a Fully Connected Network of 32, 96, 160 and then 192 units which used ReLU activation, L2 regularization, and a dropout of 0.5 which helped mitigate overfitting. Finally the output layer used softmax activation function for binary classification problem.

$$L = -\sum_{i=1}^{C} y_i \widehat{\log y}_i$$

Where, y_i represents the true label (1 for malignant, 0 for benign) and $\hat{y}_i$ is the predicted probability for $i$thclass. Optimization is carried out using the Adam optimizer, and learning rates are scheduled to decay over time.

Training and Evaluation

Data augmentation was applied to enhance variability of the model. Sparse categorical cross entropy loss and validation accuracy were used as the performance metrics. Early stopping and reduce learning rate callbacks were used by monitoring the loss function to optimize the training process. For evaluation, confusion matrix and classification reports were analysed.

Performance Metrics

The model's performance is evaluated using:
Accuracy. Proportion of correctly classified images.
Precision and Recall. To balance false positives and false negatives.
F1 Score. The harmonic mean of precision and recall.

Results

The model achieved an overall accuracy of 97%. More evaluation metrices like Precision, Recall, and F1-score are shown next (Table 4). Figure 9 shows the confusion matrix which tells the correct and incorrect number of predictions per classes. The high accuracy and well-balanced F1-scores of the model indicate neural networks have a high potential to improve diagnostic processes significantly by minimizing mistakes and assisting pathologists, particularly in low-resource environments.

Figure 9. Confusion matrix

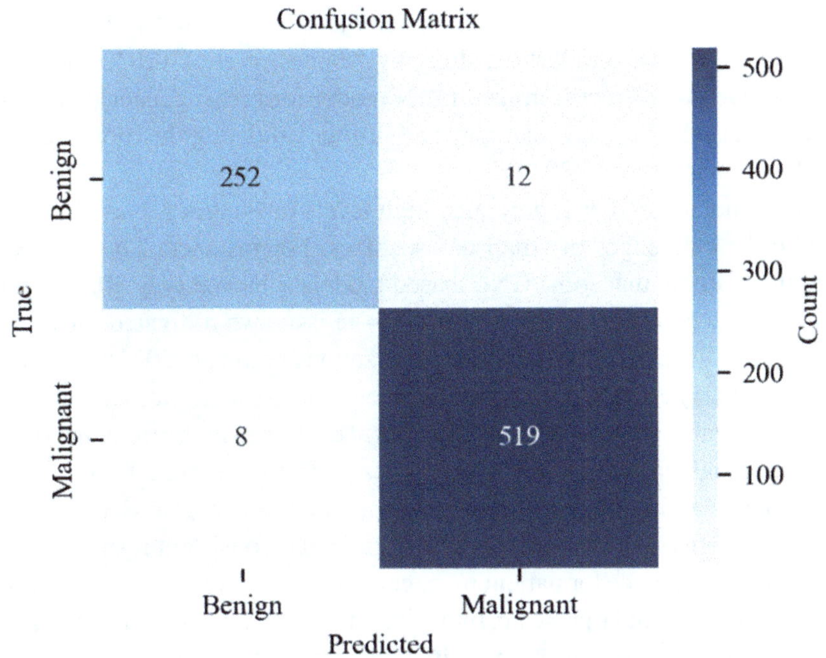

Table 4. Classification report of breast cancer image classification

	Precision	*Recall*	*F1-score*
Benign	0.95	0.95	0.95
Malignant	0.97	0.98	0.98
Weighted avg	0.96	0.96	0.96
Macro avg	0.97	0.97	0.97

These results show high sensitivity and specificity values which are essential for accurate medical diagnosis.

Discussion

The use of deep learning on the BreakHis dataset highlights the revolutionizing capability of AI in histopathological diagnosis. Our CNN model, leveraging the ResNet-50 architecture, achieved an impressive 97% accuracy in classifying breast cancer images into benign and malignant categories. This result builds upon the foundational work of Spanhol et al. (2016), who introduced the BreakHis dataset and reported classification accuracies ranging from 80% to 90% using various CNN architectures, thereby underscoring the potential of deep learning in this domain (Spanhol et al., 2016). Similarly, a study by Abunasser et al. (2023) demonstrated the effectiveness of a customized CNN model for breast cancer detection and classification, achieving high accuracy and further validating the robustness of our approach (Abunasser et al., 2023).

However, not all studies report such high levels of accuracy, particularly when faced with the challenges of small dataset sizes. For instance, Zou et al. (2023) noted in their survey that some CNN-based models achieved only 80.5% accuracy on certain datasets, often due to overfitting—an issue we mitigated through techniques such as data augmentation and regularization (Zou et al., 2023). Additionally, Lotter et al. (2021) emphasized the importance of large-scale datasets for ensuring model generalizability, highlighting a persistent challenge in the field that our study addressed through careful methodological design (Lotter et al., 2021).

Automated classification of breast cancer not only reduces the diagnostic workload for pathologists but also offers reproducible and consistent results, which are of paramount importance for patient management. Nevertheless, challenges persist, such as the necessity for large-scale, multi-institutional datasets to further test model performance and mitigate variations in imaging protocols. Future directions involve federated learning methodologies to maintain patient anonymity while tapping into multiple datasets, as well as developing explainable AI techniques to enhance the transparency of decision-making systems. These advances will be central in closing the research prototype-clinical deployment gap.

CHALLENGES

Despite the remarkable progress in neural network-based medical imaging, several challenges remain that must be addressed to translate these technologies into widespread clinical practice. This section discusses the key challenges and outlines promising future research directions.

Data Scarcity and Quality

One of the primary obstacles is the very limited availability of large-scale, well-annotated datasets. Medical images are subject to privacy regulations, and obtaining expert annotations is both time-consuming and costly. This also makes the datasets but those are usually highly imbalanced between normal and pathological cases, which can make the model's focus to shift or align towards the majority class which further reduces the quality of training and performance (Litjens et al., 2017). Although techniques such as data augmentation, transfer learning, and self-supervised learning have partially mitigated these issues (Zeng et al., 2024), there is still a pressing need for larger, more diverse datasets. Future research should focus on:

- ***Developing standardized datasets.*** that encompass a wide range of demographics and imaging modalities.
- ***Leveraging self-supervised and semi-supervised learning approaches.*** to extract useful representations from unlabeled data.
- ***Establishing data-sharing frameworks.*** that maintain patient privacy through federated learning, as demonstrated by Tian et al. (2023).

Model Interpretability and Explainability

The "black-box" nature of deep learning models continues to be a significant barrier to clinical adoption. Clinicians require transparency to trust and effectively use AI-based diagnostic tools. While tools like feature maps and class activation maps offer some insight, they're not trusted enough as they're unable to provide clinically meaningful explanations that raises concerns for regulatory approval and patient trust (Wei et al., 2023). Although, transformer-based models and attention mechanisms have improved interpretability by highlighting salient image regions (Liu et al., 2023).

Further work is needed to:

- ***Enhance explainability.*** using advanced XAI techniques that provide intuitive visual explanations.

- ***Integrate interpretable models.*** into clinical decision support systems, ensuring that model predictions can be easily understood and validated by medical professionals.
- ***Develop standardized evaluation metrics.*** for model interpretability, which would facilitate the comparison and improvement of different approaches.

Integration into Clinical Workflows

Another challenge lies in the seamless integration of AI models into existing clinical workflows. Many hospitals still rely on legacy systems, and incorporating advanced deep learning tools requires significant infrastructure upgrades. Additionally, there is a risk of over-reliance on these AI models which may potentially lead to errors if clinicians are unaware of the models' limitations (Litjens et al., 2017).

To bridge this gap, future work should consider:

- ***Developing user-friendly interfaces.*** that allow clinicians to interact with AI models without needing extensive technical expertise.
- ***Ensuring compatibility with existing electronic health record (EHR) systems.*** to facilitate data exchange and workflow integration.
- ***Conducting rigorous clinical trials***. to validate the effectiveness of these AI systems in real-world settings, thereby building clinician trust and regulatory approval.

Generalization Across Diverse Populations

Deep learning models often struggle with generalization when applied data originates from different sources, imaging conditions, and patient populations. Variations in image quality, acquisition parameters, and patient demographics can lead to significant performance degradation. For instance, a model trained on data from one institution may underperform when tested on data from another due to disparities in imaging protocols or population traits (Miotto et al., 2018).

To improve model robustness, future research should focus on:

- ***Domain adaptation techniques.*** that allow models to adjust to new data distributions.
- ***Multi-center studies.*** that evaluate model performance across diverse clinical environments.
- ***Hybrid models.*** that combine the strengths of CNNs, GANs, and transformers, thereby leveraging complementary features to improve generalization (He et al., 2023).

Real-Time Performance and Computational Efficiency

The practical implementation of AI in medical imaging requires models that not only provide high accuracy but also operate in real-time to support clinical decision-making. Many state-of-the-art models are computationally intensive, which limits their deployment in time-sensitive settings such as emergency departments. The training and deployment of deep learning models demand significant computational resources, including high-performance GPUs, which may not be feasible in all healthcare settings.

Addressing these issues involves:

- ***Optimizing model architectures***. to reduce computational load without sacrificing accuracy.
- ***Exploring hardware acceleration.*** techniques, including the use of GPUs and specialized AI chips.
- ***Employing model compression and quantization techniques***. to create lightweight models suitable for real-time applications.

FUTURE RESEARCH DIRECTIONS

The future of neural network-based medical imaging is promising, with several emerging trends that have the potential to overcome current limitations:

Federated Learning

It facilitates collaborative training across institutions without compromising patient privacy (Tian et al., 2023). By utilizing distributed datasets, this approach can mitigate data scarcity and improve model robustness, making it ideal for multicentre research (Rieke et al., 2020).

Self-Supervised Learning

It leverages vast amounts of unlabelled data to enhance model performance (Zeng et al., 2024).

Hybrid Architectures

It integrates CNNs, GANs, and transformer models to exploit their unique strengths for improved diagnostic accuracy (Liu et al., 2023; He et al., 2023).

Explainable AI (XAI)

Further development in interpretability methods to ensure that AI-driven decisions are transparent and clinically actionable. These methods ensure that a model's decisions are transparent which further builds trust among researchers, clinicians and patients (Wei et al., 2023).

Large-scale Data Sharing and Analysis

There's a need to make secure, standardized frameworks so that sensitive data can be shared among instituitions which can further support the large-scale study and help provide useful insights (for example, in the case of a global pandemic). This requires robust infrastructure and new privacy regulations if it provides assurance of helping understand disease detection and progression in a more advanced manner (Rieke et al., 2020).

Regulatory and Ethical Frameworks

There's a pressing need to establish standardized protocols and ethical guidelines for the deployment of AI in clinical practice.

Personalized Medicine

AI models can be used to customize medicines as per the need of individual patients by incorporating their medical histories and prognosis can help proper treatment planning further improving patient outcomes (Castro et al., 2020).

CONCLUSION

The results presented in this chapter demonstrate that neural networks have significantly advanced medical imaging analysis, offering substantial improvements in diagnostic capabilities. Deep learning models, such as Convolutional Neural Networks (CNNs), have consistently achieved high accuracy in detecting diseases, often surpassing traditional imaging techniques in sensitivity and specificity. Generative Adversarial Networks (GANs) have proven effective in overcoming data scarcity by producing synthetic images, enhancing the robustness and generalizability of diagnostic models across varied datasets. Hybrid architectures, combining CNNs with transformer models, have further elevated performance by effectively capturing both local and global image features, making them well-suited for complex medical imaging tasks.

Innovative learning paradigms have also broadened the applicability of these technologies. Federated Learning has enabled collaborative model development across institutions while safeguarding patient privacy, yielding models that perform reliably across diverse populations. Similarly, Self-Supervised Learning has reduced dependency on labeled datasets, allowing the efficient use of large, unlabeled medical image archives to train effective models.

However, these advancements are tempered by persistent challenges. Issues such as data sparsity, limited model interpretability, and difficulties in generalizing across heterogeneous datasets continue to hinder the full clinical integration of neural network-based tools. These findings underscore the need for ongoing efforts to enhance data availability, improve model transparency, and establish standardized validation practices.

In conclusion, neural networks have collectively enhanced the precision, efficiency, and potential of medical imaging, positioning them as transformative tools in diagnostic medicine. Their ability to improve diagnostic accuracy, address data limitations, and adapt to complex tasks highlights their broad clinical promise, though overcoming the remaining challenges is essential to ensuring their reliability and widespread adoption in healthcare settings.

REFERENCES

Abunasser, B. S., Al-Hiealy, M. R. J., Zaqout, I. S., & Abu-Naser, S. S. (2023). Convolution neural network for breast cancer detection and classification using deep learning. *Asian Pacific Journal of Cancer Prevention*, 24(2), 531–544. https://doi .org/ RCP.2023.24.2.531DOI: 10.31557/AP

Ahmed, M., Tooba, B., Khan, R. A., & Nasir, S. (2024). Enhancing breast cancer diagnosis in mammography: Evaluation and integration of convolutional neural networks and explainable AI. *arXiv:2404.03892* https://doi.org//arXiv.2404.03892DOI: 10.1109/INMIC64792.2024.11004362

Arora, G., Dubey, A. K., Jaffery, Z. A., & Rocha, A. (2023). A comparative study of fourteen deep learning networks for multi skin lesion classification (MSLC) on unbalanced data. *Neural Computing & Applications*, *35*(11), 7989–8015. DOI: 10.1007/s00521-022-06922-1

BMC Medical Imaging (2024). A survey of the impact of self-supervised pretraining for diagnostic tasks in medical X-ray, CT, MRI, and ultrasound. *BMC Medical Imaging*. Available at: https://bmcmedimaging.biomedcentral.com/articles/10.1186/ s12880-024-01253-0

Castro, D. C., Walker, I., & Glocker, B. (2020). Causality matters in medical imaging. *Nature Communications*, *11*(1), 1–10. DOI: 10.1038/s41467-020-17478-w PMID: 32699250

Chan, H. P., Samala, R. K., Hadjiiski, L. M., & Zhou, C. (2020). Deep learning in medical image analysis. *Advances in Experimental Medicine and Biology*, *1213*, 3–21. DOI: 10.1007/978-3-030-33128-3_1 PMID: 32030660

Chen, J., Lu, Y., Yu, Q., Luo, X., Adeli, E., Wang, Y., Lu, L., Yuille, A. L., & Zhou, Y. (2021). *TransUNet: Transformers make strong encoders for medical image segmentation*. arXiv:2102.04306. https://doi.org//arXiv.2102.04306DOI: 10.48550

Chen, L., Jiang, H., Wang, L., Li, J., Yu, M., Shen, Y., & Du, X. (2025). Generative adversarial synthetic neighbors-based unsupervised anomaly detection. *Scientific Reports*, *15*(1), 16. Advance online publication. DOI: 10.1038/s41598-024-84863-6 PMID: 39747674

Chen, T., Kornblith, S., Norouzi, M., & Hinton, G. (2020). A simple framework for contrastive learning of visual representations. *Proceedings of the 37th International Conference on Machine Learning*, pp. 1597-1607. Available at: http://proceedings .mlr.press/v119/chen20j.html [Accessed: 2024].

Cheng, L.. (2021). Adaptive Thresholding for Improved CT Image Segmentation. *IEEE Transactions on Medical Imaging*, *40*(5), 1303–1314. PMID: 33460369

Dai, J., Wu, H., Liu, H., Yu, L., Hu, X., Liu, X., & Geng, D. (2024). FEDATA: Adaptive Attention Aggregation for Federated Self-supervised Medical Image Segmentation. *Neurocomputing*, *128691*. Advance online publication. DOI: 10.1016/j.neucom.2024.128691

Dayan, I., Roth, H. R., Zhong, A., Harouni, A., Gentili, A., Abidin, A. Z., & Summers, R. M. (2021). Federated learning for predicting clinical outcomes in patients with COVID-19. *Nature Medicine*, *27*(10), 1735–1743. Retrieved 2024, from https://www.nature.com/articles/s41591-021-01506-3. DOI: 10.1038/s41591-021-01506-3 PMID: 34526699

Dosovitskiy, A., Beyer, L., Kolesnikov, A., Weissenborn, D., Zhai, X., & Unterthiner, T.. 2020. "An Image is Worth 16x16 Words: Transformers for Image Recognition at Scale." *International Conference on Learning Representations*. https://doi.org/ DOI: 10.48550/arXiv.2010.11929

Esteva, A., Kuprel, B., Novoa, R. A., Ko, J., Swetter, S. M., Blau, H. M., & Thrun, S. (2017). Dermatologist-level classification of skin cancer with deep neural networks. *Nature*, *542*(7639), 115–118. DOI: 10.1038/nature21056 PMID: 28117445

Features, H. (2010). The role of handcrafted features in medical image processing. *Medical Image Analysis*, *14*(2), 145–158.

Fu, Y., Xu, X., Dong, N., & Zhang, S. (2023). Biology-guided deep learning predicts prognosis and cancer immunotherapy response. *Nature Communications*, *14*(1), 4089. DOI: 10.1038/s41467-023-40890-x PMID: 37612313

Gao, H., Qian, Y., & Hui, R. (2022). The State of the Art of Medical Imaging Technology: From Creation to Archive and Back. *The Open Medical Informatics Journal*, *5*(Suppl 1), 73–85. DOI: 10.2174/1874431101105010073 PMID: 21915232

Goodfellow, I., Pouget-Abadie, J., Mirza, M., Xu, B., Warde-Farley, D., & Ozair, S.. (2014). Generative adversarial nets. *Advances in Neural Information Processing Systems*.

Haralick, R. M., Shanmugam, K., & Dinstein, I. (1973). Textural features for image classification. *IEEE Transactions on Systems, Man, and Cybernetics*, *3*(6), 610–621. DOI: 10.1109/TSMC.1973.4309314

He, A., Wang, K., Li, T., Du, C., Xia, S., & Fu, H. (2023). H2Former: An efficient hierarchical hybrid transformer for medical image segmentation. *IEEE Transactions on Medical Imaging*, *42*(9), 2763–2775. DOI: 10.1109/TMI.2023.3264513 PMID: 37018111

He, J., Baxter, S. L., Xu, J., Xu, J., Zhou, X., & Zhang, K. (2019). The practical implementation of artificial intelligence technologies in medicine. *Nature Medicine*, *25*(1), 30–36. DOI: 10.1038/s41591-018-0307-0 PMID: 30617336

He, K., Zhang, X., Ren, S., & Sun, J. 2016. "Deep residual learning for image recognition." *Proceedings of the IEEE Conference on Computer Vision and Pattern Recognition*: 770–778.

Hsu, T., Qi, H., & Brown, M. (2019). Measuring the effects of non-identical data distribution for federated visual classification. *arXiv preprint arXiv:1909.06335*. Available at: https://arxiv.org/abs/1909.06335 [Accessed: 2024].

Huang, G., Liu, Z., Van Der Maaten, L., & Weinberger, K. Q. 2017. "Densely connected convolutional networks." *Proceedings of the IEEE Conference on Computer Vision and Pattern Recognition*: 4700–4708.

Isensee, F., Jaeger, P. F., Kohl, S. A., Petersen, J., & Maier-Hein, K. H. (2021). nnU-Net: A self-configuring method for deep learning-based biomedical image segmentation. *Nature Methods*, *18*(2), 203–211. DOI: 10.1038/s41592-020-01008-z PMID: 33288961

Kaissis, G. A., Makowski, M. R., Rückert, D., & Braren, R. F. (2020). Federated learning in medicine: Facilitating multi-institutional collaborations without sharing patient data. *Scientific Reports*, *10*(12595). Retrieved 2024, from https://www.nature.com/articles/s41598-020-69250-1 PMID: 32724046

Konečný, J., McMahan, H. B., Yu, F. X., Richtárik, P., Suresh, A. T., & Bacon, D. (2016). Federated learning: Strategies for improving communication efficiency. *arXiv preprint arXiv:1610.05492*. Available at: https://arxiv.org/abs/1610.05492 [Accessed: 2024].

LeCun, Y., Bengio, Y., & Hinton, G. (2015). Deep learning. *Nature*, *521*(7553), 436–444. DOI: 10.1038/nature14539 PMID: 26017442

Litjens, G., Kooi, T., Bejnordi, B. E., Setio, A. A. A., Ciompi, F., Ghafoorian, M., van der Laak, J. A. W. M., van Ginneken, B., & Sánchez, C. I. (2017). A survey on deep learning in medical image analysis. *Medical Image Analysis*, *42*, 60–88. DOI: 10.1016/j.media.2017.07.005 PMID: 28778026

Litjens, G., Kooi, T., Bejnordi, B. E., Setio, A. A. A., Ciompi, F., Ghafoorian, M., van der Laak, J. A. W. M., van Ginneken, B., & Sánchez, C. I. (2017). A survey on deep learning in medical image analysis. *Medical Image Analysis*, *42*, 60–88. DOI: 10.1016/j.media.2017.07.005 PMID: 28778026

Liu, F.. (2023). Vision Transformers in Multi-Organ Segmentation: A Comparative Study. *Medical Image Analysis*, *78*, 102498.

Liu, X., Hu, Y., & Chen, J. (2023). Hybrid CNN-Transformer model for medical image segmentation with pyramid convolution and multi-layer perceptron. *Biomedical Signal Processing and Control*, *86*, 105331. DOI: 10.1016/j.bspc.2023.105331

Lodwick, G. S., Keats, T. E., & Dorst, J. P. (1963). The coding of roentgen images for computer analysis as applied to lung cancer. *Radiology*, *80*(2), 273–275. DOI: 10.1148/80.2.273 PMID: 14053755

Lotter, W., Diab, A. R., Haslam, B., Kim, J. G., Grisot, G., Wu, E., Wu, K., Onieva, J. O., Boyer, Y., Boxerman, J. L., Wang, M., Bandler, M., Vijayaraghavan, G. R., & Gregory Sorensen, A. (2021). Robust breast cancer detection in mammography and digital breast tomosynthesis using an annotation-efficient deep learning approach. *Nature Medicine*, *27*(2), 244–249. DOI: 10.1038/s41591-020-01174-9 PMID: 33432172

Lundberg, S. M., & Lee, S. I. (2017). A unified approach to interpreting model predictions. *Advances in Neural Information Processing Systems*, **•••**, 4765–4774.

Miotto, R., Wang, F., Wang, S., Jiang, X., & Dudley, J. T. (2018). Deep learning for healthcare: Review, opportunities and challenges. *Briefings in Bioinformatics*, *19*(6), 1236–1246. DOI: 10.1093/bib/bbx044 PMID: 28481991

Peng, X., Huang, Z., Sun, X., & Saenko, K. (2020). *Domain-agnostic federated learning for multi-site medical image analysis*. International Conference on Medical Image Computing and Computer-Assisted Intervention., Available at https://link.springer.com/chapter/10.1007/978-3-030-59725-2_67, Retrieved 2024, from.

Playout, C., Duval, R., Boucher, M. C., & Cheriet, F. (2022). Focused Attention in Transformers for interpretable classification of retinal images. *Medical Image Analysis*, *82*, 102608. DOI: 10.1016/j.media.2022.102608 PMID: 36150271

Rajendran, S., Rajagopal, S. K., Thanarajan, T., Shankar, K., Kumar, S., Alsubaie, N. M., Ishak, M. K., & Mostafa, S. M. (2023). Automated Segmentation of Brain Tumor MRI Images Using Deep Learning. *IEEE Access : Practical Innovations, Open Solutions*, *11*, 64758–64768. DOI: 10.1109/ACCESS.2023.3288017

Rajpurkar, P., Irvin, J., Zhu, K., Yang, B., Mehta, H., Duan, T., ... 2017. "CheX-Net: Radiologist-level pneumonia detection on chest X-rays with deep learning." *arXiv preprint arXiv:1711.05225*. https://doi.org//arXiv.1711.05225DOI: 10.48550

Ribeiro, M. T., Singh, S., & Guestrin, C. 2016. "Why should I trust you?: Explaining the predictions of any classifier." *Proceedings of the 22nd ACM SIGKDD International Conference on Knowledge Discovery and Data Mining*: 1135–1144. https://doi.org/DOI: 10.1145/2939672.2939778

Rieke, N., Hancox, J., Li, W., Milletarì, F., Roth, H. R., Albarqouni, S., Bakas, S., Galtier, M. N., Landman, B. A., Maier-Hein, K., Ourselin, S., Sheller, M., Summers, R. M., Trask, A., Xu, D., Xu, M., & Cardoso, M. J. (2020). The future of digital health with federated learning. *NPJ Digital Medicine*, *3*(1), 1–7. DOI: 10.1038/s41746-020-00323-1 PMID: 33015372

Ronneberger, O., Fischer, P., & Brox, T. (2015). U-Net: Convolutional networks for biomedical image segmentation. In *MICCAI 2015* (pp. 234–241). Medical Image Computing and Computer-Assisted Intervention. Springer., DOI: 10.1007/978-3-319-24574-4_28

Röntgen, W. C. (1896). On a new kind of rays. *Nature*, *53*(1369), 274–276. DOI: 10.1038/053274b0 PMID: 17769966

Sakashita, N., Shirai, K., Ueda, Y., Ono, A., & Teshima, T. (2020). Convolutional neural network-based automatic liver delineation on contrast-enhanced and non-contrast-enhanced CT images for radiotherapy planning. *Reports of Practical Oncology and Radiotherapy : Journal of Greatpoland Cancer Center in Poznan and Polish Society of Radiation Oncology*, *25*(6), 981–986. DOI: 10.1016/j.rpor.2020.09.005 PMID: 33100915

Selvaraju, R. R., Cogswell, M., Das, A., Vedantam, R., Parikh, D., & Batra, D. 2017. "Grad-CAM: Visual explanations from deep networks via gradient-based localization." *Proceedings of the IEEE International Conference on Computer Vision*: 618–626. https://doi.org/DOI: 10.1109/ICCV.2017.74

Shen, D., Wu, G., & Suk, H. I. (2017). Deep learning in medical image analysis. *Annual Review of Biomedical Engineering*, *19*(1), 221–248. DOI: 10.1146/annurev-bioeng-071516-044442 PMID: 28301734

Song, L., Lin, J., Wang, Z. J., & Wang, H. (2020). An End-to-End Multi-Task deep learning framework for skin lesion analysis. *IEEE Journal of Biomedical and Health Informatics*, *24*(10), 2912–2921. DOI: 10.1109/JBHI.2020.2973614 PMID: 32071016

Sowrirajan, H., Yang, J., Ng, A. Y., & Rajpurkar, P. (2021). *Self-supervising learning for chest X-ray classification. 2021 IEEE 18th International Symposium on Biomedical Imaging*. ISBI., Available at https://ieeexplore.ieee.org/document/9434139, Retrieved 2024, from.

Spanhol, F. A., Oliveira, L. S., Petitjean, C., & Heutte, L. (2016). A Dataset for Breast Cancer Histopathological Image Classification. *IEEE Transactions on Biomedical Engineering*, *63*(7), 1455–1462. DOI: 10.1109/TBME.2015.2496264 PMID: 26540668

Tan, M., & Le, Q. V. 2019. "EfficientNet: Rethinking model scaling for convolutional neural networks." *International Conference on Machine Learning*: 6105–6114. https://doi.org/DOI: 10.48550/arXiv.1905.11946

Tian, Y., Wang, S., Xiong, J., Bi, R., Zhou, Z., & Bhuiyan, M. Z. A. (2023). Robust and Privacy-Preserving decentralized Deep federated Learning training: Focusing on digital healthcare applications. *IEEE/ACM Transactions on Computational Biology and Bioinformatics*, *21*(4), 890–901. DOI: 10.1109/TCBB.2023.3243932 PMID: 37028039

Topol, E. J. (2019). High-performance medicine: The convergence of human and artificial intelligence. *Nature Medicine*, *25*(1), 44–56. DOI: 10.1038/s41591-018-0300-7 PMID: 30617339

Vaswani, A., Shazeer, N., Parmar, N., Uszkoreit, J., Jones, L., & Gomez, A. N.. (2017). Attention is all you need. *Advances in Neural Information Processing Systems*, *30*, 5998–6008. DOI: 10.48550/arXiv.1706.03762

Wei, C., Ren, S., Guo, K., Hu, H., & Liang, J. (2023). High-Resolution Swin Transformer for Automatic Medical Image Segmentation. *Sensors (Basel)*, *23*(7), 3420. DOI: 10.3390/s23073420 PMID: 37050479

Wolterink, J. M., Dinkla, A. M., Savenije, M. H. F., Seevinck, P. R., van den Berg, C. A. T., & Išgum, I. (2017). Deep MR to CT translation using unpaired data. In *Simulation and Synthesis in Medical Imaging* (pp. 14–23). Springer., DOI: 10.1007/978-3-319-68127-6_2

World Health Organization. (2021). *Breast cancer*. https://www.who.int/news-room/fact-sheets/detail/breast-cancer

Xu, Z., Liu, Y., Xu, G., & Lukasiewicz, T. (2024). Self-Supervised Medical Image segmentation using deep reinforced adaptive masking. *IEEE Transactions on Medical Imaging*, *1*. Advance online publication. DOI: 10.1109/TMI.2024.3436608 PMID: 39088493

Yan, Z., Wicaksana, J., Zhang, Z., & Yang, X. (2023). Label-efficient self-supervising federated learning for tackling data heterogeneity in medical imaging. *IEEE Transactions on Medical Imaging*, *42*(9), 2672–2683. Retrieved 2024, from https://ieeexplore.ieee.org/document/10093728

Yang, X., Qu, S., Wang, Z., Li, L., An, X., & Cong, Z. (2024). The study on ultrasound image classification using a dual-branch model based on Resnet50 guided by U-net segmentation results. *BMC Medical Imaging*, *24*(1), 314. DOI: 10.1186/s12880-024-01486-z PMID: 39558260

Yi, X., Walia, E., & Babyn, P. (2019). Generative adversarial networks in medical imaging: A review. *Medical Image Analysis*, *58*, 101552. DOI: 10.1016/j.media.2019.101552 PMID: 31521965

You, C., Li, G., Zhang, Y., Zhang, X., Shan, H., & Ju, S. (2020). Self-supervised learning for medical image denoising. *Medical Image Analysis*, *65*, 101749. Retrieved 2024, from https://www.sciencedirect.com/science/article/pii/S1361841520301125

Zech, J. R., Badgeley, M. A., Liu, M., Costa, A. B., Titano, J. J., & Oermann, E. K. (2018). Variable generalization performance of a deep learning model to detect pneumonia in chest radiographs: A cross-sectional study. *PLoS Medicine*, *15*(11), e1002683. DOI: 10.1371/journal.pmed.1002683 PMID: 30399157

Zeng, X., Abdullah, N., & Sumari, P. (2024). Self-supervised learning framework application for medical image analysis: A review and summary. *Biomedical Engineering Online*, *23*(1), 107. DOI: 10.1186/s12938-024-01299-9 PMID: 39465395

Zhang, Q., Liu, Y., & Zhang, H. (2023). *Federated self-supervised learning for breast cancer classification. 2023 IEEE International Conference on Bioinformatics and Biomedicine*. BIBM., Available at https://ieeexplore.ieee.org/document/10385792, Retrieved 2024, from.

Zimmerer, D., Petersen, J., Köhler, G., Jäger, P. F., & Maier-Hein, K. H. (2019). Unsupervised anomaly detection in brain MRI scans using variational autoencoders. In *Medical Imaging with Deep Learning* (pp. 50–61). Springer., Available at https://link.springer.com/chapter/10.1007/978-3-030-32692-0_4, Retrieved 2024, from.

Zou, L., Yu, S., Meng, T., Zhang, Z., Liang, X., & Xie, Y. (2023). A survey of convolutional neural network in breast cancer. *Journal of Healthcare Engineering*, *2023*, 9743929. Advance online publication. DOI: 10.1155/2023/9743929

Compilation of References

Abunasser, B. S., Al-Hiealy, M. R. J., Zaqout, I. S., & Abu-Naser, S. S. (2023). Convolution neural network for breast cancer detection and classification using deep learning. *Asian Pacific Journal of Cancer Prevention*, 24(2), 531–544. https://doi .org/ RCP.2023.24.2.531DOI: 10.31557/AP

Adam, M., Wessel, M., & Benlian, A. (2020). AI-based chatbots in customer service and their effects on user compliance. *Electronic Markets*, *31*(2), 427–445. DOI: 10.1007/s12525-020-00414-7

Adams, D., Mooi, A. N. Y., & Muniandy, V. (2020). Principal leadership preparation towards high-performing school leadership in Malaysia. *Asian Education and Development Studies*, *9*(4), 425–439. DOI: 10.1108/AEDS-02-2018-0046

Aditi, B., Hafizah, H., & Hermansyur, H. (2021). The Role of E-Services, Quality System, and Perceived Value on Customer Satisfaction: An Empirical Study on Indonesian SMEs. *Journal of Industrial Engineering & Management Research*, *2*(3), 193–205. DOI: 10.7777/jiemar.v2i3.195

Ahmed, M., Tooba, B., Khan, R. A., & Nasir, S. (2024). Enhancing breast cancer diagnosis in mammography: Evaluation and integration of convolutional neural networks and explainable AI. *arXiv:2404.03892* https://doi.org//arXiv.2404.03892DOI: 10.1109/INMIC64792.2024.11004362

Al-Daihani, M., Dirie, K.A., Muneem, A., Abdul Lateb, N. and Bouteraa, M. (2025), "Islamic social finance and its potential in addressing natural disaster emergencies and advancing sustainable development goals: a proposed model", International Journal of Ethics and Systems, Vol. ahead-of-print No. ahead-of-print. DOI: 10.1108/IJOES-05-2024-0138

Alenezi, M. (2021). Deep dive into digital transformation in higher education institutions. *Education Sciences*, *11*(12), 770. DOI: 10.3390/educsci11120770

Ali, K., & Johl, S. K. (2023). Driving forces for industry 4.0 readiness, sustainable manufacturing practices, and circular economy capabilities: Does firm size matter? *Journal of Manufacturing Technology Management, 34*(5), 838–13. DOI: 10.1108/JMTM-07-2022-0254

Ali, M. S., Vecchio, M., Pincheira, M., Dolui, K., Antonelli, F., & Rehmani, M. H. (2018). Applications of blockchains in the Internet of Things: A comprehensive survey. *IEEE Communications Surveys and Tutorials, 21*(2), 1676–1717. DOI: 10.1109/COMST.2018.2886932

Ali, O., Abdelbaki, W., Shrestha, A., Elbasi, E., Alryalat, M. A. A., & Dwivedi, Y. K. (2023). A systematic literature review of artificial intelligence in the healthcare sector: Benefits, challenges, methodologies, and functionalities. *Journal of Innovation & Knowledge, 8*(1), 1. DOI: 10.1016/j.jik.2023.100333

Alkhwaldi, A. F., Alharasis, E. E., Shehadeh, M., Abu-AlSondos, I. A., Oudat, M. S., & Bani Atta, A. A. (2022). Towards an understanding of FinTech users' adoption: Intention and e-loyalty post-COVID-19 from a developing country perspective. *Sustainability (Basel), 14*(19), 12616. DOI: 10.3390/su141912616

Alotaibi, F. M. (2023). A machine-learning-inspired opinion extraction mechanism for classifying customer reviews on social media. *Applied Sciences (Basel, Switzerland), 13*(12), 7266. DOI: 10.3390/app13127266

Altheide, D. L. (2006). Terrorism and the politics of fear. *Cultural Studies Critical Methodologies, 6*(4), 415–439. https://doi.org/DOI: 10.1177/1532708605285733

Amin, H., & R.C., et al. (2011). Determinants for ar-Rahnu usage intentions: An empirical investigation. *African Journal of Business Management, 5*(20), 8181–8191.

Amin, H., Rahim Abdul Rahman, A., Laison Sondoh, S.Jr, & Magdalene Chooi Hwa, A. (2011). Determinants of customers' intention to use Islamic personal financing. *Journal of Islamic Accounting and Business Research, 2*(1), 22–42. DOI: 10.1108/17590811111129490

Amorim, M., Madureira, R. C., Demosthenous, E., Dimopoulou, M., Ferreira Dias, M., Anastassopoulos, P. G., & Vrabelj, N. (2023). *A Competence Framework for e-Leadership*. Universidad de Aveiro., Retrieved from https://www.researchgate.net/profile/Bruno_Lins3/publication/371701955_A_Competence_Framework_for_e-Leadership/links/64917e30c41fb852dd19c40b/A-Competence-Framework-for-e-Leadership.pdf

Anayat, S., & Rasool, G. (2022). Artificial intelligence marketing (AIM): Connecting-the-dots using bibliometrics. *Journal of Marketing Theory and Practice*, *32*(1), 114–135. DOI: 10.1080/10696679.2022.2103435

Andersen, J., Nielsen, M. L., & Sandholdt, H. (2018). Designing for player experience in digital games. In *Proceedings of the 2018 DiGRA International Conference*, (pp. 1–15)

Anderson, C. A. (2020). Fortnite: A case study of cultural impact. *Games Studies*, *25*(1), 34–42.

Andersson, O. (2021). Securing Electronic Health Records: A Blockchain Solution. In.

Antonopoulou, H., Halkiopoulos, C., Barlou, O., & Beligiannis, G. N. (2021). Associations between Traditional and Digital Leadership in Academic Environment: During the COVID-19 Pandemic. *Emerging Science Journal*, *5*(4), 405–425. DOI: 10.28991/esj-2021-01286

Arokiasamy, A. R. A., Abdullah, A. G. K., & Ismail, A. (2015). Correlation between cultural perceptions, leadership style and ICT usage by school principals in Malaysia. *Procedia: Social and Behavioral Sciences*, *176*, 319–332. DOI: 10.1016/j.sbspro.2015.01.478

Arora, G., Dubey, A. K., Jaffery, Z. A., & Rocha, A. (2023). A comparative study of fourteen deep learning networks for multi skin lesion classification (MSLC) on unbalanced data. *Neural Computing & Applications*, *35*(11), 7989–8015. DOI: 10.1007/s00521-022-06922-1

Ashaari, M. A., Singh, K. D., Abbasi, G. A., Amran, A., & Liebana-Cabanillas, F. J. (2021). Big data analytics capability for improved performance of higher education institutions in the Era of IR 4.0: A multi-analytical SEM & ANN perspective. *Technological Forecasting and Social Change*, *173*, 121119. DOI: 10.1016/j.techfore.2021.121119

Autonomy. (2024). *Representing a gig economy: Gender, visibility, and news coverage of on-demand work during the pandemic*. Retrieved from https://autonomy.work/wp-content/uploads/2024/10/REPRESENTING-A-GIG-ECONOMY-1.pdf

Avolio, B., Simran, K., & George, D. (2000). E-Leadership: Implications for theory, research and practice. *The Leadership Quarterly*, *11*(4), 615–668. DOI: 10.1016/S1048-9843(00)00062-X

Axie Infinity. (2023). *Axie Infinity: Blockchain-based gaming* [Video game]. Sky Mavis.

Babbar, M., & Gupta, T. (2022). Response of educational institutions to COVID-19 pandemic: An inter-country comparison. *Policy Futures in Education, 20*(4), 469–491. DOI: 10.1177/14782103211021937 PMID: 40478015

Baber, H. (2021). Religiosity and intention to participate in donation-based crowdfunding. *Journal of Management, Spirituality & Religion, 18*(3), 218–238. DOI: 10.51327/DKES9686

Baker, S. R., Baugh, B., & Sammon, M. (2020). Measuring customer churn and interconnectedness. SPGMI: Compustat Fundamentals.

Baker, L., Johnson, K., & Smith, R. (2020). Customer retention strategies in the digital age. *Journal of Business Marketing, 45*(3), 112–129.

Basil, N. N., Ambe, S., Ekhator, C., Fonkem, E., & Nduma, B. N. (2022). Health records database and inherent security concerns: A review of the literature. *Cureus, 14*(10). Advance online publication. DOI: 10.7759/cureus.30168 PMID: 36397924

Bawack, R. E., Fosso Wamba, S., & Carillo, K. D. A. (2021). A framework for understanding artificial intelligence research: Insights from practice. *Journal of Enterprise Information Management, 34*(2), 645–678. DOI: 10.1108/JEIM-07-2020-0284

Benitez, J., Arenas, A., Castillo, A., & Esteves, J. (2022). Impact of Digital Leadership capability on innovation performance: The role of platform digitization capability. *Information & Management, 59*(2), 103590. DOI: 10.1016/j.im.2022.103590

Benjamin, R. (2019). *Race after technology: Abolitionist tools for the new Jim Code*. Polity Press.

Bin-Nashwan, S. A., Bouteraa, M., Benlahcene, A., & Sadallah, M. (2025). Beyond hype: Is ChatGPT-generated content effective in class preparation among academic instructors? *The Internet and Higher Education, 101016*, 101016. Advance online publication. DOI: 10.1016/j.iheduc.2025.101016

Blizzard Entertainment. (2023). *World of Warcraft: Guilds and social group dynamics*. Blizzard Entertainment.

BMC Medical Imaging (2024). A survey of the impact of self-supervised pretraining for diagnostic tasks in medical X-ray, CT, MRI, and ultrasound. *BMC Medical Imaging*. Available at: https://bmcmedimaging.biomedcentral.com/articles/10.1186/s12880-024-01253-0

Borade, S., Paradkar, T., Takalkar, P., & Trivedi, A. (2023). Blockchain based electronic health record management system. *Available at SSRN* 4376765. DOI: 10.2139/ssrn.4376765

Bory, P., Natale, S., & Katzenbach, C. (2024). Strong and weak AI narratives: An analytical framework. *AI & Society*, *60*(3), 259–264. DOI: 10.1007/s00146-024-02087-8

Bouteraa, M., & Al-Aidaros, A.-H. (2020). The role of attitude as mediator in the intention to have Islamic will. *International Journal of Advanced Research in Economics and Finance*, *2*(1), 22–37.

Bouteraa, M., Chekima, B., Amin, H., Tamma, E., Lada, S., Ansar, R., & Lim, M. F. (2024). Does consumer religiosity matter for green banking adoption? Evidence from a Muslim-majority market. *Journal of Islamic Marketing*, *15*(7), 1807–1823. DOI: 10.1108/JIMA-02-2023-0049

Boykoff, M. T. (2011). Frontmatter. In *Who speaks for the climate?: Making sense of media reporting on climate change* (pp. i–v). Cambridge University Press. DOI: 10.1017/CBO9780511978586

Brennan, G., Tennant, M., & Blomsma, F. (2015). Business and production solutions: Closing loops and the circular economy. In Kopnina, H., & Shoreman-Ouimet, E. (Eds.), *Sustainability: Key Issues* (pp. 219–239). Routledge. DOI: 10.4324/9780203109496-11

Brennen, J. (2018). *An industry-led debate: How UK media cover artificial intelligence*. Reuters Institute for the Study of Journalism.

Brennen, J. S., Simon, F. M., Howard, P. N., & Nielsen, R. K. (2020). *Types, sources, and claims of COVID-19 misinformation*. Reuters Institute., DOI: 10.60625/risj-awvq-sr55

Bruns, A. (2008). *Blogs, Wikipedia, Second Life, and beyond: From production to produsage*. Peter Lang.

Brynjolfsson, E., & McAfee, A. (2014). *The second machine age: Work, progress, and prosperity in a time of brilliant technologies*. W.W. Norton & Company.

Bueno-Ferrer, Á., De Pablo Valenciano, J., & De Burgos Jiménez, J. (2025). Unveiling the potential of metaheuristics in transportation: A path towards efficiency, optimization, and intelligent management. *Infrastructures*, *10*(1), 4. DOI: 10.3390/infrastructures10010004

Bukhari, S. F. H., Woodside, F. M., Hassan, R., Shaikh, A. L., Hussain, S., & Mazhar, W. (2019). Is religiosity an important consideration in Muslim consumer behavior? *Journal of Islamic Marketing*, *10*(4), 1288–1307. DOI: 10.1108/JIMA-01-2018-0006

Buolamwini, J., & Gebru, T. (2018). Gender shades: Intersectional accuracy disparities in commercial gender classification. In S. A. Friedler & C. Wilson (Eds.), *Proceedings of the 1st Conference on Fairness, Accountability and Transparency* (Vol. 81, pp. 77–91). PMLR. https://proceedings.mlr.press/v81/buolamwini18a.html

Cabecinhas, D., Batista, P., Oliveira, P., & Silvestre, C. (2017). Hovercraft control with dynamic parameters identification. *IEEE Transactions on Control Systems Technology*, *26*(3), 785–796. DOI: 10.1109/TCST.2017.2692733

Caldwell, C., Dixon, R., Floyd, L., Chaudoin, J., Post, J., & Cheokas, G. (2012). Transformative Leadership: Achieving Unparalleled Excellence. *Journal of Business Ethics*, *109*(2), 175–187. DOI: 10.1007/s10551-011-1116-2

Castro, D. C., Walker, I., & Glocker, B. (2020). Causality matters in medical imaging. *Nature Communications*, *11*(1), 1–10. DOI: 10.1038/s41467-020-17478-w PMID: 32699250

Cath, C. (2018). Governing artificial intelligence: Ethical, legal, and technical opportunities and challenges. *Philosophical Transactions. Series A, Mathematical, Physical, and Engineering Sciences*, *376*(2133), 20180080. DOI: 10.1098/rsta.2018.0080 PMID: 30322996

Chaffey, D. (2023). *Why customer retention is key to improving profitability*. Smart Insights.

Chandran, S. M. C., Mukesh, V. M., Chandran, R., Sathiyabama, B., & Santhoshkumar, N. (2024). Mediating role of green finance in transforming banking activities to environmental performance. *Srusti Management Review*, *17*(2), 19–36.

Chan, H. P., Samala, R. K., Hadjiiski, L. M., & Zhou, C. (2020). Deep learning in medical image analysis. *Advances in Experimental Medicine and Biology*, *1213*, 3–21. DOI: 10.1007/978-3-030-33128-3_1 PMID: 32030660

Chavez, L. R. (2001). *Covering immigration: Popular images and the politics of the nation*. University of California Press. DOI: 10.1525/9780520925250

Chekima, B., Bouteraa, M., Ansar, R., Lada, S., Fook, L. M., Tamma, E., Abdul Adis, A.-A., & Chekima, K. (2023). Determinants of Organic Food Consumption in Narrowing the Green Gap. *Sustainability (Basel)*, *15*(11), 8554. Advance online publication. DOI: 10.3390/su15118554

Chekima, B., Chekima, S., Syed Khalid Wafa, S. A. W., Igau, O. A., & Sondoh, S. L.Jr. (2016). Sustainable consumption: The effects of knowledge, cultural values, environmental advertising, and demographics. *International Journal of Sustainable Development and World Ecology*, *23*(2), 210–220. DOI: 10.1080/13504509.2015.1114043

Chen, T., Kornblith, S., Norouzi, M., & Hinton, G. (2020). A simple framework for contrastive learning of visual representations. *Proceedings of the 37th International Conference on Machine Learning*, pp. 1597-1607. Available at: http://proceedings.mlr.press/v119/chen20j.html [Accessed: 2024].

Cheng, L.. (2021). Adaptive Thresholding for Improved CT Image Segmentation. *IEEE Transactions on Medical Imaging, 40*(5), 1303–1314. PMID: 33460369

Chen, H., & Lee, S. (2023). Blockchain technology in gaming: Fairness and transparency. *Journal of Digital Economics, 5*(2), 112–126.

Chen, L., Jiang, H., Wang, L., Li, J., Yu, M., Shen, Y., & Du, X. (2025). Generative adversarial synthetic neighbors-based unsupervised anomaly detection. *Scientific Reports, 15*(1), 16. Advance online publication. DOI: 10.1038/s41598-024-84863-6 PMID: 39747674

Chen, S., Ke, S., Han, S., Gupta, S., & Sivarajah, U. (2024). Which product description phrases affect sales forecasting? An explainable AI framework by integrating Wave Net neural network models with multiple regression. *Decision Support Systems, 176*, 114065. DOI: 10.1016/j.dss.2023.114065

Chenthara, S. (2021). *Privacy Preservation of Electronic Health Records Using Blockchain Technology: Healthchain.* Victoria University, Ding, Y., Feng, L., Qin, Y., Huang, C., Dong, P., Gao, L., & Tan, Y. (2020). *Blockchain-based access control mechanism of federated data sharing system.* Paper presented at the 2020 IEEE Intl Conf on Parallel & Distributed Processing with Applications, Big Data & Cloud Computing, Sustainable Computing & Communications, Social Computing & Networking (ISPA/BDCloud/SocialCom/SustainCom).

Chen, Y., & Wang, X. (2022). Analyzing customer churn: A comprehensive approach. *International Journal of Business Analytics, 9*(2), 45–62.

Chen, Z., Liu, Y., & Xu, B. (2020). Examining player satisfaction in online multiplayer games: The role of performance and fairness. *Entertainment Computing, 35*, 100372. DOI: 10.1016/j.entcom.2020.100372

Cheung, G., Zimmermann, T., & Nagappan, N. (2014). The first hour experience: How the initial play can engage (or lose) new players. In *Proceedings of the first ACM SIGCHI Annual Symposium on Computer-Human Interaction in Play*. DOI: 10.1145/2658537.2658540

Chintalapati, S., & Pandey, S. K. (2022). Artificial intelligence in marketing: A systematic literature review. *International Journal of Market Research, 64*(1), 38–68. DOI: 10.1177/14707853211018428

Chugh, P., & Jain, V. (2024). Artificial intelligence (AI) empowerment in e-commerce: A bibliometric voyage. *NMIMS Management Review, 32*(3), 159–173. DOI: 10.1177/09711023241303621

Cohen, J. (1988). *Statistical power analysis for the behavioral sciences* (2nd ed.). L. Erlbaum Associates.

Cortellazzo, L., Bruni, E., & Zampieri, R. (2019). The Role of Leadership in a Digitalized World: A Review. *Frontiers in Psychology, 10*, 1938. DOI: 10.3389/fpsyg.2019.01938 PMID: 31507494

Coussement, K., Abedin, M. Z., Kraus, M., Maldonado, S., & Topuz, K. (2024). Explainable AI for enhanced decision-making. *Decision Support Systems, 184*, 114276. DOI: 10.1016/j.dss.2024.114276

Crawford, K. (2021). *Atlas of AI: Power, politics, and the planetary costs of artificial intelligence*. Yale University Press.

Creswell, J., & Creswell, J. D. (2018). *Research design: Qualitative, quantitative, and mixed methods approaches* (5th ed.). Sage Publications, Inc.

Culot, G., Nassimbeni, G., Orzes, G., & Sartor, M. (2020). Behind the definition of Industry 4.0: Analysis and open questions. *International Journal of Production Economics, 226*, 107617. DOI: 10.1016/j.ijpe.2020.107617

Dai, H., Xiao, Q., Yan, N., Xu, X., & Tong, T. (2022). What influences online sales across different types of e-commerce platforms. *International Journal of Electronic Commerce, 26*(3), 311–330. DOI: 10.1080/10864415.2022.2076196

Dai, J., Wu, H., Liu, H., Yu, L., Hu, X., Liu, X., & Geng, D. (2024). FEDATA: Adaptive Attention Aggregation for Federated Self-supervised Medical Image Segmentation. *Neurocomputing, 128691*. Advance online publication. DOI: 10.1016/j.neucom.2024.128691

Dayan, I., Roth, H. R., Zhong, A., Harouni, A., Gentili, A., Abidin, A. Z., & Summers, R. M. (2021). Federated learning for predicting clinical outcomes in patients with COVID-19. *Nature Medicine, 27*(10), 1735–1743. Retrieved 2024, from https://www.nature.com/articles/s41591-021-01506-3. DOI: 10.1038/s41591-021-01506-3 PMID: 34526699

Demir, İ. (2022). Gig economy and evaporated risks through media. In Kayıhan, B. (Ed.), *Understanding risks and crises through the media* (pp. 65–86). Cambridge Scholars Publishing.

Deng, Z., & Guo, M. (2024). Research on the impact of the application of artificial intelligence technology on the sustainable development of mobile e-commerce. *Benchmarking*, *31*(9), 3349–3372. DOI: 10.1108/BIJ-11-2022-0697

Dery, K., Sebastian, I. M., & Van der Meulen, N. (2017). The digital workplace is key to digital innovation. *MIS Quarterly Executive*, *16*(2), 135–152. https://aisel.aisnet.org/misqe/vol16/iss2/4

Desai, P., & Ganatra, K. (2022). *Artificial intelligence in strengthening the operations of e-commerce-based business. Interdisciplinary Research in Technology and Management*. IRTM., DOI: 10.1109/IRTM54583.2022.9791598

Deterding, S., Dixon, D., Khaled, R., & Nacke, L. (2011). From game design elements to gamefulness: Defining "gamification". In *Proceedings of the 2011 Annual Conference on Human Factors in Computing Systems* (pp. 2425–2434). ACM. DOI: 10.1145/2181037.2181040

Dhanalakshmi, A., Hui, X., Roopini, R., & Supriya, R. (2020). Technological Advancements in E-Commerce and Customer Relationship Management. *International Journal of Engineering and Management Research*, *10*(6), 9–20. DOI: 10.31033/ijemr.10.6.2

Dosovitskiy, A., Beyer, L., Kolesnikov, A., Weissenborn, D., Zhai, X., & Unterthiner, T.. 2020. "An Image is Worth 16x16 Words: Transformers for Image Recognition at Scale." *International Conference on Learning Representations*. https://doi.org/ DOI: 10.48550/arXiv.2010.11929

Drachen, A., Seif El-Nasr, M., & Canossa, A. (2013). Game analytics – The basics. In Seif El-Nasr, M., & Canossa, A. (Eds.), *Game Analytics* (pp. 13–40). Springer. DOI: 10.1007/978-1-4471-4769-5_2

Drachen, A., Sifa, R., Runge, J., Thurau, C., Bauckhage, C., & Klabjan, D. (2013). Guns, swords and data: Clustering of player behavior in computer games in the wild. In *Proceedings of IEEE Conference on Computational Intelligence and Games* (pp. 163–170). IEEE. DOI: 10.1109/CIG.2013.6633613

Draxler-Weber, N., Voigt, C., & Blömer, L. (2022). Teachers' barriers to digital higher education teaching during the COVID-19 pandemic. *Wirtschaftsinformatik 2022 Proceedings*, 4. https://aisel.aisnet.org/wi2022/digital_education/digital_education/4

Drèze, J., & Khera, R. (2017). Recent social security initiatives in India. *World Development*, *98*, 555–572. DOI: 10.1016/j.worlddev.2017.05.035

Ducheneaut, N., Yee, N., Nickell, E., & Moore, R. J. (2007). The life and death of online gaming communities: A look at guilds in World of Warcraft. *Proceedings of the SIGCHI Conference on Human Factors in Computing Systems*, 839–848. DOI: 10.1145/1240624.1240750

Duflo, E. (2020). Field Experiments and the Practice of Policy. *The American Economic Review, 110*(7), 1952–1973. DOI: 10.1257/aer.110.7.1952

Dunn, T. J., & Kennedy, M. (2019). Technology Enhanced Learning in higher education; motivations, engagement and academic achievement. *Computers & Education, 137*, 104–113. DOI: 10.1016/j.compedu.2019.04.004

Eberl, J. K., & Drews, P. (2021). Digital Leadership - Mountain or Molehill? A Literature Review. In Ahlemann, F., Schütte, R., & Stieglitz, S. (Eds.), *Innovation Through Information Systems. Lecture Notes in Information Systems and Organisation* (pp. 223–237). Springer., DOI: 10.1007/978-3-030-86800-0_17

Ehlers, U. D. (2020). Digital leadership in higher education. *Journal of Higher Education Policy and Leadership Studies, 1*(3), 6–14. DOI: 10.29252/johepal.1.3.6

El Sawy, O., Henrik, A., Kræmmergaard, P., & Vinther, A. (2016). How LEGO built the foundations and enterprise capabilities for digital leadership. *MIS Quarterly Executive, 15*(2), 141–166.

Entman, R. M. (1993). Framing: Toward clarification of a fractured paradigm. *Journal of Communication, 43*(4), 51–58. DOI: 10.1111/j.1460-2466.1993.tb01304.x

Erhan, T., Uzunbacak, H. H., & Aydin, E. (2022). From conventional to Digital Leadership: Exploring digitalization of leadership and innovative work behavior. *Management Research Review, 45*(11), 1524–1543. DOI: 10.1108/MRR-05-2021-0338

Esmeli, R., & Gokce, A. (2025). An analysis of consumer purchase behavior following cart addition in e-commerce utilizing explainable artificial intelligence. *Journal of Theoretical and Applied Electronic Commerce Research, 20*(1), 28. DOI: 10.3390/jtaer20010028

Esteva, A., Kuprel, B., Novoa, R. A., Ko, J., Swetter, S. M., Blau, H. M., & Thrun, S. (2017). Dermatologist-level classification of skin cancer with deep neural networks. *Nature, 542*(7639), 115–118. DOI: 10.1038/nature21056 PMID: 28117445

Eubanks, V. (2018). *Automating inequality: How high-tech tools profile, police, and punish the poor*. St. Martin's Press.

European Commission. (2021). *The role of Digital Leadership in higher education*. European Commission.

Fantoni, I., Lozano, R., Mazenc, F., & Pettersen, K. Y. (1999, December). Stabilization of a nonlinear underactuated hovercraft. In *Proceedings of the 38th IEEE Conference on Decision and Control (Cat. No. 99CH36304) 3,* 2533-2538. IEEE. https://doi.org/DOI: 10.1109/CDC.1999.831309

Fareen, J. A. M. (2022). Digital Learning in Higher Education: A Road to Transformation and Reform. *European Journal of Interactive Multimedia and Education, 3*(1), e02206. DOI: 10.30935/ejimed/11493

Farhat, R., Yang, Q., Ahmed, M. A. O., & Hasan, G. (2025). E-commerce for a sustainable future: Integrating trust, product quality perception, and online-shopping satisfaction. *Sustainability (Basel), 17*(4), 1431. https://doi.org/10.xxxx/su17041431. DOI: 10.3390/su17041431

Fast, E., & Horvitz, E. (2017). Long-term trends in the public perception of artificial intelligence. *Proceedings of the AAAI Conference on Artificial Intelligence, 31*(1). Advance online publication. DOI: 10.1609/aaai.v31i1.10635

Faturohman, T., Kengsiswoyo, G. A. N., Harapan, H., Zailani, S., Rahadi, R. A., & Arief, N. N. (2021). Factors influencing COVID-19 vaccine acceptance in Indonesia: An adoption of Technology Acceptance Model. *F1000 Research, 10*, 476. DOI: 10.12688/f1000research.53506.1 PMID: 34621508

Features, H. (2010). The role of handcrafted features in medical image processing. *Medical Image Analysis, 14*(2), 145–158.

Federoff, M. A. (2002). Heuristics and usability guidelines for the creation and evaluation of fun in video games. Master's thesis, Indiana University.

Feldstein, S. (2019). *The global expansion of AI surveillance*. Carnegie Endowment for International Peace.

Fernández del Río, A., Guitart, A., & Periáñez, Á. (2021). A time series approach to player churn and conversion in videogames. *Intelligent Data Analysis, 25*(1), 177–203. DOI: 10.3233/IDA-194940

Fernández, A., Gómez, B., Binjaku, K., & Meçe, E. K. (2023). Digital transformation initiatives in higher education institutions: A multivocal literature review. *Education and Information Technologies, 28*(10), 12351–12382. DOI: 10.1007/s10639-022-11544-0 PMID: 37361743

Financial Stability Board (FSB). (2018). *Financial stability implications from FinTech*.

Fintech Middle East. (2021). *Fintech News Middle East: UAE Fintech Report 2021.* Abu Dhabi.

Fu, L., Li, J., & Chen, Y. (2023). An innovative decision-making method for air quality monitoring based on big data-assisted artificial intelligence technique. *Journal of Innovation & Knowledge*, *8*(2), 100294. DOI: 10.1016/j.jik.2022.100294

Fu, Y., Xu, X., Dong, N., & Zhang, S. (2023). Biology-guided deep learning predicts prognosis and cancer immunotherapy response. *Nature Communications*, *14*(1), 4089. DOI: 10.1038/s41467-023-40890-x PMID: 37612313

Gai, K., Qiu, M., & Sun, X. (2018). A survey on FinTech. *Journal of Network and Computer Applications*, *103*, 262–273. DOI: 10.1016/j.jnca.2017.10.011

Gallardo-Echenique, E. E., de Oliveira, J. M., Marqués-Molia, L., & Esteve-Mon, F. (2015). Digital competence in the knowledge society. *Journal of Online Learning and Teaching*, *11*(1), 1–16.

Ganapathy, V., Gupta, C., & Chavadi, C. (2023). Building a sustainable e-commerce grocery business model in India: Challenges and opportunities. *Journal of Services Research*, *23*(2), 125–151.

Ganesan, S., & Esakki, B. (2019). Design and development of unmanned hovercraft. *International Journal of Mathematical. Engineering and Management Sciences*, *4*(5), 1180–1195. DOI: 10.33889/IJMEMS.2019.4.5-093

Gao, H., Qian, Y., & Hui, R. (2022). The State of the Art of Medical Imaging Technology: From Creation to Archive and Back. *The Open Medical Informatics Journal*, *5*(Suppl 1), 73–85. DOI: 10.2174/1874431101105010073 PMID: 21915232

Gebauer, J. E., & Sedikides, C. (2021). Cultural religiosity: A neglected but powerful dimension of culture. *Current Opinion in Psychology*, *40*, 73–78. DOI: 10.1016/j.copsyc.2020.08.027 PMID: 33027746

Gfrerer, A., Hutter, K., Fuller, J., & Strohle, T. (2021). Ready or not: Managers' and employees' different perceptions of digital readiness. *California Management Review*, *63*(2), 23–48. DOI: 10.1177/0008125620977487

Ghosh, P. K., Chakraborty, A., Hasan, M., Rashid, K., & Siddique, A. H. (2023). Blockchain application in healthcare systems: A review. *Systems*, *11*(1), 38. DOI: 10.3390/systems11010038

Gidh, P. G. (2020). A multi-dimensional research study in E-commerce to capture consumer expectations. *International Journal for Research in Applied Science and Engineering Technology*, *8*(11), 411–415. DOI: 10.22214/ijraset.2020.32169

Gkrimpizi, T., Peristeras, V., & Magnisalis, I. (2023). Classification of barriers to digital transformation in higher education institutions: Systematic literature review. *Education Sciences, 13*(7), 746. DOI: 10.3390/educsci13070746

Gold, C. (2020). *Fighting churn with data: The science and strategy of customer retention*. Manning Publishing.

Goodfellow, I., Pouget-Abadie, J., Mirza, M., Xu, B., Warde-Farley, D., & Ozair, S.. (2014). Generative adversarial nets. *Advances in Neural Information Processing Systems*.

Guerra, J. M. M., Danvila-del-Valle, I., & Méndez-Suárez, M. (2023). The impact of digital transformation on talent management. *Technological Forecasting and Social Change, 188*, 122291. DOI: 10.1016/j.techfore.2022.122291

Hadiji, F., Sifa, R., Drachen, A., Thurau, C., Kersting, K., & Bauckhage, C. (2014). Predicting player churn in the wild. In *2014 IEEE Conference on Computational Intelligence and Games* (pp. 1–8). IEEE.

Hair, J. F.Jr. (2018). *Advanced issues in partial least squares structural equation modeling*. SAGE Publications, Inc.

Hair, J. F., Risher, J. J., Sarstedt, M., & Ringle, C. M. (2019). When to use and how to report the results of PLS-SEM. *European Business Review, 31*(1), 2–24. DOI: 10.1108/EBR-11-2018-0203

Hair, J. F., Sarstedt, M., Ringle, C. M., & Mena, J. A. (2012). An assessment of the use of partial least squares structural equation modeling in marketing research. *Journal of the Academy of Marketing Science, 40*(3), 414–433. DOI: 10.1007/s11747-011-0261-6

Hair, J.. (2021). *A primer on partial least squares structural equation modeling (PLS-SEM)* (3rd ed.). SAGE Publications, Inc. DOI: 10.1007/978-3-030-80519-7

Hamari, J., & Järvinen, A. (2011). Building customer relationship through game mechanics in social games. In Business, Technological, and Social Dimensions of Computer Games: Multidisciplinary Developments (pp. 348–365). IGI Global. DOI: 10.4018/978-1-60960-567-4.ch021

Hamari, J., Alha, K., Hämäläinen, P., Linturi, H., & Ihonen, M. (2017). Why do people play games? A review of game motivations. In *Proceedings of the 2017 Annual Symposium on Computer-Human Interaction in Play* (pp. 9–20). ACM.

Hamari, J., Alha, K., Järvelä, S., Kivikangas, J. M., Koivisto, J., & Paavilainen, J. (2020). Why do players buy in-game content? An empirical study on concrete purchase motivations. *Computers in Human Behavior*, *68*, 538–546. DOI: 10.1016/j.chb.2016.11.045

Hamari, J., & Koivisto, J. (2015). Why do people use gamification services? *International Journal of Information Management*, *35*(4), 419–431. DOI: 10.1016/j.ijinfomgt.2015.04.006

Hamari, J., Koivisto, J., & Sarsa, H. (2014). Does gamification work? A literature review of empirical studies on gamification. In *47th Hawaii International Conference on System Sciences* (pp. 3025–3034). IEEE. DOI: 10.1109/HICSS.2014.377

Hamzah, N. H., Nasir, K. M., & Wahab, A. J. (2021). The Effects of Principals' Digital Leadership on Teachers' Digital Teaching during the Covid-19 Pandemic in Malaysia. *Journal of Education and e-learning Research*, *8*(2), 216–221. DOI: 10.20448/journal.509.2021.82.216.221

Han, Y.-J., Moon, J., & Woo, J. (2024). Prediction of churning game users based on social activity and churn graph neural networks. *IEEE Access : Practical Innovations, Open Solutions*, *12*, 101971–101984. DOI: 10.1109/ACCESS.2024.3429559

Han, Y., Zhang, Y., & Vermund, S. H. (2022). Blockchain technology for electronic health records. *International Journal of Environmental Research and Public Health*, *19*(23), 15577. DOI: 10.3390/ijerph192315577 PMID: 36497654

Haralick, R. M., Shanmugam, K., & Dinstein, I. (1973). Textural features for image classification. *IEEE Transactions on Systems, Man, and Cybernetics*, *3*(6), 610–621. DOI: 10.1109/TSMC.1973.4309314

Hashim, M. M. A., Tlemsani, I., & Matthews, R. (2022). Higher education strategy in digital transformation. *Education and Information Technologies*, *27*(3), 3171–3195. DOI: 10.1007/s10639-021-10739-1 PMID: 34539217

Hasnain, M., Albogamy, F. R., Alamri, S. S., Ghani, I., & Mehboob, B. (2023). The Hyperledger fabric as a Blockchain framework preserves the security of electronic health records. *Frontiers in Public Health*, *11*, 1272787. DOI: 10.3389/fpubh.2023.1272787 PMID: 38089022

He, D. et al. (2017). Fintech and financial services: Initial considerations.

He, A., Wang, K., Li, T., Du, C., Xia, S., & Fu, H. (2023). H2Former: An efficient hierarchical hybrid transformer for medical image segmentation. *IEEE Transactions on Medical Imaging*, *42*(9), 2763–2775. DOI: 10.1109/TMI.2023.3264513 PMID: 37018111

Hein, S. M., & Liaw, H. C. (2013, July). Design and development of a compact hovercraft vehicle. In *2013 IEEE/ASME International Conference on Advanced Intelligent Mechatronics,* 1516–1521 IEEE https://doi.org/DOI: 10.1109/AIM.2013.6584310

He, J., Baxter, S. L., Xu, J., Xu, J., Zhou, X., & Zhang, K. (2019). The practical implementation of artificial intelligence technologies in medicine. *Nature Medicine*, *25*(1), 30–36. DOI: 10.1038/s41591-018-0307-0 PMID: 30617336

He, K., Zhang, X., Ren, S., & Sun, J. 2016. "Deep residual learning for image recognition." *Proceedings of the IEEE Conference on Computer Vision and Pattern Recognition*: 770–778.

He, X., & Liu, Y. (2024). Knowledge evolutionary process of Artificial intelligence in E-commerce: Main path analysis and science mapping analysis. *Expert Systems with Applications*, *238*, 121801. DOI: 10.1016/j.eswa.2023.121801

Hidayat, R., Akhmad, S., & Machmud, M. (2015). Effects of service quality, customer trust, and satisfaction toward customer loyalty of Islamic banks in Indonesia. *The 6th International Conference on Entrepreneurship, Business, and Economics.*

Hidayat, R., & Akhmad, S. (2015). Commitment and trust on the customers. *Al-Ulum*, *15*(1), 57–90. DOI: 10.30603/au.v15i1.45

Howard, P. N. (2011). Reply to Evgeny Morozov's review of *The Digital Origins of Dictatorship and Democracy: Information Technology and Political Islam. Perspectives on Politics*, *9*(4), 896–897. DOI: 10.1017/S1537592711004853

Hsu, T., Qi, H., & Brown, M. (2019). Measuring the effects of non-identical data distribution for federated visual classification. *arXiv preprint arXiv:1909.06335.* Available at: https://arxiv.org/abs/1909.06335 [Accessed: 2024].

Huang, G., Liu, Z., Van Der Maaten, L., & Weinberger, K. Q. 2017. "Densely connected convolutional networks." *Proceedings of the IEEE Conference on Computer Vision and Pattern Recognition*: 4700–4708.

Huang, H., Zhu, P., Xiao, F., Sun, X., & Huang, Q. (2020). A blockchain-based scheme for privacy-preserving and secure sharing of medical data. *Computers & Security*, *99*, 102010. DOI: 10.1016/j.cose.2020.102010 PMID: 32895584

Hunicke, R., LeBlanc, M., & Zubek, R. (2004). MDA: A formal approach to game design and game research. In *Proceedings of the AAAI Workshop on Challenges in Game AI* (pp. 1–5). AAAI Press.

Hussein, S. M., & Al-Araji, A. S. (2024). Enhancement of a Path-Finding Algorithm for the Hovercraft System Based on Intelligent Hybrid Stochastic Methods. *International Journal of Intelligent Engineering & Systems*, *17*(2), 346–364. DOI: 10.22266/ijies2024.0430.29

International Labour Organization. (2018). *Representation, voice, and collective bargaining in the gig economy*. Retrieved from https://www.ilo.org

Isbister, K., & Schaffer, N. (2008). *Game usability: Advice from the experts for advancing the player experience*. Morgan Kaufmann. DOI: 10.1201/b14580

Isensee, F., Jaeger, P. F., Kohl, S. A., Petersen, J., & Maier-Hein, K. H. (2021). nnU-Net: A self-configuring method for deep learning-based biomedical image segmentation. *Nature Methods*, *18*(2), 203–211. DOI: 10.1038/s41592-020-01008-z PMID: 33288961

Iyengar, S. (1991). *Is anyone responsible? How television frames political issues*. University of Chicago Press., DOI: 10.7208/chicago/9780226388533.001.0001

Jameson, J., Rumyantseva, N., Cai, M., Markowski, M., Essex, R., & McNay, I. (2022). A systematic review and framework for Digital Leadership research maturity in higher education. *Computers and Education Open*, *3*, 100115. DOI: 10.1016/j.caeo.2022.100115

Jarad, G. A., & Shaalan, M. A. (2020). Assessment of digital competence of employees and teaching staff at the technical college of management – Kufa. *International Journal of Innovation, Creativity and Change*, 12(12), 1027-1043. https://bit.ly/3BFCrVz

Jatmika, R. T. D., Ratnasari, V., & Nadlifatin, R. (2024). Empowering micro-entrepreneurs through artificial intelligence: A conceptual framework for AI-based marketing. *Procedia Computer Science*, *234*, 1087–1094. DOI: 10.1016/j.procs.2024.03.103

Jena, R. K. (2025). Factors influencing the adoption of FinTech for the enhancement of financial inclusion in rural India using a mixed methods approach. *Journal of Risk and Financial Management*, *18*(3), 150. DOI: 10.3390/jrfm18030150

Jha, J., & Ghatak, N. (2023). Open schools in developing countries. In Zawacki-Richter, O., & Jung, I. (Eds.), *Handbook of Open, Distance and Digital Education* (pp. 493–508). Springer Nature Singapore., DOI: 10.1007/978-981-19-2080-6_27

Jiang, H. (2024). The economic impact of customer churn in modern enterprises. *Strategic Management Review*, *16*(1), 78–95.

Jiang, X. (2024). Customer churn data analysis using data mining. *Applied and Computational Engineering*, *77*(1), 17–24. DOI: 10.54254/2755-2721/77/20240496

Johari, R., Kumar, V., Gupta, K., & Vidyarthi, D. P. (2022). BLOSOM: BLOck-chain technology for Security of Medical records. *ICT Express*, *8*(1), 56–60. DOI: 10.1016/j.icte.2021.06.002

Johnson, M. (2018). Monetization strategies in free-to-play games: The case of League of Legends. *Journal of Game Design and Development*, *12*(3), 118–131. DOI: 10.1016/j.jgdd.2018.04.001

Johnston, H., & Land-Kazlauskas, C. (2018). *Organizing on-demand: Representation, voice, and collective bargaining in the gig economy*. International Labour Organization. Retrieved from https://www.ilo.org/media/412401/download

Juul, J. (2010). *A casual revolution: Reinventing video games and their players*. MIT Press.

Kahneman, D. (2011). *Thinking, fast and slow*. Farrar, Straus and Giroux.

Kaissis, G. A., Makowski, M. R., Rückert, D., & Braren, R. F. (2020). Federated learning in medicine: Facilitating multi-institutional collaborations without sharing patient data. *Scientific Reports*, *10*(12595). Retrieved 2024, from https://www.nature.com/articles/s41598-020-69250-1 PMID: 32724046

Kakkar, V. M. S. (2017). A study on artificial intelligence in e-commerce. *International Journal of Advances in Engineering & Scientific Research*, *4*(4).

Kaputa, V., Loučanová, E., & Tejerina Gaite, F. A. (2022). Digital Transformation in Higher Education Institutions as a Driver of Social Oriented Innovations. In Păunescu, C., Lepik, K. L., & Spencer, N. (Eds.), *Social Innovation in Higher Education. Innovation, Technology and Knowledge Management* (pp. 61–85). Springer., DOI: 10.1007/978-3-030-84044-0_4

Karakose, T., Polat, H., & Papadakis, S. (2021). Examining Teachers' Perspectives on School Principals' Digital Leadership Roles and Technology Capabilities during the COVID-19 Pandemic. *Sustainability (Basel)*, *13*(23), 13448. DOI: 10.3390/su132313448

Kelly, A. (2020). The evolution of Fortnite: Player engagement and community events. *Journal of Interactive Media*, *18*(3), 56–67. DOI: 10.1016/j.jim.2020.06.005

Khin, S., & Ho, T. C. (2020). Digital technology, digital capability and organisational performance: A mediating role of digital innovation. *International Journal of Innovation Science*, *11*(2), 177–195. DOI: 10.1108/IJIS-08-2018-0083

Kim, S., Choi, D., Lee, E., & Rhee, W. (2017). Churn prediction of mobile and online casual games using play log data. *PLoS One*, *12*(6), 1–11. DOI: 10.1371/journal.pone.0180735 PMID: 28678880

King, D. L., & Delfabbro, P. H. (2018). The cognitive psychopathology of internet gaming disorder. *Clinical Psychology Review*, *59*, 61–78.

Kingdon, J. W. (1984). *Agendas, alternatives, and public policies*. HarperCollins.

Knaus, T. (2020). Technology criticism and data literacy: The case for an augmented understanding of media literacy. *The Journal of Media Literacy Education*, *12*(3), 6–16. DOI: 10.23860/JMLE-2020-12-3-2

Konečný, J., McMahan, H. B., Yu, F. X., Richtárik, P., Suresh, A. T., & Bacon, D. (2016). Federated learning: Strategies for improving communication efficiency. *arXiv preprint arXiv:1610.05492*. Available at: https://arxiv.org/abs/1610.05492 [Accessed: 2024].

Kovach, B., & Rosenstiel, T. (2014). *The elements of journalism: What newspeople should know and the public should expect* (3rd ed.). Three Rivers Press.

Kulkarni, A., Patel, S., & Rodriguez, M. (2023). Understanding and mitigating customer churn: A multi-industry analysis. *Journal of Customer Insights*, *38*(4), 201–220.

Kulkarni, S. A., Upadhyay, Y. D., Shah, N., & Nair, S. (2023). Customer churn prediction using customer data and reviews. In *2023 International Conference on Advanced Computing Technologies and Applications (ICACTA)* (pp. 1–6). IEEE. DOI: 10.1109/ICACTA58201.2023.10393246

Kumar, I., & Chidambara, . (2024). A systematic literature review and bibliometric analysis of last-mile e-commerce delivery in urban areas. *Urban, Planning and Transport Research*, *12*(1), 2357577. DOI: 10.1080/21650020.2024.2357577

Kumar, N., Anusara, J., Hossin, M. A., Sarkar, M. K., Chanthamith, B., Shah, S., & Russel, M. I. H. (2018). Challenges and opportunities of E-Commerce in India: Pathway for sustainable e-commerce. *International Journal of Engineering Business Management*, *2*(2).

Labib, E. (2024). Artificial intelligence in marketing: Exploring current and future trends. *Cogent Business & Management*, *11*(1), 2348728. Advance online publication. DOI: 10.1080/23311975.2024.2348728

Lada, S., Chekima, B., Ansar, R., Lim, M. F., Bouteraa, M., Abdul Adis, A. A., Abd Karim, M. R., & Yong, K. (2024). Strategic alternatives for Muslim-friendly homestay in Sabah Malaysia: A SWOT/TOWS analysis. *Journal of Islamic Marketing, 15*(6), 1534–1559. DOI: 10.1108/JIMA-04-2023-0133

Lari, H. A., Vaishnava, K., & Manu, K. S. (2022). Artificial Intelligence in E-commerce: Applications, Implications and Challenges. *Asian Journal of Management, 13*(3), 235–244. DOI: 10.52711/2321-5763.2022.00041

Laurillard, D. (2008). The teacher as action researcher: Using technology to capture pedagogic form. *Studies in Higher Education, 33*(2), 139–154. DOI: 10.1080/03075070801915908

Lazić, A., Milić, S., & Vukmirović, D. (2024). The future of electronic commerce in the IoT environment. *Journal of Theoretical and Applied Electronic Commerce Research, 19*(1), 172–187. DOI: 10.3390/jtaer19010010

LeCun, Y., Bengio, Y., & Hinton, G. (2015). Deep learning. *Nature, 521*(7553), 436–444. DOI: 10.1038/nature14539 PMID: 26017442

Lee, N. T., Lee, H. C., Hsin, J., & Fang, S. H. (2024). Prediction of customer behavior changing via a hybrid approach. *IEEE Open Journal of the Computer Society, 5*, 27–38. DOI: 10.1109/OJCS.2023.3336904

Lemon, K. N., & Verhoef, P. C. (2016). Understanding customer experience throughout the customer journey. *Journal of Marketing, 80*(6), 69–96. DOI: 10.1509/jm.15.0420

Libai, B., Muller, E., & Peres, R. (2009). The diffusion of services. *JMR, Journal of Marketing Research, 46*(2), 163–175. DOI: 10.1509/jmkr.46.2.163

Li, C., Hao, R., Li, N., & Zhang, C. (2025). Measuring customer experience in AI contexts: A scale development. *Journal of Theoretical and Applied Electronic Commerce Research, 20*(1), 31. DOI: 10.3390/jtaer20010031

Litjens, G., Kooi, T., Bejnordi, B. E., Setio, A. A. A., Ciompi, F., Ghafoorian, M., van der Laak, J. A. W. M., van Ginneken, B., & Sánchez, C. I. (2017). A survey on deep learning in medical image analysis. *Medical Image Analysis, 42*, 60–88. DOI: 10.1016/j.media.2017.07.005 PMID: 28778026

Liu, F.. (2023). Vision Transformers in Multi-Organ Segmentation: A Comparative Study. *Medical Image Analysis, 78*, 102498.

Liu, X., Hu, Y., & Chen, J. (2023). Hybrid CNN-Transformer model for medical image segmentation with pyramid convolution and multi-layer perceptron. *Biomedical Signal Processing and Control, 86*, 105331. DOI: 10.1016/j.bspc.2023.105331

Liu, X., Wang, Z., Jin, C., Li, F., & Li, G. (2019). A blockchain-based medical data sharing and protection scheme. *IEEE Access : Practical Innovations, Open Solutions*, *7*, 118943–118953. DOI: 10.1109/ACCESS.2019.2937685

Liu, X., Xie, M., Wen, X., Li, L., Zhang, H., Yu, P. S., & Zhao, X. (2020). Micro- and macro-level churn analysis of large-scale mobile games. *Knowledge and Information Systems*, *62*(4), 1465–1496. DOI: 10.1007/s10115-019-01394-7

Livingstone, S., Stoilova, M., & Nandagiri, R. (2019). *Children's data and privacy online: Growing up in a digital age – An evidence review*. London School of Economics and Political Science. Retrieved from http://eprints.lse.ac.uk/101283

Livingstone, S. (2004). Media literacy and the challenge of new information and communication technologies. *Communication Review*, *7*(1), 3–14. DOI: 10.1080/10714420490280152

Li, Y., Liang, Z., Wang, Y., & Chang, Y. (2023). The negative effect of service robots' affective human-likeness on consumer satisfaction in frontline service encounters. *International Journal of Hospitality Management*, *115*, 103603. DOI: 10.1016/j.ijhm.2023.103603

Lodwick, G. S., Keats, T. E., & Dorst, J. P. (1963). The coding of roentgen images for computer analysis as applied to lung cancer. *Radiology*, *80*(2), 273–275. DOI: 10.1148/80.2.273 PMID: 14053755

Lopes, J. M., Massano-Cardoso, I., & Granadeiro, C. (2025). Festivals in the age of AI: Smarter crowds, happier fans. *Tourism and Hospitality*, *6*(1), 35. DOI: 10.3390/tourhosp6010035

Lotter, W., Diab, A. R., Haslam, B., Kim, J. G., Grisot, G., Wu, E., Wu, K., Onieva, J. O., Boyer, Y., Boxerman, J. L., Wang, M., Bandler, M., Vijayaraghavan, G. R., & Gregory Sorensen, A. (2021). Robust breast cancer detection in mammography and digital breast tomosynthesis using an annotation-efficient deep learning approach. *Nature Medicine*, *27*(2), 244–249. DOI: 10.1038/s41591-020-01174-9 PMID: 33432172

Lovesey, E. J. (1970). The hovercraft environment. *Applied Ergonomics*, *1*(3), 134–139. DOI: 10.1016/0003-6870(70)90002-5 PMID: 15676324

Lundberg, S. M., & Lee, S. I. (2017). A unified approach to interpreting model predictions. *Advances in Neural Information Processing Systems*, •••, 4765–4774.

Madanchian, M. (2024). The impact of artificial intelligence marketing on e-commerce sales. *Systems*, *12*(10), 429. DOI: 10.3390/systems12100429

Majeed, M. T., & Sharif, F. (2024). The role of digitalization in driving green growth: A global panel data perspective. *Pakistan Journal of Commerce and Social Sciences*, *18*(2), 435–467.

Mandala, V., Rajavarman, R., Jamunadevi, C., Janani, R., & Avudaiappan, T. (2023). *Recognition of E-commerce through big data classification and data mining techniques involving artificial intelligence*. IEEE., DOI: 10.1109/ICCES57224.2023.10192673

Manyika, J., Chui, M., Miremadi, M., Bughin, J., George, K., Willmott, P., & Dewhurst, M. (2017). *A future that works: Automation, employment, and productivity*. Retrieved from https://api.semanticscholar.org/CorpusID:114479521

Marsh, E., Vallejos, E. P., & Spence, A. (2022). The digital workplace and its dark side: An integrative review. *Computers in Human Behavior*, *128*, 107118. DOI: 10.1016/j.chb.2021.107118

McCarthy, A. M., Maor, D., McConney, A., & Cavanaugh, C. (2023). Digital transformation in education: Critical components for leaders of system change. *Social Sciences & Humanities Open*, *8*(1), 100479. DOI: 10.1016/j.ssaho.2023.100479

McCombs, M. E., & Shaw, D. L. (1972). The agenda-setting function of mass media. *Public Opinion Quarterly*, *36*(2), 176–187. DOI: 10.1086/267990

Medler, B. (2011). Player dossiers: Analyzing gameplay data as a reward. Game Studies. *The International Journal of Computer Game Research*, *11*(1). https://gamestudies.org/1101/articles/medler

Meghwanshi, S. (2024). Artificial intelligence in agriculture: A review. *International Research Journal of Modernization in Engineering Technology and Science*, *6*(3), 4358–4372. https://www.researchgate.net/publication/379308989_ARTIFICIAL_INTELLIGENCE_IN_AGRICULTURE_A_REVIEW

Mei, L., Tang, N., Zeng, Z., & Shi, W. (2025). Artificial intelligence technology in live streaming e-commerce: Analysis of driving factors of consumer purchase decisions. *International Journal of Computers, Communications & Control*, *20*(1). Advance online publication. DOI: 10.15837/ijccc.2025.1.6871

Mercader, C., & Gairín, J. (2020). University teachers' perception of barriers to the use of digital technologies: The importance of the academic discipline. *International Journal of Educational Technology in Higher Education*, *17*(1), 4. DOI: 10.1186/s41239-020-0182-x

Miller, A. (2022). League of Legends: Building community and keeping players engaged. *International Journal of Gaming and Computer-Mediated Communication*, *25*(2), 60–75. DOI: 10.1002/ijg.2022.25.2.60

Miotto, R., Wang, F., Wang, S., Jiang, X., & Dudley, J. T. (2018). Deep learning for healthcare: Review, opportunities and challenges. *Briefings in Bioinformatics*, *19*(6), 1236–1246. DOI: 10.1093/bib/bbx044 PMID: 28481991

Mojang. (2021). Minecraft active player statistics. Mojang. Retrieved from https://www.mojang.com

Montgomery, M., & Oliver, D. (2021). Sustaining engagement in live service games: Strategies for retention through content updates. *Journal of Interactive Media*, *10*(4), 211–229.

Montrieux, H., Vanderlinde, R., Schellens, T., & De Marez, L. (2015). Teaching and Learning with Mobile Technology: A Qualitative Explorative Study about the Introduction of Tablet Devices in Secondary Education. *PLoS One*, *10*(12), e0144008. DOI: 10.1371/journal.pone.0144008 PMID: 26641454

Mukherji, A., & Ganguli, N. (2020). *Efficient and scalable electronic health record management using permissioned blockchain technology.* Paper presented at the 2020 4th International Conference on Electronics, Materials Engineering & Nano-Technology (IEMENTech). DOI: 10.1109/IEMENTech51367.2020.9270106

Musa, H. G., Fatmawati, I., Nuryakin, N., & Suyanto, M. (2024). Marketing research trends using technology acceptance model (TAM): A comprehensive review of research (2002–2022). *Cogent Business & Management*, *11*(1), 2329375. DOI: 10.1080/23311975.2024.2329375

Mustač, K., Bačić, K., Skorin-Kapov, L., & Sužnjević, M. (2022). Predicting player churn of a free-to-play mobile video game using supervised machine learning. *Applied Sciences (Basel, Switzerland)*, *12*(6), 2795. DOI: 10.3390/app12062795

Narayanan, A., & Shmatikov, V. (2010). Myths and Fallacies of "Personally Identifiable Information". *Communications of the ACM*, *53*(6), 24–26. DOI: 10.1145/1743546.1743558

Nguyen, D., & Hekman, E. (2022). The news framing of artificial intelligence: A critical exploration of how media discourses make sense of automation. *AI & Society*, *39*(2), 1–19. DOI: 10.1007/s00146-022-01511-1

Nguyen, T., Park, J., & Kim, R. (2023). *Blockchain in gaming: Ownership and real-world value*. Crypto Gaming Insights. [White paper]

Niantic. (2023). Pokémon GO: Augmented reality gaming for engagement [Video game]. Niantic.

Nichols, M. (2023). Transforming conventional education through ODDE. In Zawacki-Richter, O., & Jung, I. (Eds.), *Handbook of open, distance and digital education* (pp. 641–657). Springer Nature Singapore., DOI: 10.1007/978-981-19-2080-6_35

Nieborg, D. B. (2017). From premium to freemium: The political economy of the app. *Social Media + Society, 3*(1), 1–12.

Nieborg, D. B., & Poell, T. (2018). The platformization of cultural production: Theorizing the contingent cultural commodity. *New Media & Society, 20*(11), 4275–4292. DOI: 10.1177/1461444818769694

Northouse, P. G. (2021). *Leadership: Theory and Practice* (9th ed.). SAGE Publications, Inc.

O'Neil, C. (2016). *Weapons of math destruction: How big data increases inequality and threatens democracy*. Crown.

Oberer, B., & Erkollar, A. (2018). Leadership 4.0: Digital Leaders in the Age of Industry 4.0. *International Journal of Organisational Leadership, 7*(4), 404–412. DOI: 10.33844/ijol.2018.60332

Okafor, B. E. (2013). Development of a hovercraft prototype. *IACSIT International Journal of Engineering and Technology, 3*(3), 276–281. DOI: 10.1109/TCST.2002.804134

Ordóñez de Pablos, P. (Ed.). (2022). *Handbook of research on building greener economics and adopting digital tools in the era of climate change*. IGI Global. DOI: 10.4018/978-1-6684-4610-2

Ordu, A., & Nayır, F. (2021). What is Digital Leadership? A suggestion of the definition. *E-International Journal of Educational Research, 12*(3), 68–81. DOI: 10.19160/e-ijer.946094

Óskarsdóttir, M., Gísladóttir, K. E., Stefánsson, R., Gudmundsson, G., Gylfason, G. K., & Helgason, A. R. (2022). Social networks for enhanced player churn prediction in mobile free-to-play games. *Applied Network Science, 7*(1), 82. DOI: 10.1007/s41109-022-00524-5

Pangrazio, L., & Sefton-Green, J. (Eds.). (2022). *Learning to live with datafication: Educational case studies and initiatives from across the world* (1st ed.). Routledge., DOI: 10.4324/9781003136842

Panshin, I., Solovieva, O., Kornilova, O., & Eronin, V. (2021). The Impact of Digitalization on Leadership. In Popkova, E. G., & Sergi, B. S. (Eds.), *Modern Global Economic System: Evolutional Development vs. Revolutionary Leap. Lecture Notes in Networks and Systems* (pp. 1272–1278). Springer., DOI: 10.1007/978-3-030-69415-9_139

Pariser, E. (2011). *The filter bubble: What the Internet is hiding from you.* Penguin Press.

Park, S., & Yoon, S. (2025). Cross-national findings of factors affecting the acceptance of AI-based sustainable fintech. *Sustainability (Basel), 17*(1), 49. DOI: 10.3390/su17010049

Patil, S. M., Kharat, A. M., Jain, S., Tripathi, V. V. R., Bisen, G. K., & Joshi, A. (2024). Investigating the influence and function of artificial intelligence in contemporary marketing management: Marketing in the AI era. In Proceedings of the 2024 *International Conference on Advances in Computing, Communication and Applied Informatics,* 1-5

Patil, D. (2025). Artificial intelligence in retail and e-commerce: enhancing customer experience through personalization, predictive analytics, and real-time engagement, *SSRN*, 1-10. DOI: 10.2139/ssrn.5057420

Paul, R. H. (2024). University leadership in the digital age: challenges, opportunities and critical actions. Journal of Open, Distance and Digital Education, 1(1), 1-15. DOI: 10.25619/rp3rpr75

Paun, C., Ivascu, C., Olteteanu, A., & Dantis, D. (2024). The main drivers of e-commerce adoption: A global panel data analysis. *Journal of Theoretical and Applied Electronic Commerce Research, 19*(3), 2198–2217. DOI: 10.3390/jtaer19030107

Peng, B. (2022). Digital leadership: State governance in the era of digital technology. *Cultura e Scuola, 5*(4), 210–225. DOI: 10.1177/2096608321989835

Peng, X., Huang, Z., Sun, X., & Saenko, K. (2020). *Domain-agnostic federated learning for multi-site medical image analysis*. International Conference on Medical Image Computing and Computer-Assisted Intervention., Available at https://link.springer.com/chapter/10.1007/978-3-030-59725-2_67, Retrieved 2024, from.

Perianez, A., Saas, A., & Guitart, A. (2016). Churn prediction in mobile social games: Towards a complete assessment using survival ensembles. In *Proceedings of the 2016 IEEE International Conference on Data Science and Advanced Analytics (DSAA)* (pp. 564–573). IEEE. DOI: 10.1109/DSAA.2016.84

Petry, T. (2018). Digital Leadership. In North, K., Maier, R., & Haas, O. (Eds.), *Knowledge Management in Digital Change* (pp. 209–218). Springer., DOI: 10.1007/978-3-319-73546-7_12

Pham, T. T., Huang, H., Tseng, F., Cheng, T. C., & Teng, C. (2021). For whom does flow not enhance online gamer loyalty? *Industrial Management & Data Systems, 122*(1), 215–234. DOI: 10.1108/IMDS-05-2021-0338

Playout, C., Duval, R., Boucher, M. C., & Cheriet, F. (2022). Focused Attention in Transformers for interpretable classification of retinal images. *Medical Image Analysis, 82*, 102608. DOI: 10.1016/j.media.2022.102608 PMID: 36150271

Prasad, A., Sethi, S. P., & Naik, P. A. (2012). Understanding the impact of churn in dynamic oligopoly markets. *Automatica, 48*(11), 2882–2887. DOI: 10.1016/j.automatica.2012.08.031

Predescu, A., & Mocanu, M. (2020). A data driven survey of video games. In 2020 12th International Conference on Electronics, Computers and Artificial Intelligence (ECAI) (pp. 1–6). IEEE. DOI: 10.1109/ECAI50035.2020.9223203

Qiu, H., Zhang, X., Feng, M., Zhang, Z., Wang, J., & Wang, Z. (2024). Exploring the income-increasing benefits of rural e-commerce in China: Implications for the sustainable development of farmers. *Sustainability (Basel), 16*(17), 7437. DOI: 10.3390/su16177437

Raghavan, M., Barocas, S., Kleinberg, J., & Levy, K. (2020). Mitigating bias in algorithmic hiring: Evaluating claims and practices. *Proceedings of the 2020 Conference on Fairness, Accountability, and Transparency*, 469–481. https://doi.org/ DOI: 10.1145/3351095.3372828

Rajab, M., Gazal, A., & Alkattan, K. (2020). Challenges to Online Medical Education During the COVID-19 Pandemic. *Cureus, 12*(7), e8966. DOI: 10.7759/cureus.8966 PMID: 32766008

Rajendran, S., Rajagopal, S. K., Thanarajan, T., Shankar, K., Kumar, S., Alsubaie, N. M., Ishak, M. K., & Mostafa, S. M. (2023). Automated Segmentation of Brain Tumor MRI Images Using Deep Learning. *IEEE Access : Practical Innovations, Open Solutions, 11*, 64758–64768. DOI: 10.1109/ACCESS.2023.3288017

Ramanathan, U., Mathirajan, M., & Balakrishnan, A. S. (2024). Role of e-tailing: A new way of business during the COVID situation in India – A critical view. *Benchmarking, 31*(3), 1062–1072. DOI: 10.1108/BIJ-04-2024-785

Raman, R., Lathabai, H. H., & Nedungadi, P. (2024). Sustainable development goal 12 and its synergies with other SDGs: Identification of key research contributions and policy insights. *Discover Sustainability*, *5*(1), 150. DOI: 10.1007/s43621-024-00289-0

Ratta, R., Sodhi, J., & Saxana, U. (2025). The relevance of trust in the implementation of AI-driven clinical decision support systems by healthcare professionals: An extended UTAUT model. *Electronic Journal of Knowledge Management*, *23*(1), 47–66. DOI: 10.34190/ejkm.23.1.3499

Ratwani, R. M. (2017). Electronic health records and improved patient care: Opportunities for applied psychology. *Current Directions in Psychological Science*, *26*(4), 359–365. DOI: 10.1177/0963721417700691 PMID: 28808359

Reichheld, F. F., & Teal, T. (1996). *The loyalty effect: The hidden force behind growth, profits, and lasting value*. Harvard Business Review Press.

Respawn Entertainment. (2023). *Apex Legends: Seasonal events and player engagement* [Video game]. Respawn Entertainment.

Ribeiro, M. T., Singh, S., & Guestrin, C. 2016. "Why should I trust you?: Explaining the predictions of any classifier." *Proceedings of the 22nd ACM SIGKDD International Conference on Knowledge Discovery and Data Mining*: 1135–1144. https://doi.org/DOI: 10.1145/2939672.2939778

Richter, A., Heinrich, P., Stocker, A., & Schwabe, G. (2018). Digital work design. *Business & Information Systems Engineering*, *60*(3), 259–264. DOI: 10.1007/s12599-018-0534-4

Rieke, N., Hancox, J., Li, W., Milletarì, F., Roth, H. R., Albarqouni, S., Bakas, S., Galtier, M. N., Landman, B. A., Maier-Hein, K., Ourselin, S., Sheller, M., Summers, R. M., Trask, A., Xu, D., Xu, M., & Cardoso, M. J. (2020). The future of digital health with federated learning. *NPJ Digital Medicine*, *3*(1), 1–7. DOI: 10.1038/s41746-020-00323-1 PMID: 33015372

Riot Games. (2023). *League of Legends: The power of social groups in player retention* [Video game]. Riot Games.

Robinson, P. (2002). *The CNN effect: The myth of news, foreign policy, and intervention*. Routledge.

Rodriguez, J., & Martinez, L. (2024). Customer acquisition versus retention: A cost-benefit analysis. *Business Strategy Research*, *11*(2), 33–47.

Ronneberger, O., Fischer, P., & Brox, T. (2015). U-Net: Convolutional networks for biomedical image segmentation. In *MICCAI 2015* (pp. 234–241). Medical Image Computing and Computer-Assisted Intervention. Springer., DOI: 10.1007/978-3-319-24574-4_28

Röntgen, W. C. (1896). On a new kind of rays. *Nature*, *53*(1369), 274–276. DOI: 10.1038/053274b0 PMID: 17769966

Roohi, S., Relas, A., Takatalo, J., Heiskanen, H., & Hämäläinen, P. (2020). Predicting game difficulty and churn without players. In Proceedings of the Annual Symposium on Computer-Human Interaction in Play (CHI PLAY '20) (pp. 585–593). Association for Computing Machinery. DOI: 10.1145/3410404.3414235

Rothmeier, K., Pflanzl, N., Hüllmann, J. A., & Preuss, M. (2021). Prediction of player churn and disengagement based on user activity data of a freemium online strategy game. *IEEE Transactions on Games*, *13*(1), 78–88. DOI: 10.1109/TG.2020.2992282

Runge, J., Gao, P., Garcin, F., & Faltings, B. (2014). Churn prediction for high-value players in casual social games. In *2014 IEEE Conference on Computational Intelligence and Games* (pp. 1–8). IEEE. DOI: 10.1109/CIG.2014.6932875

Sakashita, N., Shirai, K., Ueda, Y., Ono, A., & Teshima, T. (2020). Convolutional neural network-based automatic liver delineation on contrast-enhanced and non-contrast-enhanced CT images for radiotherapy planning. *Reports of Practical Oncology and Radiotherapy : Journal of Greatpoland Cancer Center in Poznan and Polish Society of Radiation Oncology*, *25*(6), 981–986. DOI: 10.1016/j.rpor.2020.09.005 PMID: 33100915

Sak, T., Mylko, I., Ivashko, O., Chulipa, I., Wołowiec, T., & Sokołowska-Woźniak, J. (2025). How the digital economy is revolutionizing marketing management and driving sustainable development. *Sustainability (Basel)*, *17*(3), 1130. DOI: 10.3390/su17031130

Salen, K., & Zimmerman, E. (2004). *Rules of play: Game design fundamentals*. MIT Press.

Salzano, F., Marchesi, L., Pareschi, R., & Tonelli, R. (2024). Integrating blockchain technology within an information ecosystem. *Blockchain: Research Applications*, *5*(4), 100225.

Sarfraz, M., Khawaja, K. F., & Ivascu, L. (2022). Factors affecting business school students' performance during the COVID-19 pandemic: A moderated and mediated model. *International Journal of Management Education*, *20*(2), 100630. DOI: 10.1016/j.ijme.2022.100630

Saykili, A. (2019). Higher education in the digital age: The impact of digital connective technologies. *Journal of Educational Technology & Online Learning*, *2*(1), 1–15. DOI: 10.31681/jetol.516971

Schiuma, G., Schettini, E., Santarsiero, F., & Carlucci, D. (2022). The transformative leadership compass: Six competencies for digital transformation entrepreneurship. *International Journal of Entrepreneurial Behaviour & Research*, *28*(5), 1273–1291. DOI: 10.1108/IJEBR-01-2021-0087

Scholz, T. (2017). *Uberworked and underpaid: How workers are disrupting the digital economy*. Polity Press.

Seif El-Nasr, M., Drachen, A., & Canossa, A. (2013). *Game analytics: Maximizing the value of player data*. Springer., DOI: 10.1007/978-1-4471-4769-5

Selvaraju, R. R., Cogswell, M., Das, A., Vedantam, R., Parikh, D., & Batra, D. 2017. "Grad-CAM: Visual explanations from deep networks via gradient-based localization." *Proceedings of the IEEE International Conference on Computer Vision*: 618–626. https://doi.org/DOI: 10.1109/ICCV.2017.74

Selwyn, N. (2014). *Digital technology and the contemporary university: Degrees of digitization*. Routledge. DOI: 10.4324/9781315768656

Shahnaz, A., Qamar, U., & Khalid, A. (2019). Using blockchain for electronic health records. *IEEE Access : Practical Innovations, Open Solutions*, *7*, 147782–147795. DOI: 10.1109/ACCESS.2019.2946373

Shahroom, A., & Hussin, N. (2018). Industrial Revolution 4.0 and Education. *International Journal of Academic Research in Business & Social Sciences*, *8*(9), 314–319. DOI: 10.6007/IJARBSS/v8-i9/4593

Sharma, B., Halder, R., & Singh, J. (2020). *Blockchain-based interoperable healthcare using zero-knowledge proofs and proxy re-encryption*. Paper presented at the 2020 international conference on COMmunication Systems & NETworkS (COMSNETS). DOI: 10.1109/COMSNETS48256.2020.9027413

Sharma, P., Borah, M. D., & Namasudra, S. (2021). Improving security of medical big data by using Blockchain technology. *Computers & Electrical Engineering*, *96*, 107529. DOI: 10.1016/j.compeleceng.2021.107529

Shen, D., Wu, G., & Suk, H. I. (2017). Deep learning in medical image analysis. *Annual Review of Biomedical Engineering*, *19*(1), 221–248. DOI: 10.1146/annurev-bioeng-071516-044442 PMID: 28301734

Sheninger, E. (2019). *Digital Leadership: Changing Paradigms for Changing Times*. Corwin Press.

Shneiderman, B., & Plaisant, C. (2010). *Designing the user interface: Strategies for effective human-computer interaction* (5th ed.). Pearson.

Siderits, J. (2011). *Hovercraft: Body and Frame* (Doctoral dissertation, University of Cincinnati).

Singh, P., Nandi, P., Jaiswal, R. S., & Padhi, A. (2022). Impact of the E-Commerce business of India. *Journal of Emerging Technologies and Innovative Research*, *9*(6).

Sira-Ramírez, H., & Ibanez, C. A. (2000). On the control of the hovercraft system. *Dynamics and Control*, *10*(2), 151–163. DOI: 10.1023/A:1008343807817

Smart, N. (2023). Computing on encrypted data. *IEEE Security and Privacy*, *21*(4), 94–98. DOI: 10.1109/MSEC.2023.3279517

Smith, A. (2023). *The future of social gaming: Cross-platform interactions and community dynamics*. Global Gaming Strategies. [Research report]

Smith, A., & Lee, D. (2023). Immersive technologies in gaming: VR and AR's role in player retention. *Journal of Virtual Gaming*, *17*(3), 45–59.

Smith, T., & Johnson, M. (2019). Guild systems and social bonds in MMORPGs: A study of World of Warcraft. *International Journal of Game Studies*, *14*(2), 155–171. DOI: 10.1016/ijgs.2019.14.2.155

Song, L., Lin, J., Wang, Z. J., & Wang, H. (2020). An End-to-End Multi-Task deep learning framework for skin lesion analysis. *IEEE Journal of Biomedical and Health Informatics*, *24*(10), 2912–2921. DOI: 10.1109/JBHI.2020.2973614 PMID: 32071016

Song, M., Zhang, H., Xing, X., & Duan, Y. (2023). Appreciation vs. apology: Research on the influence mechanism of chatbot service recovery based on politeness theory. *Journal of Retailing and Consumer Services*, *73*, 103323. DOI: 10.1016/j.jretconser.2023.103323

Sonkamble, R. G., Bongale, A. M., Phansalkar, S., Sharma, A., & Rajput, S. (2023). Secure data transmission of electronic health records using blockchain technology. *Electronics (Basel)*, *12*(4), 1015. DOI: 10.3390/electronics12041015

Sowrirajan, H., Yang, J., Ng, A. Y., & Rajpurkar, P. (2021). *Self-supervising learning for chest X-ray classification. 2021 IEEE 18th International Symposium on Biomedical Imaging*. ISBI., Available at https://ieeexplore.ieee.org/document/9434139, Retrieved 2024, from.

Spanhol, F. A., Oliveira, L. S., Petitjean, C., & Heutte, L. (2016). A Dataset for Breast Cancer Histopathological Image Classification. *IEEE Transactions on Biomedical Engineering*, *63*(7), 1455–1462. DOI: 10.1109/TBME.2015.2496264 PMID: 26540668

Stiglitz, J. E. (2019, March 11). Market concentration is threatening the US economy [Blog post]. *Project Syndicate*. https://www.project-syndicate.org/commentary/united-states-economy-rising-market-power-by-joseph-e-stiglitz-2019-03

Stomberg, G., Schwan, R., Grillo, A., Jones, C. N., & Faulwasser, T. (2024). Cooperative distributed model predictive control for embedded systems: Experiments with hovercraft formations. *arXiv preprint arXiv:2409.13334* https://doi.org//arXiv.2409.13334DOI: 10.48550

Suerdem, A., & Akkilic, S. (2021). Cultural differences in media framing of AI. In Schiele, B., Liu, X., & Bauer, M. W. (Eds.), *Science cultures in a diverse world: Knowing, sharing, caring* (pp. 185–207). Springer., DOI: 10.1007/978-981-16-5379-7_10

Supercell. (2021). Clash of Clans: Player engagement and churn reduction strategies [Video game]. Supercell.

Suri, T., & Jack, W. (2016). The long-run poverty and gender impacts of mobile money. *Science*, *354*(6317), 1288–1292. DOI: 10.1126/science.aah5309 PMID: 27940873

Suryadi, M., Muslim, A. Q., & Setyono, L. (2024). Exploring the nexus of Digital Leadership and digital literacy on higher education performance: The role of digital innovation. *European Journal of Educational Research*, *13*(1), 207–218. DOI: 10.12973/eu-jer.13.1.207

Suryahadikusumah, A., & Nadya, A. (2020). Digital Literacy and Innovation for Guidance and Counseling Program. *Advances in Social Science, Education and Humanities Research*, *462*, 190–195. DOI: 10.2991/assehr.k.200814.041

Tagscherer, F., & Carbon, C. C. (2023). Leadership for successful digitalization: A literature review on companies' internal and external aspects of digitalization. *Sustainable Technology and Entrepreneurship*, *2*(2), 100039. DOI: 10.1016/j.stae.2023.100039

Tajfel, H., & Turner, J. C. (1979). An integrative theory of intergroup conflict. In Austin, W. G., & Worchel, S. (Eds.), *The social psychology of intergroup relations* (pp. 33–47). Brooks/Cole.

Tanaka, K., Iwasaki, M., & Wang, H. O. (2001). Switching control of an R/C hovercraft: Stabilization and smooth switching. *IEEE Transactions on Systems, Man, and Cybernetics. Part B, Cybernetics, 31*(6), 853–863. DOI: 10.1109/3477.969489 PMID: 18244851

Tan, M., & Le, Q. V. 2019. “EfficientNet: Rethinking model scaling for convolutional neural networks.” *International Conference on Machine Learning*: 6105–6114. https://doi.org/DOI: 10.48550/arXiv.1905.11946

Thompson, R., Lee, S., & Kim, J. (2023). Predictive modeling of customer churn in service industries. *Journal of Service Research, 26*(3), 267–285.

Tian, Y., Wang, S., Xiong, J., Bi, R., Zhou, Z., & Bhuiyan, M. Z. A. (2023). Robust and Privacy-Preserving decentralized Deep federated Learning training: Focusing on digital healthcare applications. *IEEE/ACM Transactions on Computational Biology and Bioinformatics, 21*(4), 890–901. DOI: 10.1109/TCBB.2023.3243932 PMID: 37028039

Tigre, F. B., Henriques, P. L., & Curado, C. (2023). The digital leadership emerging construct: a multi-method approach. Management Review Quarterly, 1-48.

Topol, E. J. (2019). High-performance medicine: The convergence of human and artificial intelligence. *Nature Medicine, 25*(1), 44–56. DOI: 10.1038/s41591-018-0300-7 PMID: 30617339

Tufekci, Z. (2017). *Twitter and tear gas: The power and fragility of networked protest.* Yale University Press.

Tygel, A. F., & Kirsch, R. (2016). Contributions of Paulo Freire for a critical data literacy: A popular education approach. *Journal of Community Informatics, 12*(3). Advance online publication. DOI: 10.15353/joci.v12i3.3279

Ukwoma, S. C., Iwundu, N. E., & Iwundu, I. E. (2016). Digital literacy skills possessed by students of UNN, implications for effective learning and performance: A study of the MTN Universities Connect Library. *New Library World, 117*(11/12), 702–720. DOI: 10.1108/NLW-08-2016-0061

Ullal, M. S., Spulbar, C., Hawaldar, I. T., Popescu, V., & Birau, R. (2021). The impact of online reviews on e-commerce sales in India: A case study. Economic Research-. *Ekonomska Istrazivanja, 34*(1), 2408–2422. DOI: 10.1080/1331677X.2020.1865179

United Nations. (2015). *Transforming our world: The 2030 Agenda for Sustainable Development* (A/RES/70/1). https://sdgs.un.org/2030agenda

van Deursen, A. J., & van Dijk, J. A. (2019). The first-level digital divide shifts from inequalities in physical access to inequalities in material access. *New Media & Society*, *21*(2), 354–375. DOI: 10.1177/1461444818797082 PMID: 30886536

Van Wart, M., Ni, A., Medina, P., Canelon, J., Kordrostami, M., Zhang, J., & Liu, Y. (2020). Integrating students' perspectives about online learning: A hierarchy of factors. *International Journal of Educational Technology in Higher Education*, *17*(1), 53. DOI: 10.1186/s41239-020-00229-8 PMID: 34778515

Vaswani, A., Shazeer, N., Parmar, N., Uszkoreit, J., Jones, L., & Gomez, A. N.. (2017). Attention is all you need. *Advances in Neural Information Processing Systems*, *30*, 5998–6008. DOI: 10.48550/arXiv.1706.03762

Vidani, J. (2024). Evaluating the influence of social media advertising on e-commerce sales. *SSRN*, *11*, 52–58. DOI: 10.2139/ssrn.4849890

Vosoughi, S., Roy, D., & Aral, S. (2018). The spread of true and false news online. *Science*, *359*(6380), 1146–1151. DOI: 10.1126/science.aap9559 PMID: 29590045

Waisbord, S. (2019). The vulnerabilities of journalism. *Journalism*, *20*(1), 210–213. DOI: 10.1177/1464884918809283

Wang, C., Ahmad, S. F., Ayassrah, A. Y. B. A., Awwad, E. M., Irshad, M., Ali, Y. A., Al-Razgan, M., Khan, Y., & Han, H. (2023). An empirical evaluation of the technology acceptance model for Artificial Intelligence in E-commerce. *Heliyon*, *9*(X), e18349. DOI: 10.1016/j.heliyon.2023.e18349 PMID: 37520947

Wang, M., Guo, Y., Zhang, C., Wang, C., Huang, H., & Jia, X. (2021). MedShare: A privacy-preserving medical data sharing system by using blockchain. *IEEE Transactions on Services Computing*, *16*(1), 438–451. DOI: 10.1109/TSC.2021.3114719

Wei, C., Ren, S., Guo, K., Hu, H., & Liang, J. (2023). High-Resolution Swin Transformer for Automatic Medical Image Segmentation. *Sensors (Basel)*, *23*(7), 3420. DOI: 10.3390/s23073420 PMID: 37050479

Weiss, I., & Vilenchik, D. (2023). Predicting churn in online games by quantifying diversity of engagement. *Big Data*, *11*(4), 282–295. DOI: 10.1089/big.2022.0109 PMID: 36940288

Williams, D., Caplan, S., & Yee, N. (2006). Who plays, how much, and why? Debunking the stereotypical gamer profile. *Journal of Computer-Mediated Communication*, *11*(4), 993–1018. DOI: 10.1111/j.1083-6101.2008.00428.x

WIRED. (2023). The best games have the smartest learning curves.

Wohn, D. Y. (2011). The role of social affordances in online games: Exploring social behavior and social networks. *Journal of Computer-Mediated Communication*, *16*(4), 451–470. DOI: 10.1111/j.1083-6101.2011.01548.x

Wolterink, J. M., Dinkla, A. M., Savenije, M. H. F., Seevinck, P. R., van den Berg, C. A. T., & Išgum, I. (2017). Deep MR to CT translation using unpaired data. In *Simulation and Synthesis in Medical Imaging* (pp. 14–23). Springer., DOI: 10.1007/978-3-319-68127-6_2

World Bank. (2016). *World Development Report 2016: Digital dividends*. World Bank., DOI: 10.1596/978-1-4648-0671-1

World Bank. (2020). *Fintech: The new frontier of finance*. World Bank.

World Health Organization. (2021). *Breast cancer*. https://www.who.int/news-room/fact-sheets/detail/breast-cancer

Wu, C. W., & Monfort, A. (2023). Role of artificial intelligence in marketing strategies and performance. *Psychology and Marketing*, *40*(4), 484–496. DOI: 10.1002/mar.21737

Wu, H., Dwivedi, A. D., & Srivastava, G. (2021). Security and privacy of patient information in medical systems based on blockchain technology. *ACM Transactions on Multimedia Computing Communications and Applications*, *17*(2s), 1–17. DOI: 10.1145/3408321

Xie, W., Cabecinhas, D., Cunha, R., & Silvestre, C. (2018). Robust motion control of an underactuated hovercraft. *IEEE Transactions on Control Systems Technology*, *27*(5), 2195–2208. DOI: 10.1109/TCST.2018.2862861

Xu, Z., Liu, Y., Xu, G., & Lukasiewicz, T. (2024). Self-Supervised Medical Image segmentation using deep reinforced adaptive masking. *IEEE Transactions on Medical Imaging*, *1*. Advance online publication. DOI: 10.1109/TMI.2024.3436608 PMID: 39088493

Yadav, U. S., & Vyas, S. Kanchan, Ghosal, I., & Yadav, A. K. (2024). Impact of entrepreneurial leadership, social media, digital technology, entrepreneurial orientation, and innovation on business performance in the handicraft sector: Talent management as mediating construct. Journal of Innovation and Entrepreneurship, 13(1). https://doi.org/10.xxxx/jie13011234

Yang, X., Qu, S., Wang, Z., Li, L., An, X., & Cong, Z. (2024). The study on ultrasound image classification using a dual-branch model based on Resnet50 guided by U-net segmentation results. *BMC Medical Imaging*, *24*(1), 314. DOI: 10.1186/s12880-024-01486-z PMID: 39558260

Yan, Z., Wicaksana, J., Zhang, Z., & Yang, X. (2023). Label-efficient self-supervising federated learning for tackling data heterogeneity in medical imaging. *IEEE Transactions on Medical Imaging*, *42*(9), 2672–2683. Retrieved 2024, from https://ieeexplore.ieee.org/document/10093728

Yaqoob, I., Salah, K., Jayaraman, R., & Al-Hammadi, Y. (2022). Blockchain for healthcare data management: Opportunities, challenges, and future recommendations. *Neural Computing & Applications*, *34*(14), 1–16. DOI: 10.1007/s00521-020-05519-w

Yee, N. (2006). Motivations for play in online games. *Cyberpsychology & Behavior*, *9*(6), 772–775. DOI: 10.1089/cpb.2006.9.772 PMID: 17201605

Yee, N. (2006). The demographics, motivations, and derived experiences of users of massively multi-user online graphical environments. *Presence (Cambridge, Mass.)*, *15*(3), 309–329. DOI: 10.1162/pres.15.3.309

Yi, C. H., Keong, L. K., & Razali, N. F., & Innovation. (2023). Blockchain-Based Medical Record Management System (BBMRMS). *Journal of Applied Technology*, *7*(4), 1.

Yi, X., Walia, E., & Babyn, P. (2019). Generative adversarial networks in medical imaging: A review. *Medical Image Analysis*, *58*, 101552. DOI: 10.1016/j.media.2019.101552 PMID: 31521965

You, C., Li, G., Zhang, Y., Zhang, X., Shan, H., & Ju, S. (2020). Self-supervised learning for medical image denoising. *Medical Image Analysis*, *65*, 101749. Retrieved 2024, from https://www.sciencedirect.com/science/article/pii/S1361841520301125

Zagal, J. P., Björk, S., & Lewis, C. (2013). Dark patterns in the design of games. In Foundations of Digital Games 2013. https://www.fdg2013.org/papers/fdg2013_paper_17.pdf

Zaman, S. I., Khan, S. A., Qabool, S., & Gupta, H. (2023). How digitalization in banking improve the service supply chain resilience of the e-commerce sector? A technological adoption model approach. *Operations Management Research : Advancing Practice Through Research*, *16*(2), 904–930. DOI: 10.1007/s12063-022-00341-0

Zavyalova, E. B., Volokhina, V. A., Troyanskaya, M. A., & Dubova, Y. I. (2023). A humanistic model of corporate social responsibility in e-commerce with high-tech support in the artificial intelligence economy. *Humanities & Social Sciences Communications*, *10*(1), 274. DOI: 10.1057/s41599-023-01764-1 PMID: 37273417

Zech, J. R., Badgeley, M. A., Liu, M., Costa, A. B., Titano, J. J., & Oermann, E. K. (2018). Variable generalization performance of a deep learning model to detect pneumonia in chest radiographs: A cross-sectional study. *PLoS Medicine*, *15*(11), e1002683. DOI: 10.1371/journal.pmed.1002683 PMID: 30399157

Zeike, S., Bradbury, K., Lindert, L., & Pfaff, H. (2019). Digital Leadership Skills and Associations with Psychological Well-Being. *International Journal of Environmental Research and Public Health,* 16(14), 2628. 2628. DOI: 10.3390/ijerph16142628

Zendle, D., & Cairns, P. (2018). Video game loot boxes are linked to problem gambling: Results of a large-scale survey. *PLoS One*, *13*(11), e0206767. DOI: 10.1371/journal.pone.0206767 PMID: 30462669

Zeng, X., Abdullah, N., & Sumari, P. (2024). Self-supervised learning framework application for medical image analysis: A review and summary. *Biomedical Engineering Online*, *23*(1), 107. DOI: 10.1186/s12938-024-01299-9 PMID: 39465395

Zhang, L., & Siewiorek, D. P. (1999). Error models for robust system design: A case study in multimedia servers. *IEEE Transactions on Reliability*, *48*(2), 101–113. DOI: 10.1109/24.784834

Zhang, Q., Liu, Y., & Zhang, H. (2023). *Federated self-supervised learning for breast cancer classification. 2023 IEEE International Conference on Bioinformatics and Biomedicine*. BIBM., Available at https://ieeexplore.ieee.org/document/10385792, Retrieved 2024, from.

Zhang, Y., & Liu, C. (2024). Unlocking the potential of artificial intelligence in fashion design and e-commerce applications: The case of Mid-Journey. *Journal of Theoretical and Applied Electronic Commerce Research*, *19*(1), 654–670. DOI: 10.3390/jtaer19010035

Zhang, Z., & Zhang, S. (2020). Financial technology and its impact on the financial services industry. *International Journal of Financial Management*, *15*(1), 34–50. DOI: 10.2139/ssrn.3318835

Zhao, M., Wang, S., & Xia, T. (2025). The social welfare effect of e-commerce product reputation information asymmetry from the perspective of network externality. *PLoS One*, *20*(1), e0313852. DOI: 10.1371/journal.pone.0313852 PMID: 39746014

Zheng, A., Chen, L., Xie, F., Tao, J., Fan, C., & Zheng, Z. (2020). Keep you from leaving: Churn prediction in online games. In Nah, Y., Cui, B., Lee, S. W., Yu, J. X., Moon, Y. S., & Whang, S. E. (Eds.), Lecture Notes in Computer Science: Vol. 12113. *Database Systems for Advanced Applications. DASFAA 2020*. Springer., DOI: 10.1007/978-3-030-59416-9_16

Zhong, Y., Guo, F., Wang, X., & Guo, J. (2024). Can e-commerce development policies promote the high-quality development of agriculture?—A quasi-natural experiment based on China's e-commerce demonstration city. *PLoS One*, *19*(5), e0299097. DOI: 10.1371/journal.pone.0299097

Zhou, R., Rau, P. L. P., & Salvendy, G. (2012). Users' trust in and satisfaction with recommendation agents. *Computers in Human Behavior*, *28*(6), 2350–2359. DOI: 10.1016/j.chb.2012.07.032

Zimmerer, D., Petersen, J., Köhler, G., Jäger, P. F., & Maier-Hein, K. H. (2019). Unsupervised anomaly detection in brain MRI scans using variational autoencoders. In *Medical Imaging with Deep Learning* (pp. 50–61). Springer., Available at https://link.springer.com/chapter/10.1007/978-3-030-32692-0_4, Retrieved 2024, from.

Ziouache, A., & Bouteraa, M. (2023). Descriptive Approach of Neo-Banking System: Conception, Challenges and Global Practices. *International Journal of Business and Technology Management*, *5*(2), 194–204.

Zou, L., Yu, S., Meng, T., Zhang, Z., Liang, X., & Xie, Y. (2023). A survey of convolutional neural network in breast cancer. *Journal of Healthcare Engineering*, *2023*, 9743929. Advance online publication. DOI: 10.1155/2023/9743929

Zou, R., Lv, X., & Zhao, J. (2021). SPChain: Blockchain-based medical data sharing and privacy-preserving eHealth system. *Information Processing & Management*, *58*(4), 102604. DOI: 10.1016/j.ipm.2021.102604

Zuboff, S. (2019). *The age of surveillance capitalism: The fight for a human future at the new frontier of power*. PublicAffairs.

About the Contributors

Patricia Ordóñez de Pablos is a professor in the Department of Business Administration in the Faculty of Business and Economics at The University of Oviedo, Spain. She completed her education in The London School of Economics, UK. Her teaching and research interests focus on the areas of strategic management, knowledge management, organizational learning, intellectual capital and information technologies, with special interest in Asia (Bhutan, China, Laos, Myanmar). She is Editor-in-Chief of the International Journal of Learning and Intellectual Capital (IJLIC) and International Journal of Asian Business and Information Management (IJABIM), respectively. She has edited books for IGI Global, Elsevier, Routledge, and Springer. In 2021, 2022 and 2023, she earned placement on Stanford University's "Ranking of the World Scientists: World's Top 2% Scientists" list. Additionally she is listed in World Top Scientists of Research.com in the Areas of Social Science and Humanities in Spain and Engineering and Technology in Spain.

Xi Zhang is the professor and department head of Information Management and Management Science, College of Management and Economics, Tianjin University, China. His research interests are knowledge management systems, digital transformation, and people analytics. He has published several papers in international journals such as Journal of Knowledge Management, Journal of MIS, CHB, IEEE TEM, IEEE TKDE, etc. He also served as editorial board of IJABIM, IJSWIS, JMSE and JSTPM.

Muhammad Anshari has been named on the Stanford University List of Top 2% World Researchers in 2022 for the categories of ICT, Business & Management. He has published many peer reviewed journal papers, book chapters, and edited books. He is a Senior Assistant Professor at the Universiti Brunei Darussalam School of Business and Economics (UBDSBE) and currently serves as Deputy Director for the Institute of Policy Studies. His professional experience started when he was IT Business Analyst at Astra International. After completion of his PhD, he worked as research fellow at National Taiwan University. Before that he pursued research fellowship at King Saud University - the Kingdom of Saudi Arabia 2009. His research interests are Business Information Systems, E-government, Health Information Systems, Digital Business and Social Computing.

Mohammad Nabil Almunawar is currently a full professor at the School of Business and Economics, Universiti of Brunei Darussalam (UBDSBE), Brunei Darussalam. He was the former dean of UBDSBE. He received his bachelor's degree in 1983 from Bogor Agricultural University, Indonesia, master's degree (MSc) from the Department of Computer Science, University of Western Ontario, London, Canada in 1991, and PhD in Computer Science/Information Systems from the University of New South Wales in 1998. Dr. Almunawar has published more than 250 papers in refereed journals, books, book chapters, and encyclopedias. He has more than 30 years of teaching experience in the area of information systems and e-business/e-commerce. His overall research interests include applications of IT in management, e-business/commerce, digital marketplace/platform, digital business ecosystem, health informatics, information security, and cloud computing. Currently, he focuses his research on digital transformation, digital marketplace platforms, and digital business ecosystems.

***

Shreya Acharjee is a M.Sc Economics student at the Department of Economics, Kristu Jayanti College, Bangalore, India. She has interested in economics and social research.

Roopa Adarsh is currently working as Associate Professor, Mount Carmel College, Bangalore, India.

Tanvir Ahmed _is an Assistant Professor (Department of English) Baba Ghulam Shah Badshah University.

Yasir Ahmed is a research scholar and journalist specializing in media discourse, post-truth politics, and digital media's role in shaping societal perceptions. He is currently pursuing a PhD in Journalism and Mass Communication at Lovely Professional University, Punjab. His research focuses on media representation, political discourse analysis, and the intersection of journalism and public policy. With experience as a journalist at The Indian Express, Yasir has published extensively on health journalism, higher education, and media ethics. His investigative reporting on PGIMER, Chandigarh, and other critical issues has earned him recognition in the field. In addition to journalism, he has contributed opinion pieces and analytical articles to newspapers such as Daily Jammu Jottings and The News Now, covering a range of socio-political and cultural topics. Yasir has presented his research at multiple national and international conferences and has published scholarly articles on media framing, AI in academia, and digital media trends. He is also a passionate educator, having conducted workshops on writing for print media.

Kaan Arık is a researcher and member who continues his academic career in the Department of Computer Technologies at Sakarya University of Applied Sciences (SUBU). He completed his PhD in Department of Informatics at Istanbul University, also, Arık specializes in advanced technological topics such as machine learning, image processing, deep learning, artificial intelligence and customer churn analysis in games. His work in these areas contributes to the development of innovative solutions, especially in the fields of digital transformation and data analysis.

Mohammed Soufiane Benmoussa holds a PhD in Accounting from Tunku Puteri Intan Safinaz School of Accountancy, College of Business (COB), Universiti Utara Malaysia (UUM), 06010 Sintok, Kedah, Malaysia. His research interests are Accounting Information Systems, Technology adoption, and E-Government. He is a distinguished academic with several publications in reputable journals and is proficient in statistical software like PLS, SPSS, VOSviewer, and RStudio.

Mohamed Bouteraa is a Senior Lecturer of Finance at the Faculty of Business - American University of Qatar. Previously, he was an Assistant Professor at the School of Business-University of Malaysia Sabah (UMS). With over 6 years of academic and research experience, Dr. Bouteraa has demonstrated expertise in both teaching and scholarly activities. He holds a Master's and PhD in Finance and Banking from the highly QS Ranked and esteemed, AACSB/ EFMD/ AMBA/ IQA/ MQA-accredited Northern University of Malaysia (UUM). His teaching portfolio includes extensive experience in developing and delivering undergraduate and postgraduate courses in finance and business management. Additionally, he is an active faculty member, contributing to various academic and administrative roles. Dr. Bouteraa's research contributions are noteworthy, with numerous publications in top-quartile, Scopus- and Web of Science-indexed journals. His works have been featured in reputable publications such as the Journal of Marketing (Emerald), Journal of Sustainable Management (MIT), SAGE Open (SAGE), Journal of Open Innovation (Elsevier), Technology in Society (Elsevier), among others. He has also actively participated in and presented at international conferences. His research interests include sustainability (SDGs), green finance, FinTech, Islamic banking, and technology acceptance. Dr. Bouteraa currently serves on an editorial board and acts as a journal assessor for various indexed publishers. Additionally, he has been invited as a guest speaker to several conferences, webinars, seminars, and workshops, further solidifying his expertise and recognition within the academic and professional communities.

Brahim Chekima is a Senior Lecturer in Marketing at the Faculty of Business, Economics and Accountancy, Universiti Malaysia Sabah. He teaches various marketing subjects at both undergraduates and postgraduate levels. He holds a Ph.D. in Marketing. In addition to his teaching experience, he is involved in many research and consulting activities in Malaysia, Qatar, Turkey and Algeria. He has more than 10 years of research experience. He authored several high-impact indexed journal articles and books chapters and his research appeared in many international journals and publications.

Aman Dubey is a PhD researcher in the Department of Electronics and Communication Engineering at Maulana Azad National Institute of Technology, specializing in the optimization of neural networks for medical imaging. Their research focuses on improving model efficiency, generalization, and robustness in medical diagnostics, leveraging techniques such as deep learning, transfer learning, and model compression. Their work aims to enhance the reliability and computational efficiency of AI-driven healthcare solutions.

Yogesh Kumar Gupta did his B.Tech. degree in Electronics and Communication Engineering in 2009 and later completed his M.Tech. degree from National Institute of Technology, Kurukshetra, in 2011. He completed his PhD degree from Maulana Azad National Institute of Technology in 2025. Currently, he is actively working within the department of School of Computer Science at UPES Dehradun. With 8 years of experience in academic roles within engineering institutes, his research encompasses several critical areas, including Free Space Optical Communication (FSO), wireless communication, high-capacity lightwave transmission systems, long-range Wavelength Division Multiplexing (WDM) networks, 5G technology, Multiple Input Multiple Output (MIMO) technology, and Machine Learning.

Sivasubramanian K is currently working as an Assistant Professor and Head of the Department of Economics at Kristu Jayanti College, Autonomous, Bangalore, India. He has 9 years of rich experience in the industry and 7 years of experience in teaching. He has completed a Ph.D. from the University of Madras. He has published 45 research papers in Scopus and 7 UGC CARE-listed journals and Book Chapters. He has presented many research papers at national and international conferences. He has also received 3 best paper awards from various conferences at national and international levels. He has received the Research Award from Kristu Jayanti College, Autonomous, for a significant contribution to research publications under the Platinum category in the 2023-2024 academic year. He is also the editorial and review board member of various international level Q1 Journals. Dr. Sivasubramanian is also the Board of Studies and Board of Examiners of various colleges in India.

Kaushik Kumar holds a Ph.D. in Engineering from Jadavpur University, India, an MBA in Marketing Management from Indira Gandhi National Open University, India and a Bachelor of Technology from Regional Engineering College (Now National Institute of Technology), Warangal, India. For 11 years, he worked in a manufacturing unit of Global repute. He is currently working as a Professor in the Department of Mechanical Engineering, Birla Institute of Technology, Mesra, Ranchi, India. He has 23 Years of Teaching and Research Experience. His research interests include Composites, Optimization, Non-Conventional Machining, CAD / CAM, Rapid Prototyping and Quality Management Systems towards product development for societal and industrial usage and has received 35+ patents for them most of which are donated to Start-ups and Industrial fraternity through Jharkhand Small Industries Association (JSIA). He has published 55+ Books (They are referred as Text Books and Reference Books by 40+ Universities / Institutes in their academic curriculum), 95+ Book Chapters and 200+ Research Papers in peer-reviewed reputed national and international journals. Kaushik has also served as Editor–in–Chief, Series Editor, Guest Editor, Editor, Editorial Board Member and Reviewers for International and National Journals. He has been felicitated with many awards and honours including Distinguished Alumnus Award for Professional Excellence 2023 under Academic and Research from National Institute of Technology, Warangal, India. He has also received Sponsored Research and Consultancy Projects of more than 1 Crore from Govt. of India and abroad. Kaushik has delivered expert lectures as Keynote Speaker at International & National Conferences, Resource Person at Various Workshops, FDP's and Short-Term Courses. He has guided many students of Doctoral, Masters and Under Graduate programmes of his home and other institutions in India and abroad. He also has served as Reviewer and Examiner of Doctoral and Masters dissertation for institutes in India and abroad.

NilamadhabMishra is an Associate Professor in the School of Computer Science and Engineering, AI-ML Division, at VIT Bhopal University, India. He received his Doctor of Philosophy (Ph.D.) in Computer Science and Information Engineering with a specialization in AI-data science and machine learning from Chang Gung University, Taiwan. He has over 23 years of national and international involvement in academic teaching and research at recognized Indian, Taiwanese, and African universities. He has over 100 publications in SCI/SCIE and SCOPUS-indexed journals, ISBN books and chapters, Indian and Australian patents, IEEE conference proceedings, etc. He has been a reviewer, associate editor, and editorial board member for SCI/SCIE-indexed journals and conferences. He has been involved with several professional bodies: "Fellow Member of "ISROSET"; Fellow Member of "ISRD"; Senior Member of "ASR" (Hong Kong); Senior Member of "IEDRC" (Hong Kong); and Member of "IEEE Collabratec". He is currently an Associate Editor for two SCOPUS-indexed journals, and his research interests span the areas of AI, Data Science, Machine Learning, and Cognitive Analytics & Applications.

Anand Motwani is Brilliant academician and researcher with 20+ years' experience of training, teaching and guiding technical scholars and corporate employees. He is an alumni of Maulana Azad National Institute of Technology (MANIT), Bhopal, (M.P., India). He has worked with renowned educational Institutions at good positions. He has been associated with different universities as a guest faculty, a counsellor, an examiner and for other academic assignments. He has experience of planning and developing customized courses and training materials. He is well adept at Data Mining, Machine Learning and analytics tools (Weka, Azure ML.) and languages like Python. He also worked with Cloud Computing Technologies like Virtualization, and is also passionate about applying 'Machine Learning and Analytics' over cloud platforms. He has authored nice research publications and a book with Pearson Education. Prof. Motwani is member of IEEE Cloud Computing and Internet of Things (IoT) Society and is working with School of Computing Science & Engineering, VIT Bhopal University since May 2019.

Kumarasamy P is currently working as Associate Professor of Commerce, Dhanalakshmi Srinivasan University, Trichy, India.

Thamilmani R is currently working as Faculty in Vel Tech Rangarajan Dr Sagunthaala R&D Institute of Science and Technology, Chennai. I have more than 6 years of experience in teaching and research.

Chikesh Ranjan is currently serving as a Project Engineer for Project SwaYaan – Capacity Building in Drone/UAS at the Department of Mechanical Engineering, NIT Rourkela, India. He holds a PhD in Mechanical Engineering from the Department of Mechanical Engineering at the Birla Institute of Technology, Mesra, Ranchi, Jharkhand, India, where he also completed his Master of Engineering (M.E.) in Mechanical Engineering, specializing in the Design of Mechanical Equipment. Additionally, he earned a Bachelor of Engineering (B.E.) in Mechanical Engineering from the Marathwara Institute of Technology, Aurangabad, Maharashtra, India, graduating with First Class with Distinction. Chikesh Ranjan has made significant contributions to the field of mechanical engineering through his research, having published 17 journal papers, authored 12 books, and written 16 book chapters. He has been actively involved in organizing 10 workshops and coordinating 13 events, in addition to participating in 31 training programs and attending 34 national and international workshops, seminars, and webinars. His innovative work has been recognized with 13 design patents and 8 foreign patents, underscoring his commitment to advancing mechanical design and technology. With 9 years of teaching and research experience, Chikesh has built a global reputation in his areas of interest, which include composites, non-conventional machining, CAD/CAM, 3D printing, robotics and drone technology. He is a proud member of the Institution of Engineers, India, and has received 7 prestigious awards and honors for his outstanding contributions to the field of Mechanical Engineering.

Hepsibah Vani is the Student Welfare officer at Kristu Jayanti College, Bangalore, India.

J S Yadav Designation: Professor, MANIT Bhopal Educational Qualification: PhD(Model Order Reduction), MANIT Bhopal, MTech. (Digital Communication), (Gold Medalist) MANIT Bhopal, BE(E & TC) GEC Jabalpur. Experience: 28 Years MANIT, Bhopal(Since 1997) Publications: Int. Journals: 27 Int. & National Conf.: 15 Total: 42 Research Area: Signal Processing, Communication Engg Thesis supervised- PhD: 04 & 04 in progress MTech.: 32 Book: Published 01 book on Signal & System, and 02 book chapters in Springer book series.

Index

A

B

C

D

E

F

G

H

I

L

M

N

P

R

S

T

U

Z

www.ingramcontent.com/pod-product-compliance
Lightning Source LLC
LaVergne TN
LVHW060003031026
849161LV00025B/1345